Lecture Notes in Computer Science 16236

Founding Editors

Gerhard Goos
Juris Hartmanis

Editorial Board Members

Elisa Bertino, *Purdue University, West Lafayette, IN, USA*
Wen Gao, *Peking University, Beijing, China*
Bernhard Steffen, *TU Dortmund University, Dortmund, Germany*
Moti Yung, *Columbia University, New York, NY, USA*

The series Lecture Notes in Computer Science (LNCS), including its subseries Lecture Notes in Artificial Intelligence (LNAI) and Lecture Notes in Bioinformatics (LNBI), has established itself as a medium for the publication of new developments in computer science and information technology research, teaching, and education.

LNCS enjoys close cooperation with the computer science R & D community, the series counts many renowned academics among its volume editors and paper authors, and collaborates with prestigious societies. Its mission is to serve this international community by providing an invaluable service, mainly focused on the publication of conference and workshop proceedings and postproceedings. LNCS commenced publication in 1973.

Maurice H. ter Beek · Simon Collart-Dutilleul ·
Thierry Lecomte

Editors

Reliability, Safety, and Security of Railway Systems

Modelling, Analysis, Verification, and Certification

6th International Conference, RSSRail 2025
Pisa, Italy, November 26–28, 2025
Proceedings

 Springer

Editors
Maurice H. ter Beek
CNR-ISTI
Pisa, Italy

Simon Collart-Dutilleul
Université Gustave Eiffel
Villeneuve d'Ascq, France

Thierry Lecomte
CLEARSY
Aix-en-Provence, France

ISSN 0302-9743   ISSN 1611-3349 (electronic)
Lecture Notes in Computer Science
ISBN 978-3-032-10761-9   ISBN 978-3-032-10762-6 (eBook)
https://doi.org/10.1007/978-3-032-10762-6

This Springer imprint is published by the registered company Springer Nature Switzerland AG
The registered company address is: Gewerbestrasse 11, 6330 Cham, Switzerland

If disposing of this product, please recycle the paper.

Preface

This volume contains the papers presented at the 6th International Conference on Reliability, Safety, and Security of Railway Systems (RSSRail 2025), held in Pisa, Italy, during November 26–28, 2025, the year in which we celebrated 200 years of modern railway: on September 27, 1825, the first train line, between Stockton and Darlington in the United Kingdom, was opened to the public.

The railway industry is currently facing increasing pressure to improve system safety, to decrease production costs and time to market, to reduce carbon emissions and running costs, and to increase the capacity of the railway. Railway systems are now being integrated into larger multi-transport networks. Such systems require an even higher degree of automation at all levels of operation. These trends dramatically increase the complexity of railway applications and pose new challenges in developing novel methods of modelling, analysis, verification, and certification to ensure their reliability, safety, and security, as well as in supporting novel mechanisms and procedures to help make the case that development processes meet the mandated standards.

The RSSRail conference series aims to bring together researchers and engineers interested in building critical railway applications and systems, as a working conference in which research challenges and advances are discussed and evaluated by both researchers and engineers, focusing on their potential to be deployed in industrial settings. It is vital to ensure that advances in research (in both academia and industry) are driven by real industrial needs, to help ensure that such advances are followed by effective industrial deployment. Another particularly important objective is to integrate advances in research into current development processes, and make them usable and scalable. Finally, a key goal is to develop advanced methods and tools that can ensure that the systems meet the requirements imposed by regulatory standards and help in building supporting arguments.

RSSRail 2025 brought together researchers and developers working on railway system reliability, security, and safety to discuss how all of these requirements can be met in an integrated way in the context of the current digital transformation in the Railway industry.

RSSRail 2025 solicited high-quality papers reporting research results and/or experience reports, in the form of regular, short, or journal-first papers, as well as tutorials and posters related to the overall theme of Reliability, Safety, and Security of Railway Systems: Modelling, Analysis, Verification, and Certification. The Program Committee (PC), with members from 11 different countries spread over 3 continents, originally received a total of 39 submissions from 14 different countries spread over 4 continents: 18 regular papers, 10 short papers, 4 journal-first papers, 2 tutorials, and 5 posters. Each research paper went through a rigorous single-blind review process according to which all papers were reviewed by three PC members, with the help of a few external reviewers, while tutorials and journal-first papers were reviewed by two PC members of which at least one was from the Steering Committee. The decision to accept or reject a submission was based not only on the review reports and scores, but also and in particular on the in-depth and sometimes intense discussions. In the end, the PC of RSSRail 2025 decided to accept 4 posters, all tutorials and journal-first papers, 5 short, and 12 regular papers, resulting in an acceptance rate of 60% for papers describing new research.

The conference also featured three inspiring keynotes by our invited speakers:

- *ETCS Moving Block in the ERJU programme* by Peter Tummeltshammer (Hitachi Rail, Austria)
- *Empirical Formal Methods in Railways: Experiences and Roadmap* by Alessio Ferrari (University College Dublin, Ireland)
- *Wireless Communications Challenges for Safety Applications in Railways* by Marion Berbineau (Université Gustave Eiffel, France)

The conference also featured three informative tutorials:

- *EN 50716 in Practice: New Requirements and Practices for Safe Railway Software* by Günther Siegel and Jair Gonzales (Ansys, France)
- *Advancements in the CLEARSY Safety Platform: From Academic Research to Industrial SIL4 Certification* by Thierry Lecomte (CLEARSY, France)
- *AC/DC and GO: An Ontology-based Approach to Requirements Validation* by Arne Borälv (Prover Technology, Sweden)

We are very grateful for the contributions of our invited speakers and tutorialists.

Thanks are due to all involved in RSSRail 2025. In particular, to all PC members and external reviewers for their accurate and timely reviewing, all authors for their submissions, and all attendees for their participation. We also thank the conference Organization Chairs, Industry Liaison, Web Chair, Publicity Chair, and of course the Steering Committee, all itemised on the following pages.

We are indebted to our sponsors: The Formal Route, a company offering unique expertise in applying formal methods to computerised railway signalling; EURNEX (EUropean rail Research Network of EXcellence), an association of scientific institutes in the area of rail transport and mobility; and DITECFER (District for Railway Technologies, High Speed, Networks' Safety & Security), a consortium of companies and research organisations in Italy.

Moreover, the RSSRail 2025 conference was organised by CNR–ISTI as part of the dissemination activities of Spoke 4 Rail Transportation within the MOST – Sustainable Mobility National Research Center, which received funding from the European Union NextGenerationEU.

Finally, we would like to thank Springer for publishing these proceedings and we gratefully acknowledge the support from EasyChair in assisting us in managing the entire process from submissions through these proceedings to the programme.

We hope you enjoyed the conference!

November 2025

Maurice H. ter Beek
Simon Collart Dutilleul
Thierry Lecomte

Organization

Conference Chairs

Maurice ter Beek	CNR–ISTI, Pisa, Italy
Simon Collart Dutilleul	Gustave Eiffel University, France
Thierry Lecomte	CLEARSY, France

Organization Chairs

Stefania Gnesi	CNR–ISTI, Pisa, Italy
Laura Semini	University of Pisa, Italy

Industry Liaison

Alessandro Fantechi	University of Florence, Italy

Web Chair

Giorgio Spagnolo	CNR–ISTI, Pisa, Italy

Publicity Chair

Giovanna Broccia	CNR–ISTI, Pisa, Italy

Steering Committee

Simon Collart Dutilleul (chair)	Gustave Eiffel University, France
Alessandro Fantechi	University of Florence, Italy
Thierry Lecomte	CLEARSY, France
Anne Haxthausen	Technical University of Denmark, Denmark
Alexander Romanovsky	The Formal Route Ltd., UK

Program Committee

Abderrahim Ait Wakrime	Mohammed V University, Morocco
Dalay Almeida	ClearSy System Engineering, France
Davide Basile	CNR–ISTI, Pisa, Italy
Maurice ter Beek (Co-chair)	CNR–ISTI, Pisa, Italy
Nikola Bešinović	Technical University of Dresden, Germany
Philippe Bon	Gustave Eiffel University, France
Alessandro Borselli	Trenord, Italy
Alessandro Cimatti	Fondazione Bruno Kessler, Italy
Sana Debbech	SNCF, France
Simon Collart Dutilleul (Co-chair)	Gustave Eiffel University, France
Alessandro Fantechi	University of Florence, Italy
Alessio Ferrari	University College Dublin, Ireland
Francesco Flammini	Mälardalen University, Sweden
Barbara Gallina	Mälardalen University, Sweden
Gloria Gori	University of Florence, Italy
Stephan Griebel	Siemens AG, Germany
Alexandra Halchin	Régie Autonome des Transports Parisiens, France
Anne Haxthausen	Technical University of Denmark, Denmark
Akram Idani	Institut National Polytechnique de Grenoble, France
Alexei Iliasov	The Formal Route Ltd., UK
Kenji Imamoto	Hitachi Ltd., Japan
Thierry Lecomte (Co-chair)	CLEARSY, France
Michael Leuschel	Heinrich Heine University Düsseldorf, Germany
Riccardo Licciardello	Sapienza University of Rome, Italy
Christophe Limbrée	UCLouvain, Belgium
Bas Luttik	Eindhoven University of Technology, The Netherlands
Davide Moroni	CNR–ISTI, Pisa, Italy
Marcel Oliveira	Federal University of Rio Grande do Norte, Brazil
Matthieu Perin	Systerel, France
Jaco van de Pol	Aarhus University, Denmark
Christophe Ponsard	CETIC, Belgium
José Proença	CISTER and University of Porto, Portugal
Vito Renò	CNR–STIIMA, Bari, Italy
Alexander Romanovsky	The Formal Route Ltd., UK
Aryldo Russo	GESTE Engineering, France
Marc Sango	SNCF, France
Monika Seisenberger	Swansea University, UK
Thai Son Hoang	University of Southampton, UK

Mariëlle Stoelinga	University of Twente, The Netherlands
Davide Tarsitano	Polytechnic University of Milan, Italy
Stefano Tonetta	Fondazione Bruno Kessler, Italy
Elena Troubitsyna	KTH Royal Institute of Technology, Sweden
Laurent Voisin	Systerel, France

Additional Reviewers

| Jan Gruteser | Heinrich Heine University Düsseldorf, Germany |
| Jean-Valentin Merlevede | Université Polytechnique Hauts-de-France, France |

Sponsors and Endorsers

Contents

Communication and Control

Industrial Experiences and Trams

Formal Modelling and Analysis

Invited Presentations

Moving Block in ERJU

Peter Tummeltshammer[✉] and Felix Schaber

Hitachi Rail, Handelskai 92, 1200 Vienna, Austria
{peter.tummeltshammer,felix.schaber}@urbanandmainlines.com
http://www.hitachirail.com

Abstract. This paper presents the ETCS Moving Block system developed within Europe's Rail Joint Undertaking (ERJU) programme to address today's railway capacity constraints by replacing classical operational rules to optimize throughput. The concept was validated through simulations and field trials and future work includes extended field tests, contributing to European interoperability standards.

Keywords: ETCS Moving Block · Europe's Rail

1 Introduction

The railway sector has already reached capacity limits in some areas, which requires new technologies to increase throughput without extensive new construction work. The ETCS moving block aims to combine new trackside safety functions with existing trainside functions resulting in higher throughput and greater flexibility in train operation.

2 ETCS Moving Block

Figure 1 provides a simplified overview of the ETCS moving block.

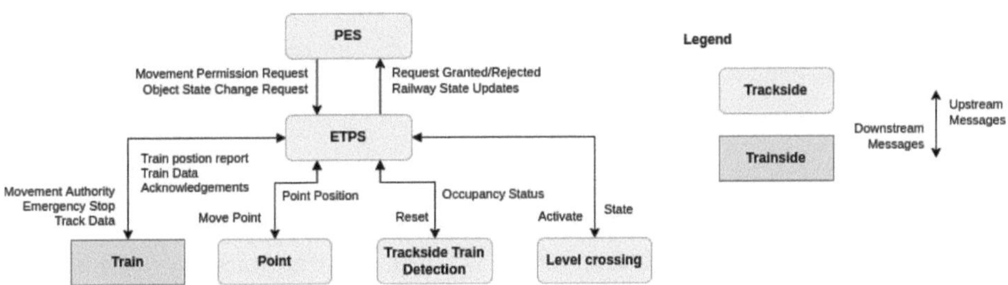

Fig. 1. Simplified overview of the ETCS moving block. Selected messages for a subset of adjacent systems are shown.

M. H. ter Beek et al. (Eds.): RSSRail 2025, LNCS 16236, pp. 3–5, 2026.
https://doi.org/10.1007/978-3-032-10762-6_1

The Plan Execution System (PES) is responsible for generating movement permission requests for individual trains based on the timetables from a traffic management system. It does not have any safety responsibility, allowing for optimization and prioritization.

The European Trackside Protection System (ETPS) is responsible for assessing the risk of movement permission commands and object state change requests (e.g., changing the position of a railway point). It only grants a request if it does not result in a hazardous situation (now or in the future) and translates it into movement authorities (MA).

In the moving block system, real-time data collection based on the geometric topology of the rail network and the physical properties of the train serves as the basis for replacing classic railway operational rules. The system thus always achieves the optimum throughput adapted to the respective situation, e.g., in the case of operational restrictions. The new approach is compatible with existing ETCS L2 systems and track vacancy detection systems, enabling the support of classical ETCS L2 operation. The system is intended to enable cloud operation with standardized EULYNX interfaces on indoor and outdoor systems.

3   Experimental Results and Outlook

Hitachi Rail already has experience in the moving block system for many years by early concept validation through simulation, prototyping and formal methods [2–4], which was continued and extended in Shift2Rail and now Europe's Rail Joint Undertaking (ERJU), where a field demonstrator reaching TRL 6 was conducted in the DB living lab. Starting in 2027, as part of ERJU Wave 2, an extended moving block field demonstrator is planned on an OEBB secondary line.

These demonstrators are based on existing standards [1,5] and the ongoing ERJU moving block specification work, paving the way towards a Technical Specifications for Interoperability (TSI) together with the European Union Agency for Railways (ERA).

Disclaimer. Funded by the European Union. Views and opinion expressed are however those of the author(s) only and do not necessarily reflect those of the European Union. Neither the European Union nor the granting authority can be held responsible for them. The project FP2-R2DATO is supported by the Europes Rail Joint Undertaking and its members.

References

1. EULYNX: Interface Specification SCI-TDS (2023). https://rail-research.europa.eu/wp-content/uploads/2023/06/20230628-Interface-specification-SCI-TDS-Eu.Doc.44-v4.0-2.A.pdf
2. Hansen, D., et al.: Validation and real-life demonstration of ETCS hybrid level 3 principles using a formal B model. Int. J. Softw. Tools Technol. Transfer **22**(3), 315–332 (2020). https://doi.org/10.1007/s10009-020-00551-6

3. Schaber, F., Mashkoor, A., Leuschel, M.: Promise-driven modeling: a structured approach for modeling cyber-physical systems. In: Remke, A., Steffen, B. (eds.) Proceedings of the 30th International Conference on Formal Methods for Industrial Critical Systems (FMICS 2025). Lecture Notes in Computer Science, vol. 16040, pp. 185–202. Springer, Heidelberg (2025). https://doi.org/10.1007/978-3-032-00942-5_10
4. Schaber, F., Mashkoor, A., Leuschel, M.: Towards a novel approach to railway safety using STPA and promise theory. In: Liu, S. (ed.) Proceedings of the First International Symposium on Software Fault Prevention, Verification, and Validation (SFPVV 2024), Lecture Notes in Computer Science, vol. 15393, pp. 263–279. Springer, Heidelberg (2025).https://doi.org/10.1007/978-981-96-1621-3_17
5. UNISIG: SUBSET-026 System Requirements Specification. https://www.era.europa.eu/system/files/2023-09/index004_-_SUBSET-026_v400.zip

Empirical Formal Methods in Railways: Experiences and Roadmap

Alessio Ferrari[(✉)] [ID]

University College Dublin (UCD), Dublin, Ireland
`alessio.ferrari@ucd.ie`

Abstract. Empirical formal methods (FMs) aim to ground the development, evaluation, and deployment of formal techniques in software engineering through systematic observation, data collection, and analysis. In the context of safety-critical domains such as railways, the need to balance mathematical rigor with practical feasibility makes empirical approaches particularly relevant. In this keynote summary, I will outline the scope and significance of empirical FMs, and present a retrospective on my experience applying these approaches in railway system development and verification. Drawing on a series of industrial and collaborative projects, I will discuss how empirical software engineering techniques such as surveys, systematic literature reviews, case studies, judgment studies, and tool evaluations have been used to assess the applicability, usability, and impact of FMs in practice. I will conclude with a roadmap for strengthening the empirical evidence base for FMs in railways, identifying research gaps and practical strategies to improve their integration into industrial processes, toolchains, and certification workflows.

Keywords: Formal Methods · Empirical Studies · Roadmap

1 Empirical Formal Methods

For more than twenty years, empirical research methods—such as controlled experiments, surveys, case studies, and systematic reviews—have been widely employed to evaluate software engineering techniques, investigate professional practice, and consolidate research outcomes [22]. In contrast, the application of these approaches to *formal methods* (FM), i.e., mathematically grounded techniques and tools aimed at producing dependable software, has been rather limited. Already in 2007, Höfer and Tichy [14] observed this gap when reviewing the state of empirical research in software engineering. Later, Jeffery et al. [16] explicitly included the need for more empirical evidence in FM within their research agenda. More recently, Gleirscher et al. [13] reinforced this perspective through the 2021 manifesto for applicable FM, which argues that the effectiveness of FM must be demonstrated through systematic evidence, e.g., by comparing outcomes with and without FM through controlled studies or real-world cases. The manifesto further emphasizes that the way FM research is conducted, written,

M. H. ter Beek et al. (Eds.): RSSRail 2025, LNCS 16236, pp. 6–13, 2026.
https://doi.org/10.1007/978-3-032-10762-6_2

and evaluated should be shaped by empirical inquiry, with case studies, experiments, and action research playing a central role. Similarly, Huisman et al. [15] underline the importance of investing in industrially grounded case studies, so as to better identify which techniques have genuine practical relevance.

Despite these calls and recommendations, FM research has predominantly concentrated on designing novel methods, addressing increasingly complex challenges, or improving tool performance. As a result, the field often maintains a method-centric orientation, rather than one driven by empirical validation. This emphasis on technical aspects tends to downplay human and organizational factors, which are known to significantly influence the adoption and use of FM tools [12]. The area of *empirical formal methods* is therefore still underdeveloped. The lack of systematic evidence on effectiveness and applicability sustains skepticism among practitioners and continues to hinder the broader industrial uptake of FM. One contributing factor is the limited awareness within the FM community of the empirical methodologies available, their theoretical underpinnings, and their practical guidance.

In software engineering at large, however, a rich body of empirical guidelines already exists. The well-known textbook by Wohlin et al. [21] surveys a range of empirical strategies and provides detailed recommendations for experimental design, particularly with human participants. Shull et al. [19] assemble contributions on qualitative research, experimental methods, and theory building. Felderer and Travassos [5] extend this foundation to cover more recent developments, such as grey literature reviews, Bayesian analysis, and data science applications. Earlier influential summaries [4,17], as well as the ABC framework of Stol and Fitzgerald [20], provide further overviews of methodological options, discussing both their advantages and inherent limitations, such as generalisability and obtrusiveness. Another community-wide effort is the Empirical Standards initiative [18], which offers structured checklists to support both the conduct and review of empirical studies. Its online repository[1] provides criteria ranging from essential to exemplary for different study types, along with references to illustrative research.

In light of this situation, my previous work [3] (co-authored with M.H. ter Beek) provides a comprehensive framework and a set of guidelines to practice empirical FMs, with pointers to existing research, and a practical guide to select the most appropriate empirical strategy for the problem at hand. In particular, nine strategies are considered to be the most relevant to FM research: (i) laboratory experiments with software artifacts, e.g., a comparison of model checkers on a pre-defined set of problems; (ii) laboratory experiments with human participants, e.g., a comparison of the performance of different subjects, when using a specific formal tool; (iii) usability studies, e.g., an analysis of the ease of use of a formal tool; (iv) surveys, e.g., a questionnaire on FMs submitted to practitioners to understand the industrial uptake of FMs; (v) qualitative investigations, e.g., analysis of interviews with practitioners on the use FMs in a company; (vi) judgment studies, e.g., evaluation of different formal tools performed by experts; (vii)

---

[1] https://github.com/acmsigsoft/EmpiricalStandards, accessed on 15 Sept. 2025.

case studies (including design science and action research), e.g., an investigation of how FMs are used in a certain company (viii) systematic literature reviews, and (ix) systematic mapping studies. While other options exist (cf. [20]), I argue that these represent the most promising approaches for FM research at present. I have applied a large subset of these different strategies in the railway context, and this keynote will provide a summary of my research in this field.

2   Experiences in Railways

The trajectory of research on empirical FMs has evolved through a series of studies that progressively applied different empirical strategies to the context of railway systems, each contributing complementary insights.

The first step in this path was a case study at General Electric Transportation Systems, where formal model-based design and code generation were introduced into the company's development process [8–10]. The study focused on defining a safe subset of Simulink/Stateflow, demonstrating behavioural conformance between generated code and specifications, and aligning modelling technologies with processes mandated by safety standards. Model-based testing and abstract interpretation were also employed to reinforce the approach. This experience demonstrated the potential of formal modelling and code generation to enhance both safety and cost-effectiveness, while also revealing the need for incremental adjustments and careful process integration.

Subsequent work broadened the perspective to capture industrial needs more systematically. Within the ASTRail European project, two surveys were conducted with railway practitioners to obtain structured information about the use of FMs and tools [1,2,7]. Responses from 147 in total stakeholders showed a fragmented tool landscape: while the B family of tools was most widely used, many other tools were adopted only sporadically. The surveys also identified the most valued features for industrial adoption, such as verification capabilities, maturity, usability, quality of documentation, and process integration.

In order to provide guidance on tool selection, a judgment study was then carried out to compare the applicability of different FM tools in the railway domain [12]. Seventeen experts evaluated nine tools, including Atelier B, ProB, SPIN, and UPPAAL SMC, through a modelling task involving a moving-block train distancing system. The resulting synthesis demonstrated that no single tool suffices for the diverse needs of railway system design, and that tool complementarity is often required. The study provided a structured perspective on when to adopt certain tools and highlighted common modelling challenges.

This line of inquiry was further extended with a systematic comparison and usability analysis of FM tools [11]. A set of 13 tools was examined, with a usability assessment of seven involving direct input from practitioners. The findings challenged common assumptions in the literature: rather than usability or maturity being the primary obstacles, the most significant barrier was the lack of support for integration into industrial processes.

Finally, a systematic mapping study provided a large-scale overview of FM applications in railway signalling over the period 1989—2020 [6]. From

328 relevant studies, trends and research gaps were identified. The analysis showed increasing interest in recent years, but also revealed that full-fledged case studies remain rare. Model checking emerged as the dominant technique, with theorem proving and simulation less frequent, and UML and B as the most common languages. The review underscored that most studies operate at higher levels of abstraction, with limited work addressing development phases closer to implementation. It also highlighted the importance of more empirically sound approaches, such as controlled experiments and industrial case studies, to strengthen the evidence base.

Overall, this body of work traces a progression from in-depth industrial case study, to surveys of industrial practice, to expert-based tool evaluations, systematic comparisons, and large-scale literature mapping. Each step has broadened the empirical understanding of how FMs are used, what challenges hinder their adoption, and what opportunities exist for more robust, evidence-driven integration into practice. Collectively, these studies illustrate a sustained effort to build the foundations of empirical FMs as a discipline.

3 Roadmap

Cost-Benefit Analysis in the Field. In the immediate future, empirical studies should provide industrial stakeholders with tangible evidence of the value of FM. Pilot projects in railway companies can play a crucial role in demonstrating concrete benefits such as reduced testing costs or earlier defect detection. These pilots should systematically collect quantitative evidence of the costs of adopting FMs and the actual benefits, by means of, e.g., field experiments [20]. Furthermore, they should also document the experiences of engineers, e.g., through interviews and observations. Such evidence can help to dispel the persistent belief that FMs are inherently difficult to learn and can guide investments in training. At the same time, transparency in tool capabilities should be improved through systematic profiling of tool features, especially with respect to usability, interoperability, and maturity. These systematic studies should be performed by independent researchers, to prevent the introduction of bias in the evaluation.

FM Tool Evaluation in Lab and in Context. The future of empirical FMs in the railway sector requires a coordinated effort among tool developers, researchers, practitioners, and certification bodies. The short-term priority is to strengthen the connection between tools and industrial processes, and provide evidence of alignment. Many formal tools still lack support for essential development functionalities such as traceability, report generation, and integration with existing railway workflows. A practical step forward is for vendors to enrich their tools with such process-oriented features and, where full certification is not feasible, to focus on providing artefact-level evidence that can still support certification arguments. A promising strategy is to maintain two parallel lines of tool development: one branch oriented to research, where novel techniques can be tested, and one branch aimed at practice, emphasising stability, usability, and customer support. While research-oriented versions should be assessed through laboratory experiments, to systematically check the performance, practice-oriented versions should be evaluated based on user acceptance and performance in context, through usability studies and case studies, respectively.

Complex Workflows Evaluated in Class. In the medium term, attention should turn to interoperability and the development of repeatable toolchain patterns. Current industrial practice shows that no single FM tool can cover all phases of the railway development process, and combinations are necessary. However, the lack of interoperability forces engineers to perform manual translations, often introducing inconsistencies. Establishing common interchange formats for models, properties, and counterexamples would allow organisations to build flexible toolchains without compromising consistency. Evaluating these complex workflows is particularly hard in real-world industrial environments. Therefore, other approaches, such as experiments with human subjects or experimental simulations should be performed, for example involving students in FMs, as common in software engineering research.

Multi-case Studies and Human-centered Aspects. Empirical research should also move beyond isolated case studies. Multi-site studies and controlled comparisons can provide stronger evidence of the costs and benefits of FM adoption. The railway community would also benefit from benchmark datasets reflecting real-world problems, enabling systematic evaluation of both tools and methodologies. Human-centred aspects should remain a central focus: longitudinal studies on training curves, investigations of team composition, and empirical work on communication between domain and FM experts can clarify how organisations should structure their engineering teams to reap the benefits of formal verification.

Evidence for Regulatory Engagement. In the long term, sustainable industrialisation of FM in the railway domain will require closer alignment with regulatory and certification practices. Regulators should be engaged early to co-develop evidence frameworks that explain how FM artefacts can contribute to safety cases and tool qualification. If FM tools can demonstrate consistent and reproducible verification results, and if traceability is maintained across the development lifecycle, their acceptance in certification contexts will be strengthened. This regulatory clarity will also encourage companies to adopt FM at scale.

Repositories and Benchmarks. Finally, broader ecosystems must emerge that combine interoperable tools, industrially maintained documentation, and *open repositories* of case studies and railway-specific benchmarks. By supporting both commercial and open-source efforts, the railway sector can ensure that FM remains accessible and that practitioners have practical pathways to adoption. In the long run, empirical FMs should be embedded not as isolated academic experiments but as an integrated, trusted part of railway engineering practice, supported by evidence, aligned with certification, and responsive to the needs of industry stakeholders.

> **Empirical FM in Railways: a Roadmap**
>
> - **Cost-Benefit Analysis:** Quantify the impact of FM adoption on testing costs and defect detection using pilot projects and field experiments, complemented by engineer feedback.
> - **Tool Evaluation:** Assess research-oriented FM tools in lab experiments and practice-oriented tools in context through usability studies and case studies.
> - **Workflow Interoperability:** Evaluate complex, multi-tool workflows and interoperability via controlled experiments or simulations with students.
> - **Human Factors and Teams:** Study team composition, learning curves, and collaboration between domain and FM experts using multi-site case studies and longitudinal observations.
> - **Regulatory Evidence:** Engage regulators to identify acceptable evidence, focusing on reproducibility, traceability, and integration with safety cases.
> - **Repositories and Benchmarks:** Promote accessible open repositories of case studies, benchmarks, and interoperable tools to support industrial adoption.

4   Conclusions

Empirical formal methods are beginning to establish themselves as a credible way to strengthen the role of rigorous techniques in the railway domain. What is still needed is a stronger body of evidence that demonstrates how these methods work in practice, together with tools that fit into real industrial processes and can be aligned with certification requirements. The roadmap presented here highlights that technical progress must go hand in hand with attention to human and organisational factors, as well as with closer engagement from regulators. With these conditions in place, formal methods can gradually move from experimental use toward routine application in railway engineering, where their value will be measured not only in terms of theoretical soundness but also through their impact on practice.

Acknowledgments. The author acknowledges the use of OpenAI's ChatGPT in assisting with language polishing and text restructuring. Responsibility for the final content rests solely with the author.

References

1. Basile, D., et al.: On the industrial uptake of formal methods in the railway domain. In: Furia, C.A., Winter, K. (eds.) IFM 2018. LNCS, vol. 11023, pp. 20–29. Springer, Cham (2018). https://doi.org/10.1007/978-3-319-98938-9_2
2. ter Beek, M.H., et al.: Adopting formal methods in an industrial setting: the railways case. In: ter Beek, M.H., McIver, A., Oliveira, J.N. (eds.) FM 2019. LNCS, vol. 11800, pp. 762–772. Springer, Cham (2019). https://doi.org/10.1007/978-3-030-30942-8_46
3. ter Beek, M.H., Ferrari, A.: Empirical formal methods: guidelines for performing empirical studies on formal methods. Software **1**(4) (2022). https://doi.org/10.3390/software1040017
4. Easterbrook, S., Singer, J., Storey, M.D., Damian, D.E.: Selecting empirical methods for software engineering research. In: Shull, F., Singer, J., Sjøberg, D.I.K. (eds.) Guide to Advanced Empirical Software Engineering, pp. 285–311. Springer, Heidelberg (2008). https://doi.org/10.1007/978-1-84800-044-5_11
5. Felderer, M., Travassos, G.H. (eds.): Contemporary Empirical Methods in Software Engineering. Springer, Heidelberg (2020). https://doi.org/10.1007/978-3-030-32489-6
6. Ferrari, A., ter Beek, M.H.: Formal methods in railways: a systematic mapping study. ACM Comput. Surv. **55**(4), 69:1 – 69:37 (2023). https://doi.org/10.1145/3520480
7. Ferrari, A., et al.: Survey on formal methods and tools in railways: the ASTRail approach. In: Collart-Dutilleul, S., Lecomte, T., Romanovsky, A. (eds.) RSSRail 2019. LNCS, vol. 11495, pp. 226–241. Springer, Cham (2019). https://doi.org/10.1007/978-3-030-18744-6_15
8. Ferrari, A., Fantechi, A., Gnesi, S.: Lessons learnt from the adoption of formal model-based development. In: Goodloe, A.E., Person, S. (eds.) NFM 2012. LNCS, vol. 7226, pp. 24–38. Springer, Heidelberg (2012). https://doi.org/10.1007/978-3-642-28891-3_5
9. Ferrari, A., Fantechi, A., Gnesi, S., Magnani, G.: Model-based development and formal methods in the railway industry. IEEE Softw. **30**(3), 28–34 (2013). https://doi.org/10.1109/MS.2013.44
10. Ferrari, A., Fantechi, A., Magnani, G., Grasso, D., Tempestini, M.: The Metrô Rio case study. Sci. Comput. Program. **78**(7), 828–842 (2013). https://doi.org/10.1016/j.scico.2012.04.003
11. Ferrari, A., Mazzanti, F., Basile, D., ter Beek, M.H.: Systematic evaluation and usability analysis of formal methods tools for railway signaling system design. IEEE Trans. Softw. Eng. **48**(11), 4675–4691 (2022). https://doi.org/10.1109/TSE.2021.3124677
12. Ferrari, A., Mazzanti, F., Basile, D., ter Beek, M.H., Fantechi, A.: Comparing formal tools for system design: a judgment study. In: Proceedings of the 42nd International Conference on Software Engineering (ICSE'20), pp. 62–74. ACM (2020). https://doi.org/10.1145/3377811.3380373
13. Gleirscher, M., van de Pol, J., Woodcock, J.: A manifesto for applicable formal methods. Softw. Syst. Model. **22**(6), 1737–1749 (2023). https://doi.org/10.1007/s10270-023-01124-2

14. Höfer, A., Tichy, W.F.: Status of empirical research in software engineering. In: Basili, V.R., Rombach, D., Schneider, K., Kitchenham, B., Pfahl, D., Selby, R.W. (eds.) Empirical Software Engineering Issues. Critical Assessment and Future Directions. LNCS, vol. 4336, pp. 10–19. Springer, Heidelberg (2007). https://doi.org/10.1007/978-3-540-71301-2_3
15. Huisman, M., Gurov, D., Malkis, A.: Formal Methods: From Academia to Industrial Practice. A Travel Guide (2020)
16. Jeffery, D.R., Staples, M., Andronick, J., Klein, G., Murray, T.C.: An empirical research agenda for understanding formal methods productivity. Inf. Softw. Technol. **60**, 102–112 (2015). https://doi.org/10.1016/j.infsof.2014.11.005
17. Kitchenham, B.A., et al.: Preliminary guidelines for empirical research in software engineering. IEEE Trans. Softw. Eng. **28**(8), 721–734 (2002). https://doi.org/10.1109/TSE.2002.1027796
18. Ralph, P. (ed.): Empirical Standards for Software Engineering Research (2020)
19. Shull, F., Singer, J., Sjøberg, D.I.K. (eds.): Guide to Advanced Empirical Software Engineering. Springer, Heidelberg (2008). https://doi.org/10.1007/978-1-84800-044-5
20. Stol, K.J., Fitzgerald, B.: The ABC of software engineering research. ACM Trans. Softw. Eng. Methodol. **27**(3), 1–51 (2018). https://doi.org/10.1145/3241743
21. Wohlin, C., Runeson, P., Höst, M., Ohlsson, M.C., Regnell, B., Wesslén, A.: Experimentation in Software Engineering. Springer, Heidelberg (2012). https://doi.org/10.1007/978-3-642-29044-2
22. Zhang, L., Tian, J.-H., Jiang, J., Liu, Y.-J., Pu, M.-Y., Yue, T.: Empirical research in software engineering—a literature survey. J. Comput. Sci. Technol. **33**(5), 876–899 (2018). https://doi.org/10.1007/s11390-018-1864-x

Wireless Communications Challenges for Safety Applications in Railways

Marion Berbineau[✉] [iD]

COSYS-LEOST, Université Gustave Eiffel, Villeneuve d'Ascq, France
`Marion.berbineau@univ-eiffel.fr`

Abstract. The rail system is a complex system of systems that is entering the era of total automation thanks to wireless sensors and advanced communication, localization and perception systems that transfer the control functions of the human driver to computers. Information must be shared between the various stakeholders in the system: Infrastructure manager, train manager, maintenance manager, timetable manager, customer manager, etc. Consequently, wireless communications are widely deployed for train operation and will carry mission critical information. The question of safety demonstration and then dependability analysis of a wireless link is an open topic. In general, a so called "safety layer" is designed to cope with the wireless communications impairments. In particular the Euroradio philosophy will be recalled as an example of safety layer for train-to-ground communication. This protocol is not suitable for decentralized communications such as train-to-train or device-to device communications and new systems should be developed. The presentation will give an overview of the current deployment of wireless communication systems in the rail domain (train-ground, intra-train, inter-train) for train operation and the on-going developments at European level. Challenges to be solved will be highlighted and possible methodologies for dependability analysis will be presented.

Keywords: wireless communications · dependability analysis · safety · railways

1 Introduction

The rail system is a complex system of systems that is entering the era of total automation thanks to wireless sensors and advanced communication, localization and perception systems that transfer the control functions from the human driver to computers. Information must be shared between the various stakeholders in the system: Infrastructure manager, train manager, maintenance manager, timetable manager, customer manager, etc. Consequently, wireless communications are widely deployed for train operation, train maintenance and passenger information. They constitute a cornerstone for railway digitalization.

Today, wireless communication systems are deployed everywhere to answer a large range of communication needs. In this keynote, we will focus on wireless communications related to mission critical applications. The question of safety demonstration and

© The Author(s), under exclusive license to Springer Nature Switzerland AG 2026
M. H. ter Beek et al. (Eds.): RSSRail 2025, LNCS 16236, pp. 14–21, 2026.
https://doi.org/10.1007/978-3-032-10762-6_3

then dependability analysis of a wireless link is an open topic. In general, a so-called "safety layer" is designed to cope with the wireless communications impairments. In particular the Euroradio philosophy will be recalled as an example of safety layer for train-to-ground communication. This protocol is not suitable for decentralized communications such as train-to-train or device-to device communications and new systems should be developed. The presentation will give an overview of the current deployment of wireless communication systems in the rail domain (train-ground, intra-train, inter-train) for train operation and the on-going developments at European level. Challenges to be solved will be highlighted and possible methodologies for dependability analysis will be presented.

2 Wireless Communications: A Cornerstone for Railway Digitalization

For a very long time, there was no communication between the ground and trains, and the only information available to the driver on board his engine was visual information provided by trackside signalling. The first transmission systems between the ground and trains were designed for safety purposes. They involved repeating the signals along the track, particularly the most restrictive ones, on board the locomotive in order to draw the driver's attention to their status. This is also known as "cabsignal". In France, the "crocodile brush" system appeared in 1872 [1]. For regulatory purposes in certain difficult areas, such as mountainous regions, analogue radiotelephone links between control centres and traction units appeared in the early 1960s. This type of link then evolved significantly and spread to most networks across many countries. This system, which is based on the 1G standard, operates in the 450 MHz band and is known as the UIC system. The late 20th century saw a transition to digital communication with the adoption of the Global System for Mobile Communications—Railway (GSM-R), based on the 2G GSM standard, which became the standard for railway voice and data communication across Europe [2]. More recently, transmission requirements have multiplied due to the increasing complexity of train and metro control/command systems, the need to increase the capacity of existing lines and optimize their management and operation. In order to improve the quality of public transport, new transmission requirements have emerged in association with new customer services. The transmissions that exist today in the Railway domain can be divided into two categories:

- voice, data and image transmissions related to control/command installations, safety requirements and operational requirements, also called mission-critical applications;
- voice, data and image transmissions related to the needs of passengers or freight customers also known as non-critical applications.

Three main types of wireless transmission media exist: Point-to-point communication media also known as beacons or balises; continuous wired communication media using magnetic coupling (induction) and radio communication media [1]. These technologies are typically classified according to their application: Train-to-Ground (T2G), Train-to-Train (T2T), and intra-train communications.

Point-to-Point Communication Systems (Beacons). As the name suggests, these systems enable the transmission of information—not necessarily bidirectional—between two relatively close points. Known as short-range communications, the data transmitted is only valid locally within the beacon's coverage area. When a vehicle enters the range of another beacon, any previously received information must be updated or changed. The frequency range for these systems spans from a few kHz to several GHz, but their coverage area must be limited to prevent interference, especially with other systems of the same type. In practice, this means that a beacon at point X must not disrupt the operation of a beacon at point Y, nor should it corrupt the information transmitted by the beacon at point Y. In guided transport, point-to-point communications via beacons are primarily used for: Vehicle identification and location; repeating lateral signalling; speed and integrity control; transmitting information that assists driving, manages onboard automation systems, and, in some cases, supports diagnostics and maintenance.

Continuous   Wired   Communication   Media   Using Magnetic Coupling (Induction). These systems have long been—and remain—highly relevant, especially for communication applications in guided transport. Typically, they are designed as dedicated systems. In their most common configurations, they offer the significant benefit of being cost-effective. However, operating at low frequencies, they face inherent limitations: Restricted useful bandwidth and a poor signal-to-noise ratio. The still existing systems are:

- Single-Conductor Cable System laid between the rails, with the return current flowing through the rails themselves. This configuration is prone to significant crosstalk between parallel tracks, especially on double-track lines.
- Twin-Wire Transmission Line is installed at track level, running alongside the rails. A typical application is the onboard repetition of wayside signalling for trains. Crossed Twin-Wire Line also known as "pilot ribbon".
- Track circuits that are electrical circuits created by isolating a section of track, known as a block. They are used to detect the presence of a train within the block and to transmit wayside signalling information to trains, including maximum authorized speed, the next speed restriction, and the distance to that restriction.

Radio Communication. This is the most suitable method for medium- and long-distance communication. The first system developed for Railway applications was the 1G standard based analogue UIC system in the 450 MHz band as mentioned previously. Significant works have been carried out at the European level for the new ERTMS (European Rail Traffic Management System) control-command system. Its Level 2 and Level 3 functionalities rely on the use of the EIRENE (European Integrated Railway Radio Enhanced Network) digital radio system in the 900 MHz band, which is derived from the GSM Phase 2 + public cellular telephony standard also known as GSM-R. The most widely used frequency bands today are in the sub-6 GHz bands with all the digital cellular systems and the wide deployment of WLAN (Wireless Local Area Network) technologies for Internet of Things. Due to their propagation characteristics, these waves are well-suited for mobile communications. However, the spectrum for vehicular applications is now highly congested, leading to a shift toward higher frequency bands to increase the number of available channels.

One of the primary challenges facing the railway industry in Europe is spectrum scarcity. For example, the European Conference of Postal and Telecommunications Administrations (CEPT) allocated only 2×4 MHz in 874.4–880.0 MHz and 919.4–925.0 MHz for railway control and command, and only 10 MHz in the 1,900 MHz band [3]. This allocation was formalized in the Commission Implementing Decision (EU) 2021/1730 of 28 September 2021, which harmonizes the use of these bands for Railway Mobile Radio (RMR), including both GSM-R and FRMCS. This decision ensures dedicated spectrum for FRMCS across Europe, supporting the transition from GSM-R and enabling the digitalization of rail operations. To address these limitations, millimetric Waves frequency bands (24–100 GHz) are explored to meet the growing demands of railway communications and complement existing standards [4].

3   Railway Wireless Environments: Complexity and Constraints

The various obstacles in the environment between a transmitter and a receiver (terrain or indoor geometry, buildings, vegetation…) create various effects on the propagating radio waves. These effects are related to well-known physical phenomena such as reflection, diffraction and diffusion. These phenomena generate multipath between the transmitter and the receiver, affecting the wave direction, amplitude, phase and polarisation. In addition, when the vehicle is moving, frequency shift, called Doppler shifts, are introduced on each path arriving to the receiver and create a Doppler spectrum that affects the signal. The multipath phenomenon determines the main properties of the radio wave propagation channel [5]:

- Time variability due to dynamic modifications of the radio propagation environment;
- Space variability that describes a different behaviour of the propagation channel when the transmitter and the receiver are moving. This provokes the large- and small-scale variations of the signal also called slow and fast fading.
- Frequency selectivity directly linked to multipaths phenomenon is illustrated on the impulse response or the transfer function respectively in time or in frequency.

All the physical phenomena can be represented from a mathematical point of view considering the system model between the transmitter and the receiver. The complex channel impulse response (response in time) or the complex transfer function of the channel (response in frequency) perfectly represent the channel's behaviour. These models are called channel models. Different statistical representations are generally considered.

Railway environments significantly differ from those typically considered for cellular systems or other transport sectors (such as automotive, maritime, or aeronautical). Moreover, these environments widely vary depending on the train category. Four main categories are generally recognized: Urban, regional, intercity, and high-speed. For High-Speed Lines (HSL), the track profile is usually linear or nearly linear, with large curvature radii. Common HSL environments include open spaces, cuttings, viaducts, tunnels, and stations, with train speeds typically ranging from 300 to 320 km/h. Intercity and regional lines are primarily located in rural areas, which may include open fields, forests, mountains, suburban zones, and medium-sized tunnels. The maximum train speed on these lines is generally around 180 km/h. Areas densely populated with pylons and catenaries are often found near major cities or marshalling yards. Metro systems are predominantly deployed in underground environments. The type and size of tunnels vary depending on whether the line is old or new. One can find different tunnel shape, with one or two tracks. Metro trains usually operate at speeds of 60–80 km/h, though some lines may reach 110–120 km/h.

Beyond the direct influence of the transmitter and receiver surroundings, it is also crucial to consider the potential impact of the numerous wireless systems operating in the vicinity. Electromagnetic interference may arise from poor contact between the catenary and pantograph, which can generate sparks and electromagnetic fields—particularly in low-frequency bands. These disturbances may also produce frequency harmonics, further complicating the electromagnetic environment. Development of channel models for railways is a very active research field in recent years, particularly for HSL and metro. A literature analysis is proposed in [6].

The degradation of radio signals due to propagation challenges directly affects the system performance, availability, reliability, and finally the safety of railway applications. Dynamic variations of the signal and electromagnetic interferences will cause dropped calls, loss of connectivity, delayed messages, increase of packet delivery ratio, errors in time-sensitive messages, decrease of throughput, reduced bandwidth, latency and jitter.

Generally, the effects of radio channels on the radio system are observed at the application layer and not directly on the physical layer. In general a given quality of service (QoS) is required. A lot of mitigation strategies exist depending on the wireless communication system. System performance can be measured at the application level using metrics such as throughput, end-to-end delay, jitter and packet loss. Currently, there is no standard for QoS performance measurement, hence various methods are used, namely actively by insertion of test traffic and passively by observing user-generated traffic. An example of such analysis is proposed in [7].

4 Dependability Assessment in Railway Systems: Risk Analysis and Safety Integrity

Dependability is a collective term used to describe the ability of a system to deliver a service that can justifiably be trusted. It encompasses the following key attributes:

- Availability: The readiness of the system to perform its function when required.
- Reliability: The system's ability to operate without failure for a specified period.
- Safety: The absence of catastrophic consequences for users and the environment.
- Integrity: The system's resistance to unauthorized alterations or corruption.
- Maintainability: The ease with which the system can be repaired or restored after a failure.
- Confidentiality (in some contexts): Protection against unauthorized disclosure of information.

In railway systems, dependability is closely tied to safety integrity levels (SIL) and fault avoidance/mitigation strategies. It goes beyond reliability by addressing both accidental faults and malicious threats (e.g., cybersecurity).

The foundational step in dependability assessment is risk analysis, which systematically identifies and evaluates potential hazards during a system's operational phase. In the railway domain, this process is governed by two key frameworks: The Common Safety Method for Risk Analysis (CSM-RA) and the EN 50126 standard. While EN 50126 establishes the overarching safety framework, CSM-RA provides the specific rules for its implementation. When wireless communication is integrated into an existing railway system, the baseline safety reference remains the legacy systemdblp.org. In such cases, the analysis prioritizes new hazards introduced by wireless technologies, weighing them against the safety benefits they offer. For communication-specific safety aspects, the EN 50159 standard provides a structured methodology to assess and demonstrate the integrity of communication systems.

Given that railway safety is primarily ensured at the application layer, risks related to message handling—such as repetition, deletion, insertion, re-sequencing, corruption, and masquerading—are of paramount concern.

System safety in railway applications is quantified using Safety Integrity Levels (SIL), as defined by the IEC 61508 standard—a cross-domain framework applicable beyond railways. Within the railway sector, EN 50176 and EN 50129 supplement IEC 61508 by addressing domain-specific safety requirements. SIL levels are categorized based on the maximum permissible probability of failure per hour (PFH):

- SIL-1: $\leq 10^{-5}$ PFH
- SIL-2: $\leq 10^{-6}$ PFH
- SIL-3: $\leq 10^{-7}$ PFH
- SIL-4: $\leq 10^{-8}$ PFH

Wireless systems are widely deployed in the rail domain to replace wired systems. Despite the well-defined safety frameworks, there is an urgent need to develop a clear methodology linking the safety requirements of wireless communication links with those of control-command systems remains. It is fundamental to establish this critical relationship to ensure that wireless solutions adhere to the same stringent safety benchmarks as traditional wired systems, thereby maintaining the integrity and reliability of railway operations. The safety layer Euroradio has been developed for centralized system and it is based on GSM-R performances to answer ETCS2 requirements. With the evolution toward IP technology and 5G NR, the performance of the wireless system in terms of robustness and latency, the initial requirements will be impacted and should be analysed.

5   Railway Requirements Related to Wireless Systems Performance

Railway requirements for mission-critical applications relying on wireless communication must define precise Key Performance Indicators (KPIs) at the application level to ensure Reliability, Availability, Maintainability, Safety, Integrity, and Confidentiality. These KPIs typically include metrics such as message loss rate, end-to-end latency, and throughput. Their values are highly influenced by the underlying wireless technology (e.g., GSM-R, LTE, 5G, Wi-Fi) as well as the operational context—train speed, environmental conditions and infrastructure layout.

Additional parameters, such as "coverage continuity"—ensuring signal strength remains above receiver sensitivity thresholds across all environments—and "seamless connectivity", particularly during handover between transmitters at any speed, are equally critical. Handover performance must guarantee uninterrupted data transmission without packet loss.

To define these KPIs accurately, a comprehensive system performance analysis across diverse use cases and operational scenarios is essential and should be performed. Such in-depth evaluations have already been conducted for Train-to-Ground (T2G) systems like GSM-R and they are still on-going for 5G NR based FRMCS, forming the basis for future wireless deployments in railway environments. Examples of requirements will be given during the Key note. These performance evaluations should be done by simulations or using emulators in the case for example of T2T communications for Virtual coupling of trains. In this case new safety layer protocol should be design and evaluated.

6 Methodologies for Dependability Analysis

Evaluating the dependability of railway applications involves a range of analytical methods aimed at measuring key attributes such as reliability, availability, maintainability and safety (RAMS). Here after we list widely recognized techniques.

- Failure Mode, Effects, and Criticality Analysis (FMECA) is a systematic approach used to identify potential failure points in the wireless system and assess their impact on train operations.
- Fault Tree Analysis (FTA) provides a graphical representation of failure pathways, helping to trace root causes and understand how communication disruptions may compromise safety and operational performance.
- Markov models offer a probabilistic framework for capturing the dynamic behaviour of wireless links.
- Petri Nets serve as a flexible modelling tool capable of representing concurrent processes and complex system interactions. These are particularly effective for analysing metrics such as packet loss, system availability and latency in railway communication systems.
- Reliability Block Diagrams (RBD) focus on the reliability of individual system components and their collective influence on overall performance.
- Simulation techniques, including discrete-event and system dynamics models, are commonly employed to study wireless system performance under various railway conditions.
- A multi-method approach, combining tools like FMECA, FTA and simulation, enables a more holistic evaluation of system dependability. This integration provides deeper insights into how different failure mechanisms interact and affect the robustness of railway communication systems.

Today, on-going research related to this topic propose to consider Coloured Peri Nets tool [8, 9] [10]. We will highlight some existing results but the work is still in progress. One fundamental point will be to bridge 5G NR technology characteristics and performances to CPN modelling.

7 Conclusion, Vision of the Future

The evaluation of dependability of wireless-based solutions for mission critical applications will need the development of new methodologies and tools in order to easily consider the wireless systems KPI depending of the railways use cases and scenarios. Can experimentation help for this performance quantification? How can we reach zero-on-site testing and what are the platform to be developed?

In addition, a lot of cutting-edge technologies will help dependability analysis in the future such as: AI-driven, adaptive wireless systems with real-time dependability monitoring and Digital twins for continuous validation of wireless performance.

Dependability is not just a technical requirement; it is the key to trust in Europe's digital rail future.

References

1. Berbineau M.: Les systèmes de télécommunication existants ou émergents et leur utilisation dans le domaine des transports guidés. Synthèse INRETS N°40 (2001). https://www.univ-gus tave-eiffel.fr/fileadmin/user_upload/editions/inrets/Syntheses/Syntheses_INRETS_S40.pdf
2. Sniady, A., Soler, J.: An overview of GSM-R technology and its shortcomings. In: 12th International Conference on ITS Telecommunications. pp. 626–629. IEEE (2012). https://doi.org/10.1109/ITST.2012.6425256
3. https://www.etsi.org/technologies/rail-communications. Accessed 28 Sept 2025
4. Berbineau, M., et al.: Millimetric waves communications for railways. Transportation Research Procedia. 72, 1248–1255 (2023). https://doi.org/10.1016/j.trpro.2023.11.584
5. Parsons, J. D.: The mobile radio propagation channel. Copyright © 2000 John Wiley & Sons, Ltd (2001). ISBN:9780471988571. Online ISBN:9780470841525. https://doi.org/10.1002/0470841524
6. Berbineau, M. et al.: Channel models for performance evaluation of wireless systems in railway environments. In: IEEE Access, vol. 9, pp. 45903–45918 (2021). https://doi.org/10.1109/ACCESS.2021.3066112
7. Berbineau, M. et al.: IP impairment models for performance evaluation of wireless systems in railway environments. In: IEEE Access, vol. 11, pp. 69928–69938 (2023). https://doi.org/10.1109/ACCESS.2023.3292794
8. Verma, S., Mohamed, G., Marion, B.: Model-based dependability evaluation of a wireless communication system in a virtually coupled train set. IFAC-Papers Online 54.2. 179–186 (2021). https://doi.org/10.1016/j.ifacol.2021.06.045
9. Li, R., Wu, D.: A CPN -based reliability analysis of a wireless communication system in a virtually coupled train set.: 2023 China Automation Congress (CAC), Chongqing, China, pp. 1954–1959 (2023). https://doi.org/10.1109/ICPICS52425.2021.9524226
10. Geleta, G.H., Berbineau, M., Collart-Dutilleul, S., Francesco F.: CPN-based modelling to assess dependability of train-to-train wireless communication for virtual coupling. In: Proceedings RSSRAIL2025, Pisa. LNCS 16236

AI and Planning

From Relay-Based Railway Interlocking Circuits to Formal Specification: An AI-Driven Approach

Dalay Almeida[(✉)] [iD] and Loïc Glemarec

CLEARSY, Aix-en-Provence, France
`{dalay.almeida,loic.glemarec}@CLEARSY.com`

Abstract. Relay-based Railway Interlocking Systems (RIS) control railway components like signals and turnouts safely but are still analysed manually through their relay diagrams, a process prone to errors. Previous works proposed formal methods and industrial tools for RIS analysis, but digitalizing and automatically transforming these diagrams into formal specifications remained challenging. This paper presents a proof of concept using an existing Multimodal Language Model to analyse relay diagrams and automatically generate formal specifications in propositional logic. Our method adopts a prompt-based methodology to guide the expected outcome (model in propositional logic) which is then applied to new diagrams. The results confirm that automatic formalization is feasible and accessible. This work opens promising perspectives for further improving correctness through dedicated prompt engineering or fine-tuning, advancing automation of the formal verification of relay-based railway systems.

Keywords: Relay-based Railway Interlocking Systems · Artifical Intelligence · Formal Methods · Large Language Models (LLMs) · Prompt Engineering · Multimodal Language Models · B-method

1 Introduction

Relay-based Railway Interlocking Systems (RIS) are used to control electrical components such as signals and turnouts, ensuring the safe movement of trains. These legacy systems are typically modelled as electrical circuit diagrams, known as relay diagrams, which depict how components are interconnected through cables. Despite the safety-critical nature of these systems, their analysis is still predominantly manual, that is, engineers interpret the diagrams and draw conclusions, a process that is inherently error-prone [12].

In previous works, we have proposed several methodologies for analysing these systems using Formal Methods [3–5,7]. However, the automatic translation of relay diagrams, from graphical representations to formal specifications, remains a significant challenge. Current approaches often require either a prior manual analysis of the system's structure or the time-consuming task of redrawing the diagrams within specialised tools [16]. An ideal solution would eliminate the need for

M. H. ter Beek et al. (Eds.): RSSRail 2025, LNCS 16236, pp. 25–34, 2026.
https://doi.org/10.1007/978-3-032-10762-6_4

reinterpretation or redrawing, offering a more streamlined and universally accessible approach.

Building on the idea of automating the manual analysis of relay-based Railway Interlocking Systems, this work explores the use of Artificial Intelligence (AI) to derive formal specifications directly from relay diagrams. As a proof of concept, we evaluate the capabilities of a state-of-the-art multimodal AI model, o3 from OpenAI, in interpreting these diagrams and generating formal specifications in propositional logic. Our results demonstrate that what was once a complex and specialized task can now be achieved with accessible and general-purpose AI tools, opening new perspectives for the automation of safety-critical system analysis.

Several studies have explored the use of artificial intelligence for diagram digitalisation, including applications in the railway domain [10,11,14,15,17,19, 20,26,27]. A notable recent contribution addresses the digitalisation of diagrams used by the Italian Railway Company [21–23], focusing on their specific conventions and representations. However, many of these approaches were developed at a time when AI models were neither as accessible nor as powerful as they are today. The key contribution of our work lies in demonstrating how a readily available AI model can be employed not only to digitalise relay diagrams but also to automatically generate the corresponding formal specifications, eliminating the need for intermediate steps. This highlights how technological advances have significantly lowered the barriers to such tasks. Moreover, as relay diagram conventions vary between railway companies, our study focuses on the French context, specifically the SNCF's diagrammatic standards, which pose particular challenges for generic AI models. Additionally, our work targets the automated generation of formal specifications in propositional logic, structured to support B-Method [1] specifications, building upon our prior work presented in [5].

The remainder of this paper is structured as follows. Section 2 provides an overview of relay diagrams and their formal specification. Section 3 describes the AI model used in our study. Section 4 details our methodology for preparing the prompt for the AI model, along with the results obtained. Section 5 presents a discussion of the findings, and Sect. 6 concludes the paper, outlining potential directions for future work.

2   Analysis and Formal Specification of Relay-Based RIS

Relay-based Railway Interlocking Systems (RIS) use electrical circuit logic based on relays to safely control components such as signals and turnouts. Despite the availability of modern technologies, these legacy systems are still in use in the majority of the french installations [24]. Their core component, the relay, consists of an electromagnetic coil and one or more contacts that open or close connections when the coil is energized. Additionally, several other components may be included in the circuits, such as capacitors, buttons, levers, and even more complex elements, like special-purpose blocks that encapsulate their own internal circuitry. More details about these diagrams can be found in [4,5].

As the analysis of these systems is generally performed manually, we have proposed some methodologies for their analysis based on Formal Methods. In this context, two distinct works stand out. In [5], we proposed a formal specification approach using the propositional logic supported by the B-method. In this approach, the activation condition of a component A can be expressed in terms of the activation of other components: B1 = TRUE &...& Bn = TRUE => A = TRUE, where TRUE indicates that a component is activated, and FALSE otherwise. Although propositional logic suits the specification of functional properties, it cannot detect RIS-specific issues such as ringbell effects[1] or short circuits[2]. To complement this, in [7] we proposed using CSP (Communicating Sequential Processes) [13], a formal language for specifying concurrent systems. That work showed how CSP assertions enable a concurrency-oriented analysis of relay-based RIS, allowing the verification of properties that could not be checked before.

A key challenge in previous works remains: converting relay diagrams into formal specifications. Despite advances in formal methods, this step still relies on manual analysis or redrawing [16], which is time-consuming and prone to errors. In this work, we explore how AI tools can automate this process for relay-based Railway Interlocking Systems, making the specification and analysis of these systems more efficient.

3   AI Model

In this work, we leveraged the o3[3] model of ChatGPT [2], a state-of-the-art large language model (LLM) developed by OpenAI, to support the formalization of legacy railway interlocking circuits [8]. The o3 model stands out for its improved reasoning capabilities, prompt sensitivity, and contextual comprehension, making it particularly suitable for translating low-level, domain-specific knowledge into structured formal specifications. A key advantage of using this model in our railway application is its ability to interpret and reorganize complex relay-based logic into higher-level representations when guided by well-crafted prompts.

Unlike earlier models, o3 demonstrates remarkable robustness in handling long contextual dependencies and domain-specific jargon, both of which are essential in the safety-critical context of railway systems. Our methodology emphasizes prompt engineering [18] as a central element: clear, precise prompts significantly enhance the model's performance, enabling efficient extraction, abstraction, and transformation of circuit-level information. This prompt-driven interaction is central to our methodology: rather than relying on extensive retraining or handcrafted rule sets, we provide the o3 model with a minimal but representative example of the reasoning process we expect (often a simplified instance of relay logic interpretation) and instruct it to extend that reasoning across more complex cases. This approach enables domain experts to guide the

---

[1] when two or more relays repeatedly activate and deactivate each other in a loop, potentially leading to overheating or unstable behaviour.

[2] when there is a direct connection between power lines, allowing uncontrolled current flow, which may cause severe damage or fire.

[3] https://openai.com/index/introducing-o3-and-o4-mini/.

model's behaviour with high precision, ensuring consistency with domain-specific logic while maintaining scalability and efficiency [9] [25].

Overall, the integration of o3 within our AI-driven framework has the potential to demonstrate how modern LLMs can be effectively directed toward formal abstraction tasks, offering a powerful bridge between legacy engineering artifacts and formal verification practices in safety-critical railway systems.

4   Transformation from Relay Diagram to Formal Specification

To analyse relay diagrams and generate the corresponding formal specifications using the AI model, we adopted a two-step approach. First, we crafted a prompt explaining and specifying the logic of a simple diagram in a format close to that used by SNCF, instructing the AI to follow the same method for subsequent ones. Then, we submitted increasingly complex diagrams, ending with an industrial relay-based RIS example from SNCF.

4.1   Initial Prompt

The proposed prompt, illustrated in Fig. 1, is structured into four parts: (1) a description of the task given to the AI, (2) an explanation of relay-based systems and the provided diagram, (3) a representation of the propositional logic describing the system's behaviour, and (4) an instruction for the AI to alert on potential issues in the diagrams.

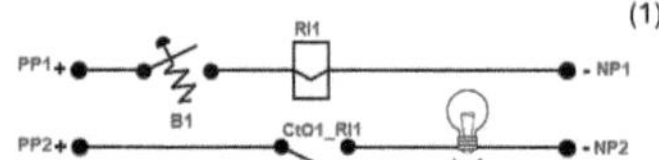

(1) I need you to read some relay-based electrical circuit diagrams for me, describe them, and explain the logic behind the behavior shown in these diagrams. I will start by giving you an example of a diagram, in which I explain its components and logic. After that, you will do the same for other diagrams that I will present.

(2) The diagram in the image contains several components connected by wires. A component is activated when it is connected to both the positive and negative poles at the same time. In this diagram, between the positive pole PP1 and the negative pole NP1, we have a button B1 and the coil of relay Rl1. Between the positive pole PP2 and the negative pole NP2, we have the contact CtO1_Rl1 and a lamp Lp1. The contact is vertically aligned with the relay coil, indicating that they are related. The behavior of this diagram works as follows: when button B1 is pressed, a connection is established between the positive and negative poles that powers the coil of relay Rl1. Once activated, the coil switches the contact CtO1_Rl1, creating a connection between the positive and negative poles that powers the lamp Lp1, turning it on. In this sense, the coil activation depends on B1 to close the connection between the poles, while Lp1's activation depends on Rl1 being energized so that the contact can close the connection. The logic of the behavior is as follows:

(3) B1 = TRUE => Rl1 = TRUE
Rl1 = TRUE => Lp1 = TRUE

Note that the logic does not describe the states of the contacts, which are completely abstracted by the states of their corresponding relays. In this case, it is important not to describe the contact states. As for the buttons, we define the closed (pressed) state as TRUE and the open state as FALSE. Other components have TRUE for activated and FALSE for deactivated. If at any point you need to describe time, you may use a Boolean variable to indicate whether time has passed or not. It is important that everything is expressed in propositional logic.

(4) During the analysis, if you encounter issues such as the ringbell effect or short circuits, do not hesitate to let me know.

Fig. 1. Image and text used in the AI prompt

While we aimed to be exhaustive in describing what the AI should reason about, we intentionally omitted certain key information to evaluate the model's ability to infer it autonomously. For example, we did not mention all component types or the specific issues the model should detect. Nevertheless, with respect to the system logic, we were as explicit as possible to ensure that the AI could generate outputs suitable for integration into a formal specification.

For the initial diagram, we selected a simple example in which a button activates a relay, which in turn closes a contact that switches on a light. The symbols for the relay, button, and contact follow the same graphical conventions used in SNCF diagrams, including the vertical alignment between a relay and its corresponding contact. However, some details were intentionally simplified. For instance, lamps are not typically represented in this way in real SNCF diagrams; we omitted the vertical semi-dotted line that usually links relays to their contacts, and we assigned explicit names to each component—something that does not usually appear in actual systems.

4.2   Experimentation on Various Diagrams

After the initial prompt, we submitted a series of diagrams (shown in Fig. 2) to be analysed and specified by the AI model, allowing it to reason about each diagram before introducing the next one. The model's responses consistently demonstrated accurate reasoning about system behaviour, followed by meaningful formal specifications expressed in propositional logic. In this paper, we do not present the full reasoning process, as the model was exhaustive in its output. Instead, we focus on the resulting formal specifications, which reflect the underlying reasoning. The complete responses are available elsewhere[4].

Diagram (1) illustrates a typical ringbell effect configuration, in which two relays are connected in a feedback loop and activated by a button within the same circuit. The model produced a long, detailed, and accurate explanation of the logic, followed by the following formal specification:

```
B1 & ¬R11 => R12    Button pressed and R11 not energised drives
   R12 TRUE.
R12 => R11    Whenever R12 is TRUE, R11 is driven TRUE.
R11 => ¬R12    An energised R11 forces R12 FALSE.
¬R12 => ¬R11    When R12 is FALSE, R11 is forced FALSE.
Lp1 <=> R11    The lamp follows the state of R11.
```

The logic is indeed correct, although we intentionally provided an example whose conditions can never be satisfied due to the ringbell effect. In this context, the AI produced a valuable observation: *"because these implications form a closed contradictory loop when B1 = TRUE, no stable truth assignment exists: the system oscillates. Technical note – ring-bell effect"*. This shows that the AI was not only capable of reasoning about the diagram and producing a propositional logic

---

[4] https://zenodo.org/records/15525212.

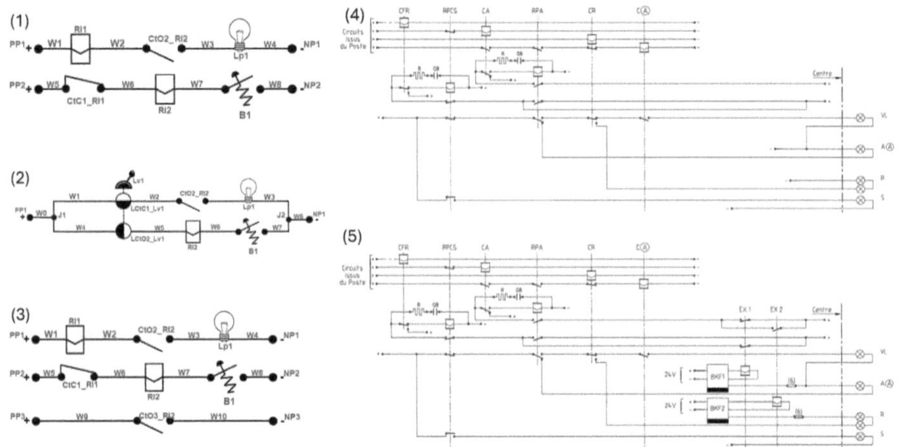

Fig. 2. Diagrams provided to the AI to be analysed and formally specified

specification, but also of identifying a behavioural anomaly that prevents a consistent logical specification. The response exceeded our expectations, providing insights and details beyond those explicitly given in the prompt.

Diagram (2) presents a similar configuration. However, the relay RL1 is replaced by a lever that can block or allow the flow of energy in both circuits. Additionally, junctions are introduced to reduce the number of energy sources. The propositional logic generated by the AI for this configuration is as follows:

```
Rl2 <=> (B1 & Lv1)
Lp1 <=> (Rl2 & ¬Lv1)
```

RL2 is thus activated if the button is pressed and the lever is in the true state (defined as the left position), while the lamp is activated if RL2 is active and the lever is in the false state (defined as the right position). In this example, the AI correctly identified the component LV1 as a lever, inferred its behaviour, and modelled it using Boolean logic, all without being provided with any explicit information about this component. Moreover, in its reasoning (the explanatory text provided alongside the logic), it pointed out that there was no stable condition for lamp activation, although the lamp might pulse briefly during contact crossover.

Diagram (3) reproduces the same ringbell effect observed in diagram (1), but introduces an additional short circuit at the bottom of the diagram, which occurs when RL2 is activated. In this case, the AI reproduced the logic from (1) and correctly captured the short-circuit behaviour, expressing it with an additional line in the logical specification: `Short PP3 <=> RL2`. Here, `Short PP3` represents a boolean value indicating whether a short circuit exists in `PP3` (TRUE) or not (FALSE).

Diagrams (4) and (5) are based on an industrial example provided by SNCF and detailed in [6,7]. While diagram (4) avoids the use of blocks, components that in the SNCF diagram represent time-based behaviours, diagram (5) includes such a block. These final diagrams were intended as a challenge for the AI as they replicate real-world relay-based systems used by a company within a specific railway context. The results for these examples were interesting, though not entirely satisfactory.

The AI correctly identified the nature of the diagrams as light panels, recognized capacitors, resistors, and lights, and reasoned correctly about the vertical alignment between relays and their contacts, marked by semi-dotted vertical lines. However, in terms of system behaviour, we believe the AI relied more on its prior knowledge of similar systems than on the actual logic depicted in the diagrams. For example, in the logic it provided for the activation of S in diagram (4), the AI included `CFR & RPCS & CR`, based on the assumption that R and S should be activated together. However, in this specific diagram, the activation of S depends solely on the deactivation of `RPCS`.

A similar issue occurred in the analysis of diagram (5): while the AI did an excellent job describing the components, it again prioritized its general knowledge over the specific behaviour shown in the diagram. For instance, it assumed that the BFK blocks are used to flash the lights. Although this is true in the original diagram from which this example was derived, the version we provided is modified, and the flashing behaviour is no longer possible. Nevertheless, the AI accurately described the relays `EX.1` and `EX.2` as responsible for creating failure alerts intended for maintenance staff.

5   Discussion

The transformation from relay diagrams to formal specification typically involves several steps: interpreting the diagrams, reasoning about their logic, describing the system behaviour, and finally producing a formal specification. In some cases, diagrams are redrawn using machine-readable formats such as XML to facilitate automated analysis. However, the o3 model, as a multi-modal AI system, is capable of performing all these steps autonomously, identifying components and connections, deducing activation logic, and generating the corresponding formal specification. This opens the possibility of developing a powerful translator that could significantly impact the relay-based RIS domain. Nevertheless, as this is a safety-critical application domain, it is essential that any generated specification be thoroughly reviewed and validated by domain experts before use. Despite its efficiency, the AI model may produce inaccurate results due to incorrect assumptions about the system and its context, as observed in our experiments.

Another critical aspect concerns the limitations of the model when dealing with diagrams from specific railway contexts, such as SNCF. In these cases, while the AI generally identified most components and connections, it began to rely on prior knowledge and expectations about how such systems typically function, sometimes overlooking the actual structure and logic of the given diagram.

This behaviour stems from our strategy of omitting certain contextual details to test whether the AI could infer them autonomously. Based on the results, we believe that providing more explicit information about components and their intended behaviour may improve performance on complex, context-specific relay diagrams.

The syntax of the propositional logic initially provided by the AI does not fully match the one used in the B-method. Nevertheless, the AI is able to adjust the expressions accordingly once our expectations are clarified. In this context, providing more detailed instructions in the initial prompt could prevent the need for this additional correction step.

6   Conclusions and Perspectives

The work presented in this paper is a proof of concept for using an existing AI tool to automatically transform relay-based Railway Interlocking System diagrams into formal specifications for analysis purposes. Rather than training new models or designing step-by-step pipelines for parsing and interpreting the diagrams, we explore the use of OpenAI's o3 model as a comprehensive solution. As a multimodal model, o3 is capable of independently performing all the required steps to reason about the system behaviour and to produce a formal specification of its logic. This demonstrates the potential of such AI models to act as end-to-end translators from circuit diagrams to formal specifications, offering a powerful and efficient tool for the analysis of legacy railway systems.

However, given the safety-critical nature of Railway Interlocking Systems, it is essential to emphasize that the outputs produced by the model must always be reviewed by a domain expert. The formal specification generated by the AI should not be used directly in safety analyses or system design without prior validation, as the model may introduce incorrect assumptions or overlook critical details. Expert verification remains a fundamental step in ensuring the reliability and safety of the resulting specification.

This work opens up several promising perspectives, especially given that the AI technology employed is both efficient (able to generate formal specifications rapidly without human intervention) and widely accessible. The results show that the model exhibits strong reasoning capabilities, and there is much to explore in this direction. Rather than training a new model, we plan to develop a structured dataset that can be directly used to enrich prompts with domain-specific knowledge. In particular, this dataset would cover the various types of components and circuit patterns commonly used in the railway industry, providing detailed and context-relevant information without departing from the prompting principle. The goal is to supply the model with a stronger knowledge base through carefully designed inputs, enabling it to generate more complete and well-grounded formal specifications. Such a curated dataset would reflect the specificities of relay-based RIS, supporting more robust reasoning and reducing the need for implicit assumptions. Finally, we observed that the AI sometimes relies on its general knowledge or assumptions about system behaviour, rather than strictly following the logic depicted in the provided diagrams. Addressing this limitation will be an important focus of future work.

A further point for future work concerns scalability. The examples used in this study were relatively simple, with a limited number of components and straightforward connections. Larger diagrams, with more components and complex interconnections, may increase the computational time required by the model; however, this remains purely machine-time and does not require additional human intervention. Evaluating strategies to maintain efficiency with growing diagram complexity will be explored in subsequent studies.

Additionally, future work could investigate the benefits of fine-tuning a multimodal AI model specifically for the railway domain. By training on real-world diagrams, component specifications, and safety-critical scenarios, it may be possible to significantly improve the model's precision and reliability when interpreting relay logic and producing formal specifications. Such specialization would contribute to the safe and effective application of AI tools in the context of railway system engineering.

References

1. Abrial, J.-R., Lee, M.K.O., Neilson, D.S., Scharbach, P.N., Sørensen, I.H.: The B-method. In: Prehn, S., Toetenel, H. (eds.) VDM 1991. LNCS, vol. 552, pp. 398–405. Springer, Heidelberg (1991). https://doi.org/10.1007/BFb0020001
2. Achiam, J., et al.: Gpt-4 technical report. arXiv preprint arXiv:2303.08774 (2023)
3. Almeida, D., Jamain, F., Lecomte, T.: Formal analysis and monitoring of legacy safety-critical interlocking systems with the use of certified industrial tools. In: International Conference on Formal Methods for Industrial Critical Systems, pp. 182–198. Springer, Heidelberg (2024). https://doi.org/10.1007/978-3-031-68150-9_11
4. de Almeida Pereira, D.I.: Analysis and formal specification of relay-based railway interlocking systems. Ph.D. thesis, Centrale Lille Institut (2020)
5. de Almeida Pereira, D.I., Deharbe, D., Perin, M., Bon, P.: B-specification of relay-based railway interlocking systems based on the propositional logic of the system state evolution. In: Collart-Dutilleul, S., Lecomte, T., Romanovsky, A. (eds.) RSSRail 2019. LNCS, vol. 11495, pp. 242–258. Springer, Cham (2019). https://doi.org/10.1007/978-3-030-18744-6_16
6. Bezerra, P.E.R.: CSP Specification and Verification of a Relay-Based Rail Interlocking System. Master's thesis, Universidade Federal do Rio Grande do Norte (2023)
7. Bezerra, P., Oliveira, M.V.M., Lecomte, T., de Almeida Pereira, D.I.: CSP specification and verification of a relay-based railway interlocking system. In: Brazilian Symposium on Formal Methods, pp. 36–54. Springer, Heidelberg (2023). https://doi.org/10.1007/978-3-031-49342-3_3
8. Bommasani, R., et al.: On the opportunities and risks of foundation models. arXiv preprint arXiv:2108.07258 (2021)
9. Brown, T., et al.: Language models are few-shot learners. Adv. Neural. Inf. Process. Syst. **33**, 1877–1901 (2020)
10. Dey, M., et al.: A two-stage cnn-based hand-drawn electrical and electronic circuit component recognition system. Neural Comput. Appl. **33**, 13367–13390 (2021)

11. Elyan, E., Jamieson, L., Ali-Gombe, A.: Deep learning for symbols detection and classification in engineering drawings. Neural Netw. **129**, 91–102 (2020)
12. Haxthausen, A.E., Le Bliguet, M., Kjær, A.A.: Modelling and verification of relay interlocking systems. In: Choppy, C., Sokolsky, O. (eds.) Monterey Workshop 2008. LNCS, vol. 6028, pp. 141–153. Springer, Heidelberg (2010). https://doi.org/10.1007/978-3-642-12566-9_8
13. Hoare, C.A.R.: Communicating sequential processes. Commun. ACM **21**(8), 666–677 (1978)
14. Kang, S.O., Lee, E.B., Baek, H.K.: A digitization and conversion tool for imaged drawings to intelligent piping and instrumentation diagrams (p&id). Energies **12**(13), 2593 (2019)
15. Kim, H.: Deep-learning-based recognition of symbols and texts at an industrially applicable level from images of high-density piping and instrumentation diagrams. Expert Syst. Appl. **183**, 115337 (2021)
16. Lecomte, T., Deharbe, D., Fournier, P., Oliveira, M.: The clearsy safety platform: 5 years of research, development and deployment. Sci. Comput. Program. **199**, 102524 (2020)
17. Li, L., Yuhui, C., Xiaoting, L.: Engineering drawing recognition model with convolutional neural network. In: Proceedings of the 2019 International Conference on Robotics, Intelligent Control and Artificial Intelligence, pp. 112–116 (2019)
18. Liu, P., Yuan, W., Fu, J., Jiang, Z., Hayashi, H., Neubig, G.: Pre-train, prompt, and predict: a systematic survey of prompting methods in natural language processing. ACM Comput. Surv. **55**(9), 1–35 (2023)
19. Mani, S., Haddad, M.A., Constantini, D., Douhard, W., Li, Q., Poirier, L.: Automatic digitization of engineering diagrams using deep learning and graph search. In: Proceedings of the IEEE/CVF Conference on Computer Vision and Pattern Recognition Workshops, pp. 176–177 (2020)
20. Shi, B., Bai, X., Yao, C.: An end-to-end trainable neural network for image-based sequence recognition and its application to scene text recognition. IEEE Trans. Pattern Anal. Mach. Intell. **39**(11), 2298–2304 (2016)
21. Stefenon, S.F., Cristoforetti, M., Cimatti, A.: Towards automatic digitalization of railway engineering schematics. In: International Conference of the Italian Association for Artificial Intelligence, pp. 453–466. Springer, Heidelberg (2023). https://doi.org/10.1007/978-3-031-47546-7_31
22. Stefenon, S.F., Cristoforetti, M., Cimatti, A.: Automatic digitalization of railway interlocking systems engineering drawings based on hybrid machine learning methods. Expert Syst. Appl. **281**, 127532 (2025)
23. Stefenon, S.F., Cristoforetti, M., Cimatti, A.: Conditional diffusion to enhance performance of object detection in unbalanced data engineering drawings. Neural Comput. Appl. 1–30 (2025)
24. Theeg, G., Vlasenko, S., et al.: Railway signalling & interlocking. Int. Compendium **448** (2009)
25. Wei, J., et al.: Chain-of-thought prompting elicits reasoning in large language models. Adv. Neural. Inf. Process. Syst. **35**, 24824–24837 (2022)
26. Yu, E.S., Cha, J.M., Lee, T., Kim, J., Mun, D.: Features recognition from piping and instrumentation diagrams in image format using a deep learning network. Energies **12**(23), 4425 (2019)
27. Yun, D.Y., Seo, S.K., Zahid, U., Lee, C.J.: Deep neural network for automatic image recognition of engineering diagrams. Appl. Sci. **10**(11), 4005 (2020)

SMT-Based Verification of Railway Plannings

Stefan Dillmann$^{(\boxtimes)}$ and Reiner Hähnle

Department of Computer Science, Technische Universität Darmstadt, Darmstadt,
Germany
`{dillmann,haehnle}@cs.tu-darmstadt.de`

Abstract. Each planning phase of ETCS-compliant railway tracks at
Deutsche Bahn (DB) prescribes a concluding review, now performed
by manually inspecting printed diagrams and tables. This is time-
consuming and bears the risk to overlook critical mistakes. We present a
concept and a tool for fully automated formal verification of railway plannings against ETCS planning rules. The approach is based on a modular
translation of track models, as well as planning rules, to the SMT-LIB
language understood by Satisfiability Modulo Theories (SMT) solvers,
which are used as a backend. Track models are assumed to be available in
the standardized object-oriented PlanPro format and are automatically
translated to SMT-LIB constraints. The planning rules themselves are
given in natural language in rule books and cannot be translated automatically. Instead, we provide a translation schema that lets a planning
engineer render planning rules almost one-to-one as first-order formulas. No specific knowledge of logic or SMT solver internals is required
to perform this task, and it is sufficient to do it once and for all for
each planning rule. Subsequent verification of a track model against a
planning rule is fully automatic. Deviations are visually highlighted for
manual inspection. To this end, we integrated rule verification with an
existing track visualization tool into a GUI. Our approach was evaluated with real DB infrastructure data, showing that it is easy to use and
sufficiently powerful to be integrated into existing planning workflows.

Keywords: Railway Track Planning · ETCS · Verification · SMT

1 Introduction

The program *Digitale Schiene Deutschland*[1] (Digital Rail Germany) intends to
equip the entire German railway network with digital interlocking systems and
the European Train Control System (ETCS) within the next 20 years. This
implies the need to speed up the existing planning process, which is divided
into a plan creation part and a review part, both predominantly performed
manually, with limited tool support. Some work has already been done towards
a digital planning workflow: The *PlanPro* data format [5] was specified as a

---

[1] https://digitale-schiene-deutschland.de/en.

© The Author(s), under exclusive license to Springer Nature Switzerland AG 2026
M. H. ter Beek et al. (Eds.): RSSRail 2025, LNCS 16236, pp. 35–52, 2026.
https://doi.org/10.1007/978-3-032-10762-6_5

standardized object-oriented data exchange format between planners and the signalling industry [13], while the traditional manual approach for plan creation and review was retained.

Previous work [6] on the ETCS planning demonstrator EPLAN[2] proved that it is possible to use the PlanPro format as a basis for fully-automated ETCS plan creation. This leaves the mandatory review of the automatically created plans. That is still performed by inspecting paper-based drawings of track layouts and corresponding data tables that list the properties of all relevant objects, such as signals and ETCS balises.

Tool-supported verification of plans would not only speed up the review process, but also increase the quality by minimizing the amount of undetected errors. To guide the development of such a verification concept, we formulate the following research questions:

RQ1: How can one verify a plan for correctness, and how can one formalize the planning rules for this purpose?

RQ2: How can one hide the technical details to a degree such that a domain expert without knowledge of formal methods can use it?

RQ3: How can one deal with incomplete and changing requirements, such as revised planning rules?

Our primary approach is to use existing data formats and technologies as much as possible for seamless integration into existing planning workflows. We use PlanPro as input format, because is intended as the new standard for digital plannings in the DB network. To formalize and to solve the ensuing verification problems, we use the *SMT-LIB* [2] format, which is supported by a wide array of *Satisfiability Modulo Theories* (SMT) solvers. The advantage is that we can employ different solvers with orthogonal strengths, and we profit from the rapid advance of the SMT community. We also want to provide an executable demonstrator, capable to work on real infrastructure data, and not only a pen-and-paper concept. The implementation should be as minimal as possible to keep the knowledge barrier for railway domain experts low, yet flexible enough to handle changing requirements. To this end, we implement the principle of *knowledge separation*: The tool is modularized along barriers that separate different kinds of expertise, not along technical subsystems. As software developers, we do not require knowledge about railway engineering or theorem proving. These tasks can be ceded to the respective domain experts. The modules communicate via the standardized interfaces PlanPro or SMT-LIB (see Fig. 1).

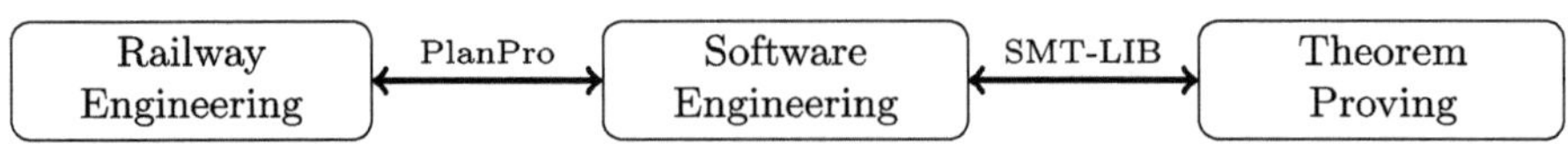

Fig. 1. Knowledge Separation in Tool-Supported Planning and Verification

---

[2] https://github.com/formetcs/eplan.

```
1  (set-option :print-success false)
2  (set-option :produce-models true)
3  (set-logic QF_LIA)
4  (declare-fun x () Int)
5  (declare-fun y () Int)
6  (assert (= (+ x (* 2 y)) 20))
7  (assert (= (- x y) 2))
8  (check-sat)
```

Listing 1.1. Example SMT-LIB File

Accordingly, the contributions of this paper are (i) a *concept* for fully auto-mated, SMT-based verification of ETCS plans in PlanPro format, (ii) an exe-cutable plan *verification tool*, integrated in the existing track visualization tool PLANPRO VIEWER[3], and (iii) an *evaluation* on realistic case studies.

In Sect. 2 we give a short description of SMT and the SMT-LIB language, as well as the German ETCS planning rules and the PlanPro format. In Sect. 3 we present the architecture and in Sect. 4 we show how to translate the PlanPro types into SMT-LIB formulas. Section 5 shows a simple usage example, while Sect. 6 covers the evaluation of our approach. Finally, in Sect. 7 we discuss related work and in Sect. 8 we conclude.

2   Background

In this section we briefly introduce the concepts and notations necessary for this paper, including basic SMT concepts, the German ETCS planning rules, and the PlanPro data format.

2.1   Satisfiability Modulo Theories and SMT-LIB

The *Satisfiability Modulo Theories (SMT)* problem is about checking whether a given first-order logic formula φ is *satisfiable* in the context of some background theory that constrains the interpretation of the symbols occurring in the formula. *Satisfiability* means that there is at least one assignment of values to uninter-preted symbols (a *model*) that evaluates φ to true, whereas *validity* means that every model evaluates φ to true. An SMT solver only proves satisfiability and finds satisfying assignments for uninterpreted symbols. To determine whether a formula φ is *valid*, we ask whether the negated formula $\neg\varphi$ is *unsatisfiable*. A satisfying assignment of values to $\neg\varphi$ is called a *counter example*.

A software tool that implements an SMT procedure is called *SMT solver*. A standardized input language for these solvers is *SMT-LIB*, using a LISP-style syntax [2]. SMT-LIB expresses logical problems in many-sorted first-order logic. Listing 1.1 shows an example SMT-LIB file [3]. The background theory and the

---

[3] https://github.com/formetcs/ppview.

used logic is set to `QF_LIA`, which includes linear integer arithmetic and restricts the input to quantifier-free formulas. Two uninterpreted symbols x and y are declared as constant integer functions, formulas are specified using the **assert** statement. When this file is sent to an SMT solver, the response will be "`sat`", meaning that it is satisfiable.[4] With an additional **get−value** command, one can query the satisfying assignments for x and y (here, for example, x=8 and y=6).

2.2 ETCS Planning Rules

The planning rulebook for signalling systems in Germany is Ril 819 [4]. It is divided into several modules covering different subsystems. Relevant for our scenario is module 819.1344 for planning at ETCS Level 2. The module defines various types of *data points*. These are balise groups with a specific meaning and a common set of included ETCS packets, as well as rules for placement, mostly relative to a reference point.

The rulebook is not written as a procedural (step-by-step) instruction of how to obtain a valid ETCS plan. Instead, the rules describe constraints which a final plan has to satisfy in a *declarative* manner. They are written rather from the perspective of a plan reviewer than a plan creator. *This makes logical formulas a natural fit for their formalization and permits automated plan verification using logic-based solvers.* For example, consider the following rule (ignore the vertical bars for the moment, these are not part of the rule text):

"For every signal, | a data point | of type 24 | has to be placed 50 m (±5 m) in front of the signal."

Assuming we provide a library with predefined common functions like *type* or *dist*, then the constituents of the rule indicated by the bars is formalized in a nearly one-to-one manner as a first-order formula:

$$\forall s \in Signal : \exists d \in Datapoint : type(d) = 24 \land 45 \le dist(s, d) \le 55$$

Even a railway expert without formal methods knowledge can understand and write such formulas. Moreover, it would be easy to provide a visual interface with menu selections to enter such formulas in a structured manner, without having to know the formal syntax.

2.3 The PlanPro Data Format

PlanPro [5] is an XML-based object-oriented data model intended as an interchange standard between planners and signal manufacturers [13]. It defines objects for all elements in a signalling system: The track layout (modeled as a graph with nodes and edges), switches, signals, block definitions, components

---

[4] Other possible responses are "`unsat`", meaning that the formula is unsatisfiable, or "`unknown`", meaning that the result could not be determined (because of resource limits or solver incompleteness).

for train control systems (ETCS balises or components for the German PZB system) and train detection devices.

All objects have properties, including a unique object id. The object classes form a hierarchy, and properties common to subclasses are defined in their parent class. For example, all objects that have a location (such as signals or balises) inherit from the parent class `Punkt_Objekt` (point object), where the position information is defined. Cross references between objects are realized by referencing the object id, which is a 128 bit UUID conforming to RFC 4122 [10].

PlanPro actually defines two graph layers for the track layout: The *geometric* layer, where edges represent straight lines or curves, i.e. the exact actual layout, and the more abstract *topological* layer, where each node (`TOP_Knoten`) is a switch and the edges (`TOP_Kante`) are the connections between them. Each `Punkt_Objekt` subtype references a `TOP_Kante`, and the position is modeled as longitudinal and lateral distance relative to the beginning of the edge.

3   Approach

To prove the validity of a railway planning using an SMT-based approach, we need to rewrite the planning rules towards the error case perspective. For example, a rule like "For every exit signal, a data point of type 21 has to be planned" has to be written as "There is an exit signal, where no data point of type 21 has been planned". If the latter statement is unsatisfiable, the plan is correct regarding this particular rule. If the statement is satisfiable, the satisfying symbol assignment denotes the error location (here, the exit signal without data point). This corresponds exactly to the workflow of a plan reviewer, who checks that a rule is globally fulfilled by searching for locations where the rule is not fulfilled, and who implicitly translates the rules to the negated form to do so.

The verification tool is realized as an extension of PLANPRO VIEWER, a graphical track visualization tool, written in C++ using the Qt GUI Framework[5]. From a user's perspective, this simplifies the verification workflow: Given a currently loaded ETCS plan, the plan reviewer opens a file containing planning rules in SMT-LIB format, pushes a button, and the verification program checks whether the current plan fulfills these rules. In case a counter example is found, the violating object can be directly selected in the visual user interface for further investigation. All technical details are hidden from the user, specifically, no knowledge about formal methods or SMT solving is required (following the principle of knowledge separation in Fig. 1). Thus the verification can be conducted by a railway expert without the need of additional training. From a technical perspective, the integration of plan verification into the PLANPRO VIEWER makes the implementation easier: The whole PlanPro object structure is already available as DOM tree and can easily be accessed and converted into an SMT-LIB representation, and the found counter examples can be located in the user interface using the existing object search function.

---

[5] https://www.qt.io/.

To perform the verification, we need two main sources of input for the SMT solver: (i) the formalized planning rules and (ii) the PlanPro objects that represent the track layout. The planning rules are loaded as *verification cases* from separate files and are written in SMT-LIB syntax from the start. However, the track model in SMT-LIB syntax has to be constructed from the PlanPro DOM tree. To represent the PlanPro type system, we need to create corresponding SMT-LIB data types. When a verification case is loaded, the tool iterates through the list of PlanPro objects in the current ETCS plan and creates for each PlanPro type an SMT-LIB counter part. These types, merged together with the formulas from verification case file (and a library with fixed definitions), constitute the input of the SMT solver.

We also need the possibility to specify control commands. For example, to control how PlanPro objects are extracted for a specific verification scenario, and how possible counter examples are rendered in the user interface. It must also be possible to specify SMT solver options. All these commands are specific to a particular verification case, so they should be defined together with the verification rules in the verification case file. To avoid the need of a separate parser or a specific file format, we use tags inside structured comments, similar to code documentation tags (such as Javadoc), to specify these options. Such comment lines can be easily parsed with simple string functions and the verification case file still contains valid SMT-LIB syntax and is accepted by any SMT solver without problems. The entire architecture is illustrated with the diagram in Fig. 2.

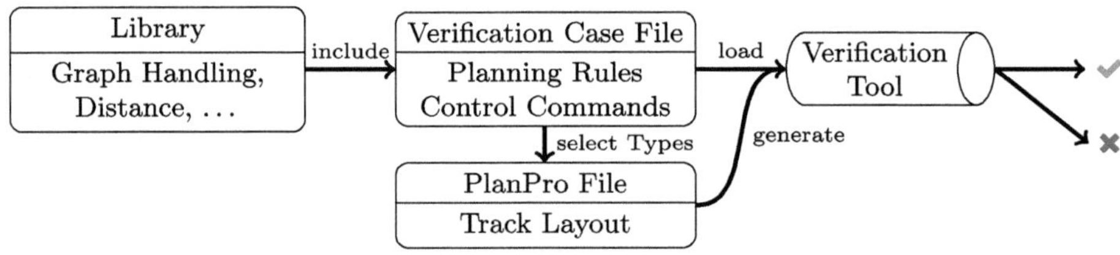

Fig. 2. Verification Architecture

A central design goal of our approach is to hide details about the technical realization from the user. In most usage scenarios, a plan reviewer loads an existing verification case file, starts the verification, and knows from the planning rule description what kind of error a possibly found counter example represents. It is unnecessary to know the content of the verification case file, neither is knowledge about the SMT-LIB language or formal methods required. But even the *author* of the verification case only needs minimal technical knowledge to write the rules in a formal syntax, because (i) each verification case corresponds one-to-one to a planning rule from the rule book and (ii) everything else that is sent to the SMT solver (types, plan, library functions) is automatically generated.

To realize this design, we use a 3-layer architecture to create the SMT formulas (see Table 1). The top layer represents the actual planning rules, written as first-order formulas, and this is the only part visible to a user. The formulas are written as a nearly one-to one translation from the rule book and are as abstract as possible. To achieve this, the formulas use functions provided in the two lower layers. The middle layer defines helper functions, such as graph handling and distance calculation, and provides them as library. On the bottom layer, the PlanPro objects of the currently loaded plan and their properties are converted into the SMT-LIB language. This is done automatically by the object extraction algorithm. Each layer uses the SMT-LIB format, together they form the input for the SMT solver process.

Table 1. Verification Input Layers

Layer	Source	Type of Information	Creation/Usage	Visible
Top	Verification Case File	Planning Rules	user-written	✓
Middle	Library	Helper Functions	included	✗
Bottom	PlanPro File	Track Layout	auto-generated	✗

4   Input Language

To formalize the planning rules in the verification case file, any legal SMT-LIB statement can be used. It is possible to use specific capabilities of a particular SMT solver, as long as these are accessible through the SMT-LIB interface and do not require a separate API. This makes the approach very flexible, because dedicated solvers can be used for each verification problem, and if new solvers with new features appear, we can immediately benefit from them.

Besides SMT-LIB built-in types, we define PlanPro-related types and control commands. These are described in the following subsections.

4.1   Static Types

Static types are SMT-LIB types that are independent of the current track plan and of the verification case. They are created once and for all by the verification tool and do not need to be defined by the user. Static types are created for every PlanPro enumeration and every PlanPro object type, and all these types are realized with SMT-LIB Algebraic Data Types (ADT) [2].

Enumeration types are one-to-one translations from the corresponding Plan-Pro enums, and the names are directly taken from the PlanPro labels. Here is an example of an enumeration type with three different values:

```
(declare-datatype ENUMWirkrichtung ((in) (gegen) (beide)))
```

Using the German PlanPro names makes object extraction later easier, because we can use the names one-to-one and do not need a translation layer. Another advantage is that we avoid name collisions with built-in SMT-LIB types, which have English names. PlanPro object types are defined in a similar way:

```
(declare-datatype PPPunktObjektExt
 ((Signal (signalArt ENUMSignal_Art)
          (signalFunktion ENUMSignal_Funktion))
  (Datenpunkt (idBezug Guid) (dpLaenge Int) (dpTyp Int))
  (BUEAnlage) ... ))
(declare-datatype PPObjektExt
 ((ProxyObjekt) (TopKnoten) ...
  (TopKante (idKnotenA Guid) (idKnotenB Guid) (laenge Int))
  (PunktObjekt (idTopKante Guid) (abstand Int)
               (wirkrichtung ENUMWirkrichtung)
               (seitlAbstand Int) (poext PPPunktObjektExt))))
(declare-datatype PPObjekt
 ((PlanProObjekt (id Guid) (objext PPObjektExt))))
```

This shows that both object inheritance and composition can be modeled using ADTs. If we read the listing from bottom to top, we see type PPObjekt as root object of the hierarchy where only the id is defined. Other properties are defined in derived objects, which are modeled as an object extension in the second data type PPObjektExt. Here the basic PlanPro types are defined, such as ProxyObjekt, TopKnoten, and TopKante. Some of those, like TopKante, define additional properties. The PunktObjekt type is the origin of another inheritance level, and defines here only the properties common to all subtypes (like position data). The actual subtypes are defined in data type PPPunktObjektExt on top of the listing. Here, the various PunktObjekt subtypes like Signal and Datenpunkt are defined with their individual properties.

4.2   Model Extraction

In contrast to the static types, some types must be defined dynamically depending on the current track plan. This is done during the Model Extraction phase: one iterates over the list of all PlanPro objects and for each object creates the corresponding SMT-LIB type.

The first type we consider is the Guid type, representing the PlanPro object id. We could convert the 128 bit UUID to SMT-LIB integers or bit vectors. This has the drawback that the corresponding theory has to be included, regardless of whether it is needed for the problem at hand or not. All we need to handle object ids is the ability to compare two values for equality, no arithmetic or binary operations are required. Hence, we model object ids as enumerations with the help of ADTs, just like the PlanPro enums. After all, ADT support is needed in any case. In contrast to PlanPro enums, however, the Guid type cannot be defined a static type, because the possible values depend on the objects present in a PlanPro file. So we generate this type dynamically, adding for each extracted PlanPro object a corresponding literal to the Guid type:

```
(declare-datatype Guid
 ((ID_EA1813B3-1924-4478-A611-1C1AB7A0405F)
  (ID_8E0D5B34-1405-4F00-8074-64F044BEC8B5) ... ))
```

The code snippet shows the start of a Guid declaration with two typical values. A realistic case study gives rise to thousands of values. For each object in the PlanPro file, we simply take its UUID string and add it to the enumeration. Each string has ID_ as a prefix, so that values can start with a number.

In analogy to the Guid type, for each PlanPro object a counterpart in the SMT-LIB language is created:

```
(define−fun o1 () PPObjekt
 (PlanProObjekt ID_16E010A4−DEC4−4033−8655−5B7072562434
  (PunktObjekt ID_8C736E63−672B−4ED5−ACF0−597B97AC45B2
              188815 gegen 3850
  (Signal Mehrabschnittssperrsignal Ausfahr_Signal)))))
```

Each object is defined as a constant function. In the above example, we instantiate a signal, using the ADT definition described in the previous section. The function name is composed of the character o followed by an increasing number, and the object properties are inserted into the attributes defined in the type hierarchy.

One problem that arises during the satisfiability check is that the SMT solver, when searching for a counter example, can use any possible value for symbol assignment or quantifier instantiation. In most cases, this is not what we want to have. For example, we want to prove that a signal occurring in the current plan fulfills a certain property, and not a random assignment of values to the signal type. To restrict assignments to values that are actually available in the plan, we define the inPlan function:

```
(define−fun inPlan ((ppo PPObjekt)) Bool
 (or (= ppo o1) (= ppo o2) (= ppo o3) ... (= ppo oN)))
```

This is simply a disjunctive combination of all extracted PlanPro objects o1,...,oN. The function returns true, if the call parameter ppo (typically, an uninterpreted symbol or a quantified variable) holds a value equal to one of the objects in the plan.

4.3   Control Commands

In addition to the planning rules in the verification case file and the generated statements, we need commands to control model extraction and the presentation of the results. In most cases, these are specific to a verification problem, so it is reasonable to provide them as part of the verification case file. We introduce keywords beginning with a @ character that have to be placed inside SMT-LIB comments, so they are ignored by the SMT solver. The order of the commands is arbitrary, and each command can occur in an arbitrary position in a verification case file. However, it is recommended to place all control commands as a preamble at the beginning.

A mandatory control command is @ppview-smt which identifies the SMT-LIB file as verification case to our railway verification tool. A file is rejected if it does not contain this command. With the command @logic the SMT logic theory to be used can be set, and with `@option` additional solver options can be specified. Both commands cannot be replaced with corresponding SMT-LIB statements, because otherwise the required sequence of the statements in a file would not be correct. The command `@description` can be used to provide a descriptive text that will be displayed in the user interface. With `@include` the content of another file can be included, similar as the C preprocessor. Important are the commands `@types-required` and `@types-optional`, which specify the PlanPro types that should be considered in the model extraction process. This is useful to restrict the model size to the essential and thus improve the performance, see Sect. 6.3. The command `@variables` is used to tell the PLANPRO VIEWER which of the formula symbols denotes a counter example if a model is found, so it can be highlighted in the user interface.

4.4   Assembly of the Solver Input

The input to the SMT solver process is constructed from the given verification case file, the extracted PlanPro file and some additional statements, see also Fig. 2. A valid SMT-LIB file for plan verification contains the following components in the given order:

1. The option statements (**set–option** :print–success false) and (set-option :produce-models true)
2. Any other options provided with the `@option` control command
3. The **set–logic** statement with the value from the `@logic` control command
4. The PlanPro enum definitions
5. The generated definition of the `Guid` type
6. The PlanPro object type definitions
7. The generated constant functions for each PlanPro object
8. The generated `inPlan` function
9. The content of the verification case file, containing all included files
10. The (**check–sat**) statement

5   Usage

We illustrate the usage of the plan verification tool with the aid of a small example. Listing 1.2 shows a complete verification case file. It is divided into two parts, beginning with a preamble containing the control commands, followed by the actual formulas to prove. Objects of type TOP_Kante will be extracted in any case, and the user can choose to extract Signal, Datenpunkt and BUE_Anlage objects as well. The file can be processed with the z3 or cvc5 solver, and the logic to use is ALL[6]. The variables cex1 and k1 in the formulas contain the counter examples when a model is found.

---

[6] For the problem shown, linear integer arithmetic would be sufficient, but the simpler logics usually do not support ADTs.

```
 1  ; @ppview-smt 1
 2  ; @description Check if there is a PunktObjekt object
 3  ; @description whose distance value is out of bounds of the
 4  ; @description length of the referenced TopKante object
 5  ; @types-required TOP_Kante
 6  ; @types-optional Signal Datenpunkt BUE_Anlage
 7  ; @provers z3 cvc5
 8  ; @variables cex1 k1
 9  ; @logic ALL
10  (declare-const cex1 PPObjekt)
11  (declare-const k1 PPObjekt)
12  (assert (inPlan cex1))
13  (assert (inPlan k1))
14  (define-fun cex1ext () PPObjektExt (objext cex1))
15  (define-fun k1ext () PPObjektExt (objext k1))
16  (assert ((_ is PunktObjekt) cex1ext))
17  (assert ((_ is TopKante) k1ext))
18  (assert (= (id k1) (idTopKante cex1ext)))
19  (assert (or (< (abstand cex1ext) 0)
20              (> (abstand cex1ext) (laenge k1ext)))))
```

Listing 1.2. Example Verification Case File

The formula section declares the counter example variables cex1 and k1 as constant symbols of type PPObjekt. The type PPObjekt itself is generated (see Sect. 4) and does not need to be declared. The following two **assert** statements ensure that any assignments in a model are taken only from the set of extracted objects, present in the plan. Lines 14–15 define shortcuts for easier access to the nested substructures inside the datatype hierarchy. The actual problem to prove is specified in lines 16–20. The two objects must have the correct type, the id of the TopKante must be referenced by the PunktObjekt, and the distance (abstand) of the PunktObjekt must be less than 0 or greater than the length (laenge) of the referenced TopKante (seen from the error perspective).

The verification functionality itself is implemented in a single modeless dialog within PLANPRO VIEWER. When the user loads a verification case file using the Load Testcase button, in the first step only the control commands are read. Figure 3 shows the dialog where the verification case from Listing 1.2 has already been executed. The text provided by the @description command is shown in the text field on the top of the dialog. For each identifier from the @provers command, a corresponding entry is added to the Prover combobox, where the solver to use can be chosen. The PlanPro types specified with the @types-required and @types-optional commands are added to the list on the left side of the dialog. The types from the @types-required command are selected, but disabled, so the user cannot deselect them. In contrast, the types provided by the @types-optional command are enabled, and the user has the choice to select or deselect them.

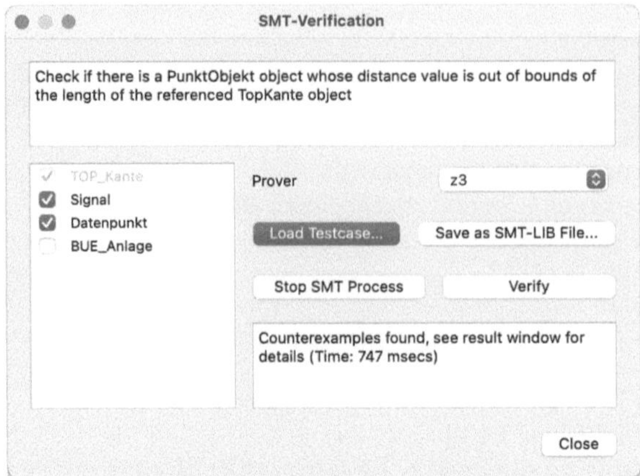

Fig. 3. Verification Dialog

Verification is started by clicking the **Verify** button. In a first step, the solver input is generated as described in Sect. 4.4. Here it is important to realize that all generated definitions are only created for PlanPro types that have been selected in the type list. The SMT input created this way is sent to the selected prover.

When the solver reports that the formula is unsatisfiable, a corresponding message is shown in the bottom right text field, announcing that the plan is valid and the elapsed time required for solving. If the formula is satisfiable, an additional **get−value** statement is sent to the solver, containing all variables from the **@variables** control command. The response from the solver contains the ids of the objects constituting the counter example and can be extracted using regular expressions. The obtained 128 bit UUID strings are then added to the **Search Results** dock window of the Main Window. In Fig. 4, the two entries Signal and TOP_Kante correspond to the variables cex1 and k1 from Listing 1.2. When the user selects one of them, the corresponding object is highlighted in all other views for further inspection (here, the error is the negative distance value).

6   Evaluation

6.1   Strategy

Even though the verification tool was designed to verify ETCS plans, in fact, we are able to prove much more. In general, the possible values of every accessible PlanPro property and relationships among them can be verified. In principle, one could check the signaling system itself and even the correct shape of the track layout. On the other hand, such an undertaking requires domain knowledge of a railway engineer (see Fig. 1). For this reason, we consider the verification of actual plans against real rules as out of scope of the present paper. What we evaluate instead, is the general applicability of our approach for such a task. Further, we cannot guarantee that the ETCS plans we use in the evaluation as

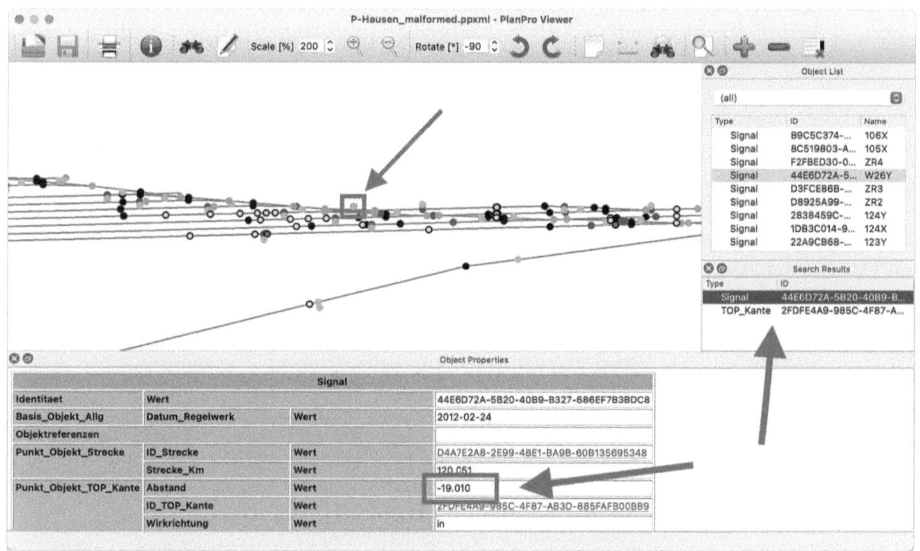

Fig. 4. Counter example selected in the Main Window

input are a priori correct, because a manually created plan can have errors, and
a plan created by EPLAN as well. So we divide the verification cases used for
our evaluation into three categories:

Verification cases ensuring that the PlanPro structure is well-formed.
Included properties are that all UUIDs are unique and all references point to
existing objects. The formulas for this kind of verification cases are mostly
very simple. Because the object references are generated by the tool in which
the plan was created, it can be assumed that they are always correct. So
it should be possible to incorporate small changes into the object structure
manually and the verification tool has to be able to detect them.

Verification cases for inconsistencies of the graph. The included properties ensure that the PlanPro files describe a valid railway track layout. For
example, each node can have a maximum of 3 connected edges, and each
object that is placed relative to an edge must be located within the edge
length. These properties are also generated and can be assumed to be correct.

Verification cases for the actual ETCS planning rules. These include as
well specification gaps, meaning rules which are intended to hold but are not
explicitly described in the rule book. In contrast to the other categories, as
mentioned above, we cannot assume correctness.

A challenge for the evaluation is the lack of publicly available PlanPro planning files. Nevertheless, it was possible to obtain three track layout files:

– P-Hausen (a fictive, but representative example station) with additional
ETCS objects created by the automated planning tool EPLAN

- A version of P-Hausen containing an ETCS planning conducted by DB using the traditional manual workflow
- Scheibenberg, a real existing, but smaller station, with additional ETCS objects created by EPLAN

We stress that P-Hausen is not a toy example, but a complex, medium size station containing a large variety of features. It is used by DB for training purposes. Real stations often tend to be smaller and less complex. In addition, we validate automatically generated plans, as well as manual plans. Together, this is a representative scenario.

In addition to the track layout and the verification case files, we use different SMT solvers as a third input variable for our evaluation. For all tests, we use z3 version 4.13.4 and cvc5 version 1.2.1. All tests are performed on an iMac with 3.8 GHz 8-core Intel Core i7, 40 GB RAM and macOS 15.5 Sequoia.

6.2   Correctness

The basic approach to evaluate the correctness of the verification approach is to take a pair of a PlanPro file and a verification case file, where the verification tool reports that the plan is valid. When we make a change at an arbitrary location in the layout, the tool has to detect this and show the manipulated location as a counter example. This approach covers the primary intended use case: To detect random errors, which are harder to find than systematic errors, and need a lot of time effort in a manual plan review.

This evaluation approach is straightforward for the PlanPro and graph structure, because these planning properties are correct by construction, i.e. we have a ground truth. The corresponding verification cases merely cover technical properties, they do not involve domain-specific railway knowledge and are easy to specify. When performing this kind of validation, we can make the following observations:

- For all combinations of unmodified PlanPro files and verification cases, the verification tool reports that the plans are valid.
- Small changes in the PlanPro files (for example the referenced IDs) cause the plan being given the verdict invalid.
- The usage of different SMT solvers (z3 and cvc5) does not affect the verdict. However, if a plan gets the verdict invalid and it contains multiple errors, then the generated counter example may be different for different tools. This indicates that the solvers operate differently and do not share the same code base. In fact this increases trust, as long as different solvers come to the same verdict.
- In no case an unknown result could be observed. Because the set of possible counter examples is finite, this behavior is also expected.

The situation is considerably different when we want to evaluate the verification of the ETCS planning rules. Here we cannot ensure that the underlying PlanPro files are correct. This is especially the case for files generated with EPLAN, where the implemented rules are incomplete and might be erroneous. But even the manually created plans by DB professionals can violate the rules, either by previously undiscovered planning errors, or else by permitted (but undocumented) deviations from the rule book. Additionally, it is possible that the planning rules are formalized incorrectly because of the lack of railway knowledge. This can lead to the situation that a valid plan is rejected because of a wrong verification case, or an invalid plan is accepted because the verification case is wrong in such a way that the verification nevertheless passes.

To evaluate planning rule verification, we claim that all PlanPro files are correct (regardless whether this is the case or not). Then we weaken the planning rules until the verification case passes. For example, if a rule is supposed to hold for all exit signals and all shunting signals, and the verification tool gives the verdict that some shunting signals do *not* satisfy the rule (intended or not), we remove the shunting signals from the rule, so that only exit signals are covered. By doing this, we compensate in our verification cases for the (possibly erroneous) real planning. Assume that now the verdict correct is returned. If we make any further modification on the PlanPro file, the verification case has to fail again, because the plan now contains more errors than permitted. In this way, we can evaluate the ability to detect errors without the need to know whether the planning file is actually correct or not.

When we run the verification cases in this way, we can make the following observations:

- After a verification case has been adapted to pass, any further modification makes it fail again.
- The EPLAN-generated and DB-planned versions of P-Hausen produce the same verdicts.
- The usage of z3 and cvc5 still shows the same behavior, modulo the values in the found counter example.
- Again no unknown result could be observed.

6.3   Performance

Table 2 shows the needed time t_{z3} (for z3) and t_{cvc5} (for cvc5) in milliseconds for some combinations of PlanPro files and verification cases with different numbers of extracted objects. The time is measured from executing the case until the SMT solver returns unsat.[7] The first two cases are derived from the rule book [4] and cover the case that there is an exit signal where no data point of type 21 has been planned (21-signal-no-datenpunkt) and the case that there is a solitary data point 21 without connected signal (21-datenpunkt-no-signal). The next two cases verify the graph structure and check that all nodes with three connected edges have the correct connection type (3-topkante) and that there are no nodes with four or more connected edges (lessthan-4-topkante).

---

[7] A response of sat is always much faster.

Table 2. Runtime for various combinations of verification cases, plans and solvers

Verification Case	PlanPro Track	Objects	t_{z3} [ms]	t_{cvc5} [ms]
21-signal-no-datenpunkt	P-Hausen (EPlan)	236	**227**	2716
21-signal-no-datenpunkt	P-Hausen (DB)	348	**436**	8714
21-signal-no-datenpunkt	Scheibenberg	104	**49**	508
21-datenpunkt-no-signal	P-Hausen (EPlan)	236	**274**	23673
21-datenpunkt-no-signal	P-Hausen (DB)	348	**538**	57387
21-datenpunkt-no-signal	Scheibenberg	104	**62**	1296
3-topkante	P-Hausen (EPlan)	91	**192**	981
3-topkante	P-Hausen (DB)	91	**193**	956
3-topkante	Scheibenberg	16	**16**	26
lessthan-4-topkante	P-Hausen (EPlan)	91	**1614**	3182
lessthan-4-topkante	P-Hausen (DB)	91	**1647**	3311
lessthan-4-topkante	Scheibenberg	16	**23**	51
datenpunkt-refs	P-Hausen (EPlan)	4187	**59595**	123900
datenpunkt-refs	P-Hausen (DB)	6625	**144061**	587650
datenpunkt-refs	Scheibenberg	1413	**5801**	6822
punktobjekt-refs-exist	P-Hausen (EPlan)	700	1910	**1743**
punktobjekt-refs-exist	P-Hausen (DB)	1268	7127	**6284**
punktobjekt-refs-exist	Scheibenberg	344	442	**429**

The final two cases check that the references are correct for data point objects (datenpunkt-refs) and general PunktObjekt subtypes (punktobjekt-refs-exist).

The first observation is that z3 is in most cases considerably faster than cvc5, but there is one case where this is reversed. Without inside knowledge of the workings of these solvers, it is not possible to find out the reason (a consequence of the knowledge separation principle in Fig. 1), but we can conclude that it makes sense to support multiple solvers and to assign an individual solver to each verification scenario. We can also see that the performance is good as long as the number of extracted objects is low. This is especially the case for the verification cases based on real planning rules, where only signals and data points have to be considered. When we have to use all objects available in the PlanPro file, the time needed can be over 10 min. We conclude that it is important to restrict the number of extracted objects to the necessary minimum, otherwise the SMT solver will need so much time that the approach would not be usable interactively. Fortunately, this is possible for most of the relevant test scenarios that verify real planning constraints (see the examples on top of Table 2).

7   Related Work

The work closest to ours is the plausibility check integrated into the PlanPro Toolbox,[8] which is performed with Schematron, a language based on XSLT to validate the content and structure of XML documents [14]. Like our tool, it is designed for the PlanPro format and the German railway context and can, in principle, be used for the same verification scenarios as our SMT approach. However, since Schematron is an XML transformation language and not a theorem prover, we believe that our SMT approach is more flexible and easier to adapt to future requirements. On the other hand, the advantage of Schematron is that it operates directly on XML and does not need the translation to SMT-LIB. Since the cited paper was published simultaneously to the present work, a detailed comparison must be deferred to future work.

We are not aware of other solutions in the German railway context. Examples outside the German scope are [12], which uses a Prolog variant, and [9], using ProB. Both are located in the Norwegian context and use railML as their track model. In general, the railway domain is a large application area for formal methods, but few papers have been concerned with plan verification. The survey [8] gives a good overview of existing solutions and the used technologies.

An earlier approach we pursued was a proposal for algorithmic verification of the planning process [7]. Once we realized that the form of the planning rules is declarative rather than algorithmic, this line of work was no longer pursued.

When the plan creation step is done using an automated tool like EPLAN, a possible alternative consists in verifying the plan creation algorithm once and for all, instead of each created plan. This can be done, in principle, with a deductive verification tool such as KeY [1] or Frama-C [11]. The drawback is that the verification of (dynamic) programs is harder to perform than the verification of static plans, the planning rules cannot be formalized one-to-one, and that manually altered plans are not covered by that approach.

8   Conclusion and Future Work

We presented a concept for automated verification of railway plans, using SMT solvers and formalized planning rules and track data in the SMT-LIB language. Our approach supports various SMT solvers for the individual test scenarios, and the flexibility of the SMT-LIB language ensures that also future requirements can be addressed. The evaluation proved that even small mistakes that can be easily overlooked in a manual review are reliably and quickly detected. As long as the number of extracted objects is limited to those necessary for each verification case, the performance is more than acceptable.

As a next step, we will formalize additional parts from the planning rule book [4], and we will also try out other SMT solvers to find out the optimal combinations of provers and rules to be verified.

---

[8] https://projects.eclipse.org/projects/technology.set.

To permit planners without any knowledge of SMT-LIB syntax to develop their own rules for verification, a graphical tool would be useful, where the planner sees only a domain-specific view and can assemble the formulas by connecting graphical blocks like a flow chart.

Acknowledgments. We thank Richard Bubel for his feedback on early drafts of this paper.

References

1. Ahrendt, W., Beckert, B., Bubel, R., Hähnle, R., Schmitt, P., Ulbrich, M. (eds.): Deductive Software Verification—The KeY Book: From Theory to Practice. LNCS, vol. 10001. Springer (2016). https://doi.org/10.1007/978-3-319-49812-6
2. Barrett, C., Fontaine, P., Tinelli, C.: The SMT-LIB Standard Version 2.6 (2021). https://smt-lib.org/papers/smt-lib-reference-v2.6-r2021-05-12.pdf
3. Cok, D.R.: The SMT-LIBv2 Language and Tools: A Tutorial (2013). https://smtlib.github.io/jSMTLIB/SMTLIBTutorial.pdf
4. Deutsche Bahn AG, Frankfurt: Richtlinie 819: LST-Anlagen planen
5. Deutsche Bahn AG: PlanPro Datenmodell Version 1.9.0 (2019). https://www.dbinfrago.com/planpro
6. Dillmann, S., Hähnle, R.: Automated planning of ETCS tracks. In: Collart-Dutilleul, S., Lecomte, T., Romanovsky, A. (eds.) RSSRail 2019. LNCS, vol. 11495, pp. 79–90. Springer, Cham (2019). https://doi.org/10.1007/978-3-030-18744-6_5
7. Dillmann, S., Pejic, M., Oetting, A., Hähnle, R.: Zeit- und Kostenersparnis bei der ETCS L2 Planung durch Digitalisierung. In: Scientific Railway Signalling Symposium, pp. 37–55. TU Darmstadt (2019). https://doi.org/10.25534/tuprints-00011296
8. Ferrari, A., ter Beek, M.H.: Formal methods in railways: a systematic mapping study. ACM Comput. Surv. **55**(4), 69:1–69:37 (2023). https://doi.org/10.1145/3520480
9. Gruteser, J., Leuschel, M.: Validation of railML Using ProB. In: Bai, G., Ishikawa, F., Aït-Ameur, Y., Papadopoulos, G.A. (eds.) Engineering of Complex Computer Systems - 28th International Conference, ICECCS, Proceedings. LNCS, vol. 14784, pp. 245–256. Springer, Cham (2024). https://doi.org/10.1007/978-3-031-66456-4_13
10. ISO: Generation of universally unique identifiers (UUIDs) and their use in object identifiers, ISO/IEC 9834-8:2014 (2014)
11. Kosmatov, N., Prevosto, V., Signoles, J. (eds.): Guide to Software Verification with Frama-C. Springer, Cham (2024). https://doi.org/10.1007/978-3-031-55608-1
12. Luteberget, B., Johansen, C.: Efficient verification of railway infrastructure designs against standard regulations. Formal Methods Syst. Des. **52**(1), 1–32 (2018). https://doi.org/10.1007/S10703-017-0281-Z
13. Maschek, U., Klaus, C., Gerke, C., Uminski, V., Girke, K.J.: PlanPro: Durchgängige elektronische Datenhaltung im ESTW-Planungsprozess. Signal+Draht **104**(9), 22–26 (2012)
14. Wunsch, S., Jaekel, B., Lehnert, M., Klaus, C., Gruteser, J., Leuschel, M.: Automated semantic validation of railway signalling data on the basis of schematron. In: ter Beek, M.H., Collart-Dutilleul, S., Lecomte, T. (eds.) Proceedings of International Conference on Reliability, Safety and Security of Railway Systems: Modelling, Analysis, Verification and Certification (RSSRail) (2025)

Using N-Version Architectures for Railway Segmentation with Deep Neural Networks

Philipp Jaß$^{(\boxtimes)}$ and Carsten Thomas

Department of Energy and Information, HTW Berlin - University of Applied
Sciences, Wilhelminenhofstraße 75A, 12459 Berlin, Germany
`philipp.jass@htw-berlin.de`

Abstract. This is an extended abstract of the journal paper [2] that
was originally published in MDPI MAKE in 2025. Autonomous trains
require reliable and accurate environmental perception to take over
safety-critical tasks from the driver. This paper investigates the application of N-version architectures to rail track detection using Deep Neural
Networks (DNNs) as a means to improve the safety of machine learning (ML)-enabled perception systems. We combine three different neural
network architectures in a 3M1I configuration. In this configuration, we
apply two prediction combination methods to increase accuracy and to
enable error detection: Maximum Confidence Voting (MCV), combining the DNN predictions at the image level, and Pixel Majority Voting (PMV), a novel approach for combining the predictions at the pixel
level. In addition, we implement a new method for evaluating and combining prediction confidence values in the N-version architecture during
runtime. We adjust the overall prediction confidence according to the
conformity of all individual predictions, which is not possible with an
individual network. Our results show that the N-version architecture
not only enables a detection of erroneous predictions by utilizing those
adjusted confidence values, but it can also partially improve the predictions by using the PMV combination algorithm. This work emphasizes
the importance of model diversity for an accurate assessment of prediction safety. These approaches can significantly improve the practical
applicability of ML-based systems in safety-critical domains such as rail
transportation.

Keywords: Autonomous Rail Systems · Safety-Critical AI · Rail
Track Detection · Machine Learning · N-Version · Semantic
Segmentation · Model diversity · Confidence Evaluation · Safety

1   Motivation and Problem Statement

Autonomous trains are being developed to achieve higher grades of automation
(GoA), such as GoA4, in the railway industry. A reliable perception system is one
of the key prerequisites for safe autonomous driving. As stated in [2] rail track

© The Author(s), under exclusive license to Springer Nature Switzerland AG 2026
M. H. ter Beek et al. (Eds.): RSSRail 2025, LNCS 16236, pp. 53–57, 2026.
https://doi.org/10.1007/978-3-032-10762-6_6

detection is one of the core perception functions that is needed for autonomous driving on rails. Due to this function, all further perception tasks, like obstacle detection, are able to distinguish the train's path, i.e., the ego-track, from the rest of the image. The ego-track is the critical area that needs supervision for obstacles of any kind, in order to ensure a safe ride of the train without collisions. Hence, the rail track detection itself is a safety-critical perception task.

However, perception systems based on deep neural networks (DNNs) lack transparency and verifiability, which are requirements demanded by safety standards in the rail sector (e.g., EN 50716 [1]). DNN model architectures pose risks due to their limited explainability and unreliable uncertainty estimation. Therefore, reliable self-assessment and fault detection at runtime are key challenges when using DNNs in safety-critical systems.

To address these issues, we are investigating the application of the N-version principle, which is well-established in classical safety engineering, to neural networks for rail segmentation, as proposed by Machida [3]. Our goal is to enhance safety, detect errors during runtime, and enable reliable confidence assessments of predictions.

2   Contribution Summary

We present the design, implementation, and evaluation of a N-version architecture for rail track segmentation [2]. This architecture has a 3M1I (3 Model, 1 Input) configuration, meaning it consists of three DNNs that are architecturally diverse, are trained independently and are all fed the same input images during testing (see Fig. 1).

The DNN architectures used are:

- WCID (a lightweight fully convolutional network (FCN) inspired by first-person lane detection),
- VGG16-UNet (a UNet variant with a VGG16 encoder),
- and MobileNet-SegNet (an efficient encoder-decoder structure for embedded systems).

In order to combine the predictions of all three individual networks, we propose two different algorithms:

1. Maximum Confidence Voting (MCV): Selection of the prediction with the highest confidence value.
2. Pixel Majority Voting (PMV): Majority voting at the pixel level across all three models.

To support safety arguments, we also introduce a novel method for evaluating confidence based on pixel-wise probability distributions. This yields image-level confidence metrics that give an estimation of how convinced a semantic segmentation DNN is of its prediction. As well as the predictions, we propose to also combine these individual confidence values into one overall and with that more

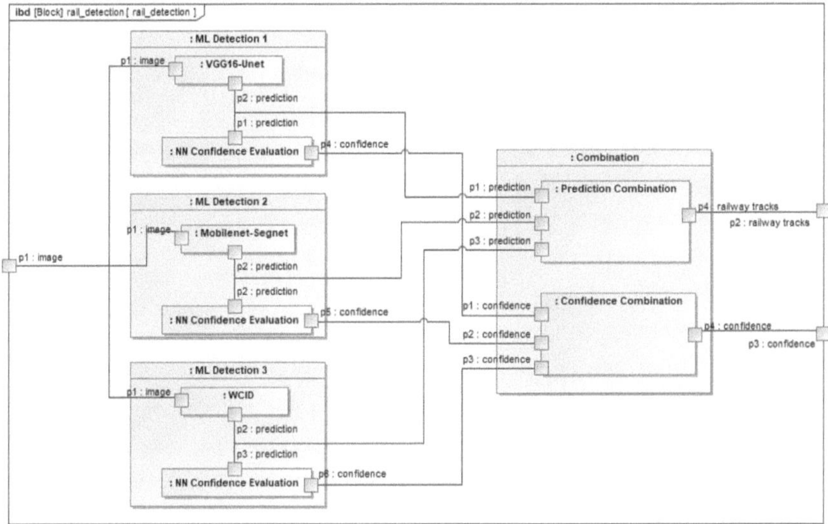

Fig. 1. N-Version architecture instantiation for rail track detection, used in this paper. It shows the 3M1I architecture pattern, using three DNNs and a combination block. Source: [2]

meaningful confidence score. This is done by validating the individual predictions against each other using model agreement metrics, such as intersection over union (IoU). This combined confidence score enables detection of potentially erroneous, i.e. unsafe, predictions at runtime and allow for implementation of fail-safe behaviours (e.g., braking under uncertainty).

Our experiments, based on a combined dataset of 15,519 annotated images from RailSem19 and Nordlandsbanen/NLB, show that:

- The introduced confidence metric correlates with actual prediction quality and allows for the detection of erroneous predictions.
- The PMV strategy can correct errors in individual models and achieves higher IoUs than the best individual model in over 30% of test cases. This can be seen in an example image from [2] in Fig. 2.

3   Relevance to RSSRail

Our contribution directly addresses several areas of interest defined by RSSRail.

- System and software safety analysis: We investigate the safety aspects of neural perception systems.
- System reliability: We design an N-version safety architecture to analyze improved overall system reliability

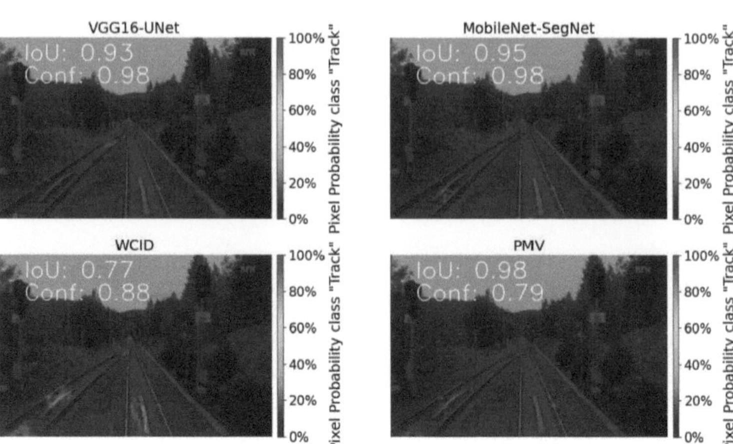

Fig. 2. Example prediction for Pixel Majority Voting (PMV) combination algorithm with higher quality than all individual networks. The image shows the predictions of all three individual neural networks (top row and bottom left), as well as the selected output from the MCV algorithm (bottom right). The respective Intersection over Union (IoU), i.e., the prediction quality, and confidence values for every prediction are shown in white in the top left corner of every prediction. Source: [2]

- Safety and security argumentation: Our architecture enables safety arguments based on diversity and plausibility during runtime.
- Safety in development processes and safety management: Using our N-version architecture, which is oriented toward safety, we are investigating a practical method for incorporating safety aspects into the development process of ML-based control systems.

Additionally, our approach addresses open questions regarding the certifiability of AI-based systems in railroad environments and supplements ongoing standardization initiatives with specific architectural and algorithmic proposals.

4   Conclusion and Outlook

N-version architectures with deep neural networks (DNNs) are a promising approach to increasing the safety and fault detection capabilities of AI-based perception systems in the railroad domain. Our results [2] demonstrate that combining architectural diversity with targeted combination mechanisms for the DNN predictions, as well as prediction confidence values, can significantly enhance reliability and facilitate integration into safety-oriented reasoning.

Future work includes:

- Expansion of diversity (e.g., alternative training data and sensor systems).
- Integrating explainable AI methods
- Expansion of evaluation metrics (e.g., mean deviation of the rail center lines).

References

1. EN 50716:2023 Railway Applications - Requirements for software development. Technical report, CENELEC (2023)
2. Jaß, P., Thomas, C.: Using n-version architectures for railway segmentation with deep neural networks. Mach. Learn. Knowl. Extract. **7**(2) (2025). https://doi.org/10.3390/make7020049. https://www.mdpi.com/2504-4990/7/2/49
3. Machida, F.: N-version machine learning models for safety critical systems. In: 2019 49th Annual IEEE/IFIP International Conference on Dependable Systems and Networks Workshops (DSN-W), pp. 48–51 (2019). https://doi.org/10.1109/DSN-W.2019.00017

Trade-Off Between Interpretability and Accuracy: How Can XAI Build Trust in Track Geometry Predictive Maintenance?

Shahab Aldin Mansouri[1]([envelope]), Rebecca Dziedzic[2], Riccardo Licciardello[1], Sepehr Abdi Goudarzi[1], Vito Renò[3], Angelo Cardellicchio[3], and Massimiliano Nitti[3]

[1] Dipartimento di Ingegneria Civile, Edile e Ambientale (DICEA), Sapienza Università di Roma, Roma, Italy
shahabaldin.mansouri@uniroma1.it

[2] Department of Building, Civil and Environmental Engineering, Concordia University, Montreal, Canada

[3] Institute of Intelligent Industrial Technologies and Systems for Advanced Manufacturing, CNR, Bari, Italy

Abstract. Machine learning (ML) offers promising capabilities for predicting rail infrastructure failure and enabling a shift from diagnostic to prognostic railway maintenance. However, the real-world adoption of high-performing ML models in safety-critical domains such as railway systems hinges on their trustworthiness, particularly their interpretability and transparency. This study, based on a case study in track geometry management, explores the trade-off between accuracy and interpretability in predicting track alignment failures by comparing six ML classifiers: Logistic Regression, Random Forest, Gradient Boosting, XGBoost, Support Vector Machine (SVM), and a Neural Network (NN). The models were trained on railway defect datasets using features such as operating speed, train traffic, total gross tonnage, and defect length. Performance was evaluated using recall as the primary metric, given the high cost of false negatives in rail safety contexts. Results showed that SVM and NN models achieved the highest recall (0.704 and 0.734, respectively), but at the cost of lower interpretability. To address this, post-hoc Explainable AI (XAI) techniques, including SHAP and LIME, were applied. These methods collectively enhance both local and global interpretability and support model transparency, stakeholder trust, and the bridging of the gap between predictive performance and decision-making needs. While XAI is increasingly applied in other sectors, its use in asset management and particularly railway predictive maintenance remains limited. This work fills that gap by demonstrating how XAI can foster more informed and confident adoption of ML models in rail infrastructure management. These explainability techniques help domain experts and end users understand why a model produced a specific result and what key factors influenced that decision, while also supporting data scientists and developers in refining model performance. For instance, feature refinement guided by SHAP improved SVM recall from 0.704 to 0.716.

Keywords: Railway Predictive Maintenance · Track Geometry Defects · Model Trustworthiness · Explainable AI (XAI)

© The Author(s), under exclusive license to Springer Nature Switzerland AG 2026
M. H. ter Beek et al. (Eds.): RSSRail 2025, LNCS 16236, pp. 58–77, 2026.
https://doi.org/10.1007/978-3-032-10762-6_7

1 Introduction

The predictive capabilities of Machine Learning (ML) have made it a powerful tool in asset management, particularly in maintenance management. However, a critical trade-off often exists between model accuracy and interpretability, primarily due to the complexity of models required to capture intricate relationships between features. Interpretability is a property of a model that provides sufficient insight into how the algorithm makes its decisions. When a model is not inherently interpretable, explainability methods are required to understand or justify its predictions. Integrating XAI methods with advanced predictive models can provide insightful explanations for predictive maintenance decisions, improving transparency and accountability in industrial systems.

The trade-off between model accuracy and interpretability is a key challenge in utilizing ML models [1]. Given the inevitable use of AI, a highly accurate model that lacks transparency can, for instance, undermine trust and raise doubts among infrastructure managers and stakeholders when used for maintenance prioritization and capital allocation. Conversely, a simple yet interpretable model may fail to capture feature complexity, resulting in suboptimal decisions and potential resource waste. Complex models such as Neural Networks often achieve high performance but lack transparency, making them difficult to trust in sensitive domains like railway systems. In such contexts, decision-makers may struggle to understand and justify the model's outputs, leading to skepticism or resistance toward AI. Explainable AI (XAI) seeks to address this by producing interpretable and transparent outputs that foster trust. However, the notion of interpretability varies across contexts. Different applications may require different forms of explanation, levels of transparency, and user understanding. While XAI has been explored in domains such as medical and clinical [2], education [3], maritime transport [4], road safety [5, 6], water quality [7], energy efficiency [8], sustainable energy [9], and livestock management [10] its application in railway systems, particularly in track geometry defect prediction remains unexplored.

Ali et al. [11] conducted an extensive review of XAI and proposed frameworks that emphasize interpretability, explainability, and the integration of trustworthiness objectives. Their work highlights how these principles can be applied in real-world contexts to ensure that AI models produce consistent, reliable, and unbiased decisions. They identified fairness, responsibility, transparency, interactivity, robustness, stability, satisfaction, and confidence as key goals that explainability methods should strive to fulfill. These dimensions underscore the role of XAI in supporting both technical reliability and user trust.

Building on this foundation, this study investigates the trade-offs between model accuracy and interpretability in track geometry defect prediction. It provides the first empirical application of XAI (SHAP and LIME) to this domain, evaluating six ML models on a real railway dataset and highlighting the balance between predictive performance and interpretability. The study further demonstrates how XAI can enhance transparency and foster trustworthiness in safety-critical railway maintenance.

This study is guided by the following research questions:

1. How do common machine learning models compare in predicting track geometry failures, particularly in terms of accuracy and recall?
2. To what extent can Explainable AI (XAI) methods, such as SHAP and LIME, improve the interpretability of these models?
3. How can the integration of XAI enhance stakeholder trust and support practical decision-making in railway maintenance management?

The remainder of this paper is structured as follows: Sect. 2 reviews related work; Sect. 3 describes the methodology and models used; Sect. 4 presents the case study, results, and analysis; and Sect. 5 concludes with key findings and future directions.

2   Literature Review

Track geometry refers to the alignment and condition of rails, which directly influence train stability, ride comfort, and derailment risk. Predicting failures in this context is critical for railway safety and maintenance planning. Geometric irregularity is one of the most critical track features influencing the safety and comfort of rail transport [12]. Data from irregularity measurement tools supports defect diagnosis and effective track management to ensure safety. With the rise of big data in railway maintenance, ML is increasingly used for track degradation prediction, enhancing both efficiency and analytical capability. These models can provide accurate results by handling large datasets and accounting for multiple factors effectively. The selection of the appropriate ML algorithm depends on the characteristics of the data, and the nature of the prediction task [13, 14]. In this context, supervised learning proves to be the most suitable approach, given the labelled nature of the datasets.

Supervised machine learning is widely applied to tasks such as defect detection, track geometry degradation prediction, rail surface assessment, and maintenance decision support. Common models include Decision Trees (DT), Random Forests (RF), Support Vector Machines (SVM), Artificial Neural Networks (ANN), and ensemble methods like Gradient Boosting Machines (GBM), XGBoost (XGB), and AdaBoost. These models effectively handle large, noisy datasets and capture complex relationships among factors like geometry, load, and environment [15].

Clear model interpretation allows users to integrate domain knowledge and build trust in model decisions. Interpretable AI follows two main approaches: Post-hoc explainability, which extracts explanations from black-box models (e.g., using surrogate models or selective querying), and intrinsic interpretability, where models are transparent by design but may struggle with complex tasks [16]. When a model is not inherently interpretable, post-hoc methods can be applied to provide interpretability and insights into its decision-making process. In his influential article, Lipton [17] argues that interpretability is not a single concept but varies by context and audience, as different stakeholders prioritize different aspects. He notes that logistic regression and linear models are often seen as interpretable, though this may not apply in high-dimensional settings. Ensemble methods such as Random Forests, Gradient Boosting, and XGBoost are considered opaque. SVM, particularly with kernels, are treated as black-box models. Neural Networks also lack transparency and typically require post-hoc explanations.

Post-hoc interpretability includes global methods, which explain overall model behavior, and local methods, which explain individual predictions. These can be model-agnostic, applicable to any ML model, or model-specific, designed for particular models using their internal structure [18].

Ali et al. [11] categorized post-hoc explainability methods in ML into six groups, each aiming to enhance the interpretability of model decisions after training. These categories include: Attribution methods, visualization methods, example-based explanation methods, game-theoretic methods, knowledge extraction methods, and neural explanation methods. The following categorization and definitions are extracted directly from their study.

Attribution methods identify which input features most influence a model's prediction. Common techniques include SHAP, LIME, saliency maps, and Integrated Gradients, all of which assign relevance scores to features to highlight their contribution. Perturbation-based approaches, which assess the effect of altering input values, also fall within this category. Visualization methods, typically applied in supervised learning, use graphical tools such as Partial Dependence Plots (PDP), Individual Conditional Expectation (ICE) plots, and Accumulated Local Effects (ALE) plots.

Other explainability techniques include example-based methods, which clarify predictions through specific instances such as prototypes (representative cases), criticisms (outliers), and counterfactuals (what-if scenarios). Game-theoretic approaches, particularly Shapley values and SHAP, view prediction as a cooperative game, distributing credit fairly among features based on their marginal contributions. SHAP unifies this fairness principle with feature attribution, offering both local and global explanations. Additionally, knowledge extraction methods aim to convert black-box models into interpretable representations. Rule extraction generates human-readable IF–THEN rules, while model distillation simplifies complex models by transferring knowledge to interpretable surrogates like decision trees. Finally, neural-specific methods such as influence functions and concept-based explanations focus on interpreting deep neural network by revealing how training data or high-level human concepts affect predictions.

Table 1 provides a structured overview of these six categories of post-hoc explainability methods, detailing their subcategories and listing specific techniques (e.g., SHAP, PDP, counterfactuals, rule extraction) used within each.

In safety-critical sectors such as railways, where transparency, accountability, and regulatory compliance are essential, the adoption of AI models requires a careful balance between accuracy and interpretability. Post-hoc methods approximate complex model logic, helping bridge the gap between performance and the need for understandable, trustworthy AI.

Numerous studies across various domains have employed XAI techniques to explain the decisions of ML models. In particular, post-hoc interpretability methods have been widely adopted to support the responsible deployment of complex models in sensitive applications. SHAP (SHapley Additive exPlanations) has been widely used by researchers for model interpretability. Sahlaoui et al. [3] applied both SHAP and LIME in their study; provided global insights while LIME offered fast local explanations. Their objective was to predict the probability of a student belonging to the lowest-performing class using classification algorithms. SHAP summary plots were used to visualize how

Table 1. Classification of post-hoc explainability methods in machine learning based on the framework proposed by Ali et al. [11]

Category	Subcategory	Method/Example
Attribution methods	Decomposition	Deep Taylor Decomposition
	Perturbation Methods	Surrogation (Local/Global), LIME, LORE, CluReFI, SP-LIME, NormLIME, Anchors, Deconvolutional Network, RISE
	Backpropagation Methods	Gradient-only methods, CAM, Guided Backpropagation, Guided Grad-CAM, Score-CAM, SmoothGrad, Integrated Gradients (IG), DeepLIFT
Visualization Methods	–	PDP, ICE Plots, ALE
Example-Based Explanation Methods	Prototypes & Criticisms	MMD-critic
	Counterfactuals	Wachter et al.'s Counterfactual Explanations MOC
	Adversarial Examples	Analogical/Contrastive Explanations
	SHAP	Kernel SHAP, Tree SHAP
Knowledge Extraction Methods	Rule Extraction	IF-THEN Rules, M-of-N Rules, Decomposition Methods (Neuron-level), Pedagogical Methods, Eclectic Methods (Hybrid)
	Model Distillation	Interpretable Mimic Learning, DarkSight
	Influence Methods	Feature Importance (LOCO, MCR), LRP, SA
Neural methods	Concept Methods	TCAV, ACE, CaCE, Concept SHAP

each feature's value influenced the model output. Similarly, Li et al. [10] applied the game-theoretic concept of Shapley values through SHAP to interpret the XGBoost model used for predicting the core body temperature of dairy cows. In the same way, in a study on the renewable energy sector, SHAP was used to enhance transparency and trust in Auto ML-selected models by analyzing and visualizing the influence of environmental features on predicted photovoltaic power output [8].

In transportation, SHAP has been used to interpret complex models and guide interventions. For instance, Yang et al. [6] predicted the severity of highway-rail grade crossing accidents using the LightGBM model and SHAP to analyze feature interactions and their effects on injury outcomes. Similarly, Wang et al. [4] applied SHAP in the maritime domain, combining it with a physics-informed neural network to improve the interpretability of ship fuel consumption predictions. Other studies, such as [5], have also used SHAP in road safety to uncover key factors in winter crash dynamics.

Understanding how a single feature influences model predictions offers key insights. Partial Dependence Plots (PDPs) illustrate this relationship, whether linear, monotonic, or complex, and highlight each feature's marginal effect. Hao et al. [7] used PDPs with Tree SHAP and Kernel SHAP to interpret regression models. PDPs showed how input features like water temperature and phosphorus levels influenced predictions, offering complementary insights into model behavior.

Combining multiple XAI methods enhances end user understanding by offering diverse interpretability perspectives, each tailored to the needs and comprehension levels of different stakeholders such as engineers, policymakers, and researchers. Bongomin et al. [9] combined PDPs, SHAP, Permutation Importance, and knowledge extraction methods like Gini Importance and Sensitivity Analysis to capture model behavior. This layered approach balances rigor with accessibility, offering intuitive visuals for non-experts and detailed insights for technical users in complex domains like gasification.

Custom interpretability methods are tailored solutions designed to meet the specific needs of a given application. In the clinical domain, for example, Lu et al. [2] enhanced a Graph Neural Network with selective classification and an interpretability module, illustrating how domain-specific adaptations can improve model reliability and trust.

Table 2 summarizes case studies that address the trade-off between accuracy and interpretability, listing the ML models used and the XAI techniques applied.

There is no single universally accepted definition for AI trustworthiness as it encompasses various aspects and dimensions. Expectations of trustworthy AI can vary significantly across sectors and stakeholders, depending on the specific risks, regulations, and intended use. The European Commission has committed to establishing principles for the trustworthy and secure use of AI in the digital society. The European Commission's Joint Research Centre highlights the need to align AI objectives with human values. It calls on industrial actors to adopt a shared set of best practices that promote interoperability and ensure the proper integration of AI into existing infrastructures; on regulators to develop effective policies that safeguard citizens' rights while maintaining economic competitiveness; and on users to understand and trust the innovations and potential disruptions introduced by AI [16]. Hamon et al. [16] argue that trustworthy AI goes beyond mere accuracy or technical security. It requires transparency, robustness, fairness, human agency, legal compliance, and accountability. While interpretability methods are essential tools to support these goals, their impact depends on rigorous validation, ethically grounded design, and alignment with existing regulatory frameworks.

Two studies by Ali et al. [11] and Rojat et al. [19] propose frameworks that stress embedding explainability into AI design to ensure consistent, reliable, and unbiased decisions in real-world applications. They outline key objectives for explainability methods,

Table 2. Summary of selected case studies on real-world data demonstrating the trade-off between model accuracy and interpretability.

Study	Sector	ML Models	XAI
[3]	Education	RF, SVM, XGB, LightGBM	SHAP, LIME
[4]	Maritime Transport	Fully-connected NN,PI-NN, XGB, MIO-BF	SHAP
[7]	Environmental Water Quality	LR, Multiple Regression, Decision Tree, RF, XGB, SVM, LSTM, MLP, KNN, Integrated	SHAP (Tree & Kernel), PDP
[9]	Energy	RF, GB, XGB, Extra Trees Regressor	SHAP, PDP, permutation importance, Gini Importance, Garson algorithm
[2]	Clinical Trials	Graph Neural Network with Selective Classification	Feature Importance Highlighting (custom)
[6]	Road Safety	LightGBM	SHAP
[5]	Road Safety	RF, XGB	SHAP
[8]	Renewable Energy	LightGBM, XGB, CatBoost, RF(AutoML selected)	SHAP
[10]	Livestock Management	LR, Decision Tree, RF, XGB, SVM, K-Nearest Neighbors, Multilayer Perceptron, AdaBoost	SHAP

including interpretability, interactivity, stability, robustness, and confidence, reflecting a shared view that explainability must support both technical performance and user trust.

The reviewed studies show that while definitions of AI trustworthiness vary, XAI methods must align with context-specific objectives. In his comprehensive literature review, Hadj-Mabrouk [20] examines AI applications in the European railway system, covering structural components such as infrastructure, energy and rolling stock, as well as functional elements like operations, traffic management, maintenance, and telematics. The study highlights the lack of prior research on XAI in this domain and emphasizes the need for transparency, explainability, robustness, accountability, and fairness (particularly in terms of bias mitigation).

Despite the growing body of work applying XAI in sectors such as healthcare, road safety, and energy, research on railway systems is sparse, and systematic evaluations of track geometry defect prediction are lacking. This gap limits the adoption of advanced ML in rail infrastructure because stakeholders cannot evaluate or trust model outputs.

Based on this identified gap, this study applies explainability methods to track defect prediction to enhance transparency, accountability, confidence, and overall trustworthiness in this safety-critical domain. The following sections present a case study that demonstrates how XAI can support maintenance management and decision-making. The empirical contribution of this work lies in providing the first systematic application of SHAP and LIME to track geometry defect prediction, through the evaluation of six ML models on a real-world railway dataset. The value of the study is in showing how explainability can improve stakeholder trust and promote the adoption of ML in safety-critical railway maintenance.

3 Methodology

This section outlines the methodology used in this study, starting with an overview of the ML models and evaluation metrics applied for track defect prediction, followed by the post-hoc explainability techniques used to interpret and validate model outputs.

3.1 Machine Learning

Machine Learning, a subset of AI, develops and improves models from data without explicit programming. It includes two main types: Unsupervised learning, which identifies patterns and structures in input data, and supervised learning, which maps input to labeled outcomes. Supervised learning is further divided into regression (for continuous outputs like age or price) and classification (for categorical outcomes) [21].

In this study, we aim to predict track failures by determining whether defect parameters of a specific track segment exceed a defined threshold. Accordingly, the output is framed as a binary classification problem: Failed or not failed.

Based on the previous literature, the most prominent ML models used in predictive maintenance are Logistic Regression, Gradient Boosting, XGBoost, Random Forest, SVM, and Neural Networks. Despite its name, Logistic Regression is a classification model and is often used for binary and linear classification tasks due to its simplicity and efficiency [22]. Logistic regression uses a logistic function for binary classification, assuming that the distribution of Y given X (Y|X) follows a Bernoulli distribution. While it can handle categorical variables using dummy encoding, it becomes impractical when many categorical variables are present in the dataset [23].

Bagging and boosting are ensemble techniques that enhance model accuracy and robustness. Bagging builds independent models in parallel and aggregates their outputs, while boosting builds models sequentially, with each one correcting errors from the previous. Gradient Boosting is a classical supervised method that improves predictions by minimizing loss iteratively. XGBoost is a fast, scalable implementation of Gradient Boosting based on tree structures, capable of handling large data and computations without sacrificing accuracy [24]. Gradient Boosting and XGBoost improve models iteratively and sequentially, making them well-suited for dynamic data environments like track recording, where factors such as climate and maintenance history change over time. This incremental learning supports continuous performance enhancement. Random Forest, a bagging method, builds multiple decision trees in parallel on random data subsets, combining their outputs by averaging (for regression) or voting (for classification). While effective for large, high-dimensional datasets, Random Forest struggles with categorical variables, unbalanced data, and time series. Class imbalance often requires preprocessing, such as resampling or class weighting. [25].

The Artificial Neural Networks does not discard any feature as it processes each data point individually rather than identifying a general trend across the dataset [26]. This characteristic makes it less effective in handling categorical variables, such as track defect types or sleeper types, as well as imbalanced datasets (e.g., for track geometry, datasets where the number of abnormalities is much smaller than that of normal track sections, which is the typical case). This individualized processing approach also limits ANN's ability to handle imbalanced data, which is common in track geometry misalignment [27].

SVM are supervised learning algorithms used for classification and regression by finding the optimal hyperplane that separates classes. They are popular for their robustness with high-dimensional data, low error rates, and ability to model non-linear relationships, making them versatile and widely used in machine learning [28].

Once a model is selected, its performance is evaluated by comparing its predictions on a portion of the data with known outcomes. Accuracy, the percentage of correct predictions (true positives and negatives), is a common metric. However, it requires setting aside data for validation, reducing the training set. Cross-validation addresses this by dividing the dataset into folds, training on some and testing on others in an iterative process, providing a more robust assessment [29]. Precision is the proportion of true positives among all predicted positives and is important when false positives are costly. Recall measures the proportion of true positives among all actual positives and becomes critical when missing a positive case (e.g., failing to detect a defective track) has serious consequences. The F1 score, the harmonic mean of precision and recall, is especially useful for evaluating performance on imbalanced datasets [30].

3.2 Post-Hoc Explainability

When models lack inherent interpretability, post-hoc explainability helps reveal how decisions are made after training. It is especially valuable when high-performance, complex models are required to reduce error and risk in safety-critical domains, yet still need to be understandable for further validation, confirmation, or audit. In railway infrastructure maintenance, key XAI objectives supported by post-hoc methods include transparency, robustness, fairness, and accountability, though these require further study in context.

Various studies have proposed post-hoc explanation methods to support key XAI goals. In a comprehensive review, Barredo Arrieta et al. [31] identify fairness, accountability, transparency, and robustness as essential for responsible AI. Transparency is enabled by LIME and SHAP, which clarify complex model behavior through local approximations and additive feature importance. SHAP also supports robustness via consistency, while fairness is addressed through SHAP and rule extraction methods that expose feature influence and bias. Accountability is linked to G-REX, which generates human-readable rules for auditing. Model simplification techniques like distillation further aid understanding, compliance, and trust.

Rule extraction is the process of transforming the internal representations of trained models, particularly artificial neural networks (ANNs), into symbolic rules that are more understandable to humans. As outlined by GopiKrishna [32], most rule extraction techniques have been developed for ANNs and categorized by rule format, translucency, and algorithmic complexity. Among these, IF–THEN rules are considered the most interpretable and user-friendly, especially for non-expert stakeholders. However, due to model complexity, this study instead adopts post-hoc methods like SHAP and LIME for their scalability and clearer balance between fidelity and interpretability.

For explaining complex model f(x), a simpler explanation model g(x) is used to explain the prediction of a ML model by assigning an importance value to each feature. Additive Feature Attribution Methods explain model predictions by assigning a contribution to each feature that adds up to the final output. Both LIME and SHAP fall under this category. Equation 1 is the core equation for all additive feature attribution methods which breaks a prediction down into a base value plus feature contributions [33]:

$$g(z') = \Phi_0 + \sum_{i=1}^{M} \Phi_i z_i' \tag{1}$$

where:

g(z'): The simplified explanation model (a local, linear approximation of the original model $f(x)$; $x \in \mathbf{R}^M$).

$z' \in \{0,1\}^M$: Binary presence vector ($z' = 1$ if i is present, else 0).

M: The total number of features.

Φ_0: The base value or intercept that represents the prediction when all input features are zero.

Φ_i: The contribution of feature i to the final prediction.

3.2.1 LIME

LIME (Local Interpretable Model-agnostic Explanations) was introduced by Ribeiro et al. [34]. This method is designed to explain predictions of any classifier and explains individual predictions rather than the entire model.

LIME is a model-agnostic, local explanation method that interprets predictions for individual instances by approximating the model locally with a simple surrogate, usually a linear model. In classification tasks, it outputs class probabilities and visualizes how each feature contributes to them [35]. This helps users understand not only which class was predicted, but also why, based on the local behavior of the model around that instance. However, surrogate models miss nonlinearity.

LIME aims to find an interpretable model g that approximates the original model f well for a given instance x, while keeping g simple enough for humans to understand. This process is formulated as an optimization problem that balances local fidelity (g mimics f) and interpretability (how simple g is). The LIME explanation is obtained by Eq. 2 where $\mathcal{L}$ is the fidelity function and Ω is the simplicity measure:

$$\xi(X) = \arg\min_{g} \mathcal{L}(f, g, \pi_x) + \Omega(g) \tag{2}$$

$\mathcal{L}(f, g, \pi_x)$ is a loss function measuring how well g approximates f around instance x, and $\Omega(g)$ is a complexity penalty encouraging interpretability.

This function balances a trade-off: g closely mimics f in the locality of x (low loss $\mathcal{L}$) while also being simple enough to be interpretable (low complexity Ω).

3.2.2 SHAP

The SHAP value of a feature is the amount of that feature's contribution to a particular prediction outcome. This approach was first introduced by Shapley [36] to fairly distribute a payoff among players based on their contribution to the total outcome. A Shapley value quantifies how much each feature (or player) contributes to the prediction (outcome) made by a ML model for a specific data point, relative to the average prediction. It indicates how the prediction would change if a specific feature were unknown.

For better intuition and visualization, Eq. 3 presents a simplified linear case of the Shapley value. In this setting, the contribution Φ_i for feature x_i is given by its actual weighted effect on the model's prediction, $w_i x_i$, minus its average contribution across the dataset, $w_i E(x_i)$:

$$\Phi_i(\hat{F}) = w_i x_i - w_i \{E(x_i)\} \tag{3}$$

SHAP (SHapley Additive exPlanations) introduced by Lundberg et al. [33] is a unified framework for measuring feature importance. SHAP is an Additive Feature Attribution method that uses Shapley values from cooperative game theory to fairly and consistently assign each feature a contribution to the model's prediction. It should be noted that if the features interact and are not independent, the order in which they are added affects the attributed contribution.

Since computing exact SHAP values is computationally intensive, practical use relies on approximation methods. As outlined by Lundberg et al. [33], SHAP approximations fall into two categories: Model-agnostic and model-specific. Model-agnostic methods, such as Shapley Sampling, estimate values by averaging contributions across many feature permutations, though they become computationally expensive with many features. Kernel SHAP, inspired by LIME and grounded in Shapley theory, improves efficiency by fitting locally weighted linear models around each prediction, ensuring local accuracy, consistency, and missingness. Model-specific methods exploit internal model structures for faster computation. Linear SHAP uses feature coefficients and expectations in linear models. Low-Order SHAP reduces complexity by limiting feature interactions, suitable for low-dimensional inputs. Max SHAP targets max functions by attributing outputs to the most influential inputs. For deep networks, Deep SHAP extends DeepLIFT, combining SHAP values recursively through layers to capture hierarchical contributions efficiently.

4   Case Study

To validate the effectiveness of XAI methods, a case study was conducted using a real-world dataset from the open-access INFORMS 2015 Railway Applications Section Problem-Solving Competition [37]. The prediction task is framed as a binary classification problem: Identifying whether a track segment has failed or not (critical or non-critical). The dataset includes 23,843 inspection records of track characteristics, operational data, and defect attributes, collected by automated track recording systems. Each record is labeled as a critical failure (RED, requiring immediate action), a non-critical failure (YELLOW, requiring intervention). The data is imbalanced, with failures (RED and YELLOW) making up 27% of segments and non-failures 73%. After merging, a correlation analysis (Fig. 1) was performed to reduce overfitting and model bias, followed by feature selection. In the European system, Yellow corresponds to the Intervention Limit (IL), while Red corresponds to the Immediate Action Limit (IAL).

The   strongest correlation was between 'TOT_CAR_WEST' and 'TOT_CAR_EAST', which reflect traffic in opposite directions on the same line, as expected. Both were initially included to capture total traffic impact, but their high collinearity provides an opportunity to assess how XAI methods handle redundant information. A final decision on retaining both will be made after applying explainability techniques. Strong correlations were also observed among 'TEST_FSPD', 'TEST_PSPD', and 'CLASS', since all represent aspects of operational speed. While 'TEST_FSPD' and 'TEST_PSPD' must be kept due to their distinct meanings, 'CLASS' was removed to avoid redundancy.

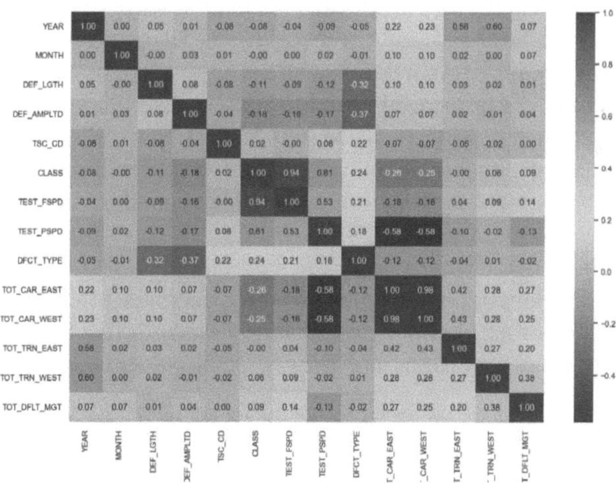

Fig. 1. Correlation coefficients

Six classification models were used: Gradient Boosting, XGBoost, Random Forest, Logistic Regression, SVM, and Neural Networks. Each was trained on seven features: DEF_LGTH (defect length), TSC_CD (track codes, tangent, spiral, and curve), TEST_FSPD (freight speed), TEST_PSPD (passenger speed), DFCT_TYPE (defect type), TOT_CAR_EAST, TOT_CAR_WEST (traffic counts in each direction), and TOT_DFLT_MGT (gross tonnage).

Model performance was assessed using test accuracy, validation accuracy, and 5-fold cross-validated recall, precision, and F1 score. Test accuracy measures performance on held-out data, while validation accuracy is based on a reserved portion of the training data, useful for detecting overfitting and guiding model tuning. Results are summarized in Table 3.

Table 3. ML model performance.

Model	Validation Accuracy	Mean Cross-Validation	Test Accuracy	Precision	Recall	F1-Score	ROC
LR	0.734	0.661	**0.734**	0.453	0.525	0.486	0.664
GB	0.713	0.780	0.712	0.434	0.621	0.510	0.683
XGB	0.702	0.760	0.710	0.426	0.605	0.500	0.674
RF	0.725	0.813	**0.732**	0.444	0.467	0.455	0.641
SVM	0.674	0.692	0.684	0.408	**0.704**	0.516	0.691
NN	0.661	0.698	0.669	0.397	**0.734**	0.516	0.693

Based on the evaluation metrics in Table 3, no single model outperformed all others across every criterion. Logistic Regression achieved the highest test accuracy (0.734), while Random Forest had the best mean cross-validation score (0.813), indicating strong consistency. However, both showed lower recall and F1-scores, which are crucial for imbalanced tasks like failure prediction. Given the high safety risk associated with undetected failures, recall was prioritized to reduce false negatives, which are more critical than false positives in this context. SVM and Neural Networks achieved the highest recall (0.704 and 0.734), making them more effective at identifying failures and reducing false negatives. Their strong F1-scores also reflect a good balance between precision and recall.

Despite this, both models are complex and less interpretable. SVM with non-linear kernels and Neural Network with multi-layered structures produce opaque decision boundaries. To address this, post-hoc explainability methods like SHAP and LIME were applied to interpret model decisions and assess their alignment with domain knowledge.

4.1 LIME Analysis

LIME plots highlight how models differ in feature interpretation and prioritization, underscoring the importance of XAI for auditability. LIME reveals unintuitive models, where explanations contradict domain knowledge, and inconsistent models, where explanations vary for similar inputs. Figure 2 shows LIME explanations for one instance, with bar charts indicating each feature's contribution (green for positive, red for negative). LIME was applied to all models, including Logistic Regression, in order to present a uniform explanation framework and to illustrate local contributions at the instance level.

For the instance, the true class is 0 (IL: Intervention Limits). Logistic Regression and Random Forest misclassify it as class 1 (IAL), while Gradient Boosting, XGBoost, SVM, and Neural Network classify it correctly. Differences in feature attributions reveal how each model interprets track conditions.

Logistic Regression overemphasizes Track Code, speed, and eastbound traffic, while misattributing a negative impact to DEF_LGTH. Combined with negative weights for gross tonnage and westbound traffic, this contradicts domain knowledge and reflects oversimplified reasoning.

Random Forest also predicts IAL, giving strong importance to DFCT_TYPE and TSC_CD but large negative weights to TEST_PSPD and TOT_CAR_WEST. While it handles some interactions, its logic still diverges from expected patterns.

Gradient Boosting and XGBoost classify the instance correctly, but LIME explanations show unexpected negative contributions from several features, with only DFCT_TYPE contributing positively. This suggests reliance on statistical patterns over physical causality, underlining the need for expert validation.

SVM and Neural Networks models not only make correct predictions but also align with domain logic, capturing nonlinear effects such as combined geometric stress and

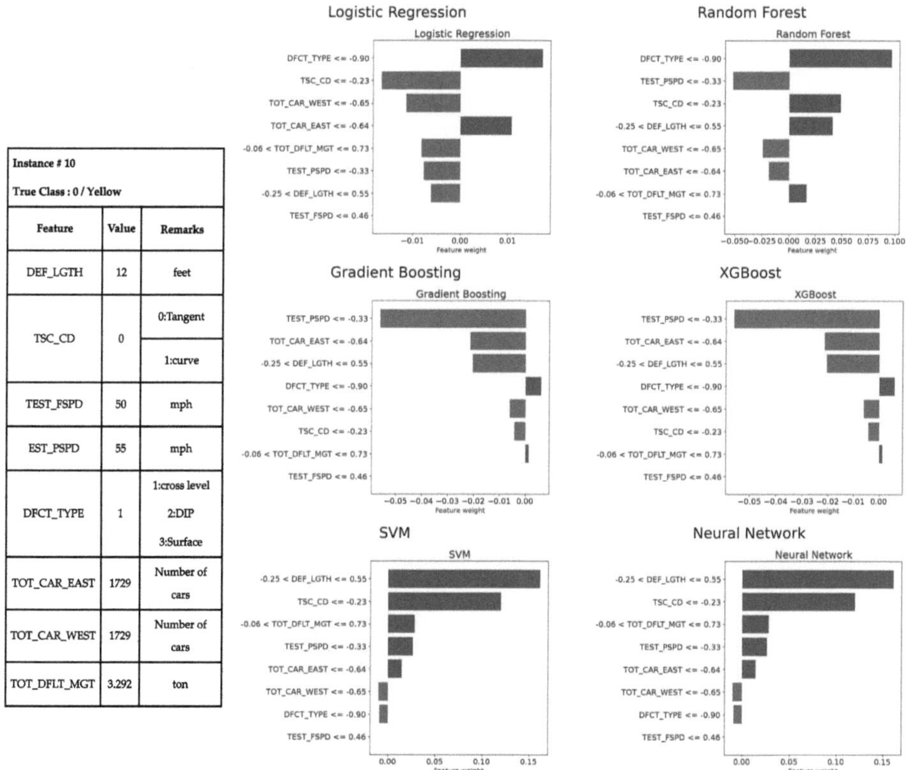

Feature	Value	Remarks
DEF_LGTH	12	feet
TSC_CD	0	0:Tangent 1:curve
TEST_FSPD	50	mph
EST_PSPD	55	mph
DFCT_TYPE	1	1:cross level 2:DIP 3:Surface
TOT_CAR_EAST	1729	Number of cars
TOT_CAR_WEST	1729	Number of cars
TOT_DFLT_MGT	3.292	ton

Fig. 2. LIME-based local explanations across models

traffic. However, their flexibility introduces variability in attributions across instances, raising concerns about explanation stability.

4.2 SHAP Analysis

In this study, Tree SHAP was applied to tree-based models (Random Forest, Gradient Boosting, XGBoost) and Kernel SHAP to SVM and Neural Networks. SHAP values are approximations of feature influence rather than exact causal effects, yet they offer a consistent and theoretically grounded framework for both local and global interpretability. The SHAP beeswarm plot in Fig. 3 illustrates feature-level contributions to the SVM model's predictions. Each point represents one instance, with color showing feature value (red for high, blue for low) and position reflecting its SHAP value (impact on output). DEF_LGTH is the strongest and most consistent contributor. High values raise failure risk, aligning with domain knowledge. The clear separation of DEF_LGTH values also suggests the model consistently captures its influence.

In the SHAP beeswarm plot, higher values of TOT_CAR_WEST (red) mostly have positive SHAP values, indicating that increased westbound traffic raises predicted failure probability. In contrast, high TOT_CAR_EAST values show neutral to slightly negative effects. Their high correlation likely leads SHAP to penalize redundancy, suggesting that including both traffic directions may be unnecessary. Though their contributions are similar, SHAP's credit depends on feature order, causing one to appear as having a negative impact. TOT_DFLT_MGT shows mixed SHAP values for both low and high values, hinting at nonlinear interactions or data skew. The model may detect trends linked to tonnage but lacks generalization across the full range.

Passenger train speeds (TEST_PSPD) tend to increase failure risk, while freight speeds (TEST_FSPD) have a neutral to slightly positive impact, possibly reflecting how higher passenger speeds amplify geometric defects.

DFCT_TYPE has a moderate, mixed influence due to its categorical nature and the varying risk levels of defect types. TSC_CD (track code) shows limited but present impact. Although curves typically increase failure risk due to lateral forces and stress, the model's low attribution may stem from data imbalance or feature confounding, such as curves occurring more in low-speed or well-maintained areas.

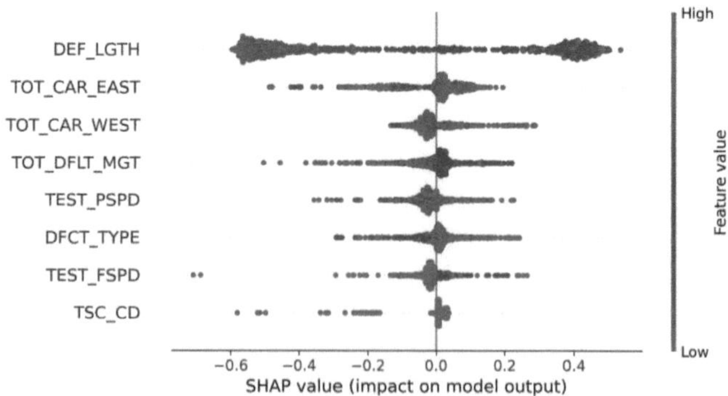

Fig. 3. SHAP beeswarm plot for SVM

Figure 4 presents the SHAP beeswarm plot for the Neural Networks model. Compared to SVM, both models identify DEF_LGTH as the most influential feature. However, secondary feature rankings differ. The SVM gives more weight to TOT_CAR_WEST and moderate importance to TOT_CAR_EAST, while the Neural Network treats both traffic directions more evenly but with weaker influence, which does not align with domain knowledge.

Both models rank TOT_DFLT_MGT highly, though the Neural Network shows a broader SHAP spread, suggesting stronger nonlinear effects. For train speed, both models associate higher passenger speeds with increased failure risk, with SVM showing slightly stronger emphasis. DFCT_TYPE is ranked slightly higher by the Neural Network, with greater SHAP variation, reflecting its strength in modeling categorical interactions. SVM also considers it relevant, but with a narrower effect range.

TSC_CD has minimal impact in both models. SVM shows slightly more variation, but both underrepresent the higher risk typically associated with curves.

SHAP analysis suggests that removing TOT_CAR_EAST and TSC_CD could improve the SVM model. Re-running the model without these features confirmed this, increasing recall from 0.704 to 0.716 and F1-score from 0.516 to 0.519.

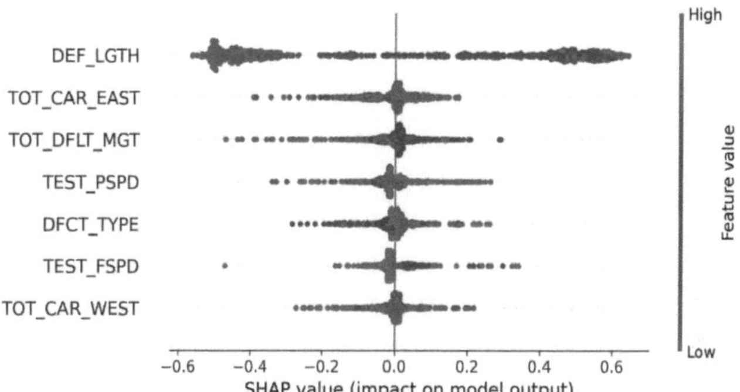

Fig. 4. SHAP beeswarm plot for Neural Network

SHAP values assume feature independence, so in cases of high correlation (such as eastbound and westbound traffic), the attributions may not fully represent causal effects. In practice, SHAP penalized redundancy by crediting one correlated feature positively and the other negatively. This underscores both the need for domain expertise in interpreting outputs and the limitations of SHAP in correlated datasets. Figure 5 shows the SHAP heatmap for the updated SVM model. Each row represents a feature, each column a prediction. Red indicates positive, blue negative, and white minimal impact on failure prediction.

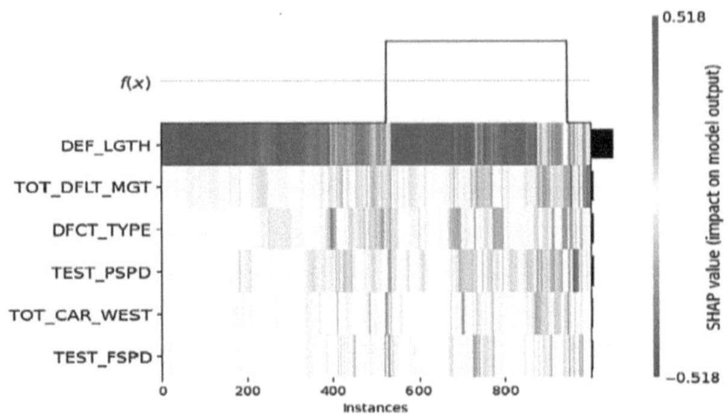

Fig. 5. SHAP heatmap for SVM second run

5 Conclusion

This paper addresses an unexplored gap in railway track maintenance research by introducing XAI into track geometry defect prediction. It contributes to both the academic understanding of trustworthy AI and its practical adoption in the rail sector. Six machine learning classifiers, including Logistic Regression, Random Forest, Gradient Boosting, XGBoost, SVM, and Neural Networks, were evaluated. SVM and Neural Networks achieved the highest recall, which is critical in safety-critical contexts. However, their inherent opacity required the application of post-hoc explainability techniques to ensure transparency, accountability, and consistency with domain knowledge.

Using SHAP and LIME, global and local explainability were achieved. SHAP identified redundant and inconsistent features, as eastbound traffic appeared to reduce failure probability and track code did the same in curved segments, both contradicting domain knowledge. Removing these features slightly improved the SVM's recall. LIME revealed that simpler models, such as Logistic Regression, misclassified defect instances due to oversimplified feature attribution, highlighting the limitations of transparent models when domain logic is not preserved.

The findings answer the research questions clearly. First, Logistic Regression achieved the highest accuracy, while SVM and Neural Network delivered the best recall, making them more effective for identifying failures. Second, SHAP and LIME improved interpretability by highlighting key features, detecting redundant variables, and aligning model logic with domain knowledge. Third, the integration of XAI enhanced transparency and auditability, thereby supporting stakeholder trust and providing actionable insights for railway maintenance.

These findings show that XAI is essential in railway track maintenance, where decisions must align with engineering logic and regulatory standards. XAI strengthens trust and supports real-world adoption. This study demonstrates that accuracy and interpretability can be balanced through effective XAI integration, with implications for both research and practice. For research, it highlights the need for systematic evaluation of this trade-off and the development of trust metrics that capture transparency. For practice, it shows how SHAP and LIME can be embedded in maintenance workflows to validate model logic, improve decision-making, and support regulatory compliance.

Future research should explore XAI in dynamic railway asset management, focusing on real-time auditing and flexible explanations. Further investigation into AI trustworthiness goals in railway infrastructure, such as transparency, robustness, fairness, and accountability, is needed for the selection of suitable XAI methods for specific operational and regulatory needs.

Some limitations should be acknowledged. First, the dataset comes from a single competition source and may not reflect all real-world conditions. Second, class imbalance could bias models toward the majority class despite resampling. Finally, SHAP and LIME also provide approximate explanations with uncertain stability.

The models were implemented in Python using the scikit-learn, XGBoost, SHAP, and LIME libraries. Data preprocessing and visualization were carried out with pandas, NumPy, and matplotlib. To support reproducibility, the code and data used in this study are available at: https://github.com/shahab-mansouri/XAI-TrackGeometry.

Acknowledgments. This study was conducted within the framework of MOST – Sustainable Mobility National Research Center and received funding from the European Union under Next Generation EU, PNRR Mission 2-Component 2-Investimento 1.4 (CUP B83C22002900007). The author gratefully acknowledges Concordia University for its research support in Canada. This manuscript reflects only the authors' views and opinions; neither the European Union nor the European Commission can be held responsible for them.

Disclosure of Interests. The authors declare no competing interests relevant to the content of this article.

References

1. Chen, Z., Xiao, L., Guo, F., Yan, J.: Interpretable machine learning for building energy management: a state-of-the-art review. Adv. Appl. Energy. **9**, 100123 (2023). https://doi.org/10.1016/j.adapen.2023.100123
2. Lu, Y., Chen, T., Hao, N., Rechem, C., Chen, J., Fu, T.: Uncertainty quantification and interpretability for clinical trial approval prediction. Health Data Sci. **4**, 0126 (2024). https://doi.org/10.34133/hds.0126
3. Sahlaoui, H., Abdellaoui Alaoui, E.A., Said, A., Nayyar, A.: An empirical assessment of SMOTE variants techniques and interpretation methods in improving the accuracy and the interpretability of student performance models. Educ. Inf. Technol. **29**, 1–37 (2023). https://doi.org/10.1007/s10639-023-12007-w
4. Wang, H., Yan, R., Wang, S., Zhen, L.: Innovative approaches to addressing the tradeoff between interpretability and accuracy in ship fuel consumption prediction. Transp. Res. Part C Emerg. Technol. **157**, 104361 (2023). https://doi.org/10.1016/j.trc.2023.104361
5. Shuai, Z., Kwon, T.: Analyzing winter crash dynamics using spatial analysis and crash frequency prediction models with SHAP interpretability. Future Transp. **5**(1), 17 (2025). https://doi.org/10.3390/futuretransp5010017
6. Yang, Z., Zhang, C., Li, G., Xu, H.: Analysis of the impact of different road conditions on accident severity at highway-rail grade crossings based on explainable machine learning. Symmetry. **17**(1) (2025). https://doi.org/10.3390/sym17010147

7. Hao, Z., Juan, H., Xian, G., Bing, S., Jian, M., Wen, D.: Model evaluation of total phosphorus prediction based on model accuracy and interpretability for the surface water in the river network of the Jiangnan Plain, China. Water Sci. Technol. **88** (2023). https://doi.org/10.2166/wst.2023.310

8. Bakht, M., Haji Mohd, M.N., Ibrahim, B., Khan, N., Sheikh, U.U., Ab Rahman, A.A.-H.: Advanced automated machine learning framework for photovoltaic power output prediction using environmental parameters and SHAP interpretability. Results Eng. **25**, 103838 (2025). https://doi.org/10.1016/j.rineng.2024.103838

9. Bongomin, O., Charles, N., Mwasiagi, J., Maube, O.: Exploring insights in biomass and waste gasification via ensemble machine learning models and interpretability techniques. Int. J. Energy Res. (2024). https://doi.org/10.1155/2024/6087208

10. Li, D., et al.: Optimized machine learning models for predicting core body temperature in dairy cows: enhancing accuracy and interpretability for practical livestock management. Animals **14**, 2724 (2024). https://doi.org/10.3390/ani14182724

11. Ali, S., et al.: Explainable artificial intelligence (XAI): what we know and what is left to attain trustworthy artificial intelligence. Inf. Fusion. **99**, 101805 (2023). https://doi.org/10.1016/j.inffus.2023.101805

12. Escalona, J.L., Urda, P., Muñoz, S.: A track geometry measuring system based on multibody kinematics, inertial sensors and computer vision. Sensors. **21**(3) (2021). https://doi.org/10.3390/s21030683

13. Sedghi, M., Kauppila, O., Bergquist, B., Vanhatalo, E., Kulahci, M.: A taxonomy of railway track maintenance planning and scheduling: a review and research trends. Reliab. Eng. Syst. Saf. **215**, 107827 (2021). https://doi.org/10.1016/j.ress.2021.107827

14. Ghofrani, F., He, Q., Goverde, R.M.P., Liu, X.: Recent applications of big data analytics in railway transportation systems: a survey. Transp. Res. Part C Emerg. Technol. **90**, 226–246 (2018). https://doi.org/10.1016/j.trc.2018.03.010

15. Chenariyan Nakhaee, M., Hiemstra, D., Stoelinga, M., Noort, M.: The recent applications of machine learning in rail track maintenance: a survey. In: Margaria, T., Steffen, B. (eds.) ISoLA 2019. LNCS, vol. 11946, pp. 91–105. Springer, Cham (2019). https://doi.org/10.1007/978-3-030-18744-6_6

16. Hamon, R., Junklewitz, H., Sánchez Martín, J.I.: Robustness and explain ability of artificial intelligence. Publications Office of the European Union, Luxembourg (2020). https://doi.org/10.2760/57493

17. Lipton, Z.C.: The mythos of model interpretability: in machine learning, the concept of interpretability is both important and slippery. Queue. **16**(3), 31–57 (2018). https://doi.org/10.1145/3236386.3241340

18. Vollert, S., Atzmueller, M., Theissler, A.: Interpretable machine learning: a brief survey from the predictive maintenance perspective. In: 2021 26th IEEE Int. Conf. Emerging Technologies and Factory Automation (ETFA), pp. 1–8. IEEE (2021). https://doi.org/10.1109/ETFA45728.2021.9613467

19. Rojat, T., Puget, R., Filliat, D., Del Ser, J., Gelin, R., Díaz-Rodríguez, N.: Explainable artificial intelligence (XAI) on time series data: a survey. arXiv abs/2104.00950 (2021). https://doi.org/10.48550/arXiv.2104.00950

20. Hadj-Mabrouk, H.: A literature review on the applications of artificial intelligence to European rail transport safety. IET Intell. Transp. Syst. **18**(12), 2291–2324 (2024). https://doi.org/10.1049/itr2.12587

21. Yu, L., Zhao, X., Huang, J., Hu, H., Liu, B.: Research on machine learning with algorithms and development. J. Theory Pract. Eng. Sci. **3**, 7–14 (2023). https://doi.org/10.53469/jtpes.2023.03(12).02

22. Subasi, A.: Machine learning techniques. In: Subasi, A. (ed.) Practical Machine Learning for Data Analysis Using Python, pp. 91–202. Academic Press (2020). https://doi.org/10.1016/B978-0-12-821379-7.00003-5

23. Banks, D.L., Fienberg, S.E.: Data mining, statistics. In: Encyclopedia of Physical Science and Technology, 3rd edn. Academic Press (2003)

24. Chen, T., Guestrin, C.: XGBoost: a scalable tree boosting system. In: Proc. ACM SIGKDD Int. Conf. Knowl. Discov. Data Min., pp. 785–794. ACM (2016). https://doi.org/10.1145/2939672.2939785

25. Zhu, T.: Analysis on the applicability of the random forest. J. Phys. Conf. Ser. **1607**, 012123 (2020). https://doi.org/10.1088/1742-6596/1607/1/012123

26. Guler, H.: Prediction of railway track geometry deterioration using artificial neural networks: a case study for Turkish state railways. Struct. Infrastruct. Eng. **10**(5), 614–626 (2014). https://doi.org/10.1080/15732479.2012.757791

27. Nisbet, R., Miner, G., Yale, K.: Classification. In: Nisbet, R., Miner, G., Yale, K. (eds.) Handbook of Statistical Analysis and Data Mining Applications, 2nd edn., pp. 169–186. Academic Press, Boston (2018). https://doi.org/10.1016/B978-0-12-416632-5.00009-8

28. Piccialli, V.: Nonlinear optimization and support vector machines. Ann. Oper. Res. **314** (2022). https://doi.org/10.1007/s10479-022-04655-x

29. VanderPlas, J.: Python Data Science Handbook. O'Reilly, Sebastopol (2016)

30. Alpaydın, E.: Introduction to Machine Learning, 4th edn. MIT Press, Cambridge (2020)

31. Barredo Arrieta, A., et al.: Explainable artificial intelligence (XAI): concepts, taxonomies, opportunities and challenges toward responsible AI. Inf. Fusion. **58**, 82–115 (2020). https://doi.org/10.1016/j.inffus.2019.12.012

32. GopiKrishna, T.: Evaluation of rule extraction algorithms. Int. J. Data Min. Knowl. Manag. Process. **4**, 9–19 (2014). https://doi.org/10.5121/ijdkp.2014.4302

33. Lundberg, S., Lee, S.-I.: A unified approach to interpreting model predictions. arXiv abs/1705.07874 (2017). https://doi.org/10.48550/arXiv.1705.07874

34. Ribeiro, M., Singh, S., Guestrin, C.: Why should I trust you? Explaining the predictions of any classifier. In: Proc. ACM SIGKDD Int. Conf. Knowl. Discov. Data Min. (2016). https://doi.org/10.1145/2939672.2939785

35. Salih, A., et al.: A perspective on explainable artificial intelligence methods: SHAP and LIME. Adv. Intell. Syst. **7** (2024). https://doi.org/10.1002/aisy.202400304

36. Shapley, L.S.: A value for n-person games. In: Kuhn, H.W., Tucker, A.W. (eds.) Contributions to the Theory of Games II, pp. 307–318. Princeton University Press, Princeton (1953). https://doi.org/10.1515/9781400881970-018

37. RAS Problem Solving Competition. https://connect.informs.org/railway-applications/new-item3/problem-solving-competition681/new-item9

Creating Synthetic Test Data for Rail Design Tools – The Case of Linear Scheme Plans

Marek T. Jezinski[1]([✉]) [iD], Markus Roggenbach[1] [iD], Monika Seisenberger[1] [iD], Victor Cai[2], and Fabio Caraffini[1] [iD]

[1] Swansea University, Wales, United Kingdom
{m.t.jezinski,m.roggenbach,m.seisenberger,fabio.caraffini}@swansea.ac.uk
[2] Siemens Mobility Limited (UK), Chippenham, United Kingdom
victor.cai@siemens.com

Abstract. Many application domains resolve to the use of synthetic test data motivated by privacy concerns and safety reasons, but also, on the positive side, due to cost and quality considerations. Genetic Algorithms have long been studied for graph optimisation, however, to the best of our knowledge, not for scheme plan generation. We present a new approach that automatically constructs scheme plans from a set of tiles. This transforms the scheme plan generation problem into a combinatorial optimisation process. The manual design of scheme plans is laborious, costly, and in itself an error-prone process. Thus, there is a demand in the rail industry for synthetic scheme plans. All constructions are given. The runtimes achieved by our tool are presented.

Keywords: testing · genetic algorithms · scheme plans · decision tables

1 Introduction

The rail industry increasingly uses software tools, for example, to design scheme plans. However, how can such tools be tested, qualified, or certified? The manual design of rail artefacts such as scheme plans is laborious, costly, and in itself error-prone. Thus, there is a demand in the rail industry for synthetic test data.

We present a technique and a tool for generating artificial scheme plans. To this end, we use genetic algorithms (GAs) with controlled fault injection. Which faults ought to be injected is steered by decision tables. This allows for a systematic case analysis for different design rules. The generated scheme plans can then be supplied to rail design tools such as the Siemens' data checker [1], the OVADO tool [2], or Luteberget's Junction tool suite [3], and one can evaluate whether the rail design tool finds injected faults or reports faults that are not there.

Fault analysis through decision tables is a manual process that requires rail engineers to determine which scenarios to consider. In contrast, the following

M. H. ter Beek et al. (Eds.): RSSRail 2025, LNCS 16236, pp. 78–87, 2026.
https://doi.org/10.1007/978-3-032-10762-6_8

steps, namely test case generation, test execution, and test evaluation, can be automated. Thus, when decision tables are given, our approach leads to a fully automatic quality evaluation of check tools for scheme plans.

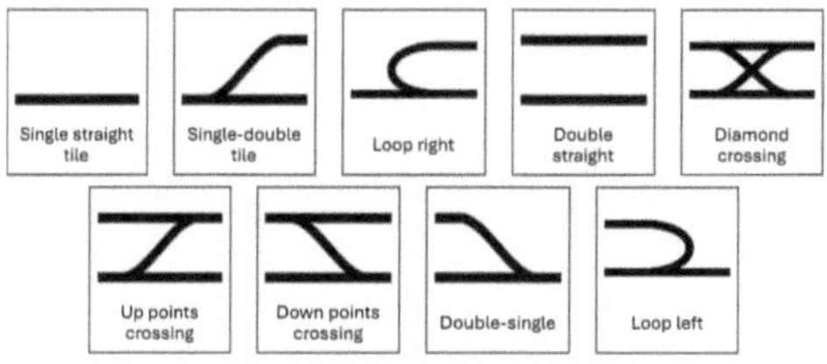

Fig. 1. Set of tiles available for generating linear, abstract scheme plans.

(a) Abstract scheme plan.

(b) Concrete scheme plans. Labels provide track start and end points with a direction label.

Fig. 2. An abstract scheme plan and two of its corresponding concrete examples; further variation comes from differing distances.

2   Scheme Plans and Design Rules

In the context of railways, a scheme plan is a graphical representation of a railway, depicting artefacts such as tracks, points, crossings, and line-side equipment, including balises (electronic beacons placed between the rails).

Following several discussions about testing coverage with industry representatives, we depicted elements of the track topology as tiles; see Fig. 1 for the tiles we have identified. A scheme plan is *linear* if it can be produced as a sequence of these tiles. For such a sequence, the following *adjacency rule* must hold for all pairs of consecutive tiles: the number of tracks at the right boundary of a given tile must be the same as the number of tracks at the left boundary of a subsequent tile. We call such a scheme plan *abstract*.

An abstract scheme plan can be turned into a *concrete* version by adding *lengths* (measured in metres) and *track directions* (DOWN and UP); see Fig. 2. The lengths are the distances from a reference point called *datum*, which in our case is to the left of the entire scheme plan. Track direction DOWN means that as the track progresses, the distances increase; on the contrary, UP denotes the distances decreasing, according to our industrial partner's conventions. One difference between the two concrete linear scheme plans in Fig. 2 (b) is that – imposed by the choices of UP and DOWN – start and end point of a line of track change position.

Table 1. Decision table reflecting the BG-03 rule.

C1: Balises	F	F	T	T	T	T	T	T	T
C2: Direction	–	–	–	UP	UP	UP	DOWN	DOWN	DOWN
C3: Distance	–	–	–	>	=	<	>	=	<
C4: Points	F	T	F	T	T	T	T	T	T
A1: Correct	X	X	X	X	X		X	X	
A2: Incorrect						X			X

2.1   Design Rules

In the railway domain, the placement of track equipment must meet strict layout requirements to ensure the safe operation of the signalling system. They can be vendor-specific, product-specific, or determined by local standard bodies.

Cai [4] studied and analysed a collection of 300+ design rules from our industrial partner Siemens. A subset of these is related to balise groups (BG). Cai identified five recurring patterns, some of which are local, some of which concern BGs separated by other infrastructure at larger distances. The rule **BG-03** is an example of a so-called local distance constraint. It specifies: *Spacing smaller than one metre between a single balise and a point toe constitutes a fault.*

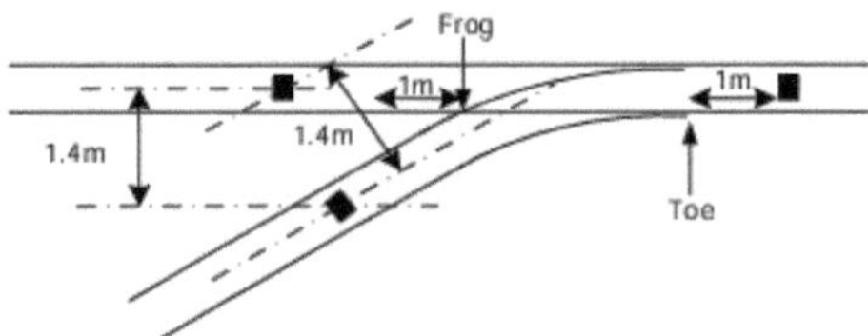

3   Testing with Decision Tables

Decision tables allow one to describe and analyse complex logical relationships. Some claim that presenting decision procedures in tabular form goes back at least to ancient Babylon [5]. In computer science, an early documented use was in 1957 for programming [6]. They are at the core of Decision Table Based Testing, an established black-box testing technique [7].

Decision tables consist of a condition and an action part; see Table 1 for an example. The condition part analyses the logical relationships between input parameters while the action part expresses the expected outcome. The entry "-"

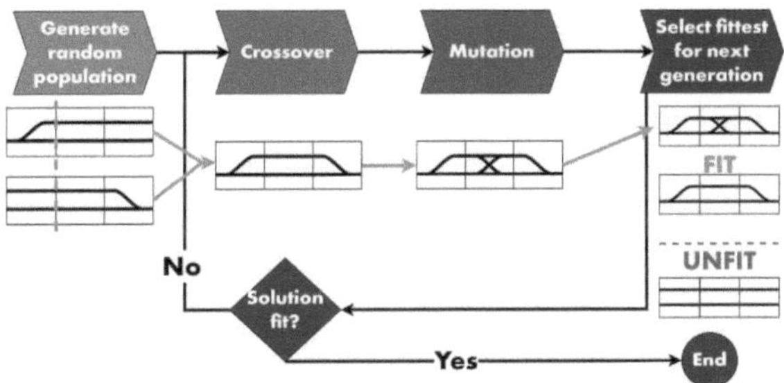

Fig. 3. Diagram depicting Genetic Algorithm utilised for scheme plan generation; for simplicity, showing only one of the two children in the crossover step.

stands for a don't care value, i.e., the decision is not influenced by the value of this parameter.

Our systematic case analysis for the design rule BG-03 led to the following conditions characterising families of concrete linear scheme plans:

C1: "Are there any balises existing in the scheme plan?"; this question can be answered with "T" (true) or "F" (false).

C2: "What is the direction of track on which the balise is placed?"; this question can be answered by one of the values "UP" or "DOWN".

C3: "How does the distance between balise and point toe relate to the 1 metre distance?"; this relation can be one of ">", "=", and "<"

C4: "Does the scheme plan include a point?"; this question can be answered with "T" (true) or "F" (false).

Depending on the answers to the questions C1 to C4, we know if a concrete scheme plan is adhering to BG-03 rule. For instance, if there is a balise in the scheme plan, the balise under discussion is on a track with direction DOWN, the balise is placed at a distance $< 1\,\mathrm{m}$ to a point node (and, naturally, there is a point in the scheme plan), then the scheme plan is failing to obey the BG-03 design rule.

The idea of testing from such a decision table is to have one test case for each of its columns. The conditions provide values or a range of the input parameters, the action determines the expected outcome.

Though the answer to question C2 does not affect the expected output, it is useful to include this criterion: the system under test might carry out different calculations depending on track direction. This is, e.g., the case in Siemens' data checker. Condition C2 illustrates that decision tables for testing also ought to consider how the system under test could be implemented.

4 Generating Abstract Scheme Plans with GAs

Building on the work of Harrison [8], we implemented a tool in Python[1] that automatically generates abstract scheme plans of length k inspired by the GA

---

[1] We refrained from using standard GA libraries to achieve better performance.

framework [9]. This is a popular randomised search heuristic inspired by Darwin's natural selection, iteratively applying operators to evolve candidate solutions whose quality is evaluated by an objective function – commonly referred to as the fitness function – based on the optimisation problem to be solved. We selected this algorithm for its simplicity, versatility, ease of use without needing training materials, and low overhead. We interpret the standard GA notation as follows:

Gene: The gene pool consists of the tiles presented in Fig. 1.
Chromosome: A chromosome is an abstract linear scheme plan.
Population: A population is a set of abstract linear scheme plans.
Fitness: A fitness value, a real number $\in [0, 1]$, allows the evaluation of newly
generated solutions tailored to meet the requirements.

Our tool works as shown in Fig. 3. First, a *random population* consisting of n scheme plans is generated. 'Parents' are selected using multiple tournament selections of size s, forming a mating pool of m solutions. Random pairs from this pool are selected 'without replacement' for crossover with a probability p_c set up by the user.

The *crossover* operation takes two linear abstract scheme plans of the same length $k \geq 2$ as input, say a sequence of tiles $p_1 = \langle s_0, \ldots, s_{k-1} \rangle$ and $p_2 = \langle t_0, \ldots, t_{k-1} \rangle$. It chooses a random value $0 \leq i < k - 1$ and produces the two new linear abstract scheme plans $c_1 = \langle s_0, \ldots, s_i, t_{i+1}, \ldots t_{k-1} \rangle$ and $c_2 = \langle t_0, \ldots, t_i, s_{i+1}, \ldots s_{k-1} \rangle$. c_1 and c_2 might be ill-formed according to the adjacency rule. Consequently, there is a post-processing repair function to ensure feasible solutions. This process checks if the tile at index $i + 1$ adheres to the adjacency rule. If not, it randomly replaces this tile with one that does.

Following this, c_1 and c_2 are mutated. The *mutation* operation takes a scheme plan $p = \langle s_0, \ldots, s_{k-1} \rangle$ as input, and has a probability p_m (set by the user) for each of its positions $0 \leq i \leq k - 1$, to change by randomly selecting a fitting tile t (a tile t is fitting if adjacency rule applies to both, s_{i-1} and t, if $i > 0$, as well as t and s_{i+1}, if $i < k - 1$), and returns a new scheme plan $m = \langle s_0, \ldots, s_{i-1}, t, s_{i+1}, \ldots s_{k-1} \rangle$. Such tile always exists, as our tiles in Fig. 1 cover all combinations of one and two tracks on the left and right boundaries. There is no need for repair at other positions, as we can presume p_1 and p_2 to be well-formed.

The newly generated solutions replace their parents in the population for the next iteration of the algorithm. Our tool terminates if the chosen *threshold* is reached.

Our *fitness functions* have a number of parameters. These include:

- the length $k \in \mathbb{N}$ of the abstract scheme plan and
- a rate $r \in \mathbb{Q}$ that determines the average expected complexity of its tiles.

The *fitness function* uses a table of values, which for each tile says how many points a tile includes and how many tracks a tile 'creates'. Here, we present an excerpt of this table for tiles from Fig. 1:

type	no. of new points $nPoints$	no. of new tracks $nTracks$
single-straight	0	0
diamond-crossing	4	2

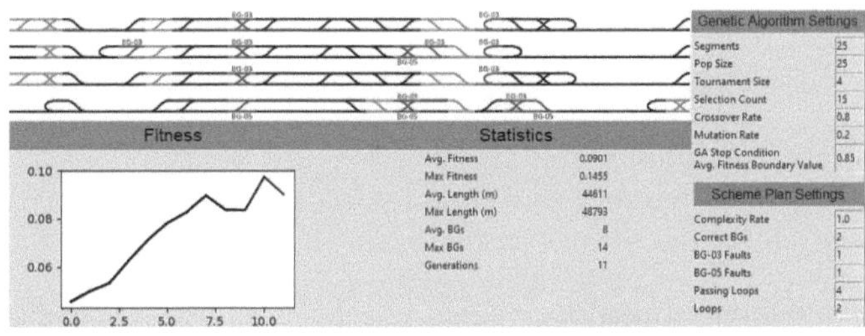

Fig. 4. Generation of abstract, linear scheme plans for BG-03 rule. The fittest solutions are at the top. Snapshot of our tool during the converging process.

With the help of the complexity rate r, we define the ideal complexity of a plan consisting of k tiles to be

$$idealComplexity(k) = r * k.$$

Given a linear abstract scheme plan T, we define its complexity to be

$$complexity(T) = \sum_{i=0}^{k-1} nPoints(T_i) + nTracks(T_i).$$

Using *complexity* as a penalty term, we define:

$$coreFitness(T) = \frac{1}{1 + 0.05(idealComplexity(k) - complexity(T))}$$

Our experiments show that, e.g., with the empirically identified parameters of $r = 2.5$, $k = 25$, $s = 4$, $m = 15$, $p_c = 0.8$, $p_m = 0.2$, and $n = 25$, our GA implementation reaches a satisfactory threshold of average fitness equal to 0.85 in less than 10 iterations. This is a very fast process.

4.1   Creating Linear, Abstract Scheme Plans for BG-03

Testing for BG-03 utilising Table 1 requires the generation of nine test cases, one for each table column, except the first.

We define a colour scheme for the tiles from Fig. 1. A tile is *black*, if it does not have a balise, it is *green* if it has a correctly placed balise around a point, and *red* if it has a balise around a point placed incorrectly. For example, a single straight tile is black. In contrast, a single-double tile can take on all three colours.

Given a linear abstract scheme plan T based on coloured tiles, we can now determine the following natural numbers:

- $cBG(T)$ how many balise groups in it are correctly placed (i.e., how many green tiles it includes),
- $fBG(T)$ how many balise groups in it are wrongly placed (i.e., how many red tiles it includes), and
- $pL(T)$ how many passing loops it includes.

Consequently, we define a number of parameters for the ideal values:

- $icBG \in \mathbb{N}$, the ideal number of correct BGs,
- $ifBG \in \mathbb{N}$, the ideal number of BG-03 faults, and
- $ipL \in \mathbb{N}$, the ideal number of passing loops in the scheme plan, respectively.

With these, we define a function

$$deviation(T) = |icBG - cBG(T)| + |ifBG - fBG(T)| + |ipL - pL(T)|$$

Finally, we set the fitness function for testing for BG-03 to

$$BG03Fitness(T) = \frac{1}{1 + deviation(T)} * coreFitness(T).$$

Our experiments show that with the choice of $r = 2.5$, $k = 25$, $p_c = 0.8$, $p_m = 0.2$, and a population $n = 25$, our GA implementation reaches a threshold of average fitness equal to 0.85 in less than 100 iterations. p_c and p_m have been chosen based on the suggested rates available in [10], while the remaining values are an effect of experimentation. Figure 4 shows our running tool with these parameters.

By choosing suitable parameters, we can guarantee the generation of scheme plans for all combinations of C1, C3, and C4. To guarantee property C2 concerning directions, we pass a parameter to the concrete scheme plan generation.

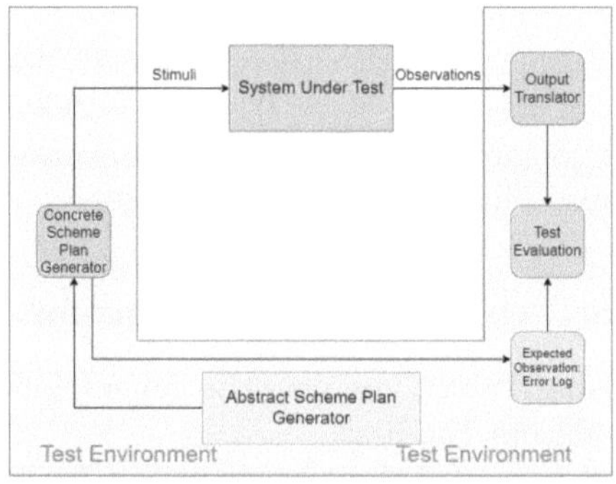

Fig. 5. Automated Test Environment

5   Generating Concrete Scheme Plans

Each abstract scheme plan corresponds to a set of concrete instantiations. This is
the case, as we are adding lengths using random number generation; furthermore,
we are adding directions according to the parameters passed. For instance, the
length of a tile is given by a randomly chosen number between 800 and 1200
metres. The point in the single-double tile is placed at $\frac{1}{4}$ of the tile length. This
data is stored in several text files, the structures of which are defined by Siemens'
proprietary "RailDNA" schemas.

On the conceptual side, the generation of concrete scheme plans is more or
less straightforward. However, it is a challenge to adhere to the specified input
format of the system under test – as usual when it comes to testing. Notably,
about 40% of our code base is related to concrete scheme plan generation.

6   Test Environment

Overall, we have established an automated test environment (see Fig. 5) for, in
our case, Siemens' Data Checker – however, open also to other tools as mentioned
in the Introduction. Using GAs and decision tables, we produce abstract scheme
plans. These are then turned into concrete realisations, encoded in the bespoke
input format of Data Checker, which is our system under test (SUT). Running
Data Checker results in an error report. This actual result can then be compared
with the expected result produced by the Concrete Scheme Plan Generator in
the form of an error log.

For test evaluation, we say that a test is passed iff the SUT's reported errors
are an exact match with the generated log file. This means that the SUT should
report all errors as mentioned in the error log, and no errors beyond those mentioned in the error log. With our test environment, we could demonstrate that
Siemens' data checker conforms to its specification w.r.t. several design rules,
BG-03 as an example of a local one, as well as others spanning over several tiles.
Therefore, our testing environment can be reused for other design rules from the
aforementioned collection of 300+ rules (see: Sect. 2.1).

7   Related Work

Many application domains resolve to the use of synthetic test data. An example of this is Behjati et al. [11]. They were motivated by privacy concerns and
safety reasons. Technically, they deal with test data (static and dynamic) in the
form of table entries. Their SUT is an electronic national registry in Norway.
In contrast, we are dealing with graphs. In the context of GAs, the generation
of (finite) graphs is a long-investigated problem with standard solutions [9,12].
Our tile graph encoding transforms the generation problem into a combinatorial
optimisation process [13]. Although the rail industry is in need of automatically
generated artificial scheme plans, to the best of our knowledge, we are the first
to address this challenge.

8   Performance

At the heart of our approach is an combinatorial optimisation process realised as a Genetic Algorithm (GA). Our approach scales, as the following run-time data for the decision table for BG-03, see Table 1, demonstrates:

Scheme Plan Length	10	25	100	200	300	400
Runtime Abstract (in s)	0.10	0.80	2.60	8.60	34.40	115.10
Runtime Concrete (in s)	0.02	0.05	0.23	0.50	0.84	1.04

Runtimes are measured in isolation, i.e., either only for abstract scheme plan generation or only for concrete scheme plan generation. The overall runtime is dominated by the GA algorithm producing an abstract scheme plan. The time for concretising such an abstract scheme plan is negligible.

9   Conclusion

As a step toward tool certification and qualification in the rail industry [14], we have presented and implemented a new, automated testing approach. Our software considers railway tools as systems under test. These railway tools shall decide if scheme plans adhere to given design rules. Our approach establishes the correctness of such tools.

The test objective is to verify that the considered checking tool treats all design rules in a correct manner. To this end, we provide one test suite per design rule, that is, for each design rule we analyse - with the help of a decision table - which scheme plan 'types' to use as a challenge for the checker. We used our tool to produce 100+ scheme plans that we manually checked to verify that Siemens' Data Checker is working correctly. In all cases, the scheme plans were as expected, i.e., our tool produced synthetic test data as required by the decision table. All tests performed were passed, i.e., Siemens' data checker correctly classified the scheme plans to be either correct or incorrect.

While the testing process itself is fully automated, characterising suitable inputs relies on human ingenuity: the quality of our testing approach is as good as the analysis of the design rules, which results in decision tables.

Future Work. An alternative use of our tool would be to utilise it for random testing [15]. Furthermore, one could argue that design rules should rather be tested in combination, i.e., decision tables for single rules should be somehow 'merged'. Finally, scheme plans 'in the wild' take the shape of long stretches of linear implementations, combined at junctions and stations.

We can rightfully claim that this paper solves the case of linear scheme plans, leaving the case of junctions and stations for future work. Experiments are underway to demonstrate that our tiling approach can be extended to 'two-dimensional' scheme plans. To create scheme plans of varying lengths, we will explore replacing the current GA with other methods like Genetic Programming.

References

1. Banerjee, M., Cai, V., Lakhsmanappa, S., et al.: A tool-chain for the verification of geographic scheme data. In: RSSRail 2023, LNCS, Vol. 14198 (2023)
2. Abo, R., Voisin, L.: Formal implementation of data validation for railway safety-related systems with OVADO. In: Counsell, S., Núñez, M. (eds.) SEFM 2013. LNCS, vol. 8368, pp. 221–236. Springer, Cham (2014). https://doi.org/10.1007/978-3-319-05032-4_17
3. Luteberget, B.: Automated Reasoning for Planning Railway Infrastructure. PhD thesis (2019)
4. Cai, V.: Show Me How It's Wrong: Counterexample Visualisation in Static Railway Verification. MA thesis. Swansea University (2023)
5. LogicGem. Decision Tables - LogicGem. https://logicgem.com/decision-tables/. Accessed 6 June 2025
6. Vanthienen, J.: The history of modeling decisions using tables (Part 1). Bus. Rules J. **13**(2) (2012). https://www.brcommunity.com/articles.php?id=b637. Accessed 6 June 2025
7. Feng, X., Parnas, D.L., Tse, T.H., et al.: A comparison of tabular expression-based testing strategies. IEEE Trans. Softw. Eng. **37**(5) (2011). https://doi.org/10.1109/TSE.2011.78
8. Harrison, T.: Exploring the feasibility of using genetic algorithms for generating railway map test data. Bachelor's Thesis. Swansea University (2024)
9. Goldberg, D.E.: Genetic Algorithms in Search, Optimization and Machine Learning. 1st. USA: Addison-Wesley Longman Publishing Co., Inc. (1989). ISBN: 0201157675
10. Eiben, A.E., Smith, J.E.: Evolutionary robotics. In: Introduction to Evolutionary Computing. NCS, pp. 245–258. Springer, Heidelberg (2015). https://doi.org/10.1007/978-3-662-44874-8_17
11. Behjati, R., Arisholm, E., Bedregal, M., et al.: Synthetic test data generation using recurrent neural networks: a position paper. In: 2019 IEEE/ACM 7th International Workshop on Realizing Artificial Intelligence Synergies in Software Engineering (RAISE), pp. 22–27 (2019). https://doi.org/10.1109/RAISE.2019.00012
12. Yang,Q., Zeng, Q.: Application of genetic algorithms in graph theory and optimization. In: 2016 3rd International Conference on Materials Engineering, Manufacturing Technology and Control, pp. 24–29. Atlantis Press (2016)
13. Alhijawi, B., Awajan, A.: Genetic algorithms: theory, genetic operators, solutions, and applications. Evol. Intell. **17**(3), 1245–1256 (2024)
14. Boulanger, J.L.: Tool qualification. In: ENELEC 50128 and IEC 62279 Standards, pp. 287–308 (2015)
15. Duran, J.W., Ntafos, S.C.: An evaluation of random testing. IEEE Trans. Soft. Eng. **4**, 438–444 (2009)

Surveys and Comparisons

Bridging Formal Verification and Domain Validation in Railway Systems

Asfand Yar[1], Akram Idani[1](✉) (ID), Yves Ledru[1], and Simon Collart-Dutilleul[2]

[1] Univ. Grenoble Alpes, CNRS, LIG, Grenoble INP, 38000 Grenoble, France
`asfand.yar@grenoble-inp.org`, {`akram.idani,yves.ledru`}`@imag.fr`
[2] Univ. Lille Nord de France, IFSTTAR, 59666 Villeneuve d'Ascq Cedex, France
`simon.collart-dutilleul@ifsttar.fr`

Abstract. Formal methods and domain-specific languages (DSLs) are now integral to the development and assurance of railway signalling systems in compliance with CENELEC EN 50128 and EN 50129. This article presents a survey and a comparison of research works and industrial initiatives that intertwine graphical DSLs with formal verification techniques. The comparison covers modelling syntax, operational semantics, adherence to industrial standards such as RailML, EULYNX and ERTMS/ETCS, and the extent to which each solution supports verification and validation. Special attention is devoted to initiatives that rely on the B Method and its associated toolchain, notably ProB, because these initiatives demonstrate how mathematically proven artefacts can be presented to, and interactively animated by, signalling engineers through user-friendly diagrams. The study highlights the added value of visual front-ends for bridging the communication gap between domain experts and formal-methods specialists while preserving traceability from informal requirements to verified systems.

Keywords: Railway Systems · Domain-Specific Languages · Formal Methods · Validation · Verification

1 Introduction

The CENELEC EN 50128[1] and EN 50129[2] norms define stringent processes for developing and certifying safety-critical railway software and its accompanying safety case. Whereas EN 50128 explicitly recommends the systematic application of formal methods, EN 50129 insists on clear, preferably graphical, system descriptions complemented by structured or formal specifications. In our works we advocate a workflow that combines both recommendations: railway systems requirements are captured with domain-specific notations tailored to railway practitioners, and the meaning of each construct is formalized in a formal approach such as the B Method [7]. In this way, the expressive power of formal techniques co-exists with intuitive domain-specific notations.

---

[1] https://standards.globalspec.com/std/2023439/afnor-nf-en-50128.
[2] https://standards.globalspec.com/std/10280790/dsf-fpren-50129.

M. H. ter Beek et al. (Eds.): RSSRail 2025, LNCS 16236, pp. 91–107, 2026.
https://doi.org/10.1007/978-3-032-10762-6_9

Over the last decade, researchers and industrial actors have contributed to a rich palette of frameworks, notably DESIGN4RAIL [3], SAFECAP [19,20] and ONTRACK [26]. These frameworks can be divided into two broad families. The first family comprises solutions that start from infrastructure computer-aided design (CAD) and inject formal models in a second stage through automated transformations; RAILCOMPLETE [5] is the archetypal representative of this line of work. The second family focuses on explicitly crafted Domain-Specific Languages (DSLs); a notable representative of this category is ONTRACK [26]. This article reviews these initiatives and positions them according to their modelling capabilities, verification depth and relation to railway standards such as RailML/EULYNX [4] and ERTMS/ETCS.

A number of clear trends emerge from this landscape. Graphical editors built on the Eclipse ecosystem currently dominate, because they shorten the distance between domain modellers and verification specialists. Tool chains that hinge on the B Method and complement it with model checking in ProB are also popular: they offer a balance between rigorous semantics, scalable proof support and human-readable models. Nevertheless, comprehensive coverage of the most recent European standards, and in particular the EULYNX reference architecture [4], remains limited. A handful of solutions provide an end-to-end path from domain-specific design to standards conformance. Our survey follows four explicit research questions; covering syntax, semantics, standards conformance and V&V capabilities. We selected nine approaches that (1) address railway signalling, (2) integrate a formal verification backend and (3) provide enough published material for analysis.

The remainder of the article is organized as follows. Section 2 contextualises and synthesizes related work. Section 3 details the modelling dimension. It separates static from dynamic semantics and analyses how each solution addresses execution. Section 4 examines verification and validation practices. Section 5 concludes with future directions.

2   Survey of Domain Modelling and Formal Approaches

In the industrial context of railway signalling, the CENELEC standards [1]—in particular EN 50128 and EN 50129—constitute the normative cornerstone for the development and certification of safety-related applications. EN 50128 explicitly encourages the systematic deployment of formal methods (FMs) when developing software for safety-critical railway equipment, whereas EN 50129 emphasises the importance of a graphical description of the system, a structured specification process, and the production of formal or semi-formal artefacts. A good framework would combine both recommendations: railway models are captured with a dedicated graphical domain-specific language (DSL), while a formal method formalises their semantics. By coupling a domain-oriented notation with a rigorous mathematical foundation, the framework simultaneously addresses the prescriptions of EN 50128 and EN 50129.

Over the past decade, numerous contributions have sought to reconcile industrial practice with advances in model-based engineering and formal verification.

Notable examples include the work of Luteberget et al. [28], Bosschaart et al. [9], James et al. [24,25], Svendsen et al. [35], and Vu et al. [37,39]; in parallel, tools such as Design4Rail [3], SafeCap [6,19,20], and OnTrack [26] have emerged to support activities ranging from graphical layout design to automated interlocking code generation.

To evaluate how these proposals advance the state of the art, the present survey considers four complementary questions. First, does an approach introduce a DSL endowed with a formally defined syntax and semantics? Second, is a graphical concrete syntax offered, so that signalling engineers—who are typically not familiar with the textual formalisms commonly used in model engineering—can actively participate in model construction? Third, to what extent do the resulting artefacts conform to exchange and operational standards such as RailML[3] (a de facto standard), its successor EULYNX, and the European Rail Traffic Management System / European Train Control System (ERTMS/ETCS)? Finally, does an approach provide explicit facilities for verification and validation (V&V), and are those facilities partially or fully automated?

Table 1 summarizes the comparison by mapping each approach onto four analytical dimensions. The first dimension, *semantics*, distinguishes frameworks that address only static infrastructure properties from those that also model dynamic train movement. The second dimension, *syntax*, records whether a graphical or purely textual notation is available. Standard conformance forms the third dimension, split between RailML/EULYNX and ERTMS/ETCS because each caters to a different layer of the railway technology stack. The final dimension, V&V, indicates whether safety properties can be analysed automatically; the symbol "P" denotes that only partial coverage or manual assistance is provided. These four analytical dimensions directly correspond to the four research questions introduced in Section 1.

2.1 Overview of Selected Approaches

We included nine state-of-the-art approaches in this comparison, which are briefed and listed below.

Luteberget et al., [28] provide methods for extracting formal railway models directly from Computer-Aided Design (CAD) drawings. Their industrial tool, RAILCOMPLETE [5], integrates seamlessly with mainstream CAD software and adopts RailML as its underlying representation format for railway infrastructure designs. Logic programming rules are employed within RAILCOMPLETE to formalize route definitions and interlocking constraints, thus facilitating automated consistency checks on large-scale networks with minimal manual intervention.

---

[3] While RailML is not formally recognized as an international standard by all major infrastructure managers, it remains the most widely used model in practice, making it a de facto standard in the railway industry.

Table 1. Comparison of State-of-the-Art Approaches

Approaches	Semantics		Syntax		Standards		V & V
	Static	Dynamic	Graphical	Textual	RailML/EULYNX	ERTMS/ETCS	
Luteberget *et al.* [27,28] RailCOMPLETE [5]	✓		✓	✓	✓		P
Chiappini *et al.* [11]	✓	✓	UML-based	✓		✓	P
Design4Rail [3]	✓		✓		✓	P	P
SafeCap [6,19,20]	✓	✓	✓				✓
James *et al.* [25] OnTrack [26]	✓		✓				P
James *et al.* [24]	✓	✓	✓	✓		P	✓
Vu *et al.* [37,39]	✓	✓		✓		P	✓
Svendsen *et al.* [35]	✓	✓	✓				✓
Idani *et al.* [16,17]	✓	✓	✓			P	✓

Yes = ✓; Partially covered = P

Chiappini et al. [11] present a structured methodology targeting the European Train Control System (ETCS). Starting from informal, natural-language descriptions of level-2 requirements, they progressively move toward a UML-based semi-formal notation, ultimately formalizing a substantial subset of the ETCS specifications. Their validation experiments were positively assessed by domain experts, confirming the practical value of this formalization approach.

Railway Infrastructure and Layout Aided Designer [3] (DESIGN4RAIL) provides railway signalling engineers with an interactive graphical editor to model track topologies intuitively. The tool maintains a synchronized tabular view of the designed infrastructure, enabling users to seamlessly alternate between graphical and tabular representations. It supports import and export operations through RailML. Additionally, DESIGN4RAIL evaluates consistency rules in real-time, automating preliminary verification tasks by ensuring structural coherence (e.g., track layout, signal placement, and detector positioning) throughout the modelling process.

SafeCap [6,19,20] is an Eclipse-based toolset integrating modelling, simulation, and formal verification for railway networks. It provides a graphical editor allowing users to intuitively construct and modify network models. These models can be rapidly prototyped and tested using the built-in discrete-event simulator under realistic operational scenarios. Additionally, SAFECAP incorporates an integrated model checker capable of verifying essential safety properties, such as the absence of conflicting routes. The synergy between lightweight simulations and rigorous formal analysis makes SAFECAP particularly appealing for practical industrial applications.

James et al. [25] propose a methodology for embedding formal methods within domain-specific languages (DSLs). Their tool, ONTRACK [26], offers a graphical editor where users design railway schemes by arranging route components on a canvas. These diagrams are then automatically translated into formal models suitable for verification. In follow-up work, the authors leveraged Real-Time Maude [30] to specify and verify temporal properties of ERTMS/ETCS Level-2, demonstrating that ONTRACK diagrams can support advanced formal analyses, including real-time safety verification.

Vu et al. [37,39] present two complementary DSLs for railway interlocking: the Interlocking Dynamic Language (IDL) for specifying behavioural aspects and the Interlocking Configuration Language (ICL) for defining structural configuration data. Their toolchain translates high-level designs into executable models, automatically generating proof obligations for safety properties. As part of the RobustRailS framework [38], the IDL/ICL combo enables a two-step verification process: static checking of well-formed configuration data, followed by instantiation of generic behavioural models with ICL data and automated verification via SMT-based model checking. This approach ensures a tight, formal correspondence between abstract domain models and their concrete implementations in realistic railway settings

Svendsen et al. [35] focus on automatically synthesizing train-station models using the Train Control Language (TCL), a domain-specific modeling language for specifying station layouts and signaling configurations. Their approach begins with concise TCL descriptions, which are processed to generate configuration code for signalling equipment. The methodology includes formal verification: the generated models are proven to preserve critical safety invariants, ensuring that station behavior conforms to safety requirements. Experimental evaluations demonstrate that this pipeline (from TCL input through code generation and verification) reliably produces safe, implementable station control models.

Idani et al. [16,17] propose a tool-supported framework that merges Model-Driven Engineering (MDE) with the B Method to support incremental railway system design. Using an Eclipse-based plug-in, engineers select components (points, signals, and routes) via a graphical palette. The tool then captures operational semantics in B, automatically generating proof obligations at each design iteration. AtelierB theorem prover is used to ensure that all safety requirements are maintained throughout the incremental development process

2.2 Discussion

Table 1 reveals a steady convergence between intuitive, domain-oriented modelling tools and the rigorous assurance provided by formal verification. Most contemporary frameworks already support the analysis of static infrastructure, and an increasing number extend their capabilities to dynamic behaviour. Verification and validation features span a wide spectrum, from basic consistency checks to fully automated theorem proving and model checking pipelines.

A recurring architectural pattern emerges: graphical or semi-formal input via domain-specific languages (DSLs), translation into formal models, and integration with verification back-ends. While this pattern enhances accessibility for signalling engineers and supports incremental validation, several limitations persist. Notably, standards such as RailML, EULYNX, and ERTMS/ETCS are only partially supported, and industrial integration into certification workflows remains uneven.

The *Standards* column in Table 1 is further divided into two sub-categories: *RailML/EULYNX* for structural modelling, and *ERTMS/ETCS* for operational semantics. This separation reflects their complementary roles in railway system development: RailML (based on the RailTopoModel (RTM)) and EULYNX (structured around the Rail System Model (RSM)) are both used to represent infrastructure data. RailML is widely adopted and has matured toward ISO/TS 4398 standardisation [28,32]. Conversely, EULYNX is gaining traction through formal interface definitions and has been applied in research prototypes such as FormaSig [10,40].

Only Luteberget et al. [28] and Design4Rail [3] explicitly support RailML. Design4Rail enables both import and export of RailML files to facilitate interoperability with external tools. EULYNX, despite its growing relevance in European projects, is not adopted by any of the surveyed tools. While partial support for railway modelling standards may seem limiting, it is also understandable: standards such as RailML/EULYNX primarily target *infrastructure data exchange* and may omit elements crucial for V&V workflows (e.g., explicit operational semantics or verification-oriented abstractions). Nevertheless, maintaining *robust import/export interoperability* with these standards should remain a priority, as it enables toolchain integration, data reuse, and smoother industrial adoption.

Support for ERTMS/ETCS specifications among the surveyed approaches is generally limited in scope. While several frameworks reference concepts from the standard, their coverage varies widely. Only a few address ERTMS/ETCS beyond superficial alignment, and typically focus on specific layers; such as trackside data (e.g., route and signal definitions) or control logic. Notably, only one approach [11] offers a substantial formalisation of the normative core of Level 2 specifications. Others selectively incorporate aspects of Level 2 or Level 3, such as interlocking semantics, RBC handovers, or decentralized block management, often for illustrative purposes rather than comprehensive modelling. The relatively low coverage of ERTMS/ETCS in current tools also reflects market reality: many European networks still operate national signalling systems, which reduces the immediate demand for comprehensive ETCS-oriented modelling and V&V toolchains. We therefore distinguish between *standards conformance as data exchange* (RailML/EULYNX) and *operational semantics coverage* (ERTMS/ETCS), and we call for incremental alignment on both axes.

3   System Modeling

In this work, *modeling* denotes the systematic design of railway systems using notations that align with practitioners' domain understanding. We classify modeling approaches across two dimensions: first, by *syntax* (graphic or diagrammatic versus textual) and second, by *paradigm* (UML-based methods common in industrial workflows versus DSL-based approaches tailored to railway semantics). As highlighted in Table 1, seven out of nine surveyed tools apply graphical syntax, reflecting a strong preference for visual representations that support layout design and animations.

3.1 UML-Based Modeling

UML (Unified Modeling Language), standardized by the Object Management Group (OMG) [29], enjoys considerable adoption by railway industry leaders such as ALSTOM and consulting firms. It is commonly employed to capture high-level requirements, scenario flows, and system structure through activity, sequence, and class diagrams. A notable example is the work of Chiappini *et al.* [11], who formalise a subset of the European Train Control System (ETCS) by first constructing UML diagrams to describe static entities, such as tracks and signals, and dynamic elements like train movement and interlocking behavior. These UML diagrams are then annotated using a Controlled Natural Language (CNL), combining concise English-like statements with mathematical constraints, before translation into a NuSMV model for formal verification. Figure 1 illustrates their use of a UML class diagram to define ETCS-related entities and constraints. Although this workflow bridges domain understanding and formal analysis, it presents several challenges. First, UML's inherent ambiguity makes it difficult to maintain precise semantics. Second, mastering UML requires significant expertise, creating a steep learning curve. Finally, the approach often fails to scale when modeling detailed interlocking systems or Level 2 traffic management logic.

3.2 DSL-Based Modeling

To overcome the limitations of semi-formal UML models, Domain-Specific Languages (DSLs) centred on railway concepts have been proposed. These DSLs typically employ graphical editors built atop Eclipse-based frameworks like GMF (Graphical Modeling Framework) or EMF (Eclipse Modeling Framework), offering notation that aligns closely with railway engineering practices. For instance, OnTrack, adopting Bjørner's DSL metamodel [8], and SafeCap are implemented with GMF. SafeCap's focus on Solid State Interlocking (SSI) programs includes embedded mechanised safety validation and has already processed over many industrial projects [21,22]. Another DSL, the Train Control Language (TCL) [13], also leverages GMF to allow the authoring of ETCS scenario models using railway-centric primitives.

Beyond GMF, we have proposed an EMF and Sirius-based approach in [16, 17] that supports multiple synchronized views and conditional styling based on OCL-like syntax, improving readability and supporting formal analysis.

Further DSL tools include RailCOMPLETE and Design4Rail. The latter, implemented with Java and JavaScript, provides a visual modeling environment for track layouts and signaling systems, illustrated in Fig. 2. These environments allow railway engineers to construct models visually, then extend them with

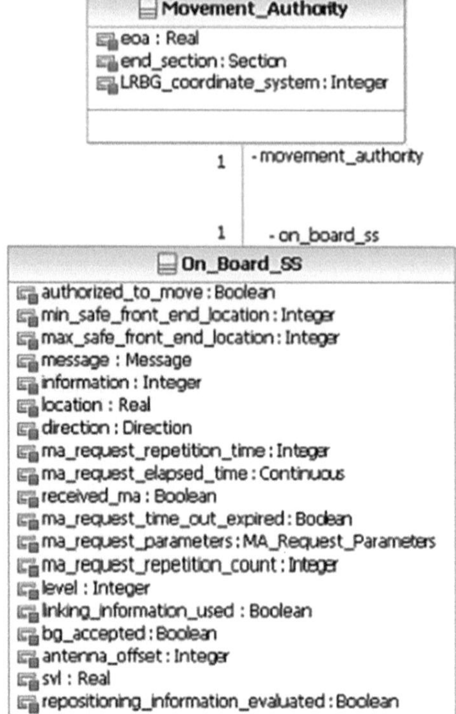

Fig. 1. UML class diagram from Chiappini *et al.* [11]

textual constraint definition using DSLs such as RailCNL [27] or Vu and Haxthausen's IDL and ICL languages [39], which support specifying interlocking configurations and behavioural rules.

Our review shows that graphical DSLs are pervasive in railway modeling, providing intuitive mapping from railway concepts to models and supporting visual animation. The dominance of the Eclipse modeling ecosystem (GMF/EMF/Sirius) across DSL tools ensures reuse of robust metamodeling infrastructures, configuration layers, and editor generation. In terms of formal analysis, DSLs like SafeCap offer direct integration with theorem proving and model checking, while UML-based workflows often rely on translation pipelines with a steep integration effort. Furthermore, DSLs frequently feature textual constraint overlays for specifying invariants and configuration properties, benefitting expressivity while requiring careful design to maintain accessibility.

Building upon the strengths of mature DSL techniques, our previous works [16,17] employ Sirius-based graphical model editors aligned with railway domain needs. Complemented by textual constraint support via OCL-like expressions, it provides a flexible yet formally grounded design workflow. The EMF-based metamodel allows automated transformation into verification artifacts compatible with model-checkers and other analysis tools. In doing so, we aim to balance

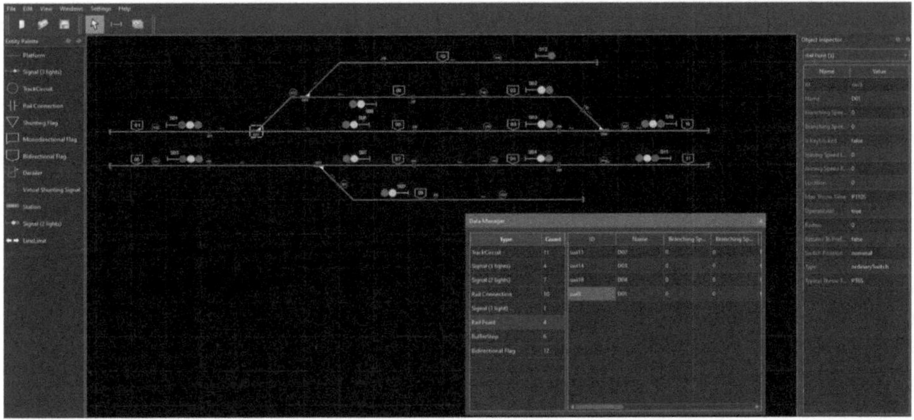

Fig. 2. Design4Rail graphical editor displaying the component palette, canvas, property sheet, and element data panel

usability (through graphical notation familiar to engineers) with rigorous semantics of DSL-based safety assurance.

3.3 Structure Vs Behavior

In system modeling, *structure* corresponds to the static semantics, defining the components of the railway system; while *behavior* corresponds to the dynamic semantics, describing how these components operate or evolve over time.

Structure. Every examined approach provides a clear structural model of the railway domain, though the representation formalism varies. Chiappini *et al.* [11] employ UML class diagrams, defining classes such as `Train`, `TrackSegment`, and `Signal`, which capture both onboard and trackside components. Similarly, Vu *et al.* [37,39] model railway topologies (tracks, signals, switches, marker boards, level crossings) using the RAISE Specification Language (RSL), grounding their interlocking DSL in formal specification semantics. The RailCOMPLETE framework uses elements from the RailML standard [32] (tracks, switches, signals) as foundational structural constructs, and Design4Rail similarly aligns with RailML. James *et al.* [24] propose a model of a station using Maude, defining switch and marker-board relationships. The OnTrack environment, extended by James *et al.* [25], relies on Bjørner's railway DSL to represent stations, lines, tracks, and routes. Svendsen *et al.* [35]'s Train Control Language (TCL) similarly supports these constructs using a GMF-based meta-model. The industrial tool SafeCap [21,22], originally targeting Solid State Interlocking (SSI) program safety checks, defines key entities such as track, line, section, switch (point), and train detection. These structural elements are further translated into B specifications. In Idani *et al.* [16,17], the EMF/Sirius-based DSL introduces static entities like train, track, axle-counter, and, in the extended version, ERTMS Level 3 concepts (trackside blocks, Movement Authority).

Behavior. Behavioral semantics address how structural components interact and evolve. Chiappini *et al.* [11] enrich their static UML models with state machines and sequence diagrams, capturing dynamic interactions such as message exchanges between train and trackside systems. James *et al.* [24] demonstrate executable behavior by animating their Maude models; commands in Real-Time Maude allow trains to progress along defined movement authorities within a station topology. The behavior in Vu *et* al. [37,39] does not provide train operations but includes an Interlocking Table Generator (ITG) which generates interlocking tables from the elements in the network layout. Svendsen *et al.* [35] incorporate an operational semantics in TCL to synthesize station topologies that reject unsafe train movements into or out of a station. SafeCap [6] introduces behavior by exporting B specifications from its graphical models and then executing safety-critical operations within the B model (though control currently remains external). Idani *et al.* [16,17] leverage the Meeduse toolkit to translate DSL structures into B, where train movement operations, respecting Movement Authority and safety, are formally defined and can be simulated within the tool, offering visual feedback on dynamic evolution of the railway system.

3.4   Discussion

All reviewed approaches define a common static vocabulary: tracks, switches, signals. But they vary in formalism: UML, general DSL, RailML, Bjørner's DSL, or RSL. On the behavior side, the implementation diverges: Chiappini's UML uses semi-formal simulations; Vu and Svendsen leverage DSL execution or code generation; James and Idani rely on formal methods through Maude or B, respectively; SafeCap integrates B (and Why3) to automate safety validation of SSI programs.

4   Verification and Validation

This section investigates the availability and use of verification and validation mechanisms in current state-of-the-art approaches. We first address verification, focusing on how safety and other critical properties are formally ensured. Then, we explore how validation is handled in these frameworks.

4.1   Verification

Verification refers to the process of proving or disproving the correctness of a system with respect to a formal specification, using mathematical and logical techniques [14]. In the railway domain, this typically involves verifying properties such as safety, topological soundness, interlocking correctness, and infrastructure capacity. Table 2 summarizes the formal tools and techniques employed by each approach, along with the classes of properties they target. The main properties verified in the surveyed works can be grouped as follows:

Safety. Safety ensures the prevention of collisions and derailments. Collisions may occur either front-to-front (two trains meeting head-on) or rear-to-front (a following train colliding with the one ahead). Derailment can result from improper switch configurations during train movement or excessive speed.

Topology. Verifying the railway topology ensures the static well-formedness of the network. This includes checking, for example, that both branches of a switch do not connect to the same track, or that a track does not form an unintended loop. Figure 3 illustrates typical static well-formedness anomalies (*e.g.*, unintended loops, conflicting switch connections) that a tool should detect.

Interlocking. Verification of interlocking ensures that the generated interlocking tables correctly assign switch positions and signal states (lights) for all possible routes. This is crucial to guarantee safe routing under dynamic train operations.

Table 2. Properties and the used formal techniques

Approaches or Tools	Formal Techniques and Tools	Properties
Luteberget *et al.* [27,28]	Datalog (Logic Programming)	Interlocking Topology
James *et al.* [25], OnTrack [26]	SPASS, eProver (Theorem Proving)	Safety
Vu *et al.* [37,39]	RSL, RT-Tester, LTL (Model-checking)	Safety Interlocking
James *et al.* [24]	Maude, Maude LTL model-checker (Model-checking)	Safety
Svendsen *et al.* [35]	Alloy, Alloy analyzer (Theorem Proving)	Capacity
SafeCap [6,19,20]	B-method, Event-B, SMT-LIB compliant SMT solver, ProB (Constraint solving, Model-checking)	Topology Safety Capacity
Idani *et al.* [16,17]	B-method Atelier B, ProB (Proofs, Model-checking)	Safety

Capacity. Capacity properties verify whether the infrastructure can handle a required number of trains simultaneously, without violating any operational or safety constraint.

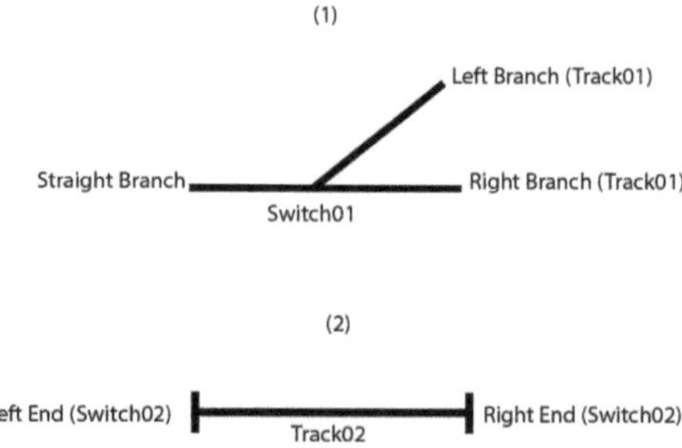

Fig. 3. Examples of static well-formedness errors in topology

Luteberget et al. [28] verify both topological correctness and interlocking using Datalog, a declarative logic programming language [36].

James et al. [25] target safety by verifying that no track is simultaneously assigned to two Movement Authorities (MAs), avoiding overlap. Their specifications are analyzed using the SPASS [41] and eProver [34] theorem provers.

Vu et al. [37,39] define interlocking correctness and safety properties in Linear Temporal Logic (LTL) [15] and verify them using RT-Tester's bounded model checker [31]. A static checker ensures compliance with well-formedness rules.

James et al. [24] use Real-Time Maude and its associated LTL model checker [12] to verify collision-freedom in ERTMS/ETCS-level train control. The key invariant enforced is that two trains must maintain a minimum distance at all times.

Svendsen et al. [35] address capacity by modeling station layouts in Alloy [23] and verifying whether the generated configurations meet required throughput. The Alloy analyzer is used to iterate through configurations until capacity constraints are met.

SafeCap [6,19,20] supports extensive verification of safety, topology, and capacity. Event-B specifications are automatically derived from the DSL schema, and constraint-based checks are discharged via SMT-LIB compliant solvers [33]. If SMT solving fails, the approach falls back to ProB model checking, which can produce diagnostic traces.

Idani et al. [16,17] integrate the B-method to verify that the modeled railway system is free of accidents. Safety properties and invariants are embedded in the translated B specifications. Verification is performed via the Meeduse tool [18], which supports animation and model-checking using ProB. Additionally, Atelier B may be employed for proof obligations to ensure the correctness of the design.

Table 2 reveals that 5 out of 7 approaches explicitly verify safety properties. These are generally framed in terms of train safety (ensuring no two trains occupy the same section simultaneously) or maintaining spatial thresholds between moving entities. While all these approaches follow a similar initial step, which is formalizing the semantics of the DSL, the tools and techniques used differ. For instance, even when the verification technique is the same (e.g., model checking), the formal language (RSL, Maude, Alloy, B) and application strategy vary. The 4SECURail project [2], funded by the European Commission, has emphasized the importance of using formal methods, particularly the B-method, for railway system modeling and verification. It recommends incorporating model checking into model-based development workflows for formal safety assurance. The similarity of this recommendation with the approaches of SafeCap [6] and Idani *et al.* [16,17], which rely on B and ProB for verification, confirms their alignment with recognized industry trends.

Note that the size and complexity of the generated formal models would provide a more operational view on scalability. Relevant indicators may include the number of states and transitions in the explored state space, the number of proof obligations, solver and/or model-checking time, and memory footprint. Although such data are often unavailable or not directly comparable across tools and back-ends, we identify this as a valuable direction for future work.

4.2 Validation

Validation aims to ensure that the developed system correctly implements the intended user requirements. Unlike verification, which primarily concerns the internal correctness from a developer's perspective, validation focuses on assessing the system from the user's viewpoint. Common validation techniques in the railway domain include reviews, simulation, animation, scenario execution, and fault injection.

Several of the surveyed approaches provide support for validation in different ways. The OpenETCS initiative[4] advocates the use of formal modeling combined with model-checking techniques to validate system behavior through fault injection. Following this direction, James *et al.* [24] experimented with injecting erroneous scenarios into railway scheme plans to observe whether the model correctly identifies and reacts to these violations. Their use of simulation further strengthens the validation process by providing a means to trace system behavior over time.

The methodology by Vu *et al.* [37,39] integrates a static checker to validate both the input data and the interlocking specifications, ensuring syntactic and semantic well-formedness before formal verification. In a different vein, Design4Rail [3] provides implicit support for validation by constraining user input: its editor prevents topological errors and inconsistencies during the modeling phase, effectively guiding the user toward correct designs.

SafeCap [6] and Svendsen *et al.* [35] do not explicitly emphasize validation, yet their simulation engines inherently enable scenario testing and behavioral exploration, thus supporting informal validation in practice.

A notable validation-oriented approach is that of Chiappini *et al.* [11], which follows a structured three-phase methodology: informal requirements analysis, formal modeling, and scenario-based validation. Their case study involves the

---

[4] https://openetcs.org/.

formalization of a representative ERTMS/ETCS subset, followed by the validation of concrete scenarios against predefined requirements.

Idani *et al.* [16,17] adopt an EMF-based graphical DSL for railway modeling that allows users to simulate the system through scenario execution. The animation of behavior is realized by executing operations derived from the B specification generated from the DSL model. This enables users to validate concrete configurations by observing operational behavior within the tool.

4.3   Discussion

Overall, most of the reviewed approaches address both verification and validation to some degree. Verification is typically performed through the use of formal methods such as logic programming, model checking, and theorem proving, with tools like ProB, Alloy Analyzer, etc. supporting property enforcement. As detailed in Table 2, safety is the most frequently addressed property, often formalized as invariants or temporal logic formulas.

In terms of validation, 7 out of 9 approaches offer some form of support; most commonly via simulation, static checks, or animation. EMF-based graphical DSLs appear particularly well-suited for this purpose, enabling users to validate models interactively. In Table 1, the V&V column reflects this distinction: a full checkmark ✓ indicates that both verification and validation are supported, while a partial (P) indicates that only one of the two is present.

5   Conclusion

This article provided a comprehensive survey and comparative analysis of contemporary modeling and verification approaches for railway systems. We examined existing tools and methods along four key dimensions: modeling syntax, semantic structuring, adherence to standards, and verification and validation (V&V) capabilities.

Our analysis shows a clear preference for graphical modeling, especially in domain-specific languages (DSLs) developed using EMF and GMF platforms. DSL-based tools such as OnTrack, SafeCap, and those developed by Idani *et al.* offer tailored visual notations and enable modular extension, making them well-suited to the specific needs of railway engineers.

Conformance to industry standards remains partial across the literature. RailML is used in a limited number of tools, while only a few approaches incorporate concepts from the ERTMS/ETCS specification, and often only partially. This highlights an opportunity for improved integration between domain-specific modeling environments and standardized railway infrastructure models such as EULYNX and ETCS.

Formal verification is a central concern in most approaches, with a focus on proving safety properties such as the absence of collisions or signal conflicts. Techniques range from model checking (e.g., ProB, Maude) to SMT solving and theorem proving. Validation, though less systematically addressed, is often enabled through simulation, animation, or fault injection, with DSL-based tools offering a promising path for domain expert involvement. In light of these observations, the article advocates for an integrated modeling approach that combines graphical DSLs grounded in standardized structural models with a formal verification backend. Such a combination fosters usability and correctness, and paves the way for the adoption of formal methods in industrial railway design workflows. Future work will also examine (i) the degree of industrial adoption and links with certification processes, and (ii) scalability aspects such as state-space size and complexity of generated proof obligations. We also plan to include the upcoming *AMS solution by SNCF* (part of RSSRail 2025) in our comparison grid, thereby broadening the coverage of industrial-grade DSLs and toolchains used in European practice.

References

1. Cenelec - railways and hyperloop systems. https://www.cencenelec.eu/areas-of-work/cenelec-sectors/transport-and-packaging-cenelec/railways-and-hyperloop-systems/. Accessed 06 July 2023
2. Deliverable d 2.1 specification of formal development demonstrator. https://projects.shift2rail.org/download.aspx?id=560cdd44-83e7-4f5d-879e-d8dcdf2e2b1b. Accessed 24 July 2023
3. Design4Rail (formerly RaIL-AiD). https://design4rail.com
4. eulynx.eu. https://eulynx.eu/. . Accessed 13 Jan 2023
5. Industrial Railway CAD software. https://www.railcomplete.com/
6. Safecap platform. http://safecap.sourceforge.net/index.shtml. Accessed 15 July 2023
7. Abrial, J.R.: The B-Book: Assigning Programs to Meanings. Cambridge University Press, Cambridge (1996)
8. Bjørner, D.: Dynamics of railway nets: on an interface between automatic control and software engineering. In: CTS2003: 10th IFAC Symposium on Control in Transportation Systems, August, Seikei University. Elsevier, United Kingdom (2003)
9. Bosschaart, M., Quaglietta, E., Janssen, B., Goverde, R.M.: Efficient formalization of railway interlocking data in railml. Inf. Syst. **49**, 126–141 (2015)
10. Bouwman, M., van der Wal, D., Luttik, B., Stoelinga, M., Rensink, A.: A case in point: verification and testing of a eulynx interface. Formal Aspects Comput. **35**(1), 2:1–2:38 (2023)
11. Chiappini, A., et al.: Formalization and validation of a subset of the European train control system. In: 2010 ACM/IEEE 32nd International Conference on Software Engineering, vol. 2, pp. 109–118 (2010). https://doi.org/10.1145/1810295.1810312
12. Eker, S., Meseguer, J., Sridharanarayanan, A.: The maude ltl model checker. Electron. Notes Theor. Comput. Sci. **71**, 162–187 (2002)
13. Endresen, J., et al.: Train control language - teaching computers interlocking. WIT Trans. Built Environ. **103**, 651–660 (2008)
14. Graham, B.T.: Formal Methods and Verification. Springer, Boston (1992). https://doi.org/10.1007/978-1-4615-3576-8_1
15. Huth, M., Ryan, M.: Logic in Computer Science: Modelling and Reasoning about Systems. Cambridge University Press, Cambridge (2004)

16. Idani, A., Ledru, Y., Ait Wakrime, A., Ben Ayed, R., Bon, P.: Towards a tool-based domain specific approach for railway systems modeling and validation. In: Collart-Dutilleul, S., Lecomte, T., Romanovsky, A. (eds.) RSSRail 2019. LNCS, vol. 11495, pp. 23–40. Springer, Cham (2019). https://doi.org/10.1007/978-3-030-18744-6_2
17. Idani, A., Ledru, Y., Ait Wakrime, A., Ben Ayed, R., Collart-Dutilleul, S.: Incremental development of a safety critical system combining formal methods and DSMLs. In: Larsen, K.G., Willemse, T. (eds.) FMICS 2019. LNCS, vol. 11687, pp. 93–109. Springer, Cham (2019). https://doi.org/10.1007/978-3-030-27008-7_6
18. Idani, A., Ledru, Y., Vega, G.: Alliance of model-driven engineering with a proof-based formal approach. Innov. Syst. Softw. Eng. 289–307 (2020). https://doi.org/10.1007/s11334-020-00366-3
19. Iliasov, A., Lopatkin, I., Romanovsky, A.: The SafeCap platform for modelling railway safety and capacity. In: Bitsch, F., Guiochet, J., Kaâniche, M. (eds.) SAFECOMP 2013. LNCS, vol. 8153, pp. 130–137. Springer, Heidelberg (2013). https://doi.org/10.1007/978-3-642-40793-2_12
20. Iliasov, A., Romanovsky, A.: The safecap toolset for improving railway capacity while ensuring its safety (2012)
21. Iliasov, A., Taylor, D., Laibinis, L., Romanovsky, A.: Industrial-strength verification of solid state interlocking programs. arXiv preprint arXiv:2108.10091 (2021)
22. Iliasov, A., Taylor, D., Laibinis, L., Romanovsky, A.: Practical verification of railway signalling programs. IEEE Trans. Depend. Secure Comput. **20**(1), 695–707 (2023). https://doi.org/10.1109/TDSC.2022.3141555
23. Jackson, D.: Software Abstractions: Logic, Language, and Analysis. The MIT Press, Cambridge (2012)
24. James, P., Lawrence, A., Roggenbach, M., Seisenberger, M.: Towards safety analysis of ERTMS/ETCS level 2 in real-time maude. In: Artho, C., Ölveczky, P.C. (eds.) FTSCS 2015. CCIS, vol. 596, pp. 103–120. Springer, Cham (2016). https://doi.org/10.1007/978-3-319-29510-7_6
25. James, P., Roggenbach, M.: Encapsulating formal methods within domain specific languages: a solution for verifying railway scheme plans. Math. Comput. Sci. **8**, 11–38 (2014)
26. James, P., Trumble, M., Treharne, H., Roggenbach, M., Schneider, S.: OnTrack: an open tooling environment for railway verification. In: Brat, G., Rungta, N., Venet, A. (eds.) NFM 2013. LNCS, vol. 7871, pp. 435–440. Springer, Heidelberg (2013). https://doi.org/10.1007/978-3-642-38088-4_30
27. Luteberget, B., Camilleri, J.J., Johansen, C., Schneider, G.: Participatory verification of railway infrastructure by representing regulations in RailCNL. In: Cimatti, A., Sirjani, M. (eds.) SEFM 2017. LNCS, vol. 10469, pp. 87–103. Springer, Cham (2017). https://doi.org/10.1007/978-3-319-66197-1_6
28. Luteberget, B., Johansen, C.: Efficient verification of railway infrastructure designs against standard regulations. Formal Methods Syst. Des. **52**(1), 1–32 (2017). https://doi.org/10.1007/s10703-017-0281-z
29. Object Managment Group: Unified Modeling Language (UML) (v251) (2017)
30. Ölveczky, P.C., Meseguer, J.: The real-time maude tool. In: Ramakrishnan, C.R., Rehof, J. (eds.) TACAS 2008. LNCS, vol. 4963, pp. 332–336. Springer, Heidelberg (2008). https://doi.org/10.1007/978-3-540-78800-3_23
31. Peleska, J.: Industrial-strength model-based testing - state of the art and current challenges. In: Petrenko, A.K., Schlingloff, H. (eds.) Proceedings Eighth Workshop on Model-Based Testing, Rome, Italy, 17 March 2013. Electronic Proceedings in

Theoretical Computer Science, vol. 111, pp. 3–28. Open Publishing Association (2013). https://doi.org/10.4204/EPTCS.111.1

32. railML.org: railml 3 – the new generation of railway data exchange. railML.org (2023). https://www.railml.org/en/user/about.html

33. Ranise, S., Tinelli, C.: The smt-lib standard: Version 1, 2 (2005)

34. Schulz, S.: E - a brainiac theorem prover. AI Commun. **15**, 111–126 (2002)

35. Svendsen, A., Haugen, Ø., Møller-Pedersen, B.: Synthesizing software models: generating train station models automatically. In: Ober, I., Ober, I. (eds.) SDL 2011. LNCS, vol. 7083, pp. 38–53. Springer, Heidelberg (2011). https://doi.org/10.1007/978-3-642-25264-8_5

36. Ullman, J.D.: Principles of Database and Knowledge-Base Systems, vol. I. Computer Science Press Inc., Henderson (1988)

37. Vu, L.H., Haxthausen, A.E., Peleska, J.: A domain-specific language for generic interlocking models and their properties. In: Fantechi, A., Lecomte, T., Romanovsky, A. (eds.) Reliability, Safety, and Security of Railway Systems. Modelling, Analysis, Verification, and Certification, pp. 99–115. Springer, Cham (2017). https://doi.org/10.1007/978-3-319-68499-4_7

38. Vu, L.H., Haxthausen, A.E., Peleska, J.: Formal modeling and verification of interlocking systems featuring sequential release. Sci. Comput. Program. **133, Part 2**, 91–115 (2017)

39. Vu, L., Haxthausen, A., Peleska, J.: A domain-specific language for railway interlocking systems. In: Schnieder, E., Tarnai, G. (eds.) Proceedings of the 10th Symposium on Formal Methods for Automation and Safety in Railway and Automotive Systems, FORMS/FORMAT 2014, pp. 200–209. Technische Universität Braunschweig (2014)

40. van der Wal, D., Gerhold, M., Stoelinga, M., Rensink, A.: Conformance in the railway industry: single-input-change testing a eulynx controller. In: Proceedings of FMICS 2023. LNCS, vol. 14291, pp. 115–131. Springer, Heidelberg (2023). https://doi.org/10.1007/s10009-025-00790-5

41. Weidenbach, C., Brahm, U., Hillenbrand, T., Keen, E., Theobald, C., Topić, D.: SPASS Version 2.0. In: Voronkov, A. (ed.) CADE 2002. LNCS (LNAI), vol. 2392, pp. 275–279. Springer, Heidelberg (2002). https://doi.org/10.1007/3-540-45620-1_22

Condition-Based Monitoring in Passenger Trains: Insights from Maintenance Logs and Accident Data

Wiryanto Dharmawan[1]([✉]) [iD], Anton Beuss[1], Raoul Schild[2], Markus Hecht[1], and Beate Bender[1] [iD]

[1] Technische Universität Berlin, Chair of Rail Vehicles, Salzufer 17-19, 10587 Berlin, Germany
`wiryanto.dharmawan@tu-berlin.de`
[2] Schild & Partner GmbH, Schäffergasse 20/52, 1040 Vienna, Austria
`rschild@schild-partner.com`
`https://www.tu.berlin/en/schienenfzg`, `http://www.schild-partner.com`

Abstract. To ensure secure and efficient transportation, railway vehicles require high levels of reliability, availability, maintainability, and safety (RAMS). These attributes are strongly influenced by the effectiveness of maintenance strategies. Due to rapid advancements in digitalization and automation, rolling stock maintenance strategies currently undergo a shift from traditional corrective and preventive methods to condition-based and predictive approaches. However, one of the main challenges in adopting condition-based maintenance (CBM) lies in the significant initial investment required. To reduce maintenance costs and maximize operational value, it is crucial to identify the subsystems, those are most prone to failure, as they can lead to unplanned downtime or safety-critical incidents. This paper analyzes maintenance logs and accident reports of passenger trains to identify recurrent failures and critical subsystems. The most failure-prone subsystems, which account for up to 80% of failures, are presented. Furthermore, the paper presents a comprehensive overview of the state-of-the-art CBM technologies used in railway vehicles, including both OnBoard systems and WaySide monitoring solutions. These findings support the development of more targeted and cost-efficient maintenance practices in the railway sector. This work was carried out within the framework of the research project "Minimum Sensor Equipment of Passenger Coaches, Multiple Units and Locomotives for Effective and Economic Condition Monitoring" on behalf of the German Centre for Rail Traffic Research (DZSF).

Keywords: Railway · Passenger train · Condition based monitoring · Condition based maintenance · preventive maintenance · reliability · availability · maintainability · safety · RAMS

M. H. ter Beek et al. (Eds.): RSSRail 2025, LNCS 16236, pp. 108–128, 2026.
https://doi.org/10.1007/978-3-032-10762-6_10

1   Introduction

The reliability, availability, maintainability, and safety (RAMS) of railway vehicles play an important role in ensuring safe and efficient transportation [7]. These factors are strongly influenced by maintenance strategies [5,36].

Currently, maintenance strategies in the European railway sector undergo a shift from scheduled and corrective maintenance to condition-based and predictive maintenance. These can be seen in some pilot projects such as "E-Check" by the German Railway (DB Long-Distance) [4,8,22,34], "Remote Maintenance and 360° Video Vehicle Inspection" by the Austrian Federal Railways (ÖBB) [29,33], and the research project "ESPEK" [38]. Furthermore, train manufacturers, like Siemens and Alstom, also offer IoT-based asset management systems integrated with condition-based and predictive monitoring systems, such as Railigent [18] and HealthHub [3]. In addition to the train manufacturers, this approach is also provided by component suppliers such as Schunk for the pantograph [37], Wabtec for the HVAC system, and Knorr-Bremse [17] as well as GlovaRail [11] for the sanitary system.

The impact of predictive maintenance is confirmed by the National Company of the French Railways (SNCF). By having more than 1,100 trains equipped with sensors to monitor the components, such as doors, mobile steps, HVAC, toilets, compressors, batteries, lighting, engines, OnBoard passenger information system (PIS), video surveillance systems, and brakes, 50% of the technical problems have been eliminated [39]. In the project "E-Check", it has been found out, that the automation of the inspection including water supply and disposal is twice as fast compared to the manual process, resulting in increasing the maintenance capacity of the workshop by 25% [4]. The project "ESPEK" showed that 60% of the vehicle safety check activities can be carried out automatically using the camera system. 27–52% inspection points are located under the vehicle, which make the manual inspection process difficult. By processing the recorded picture from the camera system and directly linking them with the maintenance activities, a time advantage can be created and used to initiate ordering and maintenance preparation before the vehicle even arrives at the workshop [29,33]. This potential is illustrated in Fig. 1.

Within the scope of the Shift2Rail project, the impact of CBM on the rolling stock's running gear maintenance was confirmed. The results show a consistent reduction in maintenance costs of around 10%. These studies were carried out on rolling stocks from different manufacturers (Siemens, Alstom, Talgo) [41]. This finding is also confirmed by a study by the Boston Consulting Group on a US transit agency and an Asian rail operator [35].

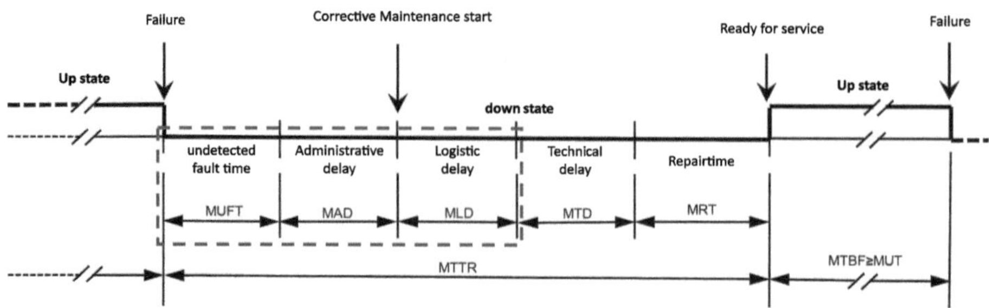

Fig. 1. Optimization potential (red) by linking fault detection and service measure [7]. (Color figure online)

The ZF connect@rail offers a monitoring system for both the bogie and the railway track. By monitoring the acceleration in the drive train, the rolling contact fatigue on the wheelsets can be detected before the inspection limit is reached. Earlier damage detection results in a reduction in the maintenance process by up to 8 days. In addition, the reprofiling of the wheelsets can be done earlier, reducing the cutting depth by about 6 mm on average compared to scheduled maintenance. This reduces the maintenance cost and prolongs the remaining useful life of the wheelset [2, 14].

Despite numerous studies on condition-based monitoring systems and their algorithms in detecting and predicting faults in specific components, an overview of the relevant components and the state-of-art of condition-based monitoring (CBM) in the passenger train is still lacking. This paper investigates the faults and defects in passenger trains, in order to identify the high-priority components that should be monitored using OnBoard (OB) or WaySide (WS) monitoring systems to enable condition-based and predictive maintenance. Furthermore, it provides an overview of the current state of the condition-based monitoring systems of these components. These insights could serve as a foundation for further studies on optimizing the railway vehicle maintenance process and developing the CBM concept in passenger trains.

2   Methodology

In order to identify the high-priority components in passenger trains, that need to be monitored, the method in Fig. 2 is used in this study. First, the data are prepared and classified for each vehicle type including locomotives, passenger coaches, and electric multiple units (EMUs). The data used in this paper consist of maintenance data provided by two German railway undertakings (RU) and the state Baden-Württemberg as well as accident data from the European Railway Accident Information Links (ERAIL) database.

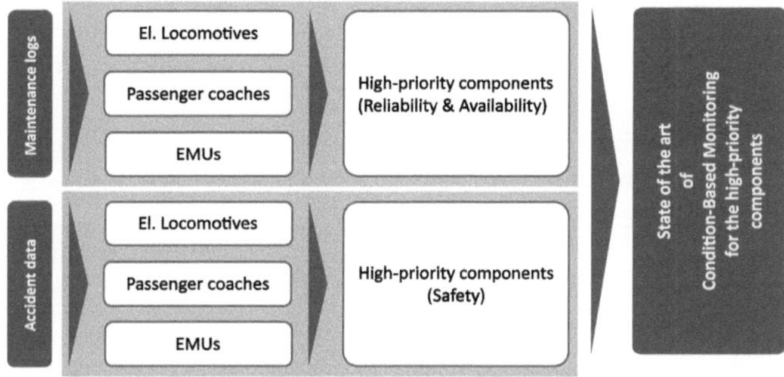

Fig. 2. Methodology for identifying the maintenance and accident data.

From the evaluation of the maintenance data, components that have high relevance to the realibility and availability of the passenger trains can be identified. On the other hand, the accident data provides information about the safety-relevant components. The classification of the faults and defects in each vehicle type is based on the irregularity catalog of the Swiss Federal Office of Transport (BAV). Based on these results, the state of the art for the condition-based monitoring of these components is established.

The summary of the maintenance data is shown in Table 1. The maintenance data includes information on 15 locomotives, 120 passenger coaches, and 320 EMUs. The data of the locomotives have a total of 1,121 entries. There are 1,829 entries for the passenger coaches and 128,783 entries for the EMUs. The data of the 12 locomotives and the 120 passenger coaches from RU-1 were recorded between November 2023 and January 2024, while the data of the other 3 locomotives from RU-2 were recorded between January 2012 and January 2024. The maintenance logs for the EMUs were recorded from January 2018 until January 2024.

Table 1. Summary of the maintenance log data.

	Locomotives	Coaches	EMUs
Number	12 (RU-1) 3 (RU-2)	120 (RU-1)	320 (RU-3)
Entries	1,121	1,829	128,783
Period	Nov 2023–Jan 2024 Jan 2012–Jan 2024	Nov 2023–Jan 2024	Jan 2018–Jan 2024

The procedure for the vehicle components classification based on BAV irregularity catalog is shown in Fig. 3. The classification was carried out in Python. The texts in the maintenance data describing the subsystems and the failure descriptions were evaluated and filtered. The first filter separates some spesific failures on spesific components e.g. "wheel flat", "wheel spalling", "WC clogging", etc. The second filter detects the more common description, e.g. "leakage", "wheelset", "spalling", etc. The filtered data are then classified under the categories "xx" and the subcategories "xx.x". The unclassified data are then put into category "20: others".

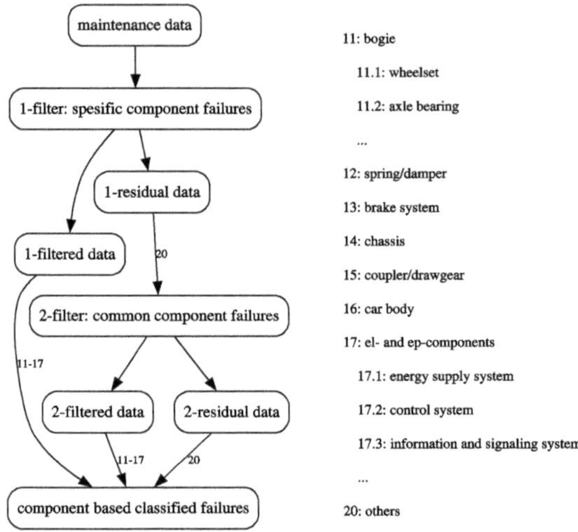

Fig. 3. Evaluation and classification process of the maintenance data.

The accident data from the ERAIL database in the last 10 years from January 2013 until June 2024 are taken into account for the evaluation. In total, there are 3782 entries. About 1000 accidents are related to passenger trains. The evaluation of the accident data relevant to passenger trains shows that only around 10% (98 accidents) are caused by technical problems. This is shown in Fig. 4.

Most accidents are the result of human error. This group includes people who work in the rail road system, such as train dispatchers, train drivers, and track construction workers. External influences include drivers at level crossings, general inattention by third parties, and severe weather events. The infrastructure group includes accidents caused by the condition of the rails, switches, or signaling technology.

The accidents caused by technical problems are filtered for further classification and evaluation. The classification method in Fig. 3 is also used here. The cause of the accident are confirmed by reviewing the accident reports manually.

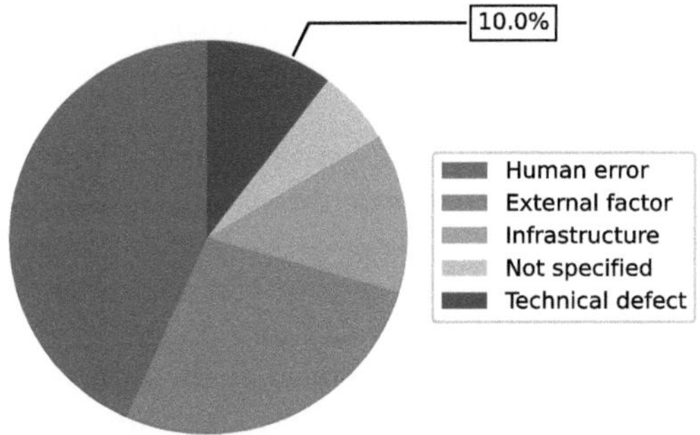

Fig. 4. Cause of passenger train accidents in Europe.

3   Data Evaluation

3.1   Maintenance Logs

The evaluation of the maintenance data revealed the high-priority component related to the reliability and availability in passenger trains. This paper only considers components for which faults and defects account for up to 80% of the total number of entries. Figure 5 presents the cumulative distribution of the most fault-prone subsystem of the locomotives, sorted in descending order. A total of 10 subsystems are responsible for 80% of the total errors. The most fault-prone subsystem in locomotives is the information and signaling system. This consists mostly of the faults in the driver machine interface (DMI), the microphone, and the head/ditch lights. The faults under the control system can be found in components such as the traction control unit and the train protection system (PZB/LZB). The energy supply system also exhibits a high numbers of errors, primarily related to components such as pantographs, transformers, and power converters. Failures in the pantograph are often linked to excessive arcing and contact strip failure. The transformers and power converters often have problems with the cooling system, such as leakage and overheating. These

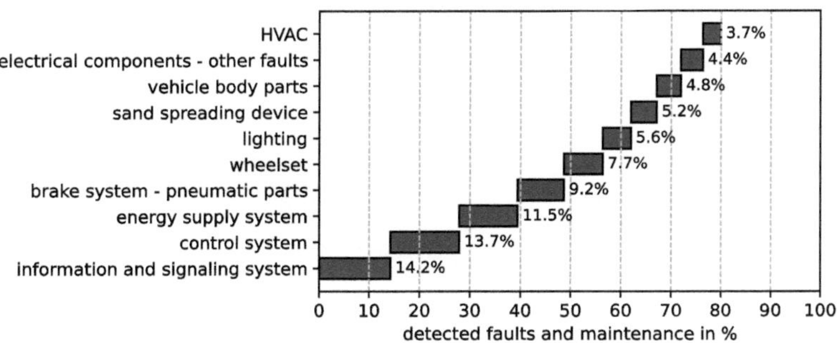

Fig. 5. The most common faults and defects in locomotives.

issues are common to be found in the locomotives considering the frequent use of these systems in operating the train and continuous communication with the passengers.

Figure 6 shows the most fault-prone subsystems in passenger coaches. Compared to locomotives, subsystems with direct interaction with the passengers are of more relevance in this case. Most faults with entrance doors occur in the door itself (door locking mechanism) and in the emergency release mechanism. Considering the number of doors in a train and its frequent operation, door systems are to be expected to be one of the most fault-prone subsystems. Inside the vehicle, defects are mainly found in seats and armrests, fire extinguishers (missing), and first aid kits (missing). In terms of sanitary system, the toilet area is where the most frequent problems occur, mainly due to clogging. In the category vehicle body parts, issues like graffiti and window defects are the predominant.

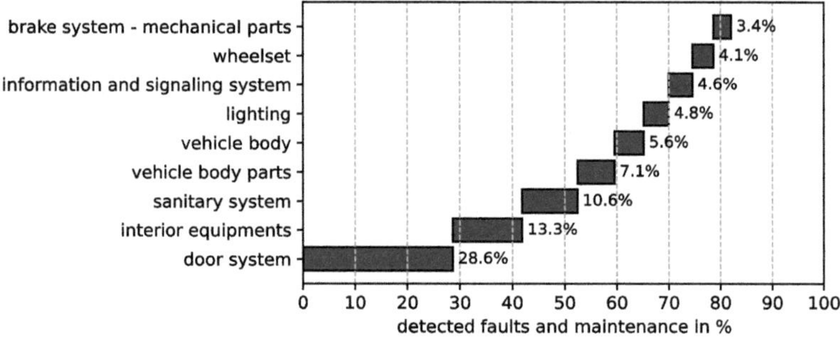

Fig. 6. The most common faults and defects in passenger coaches.

Figure 7 shows the components of the EMUs that are most prone to failure. The result shows a combination of locomotives and passenger coaches with the sanitary system in the first place, followed by information and signaling systems, door systems, and body parts of the vehicle. Other fault-prone subsystems

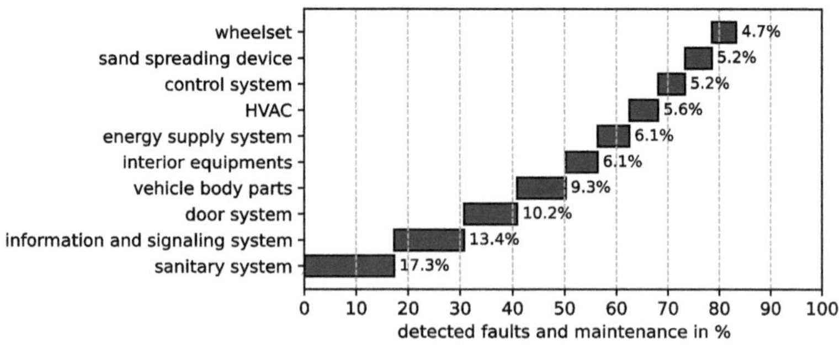

Fig. 7. The most common faults and defects in electric multiple units (EMU).

that appear, such as wheelset, HVAC, and sand-spread device, are also of great importance in this case.

3.2   Accident Data

More detailed evaluations about the technical cause of the passenger train are shown in Fig. 8. As shown in the figure, the electrical components are one of the most frequent causes of accidents in all vehicles, especially in locomotives (40%), and usually lead to short circuits and vehicle fires. Other defects in components that can lead to vehicle fire include the electric motor defects and oil leakage in the transformer's and the power converter's cooling systems.

The defects in wheelset-subsystem, especially the wheelset shaft, is the main cause for a derailment in passenger train. Around 26% of the derailments are

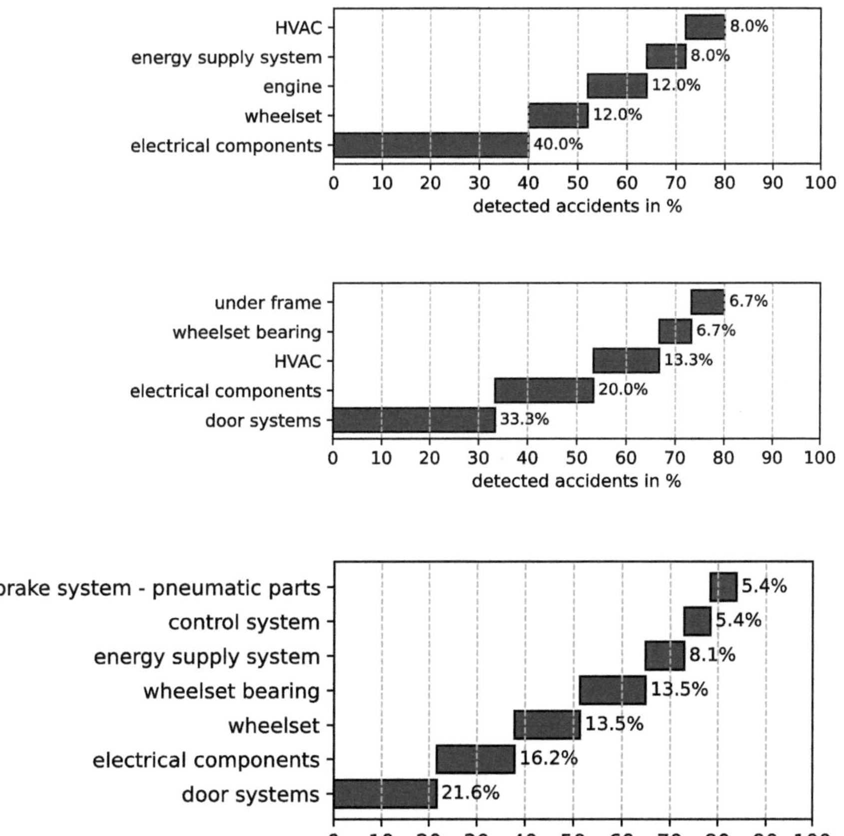

Fig. 8. Contribution of the subsystems to the detected accidents in locomotives (top), passenger coaches (middle), EMUs (bottom).

caused by this. Other causes for derailments are suspension defects and loose bolts or other attachment mounted under the wagon.

As can be seen from the diagrams of the passenger coaches (Fig. 8, middle) and the EMUs (Fig. 8, bottom), the door system is the main cause of accident for this vehicle type. The technical problems in the door locking system are the main cause of direct passenger injury (around 90%) and often lead to fatality. The remaining 10% can be attributed to the electrical components in the door system.

Based on this insight, the potential safety-critical components can be derived. According to CEN/TR 17696:2022 [12], safety-critical components are those for which a single failure is directly associated with a realistic risk of a serious accident, as defined in the article 3 (12) of Directive (EU) 2016/798 [13]. According to this directive, a "serious accident" includes train collisions or derailments resulting in at least one fatality or at least five serious injuries or significant damage to rolling stock, infrastructure or the environment, as well as other accidents involving significant damage with obvious effects on rail safety regulation or safety management. The term "significant damage" is to be understood as damage whose total costs are directly estimated by the investigating body to be at least 2 M €. Table 2 gives the summary of the potential safety-critical components in passenger train based on the ERAIL-database evaluation. The column "N" describes the number of the detected accidents in this time period.

Table 2. The potential safety-critical components in passenger trains.

Vehicle-Type	N	Event	Component	Consequence
Coach	1x	Derailment	Buffer (insufficient lubrication)	1 serious injury ¿ 2 M €
Coach	4x	Passenger injury	Door locking system	1 fatality
EMU	2x	Passenger injury	Door locking system	1 fatality
EMU	1x	Vehicle fire	Electrical cabinet	¿ 2 M €
EMU	1x	Vehicle fire	Transformer	¿ 2 M €

4 State of Art: Condition-Based Monitoring in Passenger Trains

4.1 OnBoard Monitoring

Bogie condition monitoring includes monitoring the wheel tread, wheelset bearings, wheelset axle, coupling elements, traction motor, and gearbox (driven axles). Accelerometers can detect typical damage to the wheelset, such as wheel flat, hollow wear and rolling contact fatigue (RCF). The state-of-the-art for the

CBM of bogie in freight wagon is presented by von Hinüber et al. [26]. Hermann [25] in his dissertation presented a method for detecting hollow wheel on freight wagons using accelerometers placed on the middle of the bogie frames. The lateral acceleration of the bogie, the vehicle speed and position are needed as input for the calculation. Spectral analysis is used to calculate the running frequency. By observing the dependency between the running frequency and the vehicle speed, the information about the hollow wear can be determined. The simulation results show a high level of reliability. In principle, this method can also be used for passenger trains, but further investigations are required for transferability (bogies with radial adjustment, a longitudinally flexible wheelset guide or a longer wheelset base). The system works all the better the lower the disturbances caused by the track geometry.

Siemens presented the MoComp Bogie Diagnostic Solution in 2021 [20]. The sensor system in the bogie measures the accelerations on the axlebox, the gearbox and the traction motor housings. With the MoComp-System the condition of the suspension system can also be monitored. The sensor node and the monitored components are shown in Fig. 9.

Fig. 9. Siemens MoComp Bogie Diagnostic Solution: sensor node and the monitored components [19].

The ZF connect@rail offers a monitoring system for both bogie and infrastructure. ZF connect@rail consists of sensor nodes (Heavy Duty TAG) and telematic device (VCU Pro OnBoard Unit). The acquired data, such as acceleration, temperature, vehicle speed and position, are transferred and processed further in "ZF IoT Cloud". By monitoring the acceleration in the drive train, the rolling contact fatigue on the wheelsets can be detected before the inspection limit is reached. Earlier detection of damage results in a reduction of up to 8 days to repair the damage. In addition, the reprofiling of the wheelsets can be done earlier reducing the cutting depth by about 6 mm on average compared to planned maintenance [2, 14].

Other than using acceleration signals, measuring and evaluating the acoustics emission can also be done for detecting the faults in the bogie. Usually, the sound pressure is measured using microphone. The advantages of this method are higher frequencies can be measured to maximize the fault detection limit, less stress on the sensors compared to accelerometers, and multiple faults can be detected using only one microphone. The downside of this method is the difficulty in processing the data because of other sound emissions, such as aerodynamic noise and other disturbances on trains, bridges, and tunnels [40]. Sorribes-Palmer et al. [40] presented a method for fault detection in the primary and secondary spring/damper using acoustic signal. The microphones are installed in the center of the bogie frame where the aerodynamic influence is lowest. Two measurement campaigns were carried out in which different sampling frequencies (19.2 kHz and 8 kHz) were tested. The proposed methodology shows an accuracy of over 85%. Kreuzer et al. [30, 31] have shown that an accuracy of over 94% can be achieved in detecting faults in bearing components (pitting and fatigue) using airborne sound signals and machine learning (ML) approach. Omnidirectional electret microphones of the type "M 370" with a sampling frequency of 25.6 kHz were used for the measurement. In this method, the Mel-Frequency Cepstral Coefficients (MFCC) are calculated from the measured sound signals and used to train a Multilayer Perceptron (MLP). This allows errors that are not present in the training data to be detected and classified.

Braking System condition monitoring includes mostly the pneumatic and mechanical subsystems. This can be achieved by using pressure sensors in the main brake pipe or in the brake cylinder and using strain gauges on the brake linkage [26]. Peche [32] presented in his dissertation a method to monitor the braking system on the automatic slack adjuster (ASA). In this method, the rotation angle and the angular velocity of the brake slack adjuster are measured using a linear Hall effect sensor in order to determine the brake position and the brake linkage force. The duration and number of oscillations derived from the measured data are the core of the algorithm. However, this method is not a stand-alone system for monitoring the brake system. In combination with other sensors, such as the pressure sensor in the brake cylinder, this method offers the possibility of increasing the reliability and safety of the brake system.

Galimberti et al. [16] developed a hybrid model of the air brake for fault detection. The pressure in the main brake pipe and in the weighing valve as well as the brake position are required as input variables. The model is used to determine the pressure in the brake cylinder and compare it with the brake cylinder pressure from the measurement. Errors are detected and classified based on the deviation of the brake cylinder pressure. Since all of the necessary variables are usually available in passenger trains, this method can also be used.

When braking, the uneven wear of brake pads can cause vibrations in high-speed trains, which generate noise that can affect the environment along the route and reduce passenger comfort. It can also lead to excessive wear and reduced braking force. These issues can affect the safety of high-speed trains. Zhang et al. [43–45] have presented a methodology using the Trade-Off Contrastive Learning Network (TCLN) to detect uneven wear of brake pads in high-speed trains. The tangential acceleration at the brake pad is required as input for the model. They used a piezoelectric acceleration sensor with a sensitivity of $10\,\mathrm{mV/g}$ and a measurement range of $\pm500\,\mathrm{g}$ for the measurement. The sampling frequency is $50\,\mathrm{kHz}$. The results show an accuracy of over 90%.

The "Brake-by-Wire" system from Siemens introduced a new braking system in the railway sector without the usual pneumatic subsystems. The brake actuator, which is purely electrically controlled, applies the braking force. This ensures faster braking and deceleration. Furthermore, the energy usage can also be reduced due to the elimination of the energy-intensive compressed air. With the compressed air-free brake system, only the brake actuator requires maintenance. The maintenance intervals are the same as those for air brake system. This reduces the amount of maintenance required. In the event of a fault, such as a power failure, the pressure reservoir integrated in the actuator applies braking forces. This system was developed according to Safety Integrity Level (SIL) 4, and the brake-by-wire system has been used regularly on the X-cars (subway) in Vienna since June 2023. The brake actuator is connected to the CAN bus and the brake control unit. The CAN bus exchanges all necessary set values and information about the vehicle status. This allows for the detection of brake system faults. Consequently, this system does not require an additional sensor for monitoring the condition of the brake system [21].

Door Systems in passenger trains are equipped with numerous sensors and control switches that monitor their status. Generally, the doors in modern EMUs are equipped with a door control unit. The signals from the control unit can be used to monitor the condition of the door systems. For example, the electrical current at the motor and the door's position can be measured. These can be used for control purposes as well as for anti-trap protection. With pneumatic drives in the old passenger coaches, the air pressure in the operating cylinder (3–8 bar) is measured as an indicator. Other than that, redundant anti-trap protection system is also installed in modern EMUs, such as light grids, weight sensor in the sliding step [6, 15, 23, 27].

Sanitary System. As mentioned above, clogging is the biggest problem in the passenger train's toilet system. According to GlovaRail, clogging in passenger train toilets is usually caused by foreign objects in the pipes. Modern toilet system can detect this problem by measuring the pressure in the intermediate tank. A pressure switch (Knorr/EVAC) or a pressure sensor (GlovaRail and Wabtec/Semvac) can be embedded in the diagnostic system. A diagnostic system with a pressure switch operates using fixed time sequences. A diagnostic system with a pressure sensor controls the flushing process based on the defined pressure limits. Additionally, the liquid level in the fresh water and the waste water tanks are measured using floating switches [11].

HVAC. Inadequate maintenance of HVAC systems can lead to shorter component service life and higher operating costs. Various studies on the subject of condition monitoring and predictive maintenance of HVAC systems have been carried out in recent years. The number of sensors used is essentially determined by the fault diagnosis approach used. For example, temperatures are measured at various points, and the CO_2 concentration is measured to control the supply of fresh air for circulation purposes.

Kim and Lee [28] presented a hybrid approach to detect and diagnose faults (FDD) using both data and model. This methodology requires measuring the temperature in the environment and on the refrigeration circuit using real sensors. Other physical variables, such as the pressure and airflow in the refrigeration circuit, are measured using virtual sensors in the model environment.

Ciani et al. [9] conducted a study using fuzzy logic to determine the most fault-prone components in the HVAC system. Four critical components, such as compressor, electrical control card, insulated gate bipolar transistor module (IGBT), and uninterruptible power supply (UPS), whose conditions should be monitored by sensors, were identified. The components, failure modes, and the required sensors are listed in Table 3.

Table 3. The four critical components of the HVAC system that require condition monitoring [9].

Component	Failure mode	Sensors
Compressor	sticking internal valve	position transducer, pressure transmitter
Compressor	internal overload motor protection	several sensors to monitor temperature, temperature, vibration, pressure and load
ECC	electronic control failure	humidity, vibration transducers
IGBT-Module	short/open circuit	temperature transducer, power meter
UPS	no output power	volt- and ampere meter

Energy Supply System. All new rail vehicles are equipped with an automatic dropping device (ADD) for the pantograph as standard. This device must also be installed on older traction units. In case the pantograph strip line is damaged (spalling or crack), the ADD prevents damage to the overhead contact line, which could lead to an operational interruption or very high repair costs [1].

Currently, OnBoard condition monitoring of pantographs is not cost-effective, as the camera system installed on the vehicle roof can only monitor one pantograph. Furthermore, the camera installed on the vehicle roof has a limited viewing angle compared to the WaySide monitoring system. The OnBoard monitoring system is generally only used to monitor the overhead contact line [10].

Today's challenge in pantograph overhead line system condition monitoring is developing algorithms that use simple sensors, that can detect faults both in the overhead line and on the vehicles. The Schunk OnTrack monitoring system is one example. It consists of accelerometer and optical sensors [10,37].

4.2   WaySide Monitoring

A WaySide monitoring system is a fixed, trackside monitoring system. It can detect damaged passing vehicles using mechanical sensors like strain gauges, as well as acoustic detection using microphone arrays. It can also detect damage thermally and optically using cameras and lasers [26].

Current State of WaySide-Monitoring System. Von Hinüber et al. [26] summarized conventional WS monitoring systems in rail transport. These systems include wheel impact load detectors (WILD), weigh-in-motion (WIM) systems, hot axle box detectors (HABD), acoustic monitoring systems for axle boxes (AMS), derailment detection systems (DRD), dragging equipment detection (DED), and train conformity check systems (TCCS). Other newly developed WS systems are also described. These include the camera bridge from DB Cargo as part of a German Federal Ministry of Transport (BMV) pilot project, the optical underfloor wheel inspection from DTEC and Innotec Systems and a combination of optical and acoustic methods from Vossloh/RailWatch.

There are various modular WS diagnostic systems on the market today. For example, the modular WS systems from Voestalpine is shown in Fig. 10.

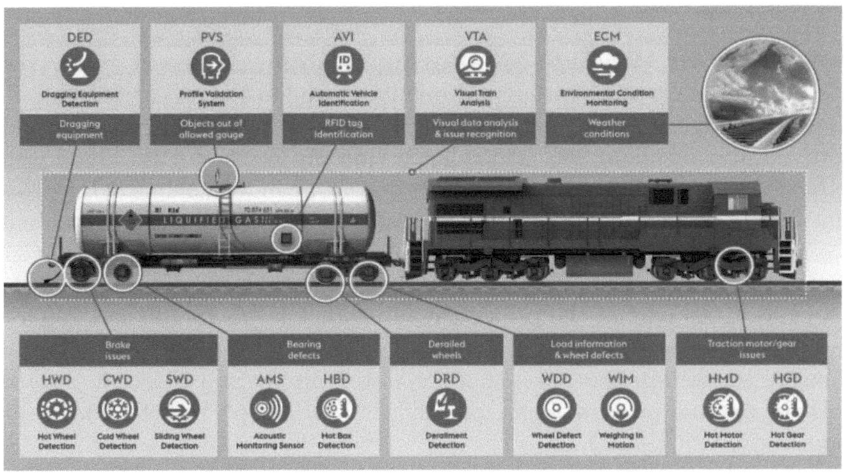

Fig. 10. Voestalpine zentrak Modular Diagnostic System [42].

These systems can identify numerous types of damage, such as wheel flat, engine/transmission damage, and brake system defects [42].

A WS monitoring system to monitor the pantograph usually works optically. Basically, the geometry of the pantograph and the surface of the contact strip are recorded using a camera and laser scanners. Figure 11 shows MERMEC's pantograph WS monitoring system. It consists of four modules. When a vehicle passes through the camera gate, the system records the geometry and height position of the pantograph. This recorded geometry can then be compared to a reference model to detect wear and cracks on the contact strip's surface. The contact pressure against the overhead contact line can be derived from vertical position measurements of the pantograph [24].

Fig. 11. MERMEC's pantograph WaySide monitoring system [24].

Development of WaySide-Monitoring System. In recent years, various research projects on semi-automated maintenance have been carried out. These include the E-Check project by DB-Long Distance, the ESPEK project, and the remote maintenance and 360° video inspection project by ÖBB. These projects aim to reduce inspection work and vehicle downtime in workshops. AI approaches are intended to speed up fault detection. Additionally, linking faults and maintenance measures can significantly reduce administrative and logistic delay time.

Since the end of 2023, Deutsche Bahn (DB) has been carrying out the E-check project. As part of the project, maintenance levels IS 100 and 200 for the ICE 401, 402, 403, 408, 411, 412, and 415 series will be partially automated. The entire inspection process, including water supply and disposal, is twice as fast as the manual process. Consequently, the workshop's maintenance capacity is increased by 25% [4, 22, 34].

The E-check consists of a camera gate, a mobile underfloor inspection device (MUFIG), and a collaborative robot (Cobot) (see Fig. 12). The camera gate can scan a train at a speed of up to 6 km/h. As the train passes through the camera gate, images and sound are recorded. This allows various external "defects" to be detected, such as damaged pictograms, graffiti, and leaking compressed brake pipes. The AI enables image-based detection of components and automatic detection and localization of anomalies on the train [4,22,34].

Fig. 12. The "E-Check" project from DB-Long Distance. The camera gate with AI (left). Mobile underfloor inspection device (top right). Collaborating robot/cobot (right, bottom) [4,22,34].

The project ESPEK was investigating whether automatic inspection is feasible for different vehicle types and series. Vehicle inspection is a demanding task that should be carried out frequently and almost exclusively visually. Trained personnel are essential for this. 27–52% of all inspection points are located under the vehicle. The approach using camera and AI is driven by the lack of qualified personnel in the last years and the risk of losing the knowledge transfer because of generational change [38].

From 2020 to 2021, the ÖBB collaborated with TU Graz and Pace University in New York to test a new maintenance concept combining remote maintenance and 360° video vehicle inspections. Remote maintenance involves automatically assigning vehicle diagnostic data to maintenance measures specified in maintenance specifications. First, the recorded diagnostic data are managed and stored in the appropriate form. Then, inspection routines are derived from the maintenance measures. Combining these two sets of findings creates a maintenance tool. The 360° video vehicle inspection can theoretically cover up to 60% of safety check activities. The status of the component for a specific vehicle is available as a digital twin and is updated each time the vehicle passes the gate. Maintenance checklists can be created directly using the "Maintenance Tool". This shortens the vehicle downtime in the workshop. [29, 33]

5 Summary and Outlook

In order to further improve the RAMS factors and also optimize the maintenance strategies for passenger trains, this paper focuses on identifying the high-priority subsystems. This was done, by analyzing maintenance logs and accident reports. Through this analysis, a small number of subsystems that account for nearly 80% of the technical failures are identified. These include service- and safety-relevant components such as information and signaling system, control system, energy supply system, door system, sanitary system, brake system and HVAC-system. Focusing condition-based monitoring (CBM) efforts on these areas can therefore generate the highest operational and safety benefits.

The review of state-of-the-art CBM technologies demonstrates that both OnBoard systems and WaySide monitoring solutions are now sufficiently mature to support this shift. Early deployments already indicate significant reductions in unplanned downtime and improved fleet availability. Through pilot projects and real applications, it can be shown, that this approach can eliminate the technical problems up to 50%, increasing the maintenance capacity of the workshop by 25%, and carried out the safety check activities automatically up to 60%. In addition, the maintenance costs of the running gear could also be reduced around 10%.

From a practical perspective, this findings could be used by the operators and maintainers in directing limited resources toward the subsystems with the greatest operational leverage. Beyond cost efficiency, these targeted strategies also align with the broader goals of improving the reliability, availability, maintainability and safety of passenger rail transport.

Nevertheless, several challenges remain. The datasets analyzed in this study represent only a subset of European operators, and cost-benefit assessments were not quantified in detail. Furthermore, the organizational implications of digital maintenance, such as the preservation of know-how and the redistribution of workload between operators, OEMs, and suppliers, require further investigation.

Future research should therefore expand on developing minimal equipment concept for passenger trains, life-cycle cost analysis of CBM deployment, integration of decision-support methods such as AHP, fuzzy logic, or AI-based models to optimize planning, and strategies for standardization, interoperability, and skills development across the sector. Addressing these aspects will be crucial for ensuring that the ongoing shift toward predictive maintenance delivers not only cost reductions but also sustainable improvements in RAMS performance and total cost of ownership.

Acknowledgments. The present study was undertaken within the framework of the research project "Minimum Sensor Equipment of Passenger Coaches, Multiple Units and Locomotives for Effective and Economic Condition Monitoring" on behalf of the DZSF (link).

Disclosure of Interests. The authors declare that they have no conflict of interests that could have appeared to influence the work reported in this paper.

References

1. Deutsche Bahn AG: Automatische Stromabnehmer-Senkeinrichtung (AS). Bahn Praxis (2001). https://www.uv-bund-bahn.de/fileadmin//Dokumente/Publikationen/BahnPraxis_B/BahnPraxisB-2002_10.pdf. Accessed 18 Sept 2025
2. Alber, J.: Erkennen von Rollkontaktermüdung bei gleichzeitigem Track-Monitoring. Moderne Konzepte für Wartung und Instandhaltung, Fachtagung (2024)
3. Alstom. HealthHub - The intelligent way to improve maintenance (2023). https://www.alstom.com/press-releases-news/2023/2/healthhub-intelligent-way-improve-maintenance. Accessed 18 Sept 2025
4. Deutsche Bahn. Digitale ICE-Wartung: Deutsche Bahn investiert 55 Millionen Euro in Roboter und künstliche Intelligenz (2023). https://www.deutschebahn.com/de/presse/pressestart_zentrales_uebersicht/Digitale-ICE-Wartung-Deutsche-Bahn-investiert-55Millionen-Euroin-Roboter-und-kuenstliche-Intelligenz-12285750. Accessed 18 Sept 2025
5. Beqiri, L., et al.: Remaining useful life estimation for railway gearbox bearings using machine learning. In: Milius, B., Collart-Dutilleul, S., Lecomte, T. (eds.) RSSRail 2023. LNCS, vol. 14198, pp. 62–77. Springer, Cham (2023). https://doi.org/10.1007/978-3-031-43366-5_4
6. Bode, S.: Bode. Die Tür. Systemlösungen für Schienenfahrzeuge (2016). https://schaltbaugroup.com/wp-content/uploads/2016/09/Bode_Bro_Schiene_DE_web.pdf. Accessed 18 Sept 2025
7. BS EN 50126-1:2017 (E). Railway Applications – The Specification and Demonstration of Reliability, Availability, Maintainability and Safety (RAMS). Part 1: Generic RAMS Process (2017). ISBN 978-0-580-91692-2
8. Cabadag, S.S.: Die DB Fernverkehr AG automatisiert die ICE-Instandhaltung. Bahn Praxis W (2023). https://www.uv-bund-bahn.de/fileadmin/Dokumente/Publikationen/BahnPraxis_W/BahnPraxisW-2023_02.pdf. Accessed 18 Sept 2025
9. Ciani, L., et al.: Condition-based maintenance of HVAC on a high-speed train for fault detection. Electronics (2021). https://doi.org/10.3390/electronics10121418. Accessed 18 Sept 2025
10. Dharmawan, W., Song, Z., Hecht, M.: Pantograph und Oberleitung - Monitoring System. Austausch mit PantoHealth. Technische Universität Berlin (2025)
11. Dharmawan, W., Song, Z., Hecht, M.: Toilettensystem im Schienenpersonenverkehr v.1.0. Austausch mit GlovaRail. Technische Universität Berlin (2025)
12. DIN CEN/TR 17696:2022–11. Railway applications - Vehicle Maintenance - Guide for identification and management of Safety Critical Components for railway vehicles; German version CEN/TR 17696:2021. Technical Report. Published by CEN and adopted as a DIN standard (2021)

13. Directive (EU) 2016/798 of the European Parliament and of the Council. of 11 May 2016 on railway safety (recast). EU Directive (2016). https://eur-lex.europa.eu/eli/dir/2016/798/oj. Accessed 26 June 2025
14. Dittrich, A., et al.: Condition Monitoring als Erfolgsmodell: ZF connect@rail bei den Graz Linien. ZEVrail (2022 (Jahrgang 146)/Ausgabe Sonderheft Graz 2022/Sprache: Deutsch). https://www.zevrail.de/artikel/condition-monitoring-als-erfolgsmodell-zf-connectrail-bei-den-graz-linien. Accessed 18 Sept 2025
15. Ultimate Europe. Unsere Türen eröffnen neue Welten!. https://www.ultimate-eur.com/ausfuehrungen-zugtueren/. Accessed 18 Sept 2025
16. Galimberti, A., Zanelli, F., Tomasini, G.: A hybrid model for freight train air brake condition monitoring. Appl. Sci. (2024). https://www.mdpi.com/2076-3417/14/24/11770. Accessed 18 Sept 2025
17. Knorr-Bremse Evac GmbH. Smart control system for next generation train toilets. https://rail.knorr-bremse.com/en/at/stories/newsforum/content-page-evac-61.json. Accessed 18 Sept 2025
18. Siemens Mobility GmbH. Digital transformation for sustainable mobility – with Railigent X. https://www.mobility.siemens.com/global/en/portfolio/digital-solutions-software/digital-services/railigent-x.html. Accessed 18 Sept 2025
19. Siemens Mobility GmbH. MoComp Bogie Diagnostic Solution. https://www.mobility.siemens.com/global/de/portfolio/fahrzeugkomponenten/bogie-diagnostic.html. Accessed 18 Sept 2025
20. Siemens Mobility GmbH. Siemens Mobility launches "MoComp" - An initiative to market its diverse portfolio of rail vehicle components (2021). https://press.siemens.com/global/en/pressrelease/siemens-mobility-launches-mocomp-initiative-market-its-diverse-portfolio-rail-vehicle. Accessed 18 Sept 2025
21. Siemens Mobility GmbH. Whitepaper - Druckluftfreies Bremssystem für Schienenfahrzeuge. Technical report. https://www.mobility.siemens.com/global/en/portfolio/rolling-stock-components/brake-systems/air-free-brake-system/whitepaper-air-free-brake-system-for-rail-vehicles.html. Accessed 18 Sept 2025
22. DB E.C.O. Group. Künstliche Intelligenz für die Instandhaltung von ICES (2023). https://db-eco.com/de/aktuelles/projekt-e-check-kuenstliche-intelligenz-fuer-die-instandhaltung-von-ices/. Accessed 18 Sept 2025
23. Hübner Group. Produktportfolio Rail & Bus (2019). https://www.hubner-group.com/fileadmin/user_upload/hubner-group.com/downloads/broschueren/HUBNER_MatSol_Rail-Bus_DE_10-2019__preview.pdf. Accessed 18 Sept 2025
24. MERMEC Group. Pantograph Parameters. https://www.mermecgroup.com/measurement-br-trains-e-systems/train-monitoring/1021/pantograph-parameters.php. Accessed 18 Sept 2025
25. Hermann, T.: Methode zur Detektion von hohlgelaufenen Rädern an Güterwagen. Ph.D. thesis. Technische Universität Berlin (2017)
26. v. Hinüber, E.L., et al.: Mindestausrüstung von Güterwagen Effektives und wirtschaftliches Condition Monitoring für zustandsorientierte Instandhaltung. DZSF (2022). https://doi.org/10.48755/dzsf.210009.01. https://www.dzsf.bund.de/SharedDocs/Textbausteine/DZSF/Forschungsberichte/Forschungsbericht_2022-26.html. Accessed 18 Sept 2025
27. Janicki, J., Reinhard, H., Rüffer, M.: Schienenfahrzeugtechnik. DB-Fachbuch. 4. überarbeitete Auflage. Bahn Fachverlag GmbH (2020). ISBN 978-3-943214-26-0
28. Kim, W., Lee, J.-H.: Fault detection and diagnostics analysis of air conditioners using virtual sensors. Appl. Thermal Eng. **191**, 116848 (2021). https://doi.org/10.1016/j.applthermaleng.2021.116848. https://www.sciencedirect.com/science/article/pii/S1359431121002970. ISSN 1359-4311. Accessed 18 Sept 2025

29. Koller, S.: Instandhaltungsstrategie "ferngesteuerte Instandhaltung Cityjet". ZEVrail (2021 (Jahrgang 145)/Ausgabe 09/Sprache: Deutsch). https://www. zevrail.de/artikel/instandhaltungsstrategie-ferngesteuerte-instandhaltung-cityjet. Accessed 18 Sept 2025

30. Kreuzer, M., et al.: Airborne sound analysis for the detection of bearing faults in railway vehicles with real-world data. In: 2023 IEEE International Conference on Prognostics and Health Management (ICPHM) (2023). https://doi.org/10.1109/ ICPHM57936.2023.10194026. Accessed 18 Sept 2025

31. Kreuzer, M., et al.: Real-world airborne sound analysis for health monitoring of bearings in railway vehicles (2024). https://doi.org/10.2139/ssrn.4923626. https:// papers.ssrn.com/sol3/papers.cfm?abstract_id=4923626. Accessed 18 Sept 2025

32. Peche, F.: Bremsgestängestellerüberwachung. Ph.D. thesis. Technische Universität Berlin (2024)

33. Pfister, M., Koller, S.: Digitalisierung in der Instandhaltung von Schienenfahrzeugen - Fernwartung und digitale 360° Video - Fahrzeuginspektion. ZEVrail (2022 (Jahrgang 146)/Ausgabe Sonderheft Graz 2022/Sprache: Deutsch). https://www.zevrail.de/artikel/digitalisierung-der-instandhaltung-von-schienenfahrzeugen-fernwartung-und-digitale-360deg. Accessed 18 Sept 2025

34. Railvolution. E-Check - DB's ICE digital maintenance (2023). https://www. railvolution.net/news/e-check-db-s-ice-digital-maintenance. Accessed 18 Sept 2025

35. Rodriguez, J., et al.: A digital approach to rolling stock maintenance (2023). https://web-assets.bcg.com/pdf-src/prod-live/a-digital-approach-to-rolling-stock-maintenance.pdf. Accessed 18 Sept 2025

36. Rösch, W.: Kompendium Schienenfahrzeuginstandhaltung. TrackoMedia (2019). ISBN 978-3-96245-197-4

37. Schunk. Digital condition monitoring: on track. https://www.schunk-group.com/ transit-systems/en/products/digital-condition-monitoring. Accessed 18 Sept 2025

38. Schymik, L., Stolpmann, A.: Erkennung von Schadmustern an Personenverkehrszügen und Evaluierung der Konfidenz zur Auswahl robuster Features für "Predictive Maintenance" Projekt ESPEK. Tagungsband AALE 2025. menschzentrierte Automation im digitalen Zeitalter. HTWK Leipzig, pp. 171–180 (2025). https://doi.org/10.33968/2025.18. Accessed 18 Sept 2025

39. SNCF. A global leader in predictive maintenance (2024). https://www.groupe-sncf. com/en/innovation/digitalization/predictive-maintenance. Accessed 18 Sept 2025

40. Sorribes-Palmer, F., et al.: Data-driven fault diagnosis of bogie suspension components with on-board acoustic sensors. English. In: PHME 2020, pp. 1–13 (2020). http://phmeurope.org/2020/. Accessed 18 Sept 2025

41. Europe's Rail Joint Undertaking. Optimising running gear (2024). https://rail-research.europa.eu/latest-news/optimising-running-gear. Accessed 18 Sept 2025

42. Voestalpine. Zentrak Modular Diagnostic System. https://www.voestalpine.com/ railway-systems/de/produkte/zentrak-modulares-diagnosesystem/. Accessed 18 Sept 2025

43. Zhang, M., et al.: A cross-domain state monitoring method for high-speed train brake pads based on data generation under small sample conditions. Measurement **226**, 114074 (2024). https://doi.org/10.1016/j.measurement.2023.114074. https:// www.sciencedirect.com/science/article/pii/S026322412301638X. ISSN 0263-2241. Accessed 18 Sept 2025

44. Zhang, M., et al.: Brake uneven wear of high-speed train intelligent monitoring using an ensemble model based on multi-sensor feature fusion and deep learning.

Eng. Failure Anal. **137**, 106219 (2022). https://doi.org/10.1016/j.engfailanal.2022.106219. https://www.sciencedirect.com/science/article/pii/S1350630722001935. Accessed 18 Sept 2025. ISSN 1350-6307

45. Zhang, M., et al.: High-speed train brake pads condition monitoring based on trade-off contrastive learning network. IEEE Trans. Instrum. Measur. (2024). https://doi.org/10.1109/TIM.2024.3485406. Accessed 18 Sept 2025

Quantitative Dependability Evaluation of Train Control Systems in Presence of Uncertainty: A Systematic Literature Review

Laura Carnevali[1], Felicita Di Giandomenico[2], Alessandro Fantechi[1(✉)], Stefania Gnesi[2], and Gloria Gori[1]

[1] Department of Information Engineering, University of Florence, Florence, Italy
{laura.carnevali,alessandro.fantechi,gloria.gori}@unifi.it
[2] Institute of Information Science and Technologies (ISTI), CNR, Pisa, Italy
{felicita.digiandomenico,stefania.gnesi}@isti.cnr.it

Abstract. Technological advances in Train Control Systems (TCSs) hold substantial promise for revolutionizing railway transportation dependability in terms of safety, availability, and operational capacity. This transformation is primarily driven by cutting-edge distancing policies such as Moving Block (MB) signaling and Virtual Coupling (VC), which are powered by sophisticated train localization technologies including satellite-based positioning systems. At the same time, these technological advances raise notable concerns about the effects that uncertainty in critical TCS parameters, such as train position and speed, may have on dependability-related attributes. This is an extended abstract of the journal paper [6], where a comprehensive systematic literature review investigating quantitative methodologies for assessing TCS dependability under uncertain conditions is presented. Through selection and analysis of 42 peer-reviewed publications spanning 2011–2023, we provide empirical insights and a taxonomic framework on research and practice in quantitative dependability assessment of TCSs.

Keywords: Train control systems · dependability · quantitative evaluation · uncertainty · systematic literature review

1   Introduction

Major technological innovations [7,8,15], such as advanced distancing [19] and satellite positioning [3], have promised to improve dependability of Train Control Systems (TCSs), while introducing *uncertainty* in vital parameters such as train position, speed, and acceleration, posing significant challenges on the assessment of dependability-related attributes. Since the pioneer results of [28], solution techniques for quantitative evaluation of stochastic models have addresses these issues [10] in research papers [2,4,13,14,23,24] and projects [1,5,9,21,22].

M. H. ter Beek et al. (Eds.): RSSRail 2025, LNCS 16236, pp. 129–134, 2026.
https://doi.org/10.1007/978-3-032-10762-6_11

Despite increasing academic and industrial efforts to investigate quantitative dependability evaluation of TCSs, only a preliminary review has been presented on this subject [10]. Few systematic reviews have focused on applications of formal methods in railways, including those capturing probabilistic features of TCSs, though not extensively investigating these aspects [11,12]. Other works have reviewed research on advanced technologies for TCSs [17,18,20,26,27].

This is an extended abstract of the journal paper [6], presenting the first Systematic Literature Review (SLR) on methods for quantitative dependability evaluation of TCSs, following the guidelines of [16]. Specifically, we selected 42 high-quality research papers published between 2011 and 2023, categorizing them based on various features, notably the addressed category of TCS, the considered dependability attributes, and the quantitative evaluation methods and tools used for their computation. We analyzed also other relevant features like the distribution over time of the papers, the geographical distribution of the research institutes of the involved scholars, the type of data used in the analysis (real or synthetic), and the availability of artifacts supporting the reproducibility and replicability of the experimental results.

2   A Systematic Literature Review

The main objective of this study is to survey studies, published from 2011, that employ rigorous modeling methodologies in the development of TCSs to assess dependability-related attributes, even in the presence of some form of (quantifiable) uncertainty about the information produced by sensors or the system itself. The study aims to answer the following Research Questions (RQs):

- RQ1: Which TCSs and measures are considered?
- RQ2: Which quantitative evaluation methods and tools are used?
- RQ3: How is quantitative evaluation performed?
- RQ4: Are experimental results reproducible?

To answer these RQs, we have set up a study, detailed in [6], following the guidelines for SLRs of [16], which define an automated process to retrieve papers published in peer-reviewed journals and conferences, and a rigorous procedure to select those that have advanced the state-of-the-art in the scientific or technological perspective. The SLR implemented investigates quantitative methodologies to assess TCS dependability under uncertain conditions.

The SLR process started with a search on relevant scientific databases as data sources, namely Scopus, IEEE Xplore, ACM Digital Library, and SpringerLink, with a search string reflecting the main RQs. This automatic search has retrieved 939 *primary studies*, which were then object of a first screening phase by the authors, employing predefined inclusion and exclusion criteria, which left 66 papers as candidates for the next step: reading and evaluating each of them has led to focus on 31 papers of interest. A secondary search has been then performed with the backward and forward *snowballing* to papers citing or cited by these 31, adding a further 11 papers of interest.

3   The Context of the Study

The study has adopted a broad definition of Train Control Systems (TCS), that is, any computer-based system that controls a relevant function related to train movement and line operation such that a failure of the system can impact on regular service and/or on performance, availability, capacity, and safety of the railway operation. This definition includes: train movement and distancing control, by means of Automatic Train Control (ATC) and Automatic Train Protection (ATP); automatic driving, known as ATO; collision avoidance in a station or junction, by means of interlocking (IXL); scheduling and optimization of railway traffic, known as Automatic Train Supervision (ATS).

The considered dependability attributes are: *reliability* (R), i.e., continuity of correct service; *safety* (S), i.e., absence of catastrophic consequences on the user(s) and the environment; *availability* (A), i.e., readiness for correct service; *railway network capacity* (C); *energy efficiency* (EE).

Dependability assessment studies through model-based approaches, especially when performed at early stages of the system development to support design choices and promptly detect potential weaknesses, have to cope with inaccurate, sometimes even unknown, information on a subset of the model parameters [25]. Thus, the analysis is conducted considering degrees of *uncertainty* about the value of quantities modeling either *i*) aspects intrinsically connected with adopted technologies, or *ii*) external phenomena impacting on the dependability-related indicators under evaluation. In the context of TCSs, measures of train position, speed, acceleration, as well as measures related to delay and loss of communication messages, are among the main sources of uncertainty.

4   Lessons Learned and Conclusions

The answers to the stated RQs unveil interesting trends and insights in the quantitative dependability assessment of TCSs considering uncertainty conditions.

First, regarding the considered dependability measures considered (RQ1), as expected within the railway domain, a significant portion of the studies (nearly 38%) focus on safety properties, followed by works focusing on reliability, availability and performability. Notably, the most frequently studied TCSs categories for safety assessment include Communication-Based Train Control (CBTC), Chinese Train Control System (CTCS), IXL, Moving Block (MB), Satellite, Train-to-train Communication (T2TC) and Train-to-train Distancing (T2TD).

Second, regarding the employed analysis techniques (RQ2), we notice a preference for advanced stochastic modeling techniques. We grouped the resulting methods into four categories; the relative majority of papers leverage techniques belonging to the stochastic modeling and simulative solution (SM-SS) group, and to the Statistical Model Checking (SMC) group (each accounting approximately 42% of studies). Moreover, most of the selected papers integrate more than one method to evaluate a given dependability measure, with the exceptions of studies on IXL, where SMC is used for the quantitative analysis in all the measures, and studies on Virtual Coupling (VC) that all leverage SM-SS. These results also highlight a pivotal shift from the concept of "absolute safety", where a system was considered either perfectly safe or unsafe (leaving no room for degrees of risk), to the different perspective of "probabilistic safety". This transition is particularly evident in the increased use of SMC, which directly enables the quantification of the probability that a system will remain safe.

Third, the results on the impact of uncertainty factors (RQ3) reveal that nearly half of the analyzed papers address communication-related uncertainties, closely followed by positioning errors and failure probability. Almost half of the selected studies address more than one (up to three) uncertainty aspect. When safety is the main objective of the analysis, communication errors, subsystem failures, and positioning errors are consistently the major areas of concern.

Finally, regarding RQ4, the experimental evaluations presented in the studies rely primarily on synthetic but realistic data, used in approximately 64% of the papers. This reliance stems from the inherent difficulty in obtaining comprehensive operational parameter values for safety-critical systems like TCSs.

The insights derived from this review are of practical utility to various stakeholders around TCSs. Researchers focused on the dependability analysis of TCSs can utilize these findings to better guide future activities, while those enhancing TCS technologies can use this information to understand the strengths and weaknesses of current solutions. For railway operators, documented studies offer additional support in guiding choices at the configuration and operational level. Finally, normative and standardization bodies can benefit from the reported studies to develop the proper recommendations for designers and operators in the field. In addition, this survey identifies several future research directions. There is a clear need for enhanced cooperation between academia and industry to strengthen the industrial application of proposed techniques and tools (only 7 reviewed studies include both academic and industrial authors). Prioritizing the development of domain-specific tools that automate (or at least ease) the translation of high-level semi-formal TCS specifications into formal stochastic models would significantly boost the adoption of quantitative evaluation tools by personnel who may not possess deep expertise in formal modeling. Furthermore, encouraging the analysis of compound dependability metrics, e.g., performability, and exploring trade-offs among different metrics of interest would promote TCS solutions with satisfactory operational capabilities across a wider dependability perspective. Finally, the application of these quantitative evaluation techniques to the field of predictive maintenance would be worth investigating, potentially in combination with emerging machine learning techniques.

Acknowledgement. This work was partially supported by the MUR PRIN 2022 PNRR P2022A492B project ADVENTURE (ADVancEd iNtegraTed evalUation of Railway systEms) and the MOST – Sustainable Mobility National Research Center and received funding from the European Union NextGenerationEU (PIANO NAZIONALE DI RIPRESA E RESILIENZA (PNRR) – MISSIONE 4, COMPONENTE 2, INVESTIMENTO 1.4 – D.D. 1033 17/06/2022, CN00000023). This manuscript reflects only the authors' views and opinions, neither the European Union nor the European Commission can be considered responsible for them.

References

1. ASTRail. http://www.astrail.eu
2. Basile, D., ter Beek, M.H., Ferrari, A., Legay, A.: Exploring the ERTMS/ETCS full moving block specification: an experience with formal methods. Int. J. Softw. Tools Technol. Transfer 1–20 (2022). https://doi.org/10.1007/s10009-022-00653-3
3. Beugin, J., Marais, J.: Simulation-based evaluation of dependability and safety properties of satellite technologies for railway localization. Transp. Res. Part C: Emerg. Technol. **22**, 42–57 (2012)
4. Biagi, M., Carnevali, L., Paolieri, M., Vicario, E.: Performability evaluation of the ERTMS/ETCS - Level 3. Transp. Res. Part C: Emerg. Technol. **82**, 314–336 (2017)
5. Capacity4Rail. http://www.capacity4rail.eu
6. Carnevali, L., Di Giandomenico, F., Fantechi, A., Gnesi, S., Gori, G.: Quantitative dependability evaluation of train control systems in presence of uncertainty: A systematic literature review. IEEE Trans. Intell. Transp. Syst. **26**(4), 4298–4314 (2025). https://doi.org/10.1109/TITS.2025.3530112
7. EEIG ERTMS User Group: ERTMS/ETCS RAMS System Requirements Specification (1999)
8. EEIG ERTMS User Group: ERTMS/ETCS Systems Requirements Specification (1999)
9. Europe's Rail. https://rail-research.europa.eu/
10. Fantechi, A., Gnesi, S., Gori, G.: Future train control systems: challenges for dependability assessment. In: Leveraging Applications of Formal Methods, Verification and Validation. Practice: 11th International Symposium, ISoLA 2022, Rhodes, Greece, 22–30 October 2022, Proceedings, Part IV, pp. 269–285. Springer, Cham (2022)
11. Ferrari, A., ter Beek, M.H.: Formal methods in railways: a systematic mapping study. ACM Comput. Surv. **55**(4), 1–37 (2022)
12. Ferrari, A., Mazzanti, F., Basile, D., ter Beek, M.H.: Systematic evaluation and usability analysis of formal methods tools for railway signaling system design. IEEE Trans. Softw. Eng. **48**(11), 4675–4691 (2021)
13. Flammini, F., Marrone, S., Nardone, R., Vittorini, V.: Compositional modeling of railway virtual coupling with stochastic activity networks. Formal Aspects Comput. **33**(6), 989–1007 (2021). https://doi.org/10.1007/s00165-021-00560-5
14. Himrane, O., Beugin, J., Ghazel, M.: Toward formal safety and performance evaluation of GNSS-based railway localisation function. IFAC-PapersOnLine **54**(2), 159–166 (2021)
15. IEEE Vehicular Technology Society: IEEE 1474.1 - Standard for Communications Based Train Control (CBTC) - Performance and Functional Requirements (2004)
16. Kitchenham, B.: Procedures for performing systematic reviews. Keele, UK, Keele University **33**(2004), 1–26 (2004)
17. Knutsen, D., Olsson, N.O., Fu, J.: ERTMS/ETCS level 3: development, assumptions, and what it means for the future. J. Intell. Connected Veh. (2023)
18. Marais, J., Beugin, J., Berbineau, M.: A survey of GNSS-based research and developments for the European railway signaling. IEEE Trans. Intell. Transp. Syst. **18**(10), 2602–2618 (2017)

19. Mitchell, I., et al.: ERTMS level 4, train convoys or virtual coupling. IRSE News **219**, 14–15 (2016)
20. Otegui, J., Bahillo, A., Lopetegi, I., Díez, L.E.: A survey of train positioning solutions. IEEE Sens. J. **17**(20), 6788–6797 (2017)
21. PERFORMINGRAIL. https://www.performingrail.com
22. Shift2Rail Joint Undertaking: Multi-annual action plan (2015)
23. da Silva, L.D., Lollini, P., Mongelli, D., Bondavalli, A., Mandò, G.: A stochastic modeling approach for traffic analysis of a tramway system with virtual tags and local positioning. J. Braz. Comput. Soc. **27**(1), 2 (2021). https://doi.org/10.1186/s13173-021-00105-x
24. Song, H., Liu, J., Schnieder, E.: Validation, verification and evaluation of a train to train distance measurement system by means of Colored Petri Nets. Reliab. Eng. Syst. Saf. **164**, 10–23 (2017)
25. Trivedi, K.S., Bobbio, A.: Reliability and Availability Engineering: Modeling, Analysis, and Applications. Cambridge University Press, Cambridge (2017)
26. Xun, J., Li, Y., Liu, R., Li, Y., Liu, Y.: A survey on control methods for virtual coupling in railway operation. IEEE Open J. Intell. Transp. Syst. **3**, 838–855 (2022)
27. Yin, J., Tang, T., Yang, L., Xun, J., Huang, Y., Gao, Z.: Research and development of automatic train operation for railway transportation systems: a survey. Transp. Res. Part C: Emerg. Technol. **85**, 548–572 (2017)
28. Zimmermann, A., Hommel, G.: Towards modeling and evaluation of ETCS real-time communication and operation. J. Syst. Softw. **77**(1), 47–54 (2005)

Comparing Model Checking
and Model-Based Simulation

Davide Basile[(✉)] and Franco Mazzanti

Formal Methods and Tools Lab, ISTI–CNR, Pisa, Italy
{davide.basile,franco.mazzanti}@isti.cnr.it

Abstract. We use a railway-related case study to illustrate the differences that can be encountered while modeling and verifying a system using an academic formal verification framework and an industrial model-based framework. The different roles and structures of the two approaches are illustrated. We analyze instances where the exclusive use of interactive simulation cannot replicate the formal verification activity, and we derive some future research directions.

Keywords: umc · Sparx enterprise architect · formal verification · uml

1 Introduction

Model-based development is an industrially adopted software engineering technique, supported by commercial tools such as PTC Windchill Modeler SySim [2], Sparx Systems Enterprise Architect [3], Dassault Cameo Systems Modeller [1]. This technique supports the creation of models to represent the behavior and structure of a system and is often based on the Unified Modeling Language (UML) OMG standard [24,25]. These models are used to generate code, documentation, test cases, system simulations, and perform other tasks.

Formal methods are used and developed mainly by academia with the goal of achieving rigorous and exhaustive analysis of a system. There is a growing body of literature on the integration of formal methods into model-based development tools, and this integration is often based on alternative approaches to the formalization of UML state machines (see, e.g. [6,8,14,21,26,28,29]).

The combination of an academic formal verification tool (UMC [5]) with an industrial model-based development tool (Sparx EA [3]) has been investigated in [10]. The models developed using the two tools were related through a mapping of their models that preserves their semantics. A set of actionable rules to map the UMC and Sparx notations have been defined, and it was shown in detail how simulations in Sparx EA can be derived from traces generated by the UMC formal verification activity. This allowed to perform model checking of models developed through an industrial model-based development tool, to enhance the validation generally performed using interactive simulations. In particular, UMC has been used to guide the transformation of the initial, ambiguous, and

M. H. ter Beek et al. (Eds.): RSSRail 2025, LNCS 16236, pp. 135–154, 2026.
https://doi.org/10.1007/978-3-032-10762-6_12

incomplete natural language requirements into more rigorous UML designs and to perform a formal analysis of them. Sparx EA has been used to introduce the initial UML designs into an industrial development framework to exploit its advanced features of simulation, documentation, and code generation.

In this paper we bring forward the activity started in [10]. We take here a wider point of view, illustrating the main differences in the formal verification of the system as done by UMC with respect to the simulations that can be performed using Sparx EA. This comparison is performed in the framework of a railway case study, and is made possible through their connection established in [10]. We show a series of examples of formal verification performed in UMC, which goes beyond the simulation capabilities offered by Sparx EA. A comparison of formal verification in UMC is conducted between modelled scenarios and a generic model of the environment, emphasizing the advantages and disadvantages of these two approaches.

The selected case study is a component of a standard railway interface called the Communication Supervision Layer (CSL) [30, 31]. This component is at the base of the handover protocol that allows a train to migrate from one RBC controlled zone to another.

Finally, we share a set of future challenges, highlighting the differences between models designed for formal verification and those designed for code generation, the handling of parallelism and others.

Related Work. This work continues the line of research published in [10]. Previously, a recent set of works [22, 23] focuses on the incremental modelling of natural language requirements as UMC state machines, and associated formal validation. Initially, a UML state machine used to verify a set of requirements under analysis is created. This initial model is not targeting any specific tool and it contains pseudo-code. Once consolidated, the state machine model will eventually be written using the UMC syntax. It is showed how, under certain notation restrictions, it is possible to automatically translate the state machines from UMC to other verification tools such as ProB [13] and CADP [16, 18, 19], where the models are formally verified to be equivalent.

In [12] it is discussed how the formal verification of UMC state machines can be used independently to transform natural language requirements into formally verified structured natural language requirements.

Still on the translation from UML-like models to other formal notations, recent works have focused on transforming these models into mCRL2 [14, 29]. Many studies also focus on the translation from UML into the B/Event-B notation [27, 28], with formal verification performed by means of Atelier B and ProB [15]. The selected case study has also been modelled and analysed in UPPAAL [9].

Structure of the Paper. In Sect. 2, we introduce the two tools used for performing simulations and model checking, respectively, and the case study. In Sect. 3, we describe the different roles that these tools have played in our investigation and the different structure of their models. Section 4 is where model checking and simulations in these environments are compared. In Sects. 5 and Sect. 6, we discuss a set of limitations and future challenges highlighted by this activity and draw some conclusions.

2   Background

Model-Based Software/System Development (MBSD) is a methodology for creating software and hardware artifacts using models expressed as graphical diagrams. Models are used throughout the development cycle. The development process is guided by a model of the software architecture, which represents a semi-formalization of the system's abstract level without implementation details. Semi-formal models can be complemented by their formal specifications, enabling formal techniques like model checking or theorem proving. Early detection of errors is possible by verifying the model against requirements using techniques such as model checking.

UML, an OMG standardized notation [24,25], is the standard for many MBSD environments. In UML, a model consists of multiple classes, each with its own set of attributes. Objects are created by instantiating these classes and assigning values to the attributes using the object-oriented paradigm. A classifier behavior can be assigned to a class in the form of a UML state machine. A state machine can be triggered by events, e.g., signals. The state machine includes various states and transitions connecting them. Transitions also have triggers, conditions and effects (denoted as `trigger[conditions]/effects`). The trigger and conditions specify when the transition is enabled, and the effects can modify the class variables and generate outgoing signals. A transition may have no trigger, in which case it is called a completion transition, and completion transitions typically take precedence over triggered transitions. A run-to-completion step represents the sequence of actions that need to be performed when a specific transition is executed in a UML state machine. Two examples of state machines, accepted by the tools UMC and Sparx EA, are in Fig. 2 and Fig. 3.

2.1   Sparx Enterprise Architect

Sparx Enterprise Architect [3] is an MBSD tool based on OMG UML [24]. Sparx EA offers an Executable State Machine (ESM) artifact specifically designed for simulating the *composition* of different state machines.

In addition to simulating a composition of state machines, the standard simulation engines of Sparx EA can be used to interact with each machine individually. Source code is automatically generated from such ESM models, which is then executed/debugged. It is possible to generate source code in Ada, JavaScript, Java, C, C++ and C#. The source code contains the implementation of the behavioral engine of state diagrams, for example the pool of events for each state machine, the dispatching method and so on. Once designed, a system composed of several interacting state machines can be simulated interactively, by sending triggers, to observe its behavior. The ESM is used for generating code, and the simulation gives an interactive graphical animation of the system being debugged. In this paper, we used Sparx EA unified edition version 15.2 build 1559.

2.2 UML Model Checker

The UML Model Checker (UMC) [11,20] is an open-access tool explicitly oriented to the fast prototyping of systems constituted by interacting state machines, developed at the Formal Methods and Tools Lab of ISTI-CNR. This tool can be easily accessed and used through its web interface at [5]. UMC allows the user to design a UML state machine using a simple textual notation, visualize the corresponding graphical representation, interactively animate the system evolutions, and formally verify (using on-the-fly model checking) UCTL [11] properties of the system behavior. Detailed explanations are given when a property is checked, when possible also in terms of simple UML sequence diagrams. With UMC it is possible to check if/how a given transition is eventually fired, if/when a certain signal is sent, if/when a certain variable is modified, or if/when a certain state is reached.

In UMC a system is specified as a set of interacting objects. Objects are instances of Classes and are possibly customized at instantiation time with specific parameters. Classes describe the behavior of their instances in the form of UML state machines. There are a few restrictions on the UML notation supported by UMC. The most important are the absence of entry/exit /do fields inside states, the absence of history/deep history/junction and choice states, and the absence of numerical types other than integers. The formal semantics of UMC models is provided by an incremental construction of a doubly labeled transition system (L2TS) [11]. In this L2TS, nodes correspond to the composition of the internal states of the objects in the system, and each edge corresponds to an object run-to-completion step. States of the L2TS can be enriched with labels that make visible the values of the local variables of the objects. Edges of the L2TS can be enriched with information on the actions executed as part of the run-to-completion step of the evolving state machine or with the label associated with the executing transition. The supported logic is called UCTL [11]: it is an ACTL-like, state- and event-based, branching time logic that supports the typical operators (e.g., eventually, globally, next, until and fix points). In [4] a more detailed interactive presentation of the supported grammar for the models and the logical properties is available.

UMC is an on-the-fly model checker. It generates the state space (L2TS) only for the fragments needed to evaluate the formula in a top-down way, starting from the initial state and the outermost level of the formula. The validity or invalidity of a formula can be analyzed interactively by traversing the L2TS graph that explains the result. Linear sequences of verification steps can be displayed also in the graphical form of a message sequence chart.

UMC is an academic tool that is primarily used for research and teaching. A comparison of UMC with other tools can be found in [17]. In these experiments, we made use of UMC version 4.9 (2024).

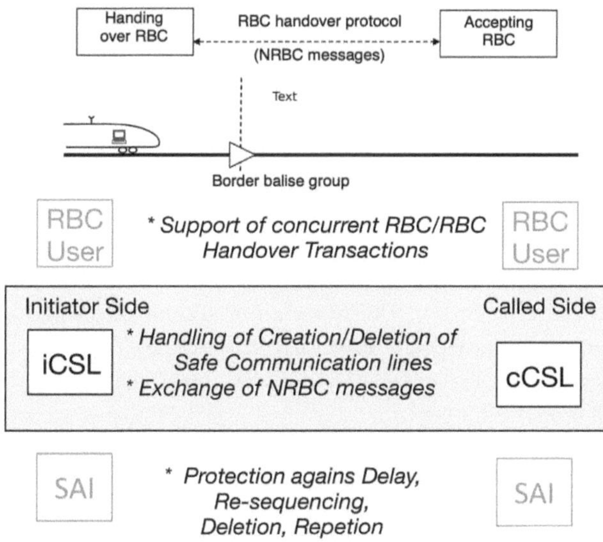

Fig. 1. The overall structure of the handover protocol

2.3   Case Study

The chosen case study is a subset of the RBC/RBC handover protocol [30, 31]. The RBC/RBC handover is a crucial aspect of the ERTMS/ETCS train control system, in which a Radio Block Centre (RBC) manages trains under its area of supervision. An RBC is a wireless component of the wayside train control system that manages trains inside its assigned geographic area (i.e., the area of supervision). When a train approaches the end of an RBC's area of supervision, a handover procedure with the neighboring RBC must take place to manage the transfer of control responsibilities. This exchange of information is supported by the communication layer specified within the documents: UNISIG SUBSET-039 [31], UNISIG SUBSET-098 [30], and the whole stack is implemented by both sides of the communication channel.

Figure 1 summarizes the overall relation between the components of the handover protocol. The RBC/RBC communication system consists of two sides that are respectively configured as "initiator" and "called". Each side is composed of levels. For example, the RBC User level is responsible for handling concurrent handover transactions involving multiple trains. The Communication Supervision Layer (CSL) of the SUBSET-039 and the Safe Application Intermediate SubLayer (SAI) of the SUBSET-098 support, respectively, the creation/deletion of safe communications and the protection of the transmission of messages exchanged. In particular, the CSL is responsible for requesting the activation – and in the event of failure, the reestablishment – of the communication, for controlling its liveliness, and for forwarding the handover transaction messages. The RBC User communicates with the CSL, and the CSL with the SAI. The SAI of the two sides communicate with each other through lower levels not reported here for brevity.

In this paper, we focus on the CSL model and show all the details of its initiator side (ICSL). In other words, the SAI, the communication network, and the RBC User are considered as the environment of the modeled CSL (both for initiator and called sides). The called side (CCSL) is also modelled, and can be inspected at [7]. It is not shown here for reasons of space.

The CSL specification is highly parametric. In particular, its behavior strictly depends on the delay values used for transmitting live signals, for triggering the reset of the communications in the absence of signals from the other side, and for triggering the restart of the connection process. Together with the modeling of the environment, the instantiation of these parameters becomes part of the scenarios under analysis.

The state machine modeling the ICSL is provided both as a formal model in UMC (see Fig. 2) and as a semi-formal model in Sparx EA (see Fig. 3). These two models are related through a mapping described in [10], and the difference relies on the underlying semantics of the two tools (formal and semi-formal). Each transition is labeled with a name (e.g., R1) to keep track of the correspondence between the two models. In both Fig. 2 and Fig. 3 transitions from R1 to R4 are grouped to enhance readability. The send and receive operations are represented, respectively, by the trigger and effect of a transition label (see Sect. 2). Communications are asynchronous and each state machine has a FIFO buffer.

The ICSL state machine is made up of two states NOCOMMS (the two RBC are disconnected) and COMMS (the two RBC are connected). The initial state is NOCOMMS. From the state NOCOMMS, a counter connect_timer is incremented at each reception of a TICK signal from the clock (R6) (note that the model is not real time and the length of the interval of time between ticks is not modelled).

If the threshold max_connect_timer is reached, a request for connection SAI_CONNECT_request is signaled to the SAI (which will be forwarded to the called CSL (CCSL)), and the counter is reset (R5).

The signal of connection SAI_CONNECT_confirm (signaling the connection of the CSL) coming from the SAI triggers the transition to state COMMS (R7). In state COMMS two counters are used. A counter receive_timer is used to keep track of the last message received. A counter send_timer is used to keep track of the last time a message was sent. These counters are incremented at the reception of a signal from the clock (R9). Each time a message is received from the SAI, the receive_timer is reset (R11,R12). Moreover, if the message is not of type LifeSign, it is forwarded to the user (R11). Similarly, if a message is received from the user, it is forwarded to the SAI (R8), and the send_timer is reset. Whenever the threshold max_send_timer is reached (R10), a LifeSign message is sent to the SAI (which will be forwarded to the CCSL) and send_timer is reset. This message is used to check if the connection is still up. Whenever the threshold max_receive_timer is reached, the connection is closed because no message has been received within the maximum allowed time. In this case, a disconnection

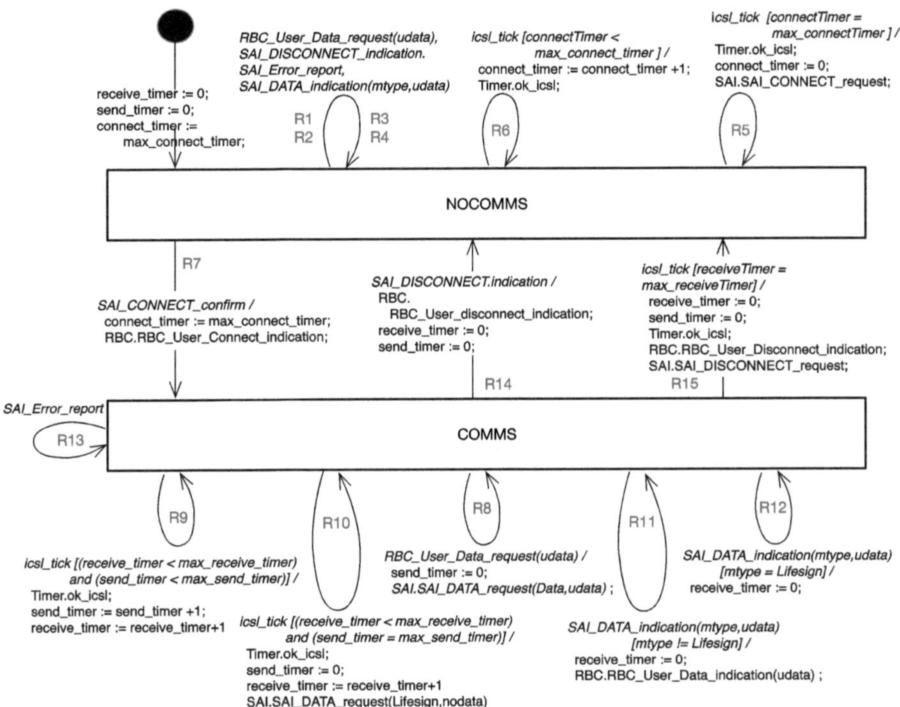

Fig. 2. The Initiator Communication Supervision Layer State Machine of UMC

signal is sent to both the user and the SAI (R15). If the disconnection message is received from the SAI (R14), then it is only forwarded to the user and the connection is closed.

3   The Different Roles and Structure of UMC and Sparx EA Environments

Starting from the initial requirements in natural language, UMC has been used to develop a clear, correct, and executable UML design. In fact, several ambiguities and uncertainties were identified and corrected during the UMC design process.

This executable UMC description is already at a lower level than the higher-level natural language requirements. For example, if we consider transition R15 in Fig. 2, the original natural language requirements stated that:

> "when ICSL is in the COMMS state, if the receive timer expires, a disconnect indication is sent to the user, and a disconnect request is sent to the SAI".

Nothing is said about the order in which these two messages should be sent. Nothing is specifically stated about how the timer expiration should be observed (here, we have used an integer **receive_timer** variable periodically incremented

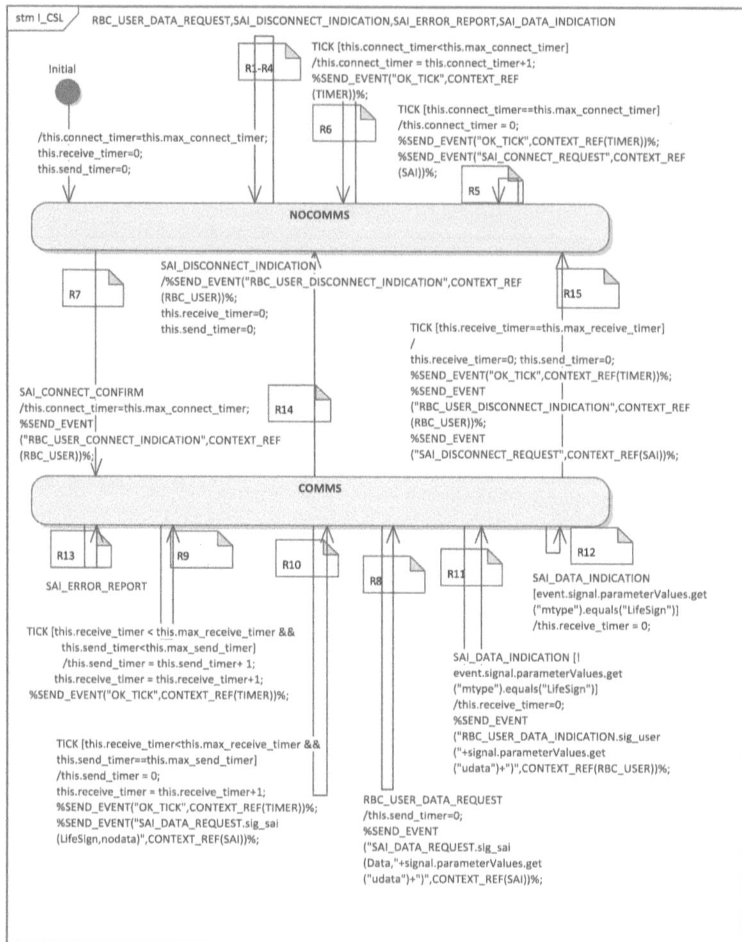

Fig. 3. The Initiator Communication Supervision Layer State Machine of Sparx EA

by tick events generated by a Timer component), and nothing is said about resetting the **receive_timer** variable. In particular, the choice to reset this variable immediately—rather than, for example, when reentering the COMMS state and restarting the timer—was made to avoid unnecessary growth of the state space during verification. We decided to adopt the same implementation choices in Sparx EA to preserve, as much as possible, a strict coherence between the two platforms. In Sect. 5, we will discuss some limitations and challenges ahead for this kind of choice.

In UMC, all nondeterministic aspects of UML are preserved and considered. All components are modeled as concurrent, and all possible interleavings among them are explored. This is the correct approach if we aim to verify the correctness of UML designs in an abstract way. However, Sparx EA uses a deterministic execution engine to execute the system components, making proprietary decisions to resolve all nondeterministic aspects of UML. The Sparx choice might be reasonable from the standpoint of constructing a sequential system that should be as deterministic as possible, to simplify monitoring and testing. However, it is important that the design is also proved correct at the more generic UMC level. This ensures that future changes in internal code generation or system simulation details will not affect the correctness of the system. From a documentation standpoint, it is also important that the correctness of the state machine diagrams describing the system does not rely on hidden assumptions about the underlying execution engine. Of course—as will be described in more detail in the next section—not all UMC executions will be repeatable in the Sparx EA setting.

UMC requires the presence of a complete, closed system to analyze all possible system evolutions. This necessitates the generation of usually nondeterministic environment stubs in addition to the specific components under design. In our case, the environment stubs that must be composed with the two initiator and called CSL components are those modeling the RBC Users, the lower levels of communication (SAI and network levels), and a Timer.

Sparx EA, instead, allows us to stimulate a system component through direct user interactions via the GUI, triggering a specific execution trace. In this case, only the code of the component under development needs to be generated, and it is the user's task to provide all the missing interactions from the RBC User, the SAI components, the Timer, and the network. Some "sink" stubs may still be needed to receive outgoing signals from the CSL components. Note that nothing prevents us from encoding in Sparx the same environment stubs as the ones used in the UMC context, but their execution within the Sparx simulation environment would be subject to all the internal deterministic choices of the execution engine, making them scarcely useful for modeling purposes. When more than one component is involved, several execution steps may be performed before control is returned to the user.

4   Comparing Model Checking and Simulations

In this section, we will analyze scenarios where it is not possible to replicate the outcome of the model checking phase (i.e., the trace) as simulations. Indeed, even if the correspondence between models is sound, this is still possible since UMC overapproximates all possible behaviors of Sparx EA.

All models are available at [7].

Example of Traces not Reproducible in Sparx EA. We consider a scenario in which the RBC User on the initiator side (as shown in Fig. 4) may nondeterministically decide to send a data request to the initiating CSL, but only if it is in a connected status (i.e., after having received from CSL a connect indication without any subsequent disconnect indication).

In this scenario, when the CSL is in state COMMS and the RBC User connected variable is true, two different signals could arrive at the CSL: a data request from the initiator RBC User, and a disconnect indication from the SAI. Both events are stored in the buffer of the initiator CSL before it can process any of them. In this case, a possible system evolution might be that the disconnect

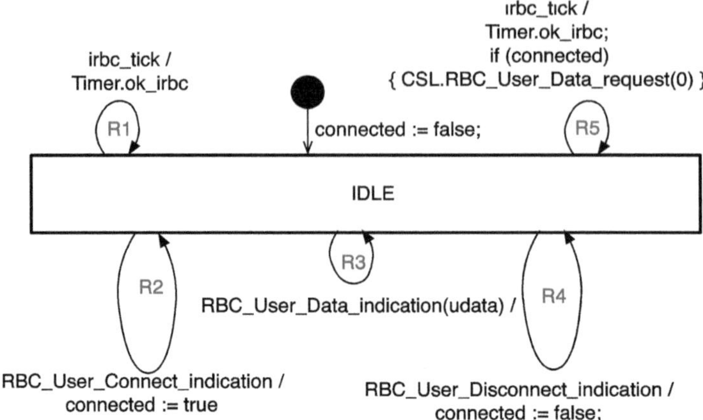

Fig. 4. The UMC state machine of the RBC User of the initiator side for the second example

indication is treated as first, changing the CSL state to NOCOMMS and forwarding a disconnect indication to the RBC User. At this point, the RBC user data request is dispatched from the event queue. In this case, being the CSL in state NOCOMMS, the signal is discarded.

This evolution is clearly represented by the sequence diagram in Fig. 5,[1] which can be produced, for example, when UMC evalutes the formula:

$$EF\{R1\_ICSL\_discard\_userdata\}$$

This formula checks whether there exists an execution in which the transition R1 of the initiator CSL is eventually fired (for brevity, in Fig. 2 the transitions are labelled with abbreviations of the original labels, e.g., R1 instead of R1_ICSL_discard_userdata).

To reproduce the trace in Sparx EA, the Sparx user assumes the role of the environment (in this case, the RBC User and the SAI). However, in the Sparx EA simulator, it is not possible for the interactive user to send to (and enqueue in) the CSL two consecutive signals, because as soon as the first event is triggered, it immediately activates its corresponding transition. In particular, when the Sparx user sends the first signal SAI_DISCONNECT_indication, this will trigger a run-to-completion-cycle of the CSL that will execute the transition R14 of the initiator CSL (see Fig. 3). This will cause the immediate emission of the signal RBC_User_Disconnect_indication from the initiator CSL to the RBC User. Therefore, the last three interactions shown at the end of the trace in Fig. 5 (i.e., SAI_DISCONNECT_indication, RBC_User_Data_request, RBC_User_Disconnect_indication) appears not to be reproducible in Sparx EA.

---

[1] The event names appearing in the formulas and in the arrows of Fig. 5 denote the event of sending a signal (and its storage in the receiver's buffer), and not the event of picking up the message from the buffer as done by the receiver.

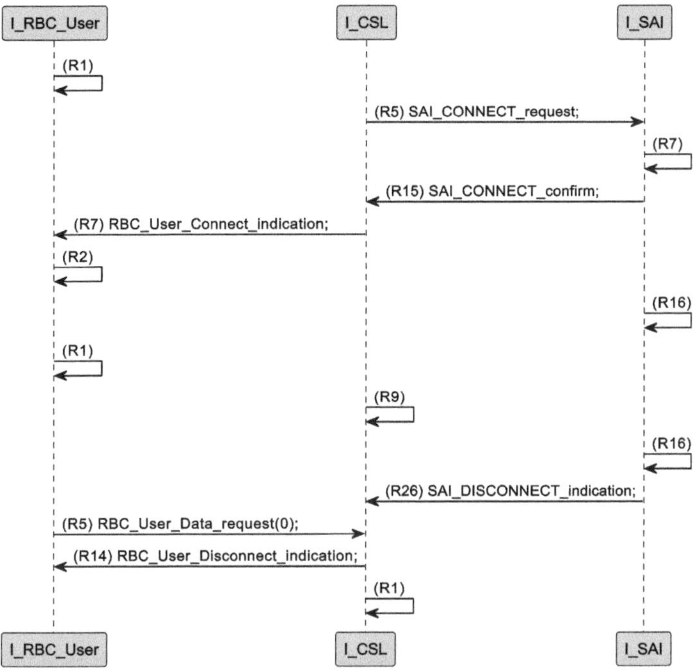

Fig. 5. The trace produced by UMC explaining the verification of the first example, not reproducible in Sparx EA

To precisely reproduce this scenario, it would be necessary for the Sparx user to send two signals to the CSL (one coming from the SAI and one coming from the RBC User) before the system executes the run-to-completion.

Example of a Formal Verification that does not Produce Any Trace. The model checking of certain formal properties (e.g. reachability) produces a trace indicating whether the property holds. However, there are instances where a formal property is confirmed (or not) to hold in the model, yet no single trace can be given as explanation. This occurs when the successful proof of a universal formula (or the counterexample of an existential formula) can be described only by reporting a complex fragment of state space of the model, usually in the form of a tree or subgraph, rather than just a single trace. Consider, for example, the following property:

```
AG(
    [IRBC_User_Connect_indication](
      A[{not IRBC_User_Connect_indication}
      W{IRBC_User_Disconnect_indication}]))
```

The formula makes use of three temporal operators: `AG phi1` stating that subformula `phi1` should hold for all states reachable from the current one; where `phi1=[cond2] phi2` stating that subformula `phi2` should hold for all states reachable after a transition satisfying `cond2` (if any); and `phi2=A[ {cond3} W phi3 ]` stating that for all paths starting from the current state the transitions should satisfy the condition `cond3` until a state is reached that satisfies the subformula `phi3` (if ever found).

This property asserts that whenever the RBC User receives a connect indication (from the CSL), no other connect indication will be received until a disconnected indication is received. The weak until operator `W` specifies that it could also be the case that no disconnect indication will ever be received by the RBC User. We verify this formula using the previous scenario. The property is formally verified by UMC to hold in the model. However, no single trace is sufficient to prove that this formula holds. In fact, UMC necessitates visiting the whole state space, which consists of 51303 states, to prove the formula.

In summary, whenever a universally quantified property is verified not to hold or an existentially quantified property is verified to hold, a trace (generated by UMC) exists to witness the verification. In such cases, it is possible to test whether the same trace also exists in the Sparx EA simulation. However, for other formulas, one can only rely on UMC for formal property verification. In this case, formal verification is useful in providing guarantees that would otherwise be hard to obtain solely by relying on the semi-formal Sparx EA model.

Example of an Infinite Trace. Finally, it could also be the case that the formal verification produces, as witness, an infinite trace. For example, consider the following property:

$$EF\{IRBC\_User\_Connect\_indication\}$$
$$(EG\{not\,IRBC\_User\_Disconnect\_indication\})$$

The formula makes use of two temporal operators: `EF {cond1} phi1` stating that there exists a state reachable from the current one with a transition satisfying `cond1` that lead to to a state satisfying `phi1`; and `phi1=EG {cond2}` stating that there exists a path starting from the current state whose transitions continuously satisfy `cond2`.

This property asserts that there exists a trace where the RBC User receives a connect indication (from the CSL), and subsequently, it may never receive a disconnect indication from the CSL. In other words, in the model, it is possible that the connection remains open forever.

The formal verification produces two sequence diagrams that explain the two nestings in the formula. The first sequence diagram illustrates the connection phase (not shown here). The second sequence diagram is shown in Fig. 6. Figure 6 contains an infinite loop, within which the initiator CSL continuously exchanges life signals with the other side. Therefore, it is not possible to entirely reproduce this trace in Sparx EA, but only a finite fragment of it. Moreover Sparx EA does

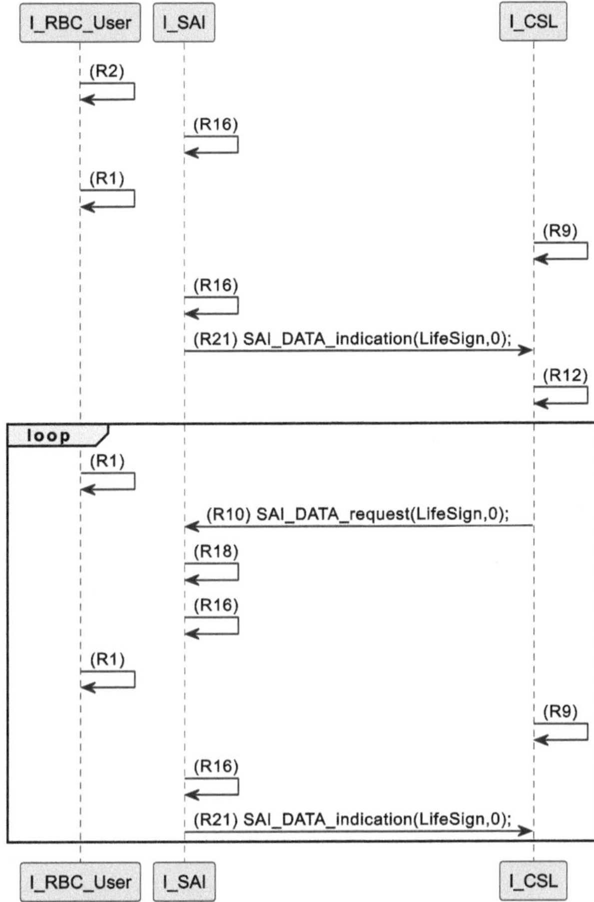

Fig. 6. An infinite trace generated by UMC

not provide the user with any help for detecting that during trace simulation we have encountered a state already seen in the same trace, therefore it becomes very difficult to understand when just a trace fragment would be sufficient.

In summary, formal verification encompasses infinite behavior that is not reproducible solely by relying on the interactive simulation capabilities of Sparx EA.

The Role of the Environment. The modeling of the environment is peculiar to the formal verification performed in UMC, while it may not be necessary for interactive simulations. In fact, during the interactive simulation, the Sparx user acts as the environment and sends signals to the state machines.

In the previous examples, the environment was used to model specific *scenarios* where the system is being analyzed. Another possible approach is to model a generic environment that does not implement any specific scenario. In this case,

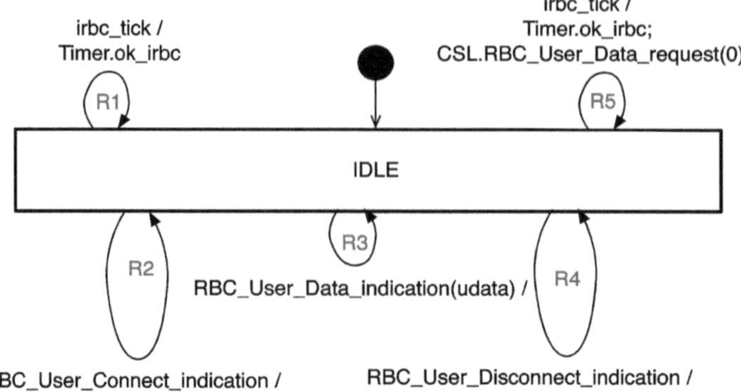

Fig. 7. The UMC state machine of a generic RBC User

the environment receives and discards all messages from the system and may nondeterministically send the available signals to the system.

The advantage of having a generic environment is that it encompasses all the behavior that can be manifested by any specific scenario. Therefore, a safety property (i.e., ensuring that nothing bad ever happens) verified to hold using the generic environment will also hold for any specifically modeled scenario. The disadvantage is that many false positives may be present, i.e., behavior manifested by the environment that is not present in the real system. The over-approximation of a generic environment may also increase the state space during formal analysis.

Consider again the first example discussed in this section (i.e., an example of traces not reproducible in Sparx EA). We replace a portion of the environment, specifically the RBC User depicted in Fig. 4, with a generic component shown in Fig. 7. The RBC User in Fig. 7 is generic: it receives and discards all signals, and nondeterministically sends signals to the system. By comparing these two RBC User components, we observe that the generic RBC User may send a signal to the CSL at any time, even when disconnected. This is an example of over-approximation: in the real system, data request signals will only be emitted when the user is connected.

We demonstrate how the verification using this generic environment impacts our analysis. Firstly, in the original example (without replacing the RBC User), the overall state space of the entire model consists of 9495 states. By switching to the generic RBC User, we observe a deterioration in the size of the state space, which now consists of 10336 states. Note that we only generalized a single component of the environment. Moreover, the formal verification of the property

$$\texttt{EF\{R1\_ICSL\_discard\_userdata\}}$$

produces a trace shown in Fig. 8. In this case, the generated trace is not significant as it represents a false positive. Indeed, the trace simply shows an execution where the disconnected RBC User sends a data request to the disconnected CSL, which discards it. This trace is not significant because in the real system it will never occur.

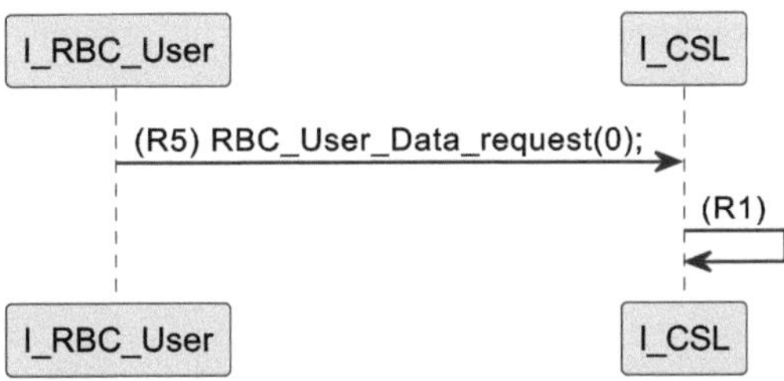

Fig. 8. The trace produced by UMC using a generic RBC User component

In summary, adopting an environment that models specific scenarios has proven to be more effective. Indeed, when switching to a generic environment, the results of formal verification may not be significant (i.e., false positives), and the performance (i.e., the state space) may deteriorate. In addition, the presence of false positives makes the discovery of true positives (if any) more difficult. The risk of not covering unexpected errors is a downside.

In the Sparx EA context, since it is the user who directly triggers the environment events, both approaches (generic user and specific user) can be easily simulated.

The use of a "generic" environment could actually be useful in evaluating the robustness of a component, even in the presence of misbehavior by the environment or other components. Indeed, transitions R1 to R4 (see Fig. 2) have been introduced to model that messages arriving at the wrong time are simply discarded and have no effect on the system.

The diagram in Fig. 2 does not explicitly describe what should happen if a `SAI_CONNECT_confirm` message arrives when the ICSL is already in the `COMMS` state. This is a situation that should be impossible in the real system but can still be triggered by user interactions in Sparx EA or by a generic ISAI stub in UMC. In any case, the UML semantics requires that the message must be discarded, but this fact is left implicit in the design. It is a design choice whether or not to make this kind of behavior explicit in the diagram. During the UMC analysis, such situations (i.e., messages implicitly discarded because they do not immediately trigger a transition when dispatched) can be identified and flagged as possible design errors.

5   Limitations and Future Research Directions

We now discuss the limitations and future research directions.

5.1 Parallelism and Atomicity

We recall that a run-to-completion of a UML state machine consists of the execution of different actions. Internally to each state machine, the run-to-completion steps appear to be executed atomically (even in the presence of parallel regions of states). Externally, when different state machines are executed in parallel, the external effects (e.g., signals) produced by different run-to-completions of different state machines may overlap and interfere. For example, this may occur when a transition of a UML state machine sends several signals (e.g., the transition R15 of the initiator CSL in Fig. 2). At the system level, the sending of these signals may interleave with signals sent by other state machines.

Currently, in the latest version of UMC, the external effects of different state machines' run-to-completions are never interleaved. Therefore, some behaviors that could be observable in the real system are not reproduced by UMC.

This is a current limit of UMC that should be overcome in future releases.

A temporary solution to this problem is to require that the effects of transitions of state machines not contain more than one communication action. This may force the splitting of a transition that sends several messages (e.g., R15 in Fig. 2) into a sequence of transitions, each sending only one message.

5.2 Differences Between Modelling Activities

The modelling activities concerning formal verification and software development, although being related, also present differences. Indeed, formal verification may require the generation of the state space, as in model checking. In this case, optimizations may be performed during modeling to reduce the state space. On the other hand, in software development, rules are followed to maintain clarity and readability of the models. These rules may be conflicting with the optimizations performed for formal verification. As already discussed in Sect. 3, consider for example the case of resetting a variable. In a model used for code generation, the variable should be reset only when strictly necessary to avoid unnecessary instructions. Conversely, in a model used for formal verification, a variable is reset as soon as possible to keep the state space from growing. We note that these changes are made in a way that does not affect the overall semantics of the model.

For example, consider Fig. 2. The variables `send_timer` and `reset_timer` are reset after moving from state `COMMS` to state `NOCOMMS`. This guarantees that, whenever the system is in state `NOCOMMS`, both variables have value zero. However, the reset operation is only needed when entering state `COMMS`. Thus, for readability, the reset should only be performed when entering the state `COMMS`, instead of being anticipated earlier. Therefore, the related model used for the development and code generation (i.e. Sparx EA) may need to be slightly adjusted to adhere to readability and other model-based development guidelines (e.g., in Fig. 3 the reset of the two variables should be moved to R7).

5.3 Automatic Translations and Sparx EA Profile for Model Checking

It might be interesting to exploit model checking on the same specific Sparx EA executable model, and not only on the abstract UML designs. To achieve this goal, two problems should be dealt with:

1. The model should be automatically regenerated from the Sparx EA model (probably by exploiting the XMI export feature of Sparx).
2. A Sparx EA profile should be introduced in UMC that constrains all the nondeterministic aspects in precisely the same way as Sparx EA does at runtime. This would require a deep analysis of Sparx EA's behavior but might actually be of great help for analyzing the actual executable system.

5.4 Sparx EA Custom Runtime

Another possibility that could be investigated is the manipulation of the default Sparx EA engine managing the deterministic choices that affect the allowed system execution traces, by introducing pseudo-random or user-guided choices instead of fixed ones. In this case, the generated code would not be suitable for the real product but could serve as a tool for more extensive testing and more controlled simulations of the system.

6 Conclusion

We have analyzed some of the benefits provided by the formal verification activity compared to interactive simulations. The tools adopted were an academic formal verification tool, UML Model Checker (UMC), and an industrial model-based development tool, Sparx Enterprise Architect (Sparx EA). This analysis is part of growing interest in the integration of formal techniques within industrial tools for the development of safety-critical systems. The selected case study belongs to the railway domain.

We have shown that formal verification enhances validation based solely on interactive simulations. We have analyzed instances where the exclusive use of interactive simulation cannot replicate the formal verification activity. From this experience, we have derived some future research directions.

Extensions to UMC are needed to manage parallelism and atomicity in the execution of run-to-completion steps of different state machines. Concerning other comparison points, a systematic evaluation (as previously done in [17]) is left for future work. Another direction is researching modeling approaches that balance modeling activities oriented towards formal verification and software development, and developing methodologies for the transformation of models between these two purposes. Finally, a custom Sparx EA profile and custom runtime could be exploited to align the execution traces of the two tools.

Acknowledgements. Part of this study was carried out within the MOST – Sustainable Mobility National Research Center and received funding from the European Union Next-GenerationEU (Piano Nazionale di Ripresa e Resilienza (PNRR) – Missione 4 Componente 2, Investimento 1.4 – D.D. 1033 17/06/2022, CN00000023), and the MUR PRIN 2022 PNRR P2022A492B project ADVENTURE (ADVancEd iNtegraTed evalUation of Railway systEms) funded by the European Union - NextGenerationEU.

References

1. Dassault Cameo Systems Modeler. https://www.3ds.com/products-services/catia/products/no-magic/cameo-systems-modeler/. Accessed Apr 2025
2. PTC Windchill Modeler SySim. https://www.ptc.com/en/products/windchill. Accessed Apr 2025
3. Sparx Systems Enterprise Architect. https://sparxsystems.com/products/ea/index.html. Accessed Apr 2025
4. UMC interactive syntax help. http://fmt.isti.cnr.it/umc/V4.9/sdhelp.html
5. UMC project website. http://fmt.isti.cnr.it/umc
6. André, É., Liu, S., Liu, Y., Choppy, C., Sun, J., Dong, J.S.: Formalizing UML state machines for automated verification-a survey. ACM Comput. Surv. (2023). https://doi.org/10.1145/3579821
7. Basile, D., Mazzanti, F.: Comparing UMC Model Checking and Sparx EA Simulation - Complementary Material (2025). https://doi.org/10.5281/zenodo.17045133
8. Basile, D., ter Beek, M.H., Ferrari, A., Legay, A.: Modelling and analysing ERTMS L3 moving block railway signalling with simulink and UPPAAL SMC. In: Larsen, K.G., Willemse, T. (eds.) FMICS 2019. LNCS, vol. 11687, pp. 1–21. Springer, Cham (2019). https://doi.org/10.1007/978-3-030-27008-7_1
9. Basile, D., Fantechi, A., Rosadi, I.: Formal analysis of the UNISIG safety application intermediate sub-layer. In: Lluch Lafuente, A., Mavridou, A. (eds.) FMICS 2021. LNCS, vol. 12863, pp. 174–190. Springer, Cham (2021). https://doi.org/10.1007/978-3-030-85248-1_11
10. Basile, D., Mazzanti, F., Ferrari, A.: Experimenting with formal verification and model-based development in railways: the case of UMC and sparx enterprise architect. In: Cimatti, A., Titolo, L. (eds.) Formal Methods for Industrial Critical Systems - 28th International Conference, FMICS 2023, Antwerp, Belgium, 20–22 September 2023, Proceedings. LNCS, vol. 14290, pp. 1–21. Springer, Cham (2023). https://doi.org/10.1007/978-3-031-43681-9_1
11. ter Beek, M.H., Fantechi, A., Gnesi, S., Mazzanti, F.: A state/event-based model-checking approach for the analysis of abstract system properties. Sci. Comput. Program. **76**(2), 119–135 (2011). https://doi.org/10.1016/j.scico.2010.07.002
12. Belli, D., Mazzanti, F.: A case study in formal analysis of system requirements. In: Masci, P., Bernardeschi, C., Graziani, P., Koddenbrock, M., Palmieri, M. (eds.) SEFM Workshops. LNCS, vol. 13765, pp. 164–173. Springer, Cham (2022). https://doi.org/10.1007/978-3-031-26236-4_14
13. Bendisposto, J., et al.: ProB 2.0 tutorial. In: Butler, M., Hallerstede, S., Waldén, M. (eds.) Proceedings of the 4th Rodin User and Developer Workshop. TUCS Lecture Notes, Turku Centre for Computer Science (2013)

14. Bouwman, M., Luttik, B., van der Wal, D.: A formalisation of SysML state machines in mCRL2. In: Peters, K., Willemse, T.A.C. (eds.) FORTE 2021. LNCS, vol. 12719, pp. 42–59. Springer, Cham (2021). https://doi.org/10.1007/978-3-030-78089-0_3

15. Butler, M., et al.: The first twenty-five years of industrial use of the B-method. In: ter Beek, M.H., Ničković, D. (eds.) FMICS 2020. LNCS, vol. 12327, pp. 189–209. Springer, Cham (2020). https://doi.org/10.1007/978-3-030-58298-2_8

16. Champelovier, D., et al.: Reference manual of the LOTOS NT toLOTOS translator (2023). https://cadp.inria.fr/ftp/publications/cadp/Champelovier-Clerc-Garavel-et-al-10.pdf. Accessed Jan 2024

17. Ferrari, A., Mazzanti, F., Basile, D., ter Beek, M.H.: Systematic evaluation and usability analysis of formal methods tools for railway signaling system design. IEEE Trans. Softw. Eng. **48**(11), 4675–4691 (2022). https://doi.org/10.1109/TSE.2021.3124677

18. Garavel, H., Lang, F., Mateescu, R., Serwe, W.: CADP 2011: a toolbox for the construction and analysis of distributed processes. Int. J. Softw. Tools Technol. Transf. **15**(2), 89–107 (2013). https://doi.org/10.1007/s10009-012-0244-z

19. Garavel, H., Lang, F., Serwe, W.: From LOTOS to LNT. In: Katoen, J.-P., Langerak, R., Rensink, A. (eds.) ModelEd, TestEd, TrustEd. LNCS, vol. 10500, pp. 3–26. Springer, Cham (2017). https://doi.org/10.1007/978-3-319-68270-9_1

20. Gnesi, S., Mazzanti, F.: An abstract, on the fly framework for the verification of service-oriented systems. In: Wirsing, M., Hölzl, M. (eds.) Rigorous Software Engineering for Service-Oriented Systems. LNCS, vol. 6582, pp. 390–407. Springer, Heidelberg (2011). https://doi.org/10.1007/978-3-642-20401-2_18

21. Horváth, B., et al.: Pragmatic verification and validation of industrial executable sysml models. Syst. Eng. (2023). https://doi.org/10.1002/sys.21679

22. Mazzanti, F., Belli, D.: Formal modeling and initial analysis of the 4SECURail case study. In: Proceedings of Fifth Workshop on Models for Formal Analysis of Real Systems (MARS), Munich, Germany, 2nd April 2022, pp. 118–144. Springer, Cham (2022). https://doi.org/10.4204/EPTCS.355.6

23. Mazzanti, F., Belli, D.: The 4SECURail formal methods demonstrator. In: Dutilleul, S.C., Haxthausen, A.E., Lecomte, T. (eds.) RSSRail. LNCS, vol. 13294, pp. 149–165. Springer, Cham (2022). https://doi.org/10.1007/978-3-031-05814-1_11

24. Object Management Group: Unified Modelling Language (2017). https://www.omg.org/spec/UML/About-UML/

25. Object Management Group: OMG Systems Modeling Language (OMG SysML) (2019). http://www.omg.org/spec/SysML/1.6/

26. Salunkhe, S., Berglehner, R., Rasheeq, A.: Automatic transformation of SysML model to event-B model for Railway CCS application. In: Raschke, A., Méry, D. (eds.) ABZ 2021. LNCS, vol. 12709, pp. 143–149. Springer, Cham (2021). https://doi.org/10.1007/978-3-030-77543-8_14

27. Snook, C.F., Butler, M.J.: UML-B: formal modeling and design aided by UML. ACM Trans. Softw. Eng. Methodol. **15**(1), 92–122 (2006). https://doi.org/10.1145/1125808.1125811

28. Snook, C.F., Butler, M.J., Hoang, T.S., Fathabadi, A.S., Dghaym, D.: Developing the UML-B modelling tools. In: Masci, P., Bernardeschi, C., Graziani, P., Koddenbrock, M., Palmieri, M. (eds.) SEFM Workshops. LNCS, vol. 13765, pp. 181–188. Springer, Cham (2022). https://doi.org/10.1007/978-3-031-26236-4_16

29. Stramaglia, A., Keiren, J.J.A.: Formal verification of an industrial UML-like model using mCRL2. In: Groote, J.F., Huisman, M. (eds.) FMICS. LNCS, vol. 13487, pp. 86–102. Springer, Cham (2022). https://doi.org/10.1007/978-3-031-15008-1_7
30. UNISIG: RBC-RBC Safe Communication Interface – SUBSET-098 (2012). https://www.era.europa.eu/system/files/2023-01/sos3_index063_-_subset-098_v300.pdf. Accessed Apr 2025
31. UNISIG: FIS for the RBC/RBC Handover – SUBSET-039 (2015). https://www.era.europa.eu/system/files/2023-01/sos3_index012_-_subset-039_v320.pdf. Accessed Apr 2025

Communication and Control

CPN-Based Modelling to Assess Dependability of Train-to-Train Wireless Communication for Virtual Coupling

Getachew Hagos Geleta[1]([⊠]) [iD], Marion Berbineau[1] [iD],
Simon Collart-Dutilleul[2] [iD], and Francesco Flammini[3,4] [iD]

[1] COSYS-LEOST, Université Gustave Eiffel, Villeneuve d'Ascq, France
`{getachew-hagos.geleta,marion.bernibeau}@univ-eiffel.fr`
[2] COSYS-ESTAS, Université Gustave Eiffel, Villeneuve d'Ascq, France
`simon.collart-dutilleul@univ-eiffel.fr`
[3] IDSIA USI-SUPSI, University of Applied Sciences and Arts of Southern
Switzerland, Lugano, Switzerland
`francesco.flammini@supsi.ch`
[4] DIMAI, University of Florence, Florence, Italy
`francesco.flammini@unifi.it`

Abstract. Virtual Coupling of Train Sets (VCTS) offers a promising way to boost railway capacity and flexibility, but it demands reliable, high-performance and safe wireless communication between trains and control centres, as well as between train sets. Current centralized systems like Euroradio are not suited for VCTS's decentralized architecture, making a dedicated safety layer essential. This paper presents a Coloured Petri Net (CPN)-based framework to assess the reliability of Train-to-Train (T2T) communication, focusing on 5G NR V2X. After introducing VCTS architecture and dependability analysis methods, we detail our CPN model and performance metrics. Simulations reveal that higher message loss rates (MLR) significantly reduce reliability, highlighting the need for robust error handling. In the absence of VCTS-specific requirements for the wireless communication performance, we use automotive benchmarks (3GPP V2X, 5G AA) for evaluation. Under low MLR, the system meets these performance criteria.

Keywords: Virtual Coupling of Train Set (VCTS) · Train-to-Train (T2T) · Coloured Petri Nets (CPN) · Train Control and Monitoring System (TCMS) · Cooperative Awareness Message (CAM) · Dependability Analysis

1 Introduction

As railways move toward automation, Virtual Coupling of Train Sets (VCTS) emerges as a key innovation, allowing trains to travel closely and in sync—like autonomous convoys—without physical coupling. This boosts line capacity

[1] [2] [3] and requires a moving block system, a dynamic safety zone updated via real-time data. Trains exchange critical information (speed, location, braking) through Cooperative Awareness Messages (CAM) to maintain safe spacing. However, VCTS relies on highly reliable communication, both Train-to-Train (T2T) and Train-to-Ground (T2G). Real-world conditions (tunnels, vegetation, interference, and speed)can disrupt signals, posing risks to system dependability.

Several European research projects, such as R2DATO, and IAM4RAIL are actively exploring the VCTS concept and related communication technologies, including the Wireless Train Backbone [4]. Within the CONNECTA project, CAF has demonstrated the concept [5]. Whatever the chosen wireless system, a dedicated safety layer should be added in the application layer. Existing safety protocol, such as Euroradio for centralized train-to-ground communication, is not suitable to support the decentralized nature of VCTS. This paper presents a preliminary model for T2T communications considering 5G side link (V2X) technology. The model is developed using Coloured Petri Nets IDE (CPN IDE). The rest of this paper is organized as follows. Section 2 introduces the VCTS architecture and illustrates how trains function within a virtual coupling setup, exploring the underlying processes. Section 3 discusses the hurdles of wireless communication in rail environments and explains the European safety standards. Section 4 presents the main different methods used to analyse dependability and reviews current research and related technologies focusing on Coloured Petri Nets. Section 5 explains the use of Coloured Petri Nets for modelling T2T communication and presents the equations and definitions for the current considered metrics. Section 6 discusses the simulation results. Section 7 summarises the conclusions and future works.

2   Virtual Coupling Train Set Description

VCTS system combines onboard sensors, communication modules, and control systems to achieve accurate synchronisation and maintain operational safety [6]. It enables multiple trains to function as a single coordinated unit while ensuring a safe separation is maintained between them. An overview of the VCTS system architecture is illustrated in Fig. 1. It includes three main elements: an onboard subsystems, a communication network, a centralized control system. The onboard subsystems include the train control and monitoring system (TCMS) serving as the central intelligence of each train. The TCMS manages essential functions such as speed regulation, braking, and door operations. Within the VCTS framework, it is adapted to support inter-train communication and coordination. The communication network enables continuous data exchange between trains and with the ground-based systems, forming the backbone of the VCTS.

Figure 2 depicts the message exchange sequence involved in the VCTS between Train A and Train B. The process is initiated by the central control system (CCS), which dispatches virtual coupling procedures to evaluate whether the two trains are ready and compatible for coupling. As part of this assessment, both Train A (the lead train) and Train B (the following train) transmit

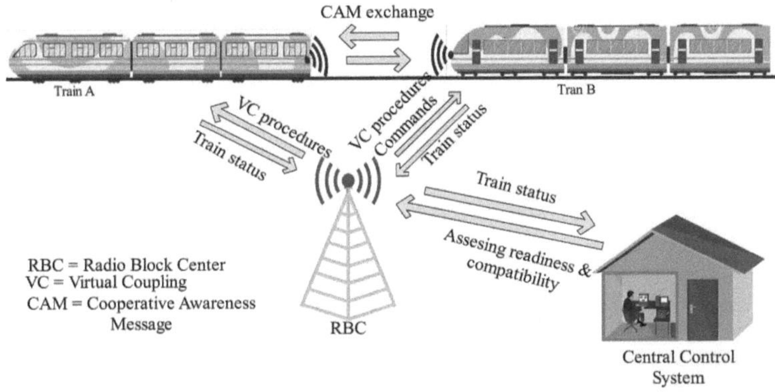

Fig. 1. Virtual Coupling Train Architecture

their operational data to the CCS. Upon verifying these parameters, the CCS instructs Train B to begin the virtual coupling. Train B then aligns its movement with Train A by continuously adjusting its parameters through real-time communication. This initial stage is critical to confirm that both trains are properly synchronized and that the communication link is stable.

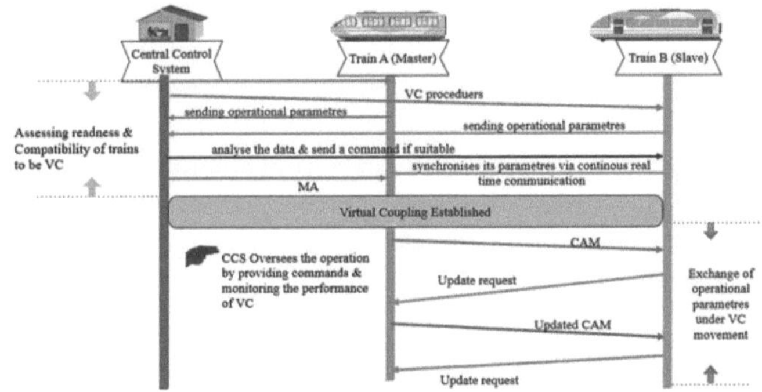

Fig. 2. Operation of trains under Virtual Coupling

After the virtual coupling is successfully established, Train A takes on the role of the master train (MT), while Train B operates as the slave train (ST) within the coupled formation. The CCS continues to supervise the process, issuing high-level commands, and monitoring the overall performance of the virtual link. Train A sends real-time updates, including its speed, position, and control instructions, to Train B through the wireless communication channel. Using these data, Train B continuously adjusts its speed and following distance to stay precisely aligned with Train A. During this phase, the system carefully monitors the end-to-end delay of messages exchanged between the trains. If a message does not reach its destination or becomes corrupted, a retransmission protocol is activated, prompting the sender to resend the message until the receiver confirms successful delivery with an acknowledgment. In order to respect safety rules, the message should be received within a given interval to avoid emergency braking.

3 Wireless Communications in the Rail Domain and Safety

3.1 Wireless Communications

Numerous wireless technologies have been explored for Vehicle-to-Vehicle (V2V) communication in platooning scenarios [7]. For Train-to-Train (T2T) communication, several options have been assessed, including LTE and LTE-V2X [8], millimeter-wave bands for high-speed V2V links [9], and ITS-G5 operating in the 5.8 GHz band [10]. All of these technologies have their own pros and cons in terms of latency, bandwidth, throughput, coverage capability, as summarized in [11]. For example, LTE-V2X can provide good coverage but may encounter latency issues in congested areas, while millimeter-wave technologies offer high data rates but are more vulnerable to environmental effects.

In this study, we consider the 5G sidelink standard (NR-V2X), which is currently under development. NR-V2X is aligned with the 5G New Radio (5G NR), the foundation of Future Railway Mobile Communication Systems (FRMCS) [12]. The performance of NR-V2X for T2T communication is influenced by various factors, including the distance between trains, potential masking effects, and possible interferences from surrounding wireless systems and nearby trains. The performance of wireless communication is measured considering key performance indicators (KPI) such as packet loss rate, end-to-end delay, and error-free throughput at the application level. These indicators can critically affect the transmission of time-sensitive information, such as braking commands or speed adjustments. Consequently, the safety level will also be affected.

3.2 Safety Aspects and Norms

The risk analysis phase plays a critical role in identifying and assessing potential hazards that may arise during a system's operational phase. In the railway industry, this process typically adheres to the EN 50126 and Common Safety Method for Risk Evaluation and Assessment (CSM-RA) standards [50126, 50126-2]. EN 50126 outlines the overall safety management framework, while CSM-RA provides specific regulatory guidance for implementation. For communication-specific safety in the railway domain, EN 50159 standard is [13]. It offers a structured approach for analysing and demonstrating the safety of communication systems used in railway operations. A distinctive feature of railway applications is that safety is inherently managed at the application level. Common message-related faults in such systems include repetition, deletion, insertion, sequencing, corruption, and masquerade. These types of error must be rigorously analysed and mitigated to ensure the safety and reliability of railway communication systems.

The safety of a system is evaluated with the safety integrity level (SIL) defined by the International Electrotechnical Commission's (IEC) standard IEC 61508, which concerns other domains than Railway. As mentioned previously, EN 50126, EN 50128, and EN 50129 standards are considered to meet railway-specific requirements. For continuous operation, SIL-1 requires at most 10^{-5} probability of failure per hour (PFH). SIL-2, 3, and 4 require at most 10^{-6}, 10^{-7}, and 10^{-8} PFH, respectively. As far as we know, the relation between the safety requirements for the wireless link and the control-command system does not exist. The aim of our work is to provide a methodology to establish this relationship in the case of T2T communications.

4   Existing Works

4.1   Methodologies to Analyse Dependability Analysis

The analysis of dependability of railway applications employs a variety of methodologies to assess key factors such as reliability, availability, maintainability, and safety (RAMS). This section highlights several prominent approaches and related research.

Failure Mode Effects and Criticality Analysis (FMECA) [14] is a structured methodology used for wireless communication in VCTS to find critical failure points in communication links and how these failures could affect train operations. Fault Tree Analysis (FTA) [15] visually represents the different pathways leading to system failures. By identifying the root causes of failures, FTA helps to understand how communication breakdowns can influence train safety and operational efficiency. Markov models [16] are used to model the probabilistic behaviour of wireless communication systems, capturing the dynamic nature of wireless links. Petri Nets [17–22] are a versatile modelling tool that can represent complex interactions and concurrent processes within communication systems. Petri Nets enable the analysis of performance metrics such as packet loss, system availability, and end-to-end delays, making them especially suitable for studying railway communication systems. Simulation techniques [23], including discrete-event simulations and system dynamics, are widely used to evaluate the performance of wireless communication systems within railway environments. Reliability Block Diagrams (RBD) [15] are useful for assessing the reliability of wireless communication systems, as they focus on the reliability of individual components and their combined effect on system performance. Combining multiple methodologies [24], such as combining FMEA, FTA, and simulation techniques, offers a more comprehensive approach to dependability analysis. These combined methods provide a deeper understanding of how different failure modes interact and how they influence the system's performance.

For our analysis of the dependability of train-to-train wireless communication for virtual coupling, we chose the Colored Petri Net (CPN) approach. It allows us to represent interactions within the communication system clearly and capture the dynamic behaviour of wireless protocols [25]. We can assess critical performance metrics such as end-to-end delay, message loss, and system reliability through simulations of different operational conditions.

4.2 Existing Works Related to Coloured Petri Nets

Coloured Petri Nets have been widely applied in railway communication and control systems for their ability to capture both logical correctness and timing behaviour. In [17], the authors applied CPN to validate a train-to-train distance measurement system, demonstrating that CPN can verify functional safety and evaluate basic timing properties of T2T subsytems. Similarly, [19] and [22] explored virtual coupling scenarios using CPN, focusing on how control parameters and vehicle-to-vehicle communication affect safety in tightly coupled train operations. The works highlight CPN's value for analysing control safety, but they do not address detailed message-level dynamics of continuous information exchange.

Several studies extend CPN towards dependability and communication reliability. [18] and [21] modeled wireless communication in virtual coupled train sets, evaluating reliability and fault-tolerance under difference conditions. [20] investigated high-speed train communication systems with CPN, optimizing communication structures to improve performance in extreme mobility scenarios. Although these contributions address communication dependability, they typically abstract wireless links as a simple loss or delay channel and do not incorporate modern cellular mechanisms.

More recently, attention has turned toward 5G and 5G-R for railway systems. CPN has been used to model 5G-based train-to- ground reliablity in [26], showing the feasibility of integrating cellular concepts into formal models. However, these works consider train-to-infrastructure or generic wireless reliability, not direct train-to-train periodic message exchanges. In these studies, performance analysis is usually expressed in terms of latency bounds, reliability, or fault probabilities at the system level. What is missing is an explicit focus on safety-related message level metrics, such as how message loss rate impacts end-to-end CAM delay, average inter-message gap, percentage of safe gaps, throughput, message delivery ratio, and percentage of safe delivery. These metrics are directly relevant to collision avoidance and cooperative awareness, and this point remains unexplored in the CPN railway literature. Existing CPN research has demonstrated strong potential for modelling railway communications, particularly for control safety and system reliability. However, no prior work has applied CPN to evaluate periodic train-to-train CAM exchanges over 5G NR sidelink, nor have quantified the above safety-related performance indicators. This paper addresses this gap providing a new perspective for safety-critical railway communication analysis.

5   The Coloured Petri Net (CPN) Model and Simulation Parameters

5.1   Coloured Petri Net Model

This section introduces a Coloured Petri Net (CPN) model for simulating the exchange of CAMs between a MT and a ST within a virtual coupling context. The model is specifically designed to capture the impact of varying T2T communication conditions, considering 5G NR V2X sidelink. By adjusting the simulation to reflect different message loss rates based on various railway environments, the model allows detailed performance evaluation. It excludes other train control operations and assumes that only one retransmission is permitted. This retransmission must occur within a predefined time window that ensures message delivery without error, before triggering emergency braking. This time constraint is also configurable within the simulation. So, retransmission of the CAM data occurs when the MT does not receive an acknowledgment from the ST within the specified CAM period, 200 ms or due to the request of the ST in case of message loss and repetition of received old messages. Each transmitted CAM data is associated with a particular sequence number and time stamps. This is initially shown in the model in the first place (P1, MT data ready), which is labelled as NUMxDATA. So, these sequence numbers can be used for different purposes during the exchange of CAM between the MT and ST. For instance, for confirmation, duplication, loss, retransmission, and updated CAM requests by the ST. The ST sends a numeric value of 2 for the reception confirmation of the first CAM and requests the next updated CAM (second CAM). Therefore, the entire CAM exchange or transmission protocol between the MT and ST continued in this way. The graphical CPN model illustrated in Fig. 3 represents the flow of tokens and interactions between transitions and places, representing the sequence of events in CAM exchanges.

The MT initiates communication by sending a message and awaits responses, while the ST processes incoming data and replies with acknowledgments or CAM requests. The model integrates mechanisms to handle message loss (transition T4) and simulates realistic network delays through functions like @+Delay () to maintain safe train operations. And the communication process is modelled in the following steps:

1. Initiation and transmission via the network (P1 → P2 → P3 → P4): The master train generates the message, begins transmission, sends it across the network, and completes delivery.
2. Reception by Slave Train (P5 → P6 → P7): The slave train receives, processes, and confirms the message.
3. Response from Slave Train (P8 → P9): The slave sends back either an acknowledgment or a new CAM request.
4. Master Train Verification (P10 → P11): The master receives and validates the response, deciding whether further action (like retransmission or update) is needed. The arc expressions defined how tokens are created, consumed, and modified as they flow through the network. For instance,

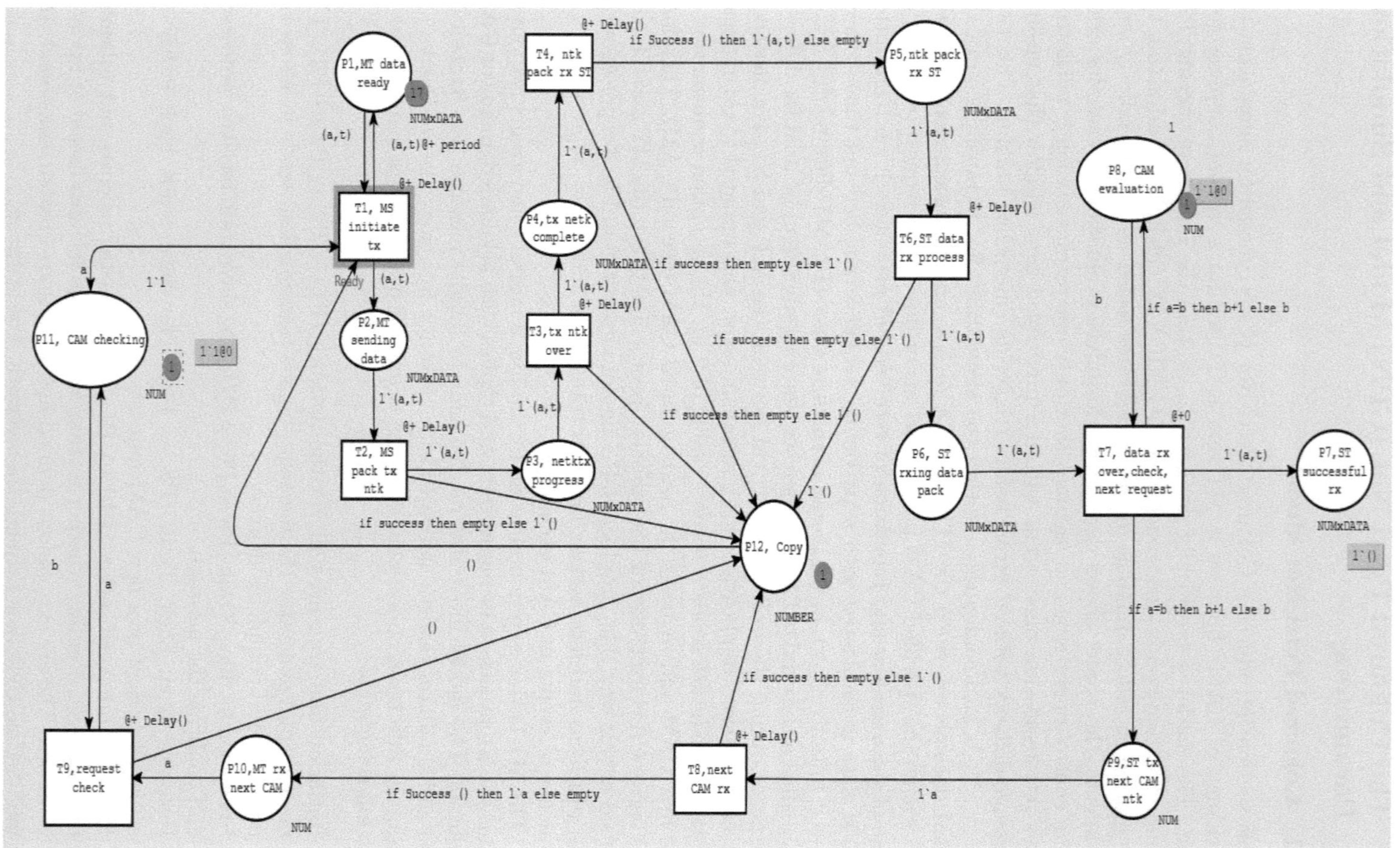

Fig. 3. Train-to-Train Data Exchange CPN Model

- 1'a: creates one token with the value of variable a.
- (a, t): A token consisting of a tuple of the CAM's data (a) and the timestamp (t).
- if a = b then b+1 else b, if success () then 1' (a, t): A conditional expression for token manipulation.

The places represent the states of the communication system. Thus, each place (P1 - P12) describes specific stages in the communication process and is represented as a circle in the Petri Net. For example, (P1, MT data ready) represents that the master train has prepared a CAM data packet to transmit, (P3, netk tx processing) represents that the CAM data packet is travelling through the network, and (P5, ntk pack rx ST) represents that the slave train has received the CAM data packet. The transitions represent the events or actions that change the state of the communication system from one state to another and are shown in rectangles in the Petri Net. For example, (T1, MS initiate tx) represents that the master train initiates CAM data transmission, (T3, tx ntk over) represents that the CAM data packet transmission to the network is completed, and (T7, data rx over, check, next request) represents that the reception of CAM data is completed, checked, and generates an updated request or confirmation by the slave train. The green symbols of the places define the data types for tokens. Thus, the colour sets represent the CAM data and associated information, such as sequence number, data, and timestamp. It is conveniently labelled in each place for the readability of a CPN model, such as NUM to represent a token containing only numbers and NUMxDATA to represent a token that contains a sequence number and data. And the green rectangular shape in the first transition (T1, MS initiate tx) shows that the readiness of the transition for firing the tokens to move from the first place (P1, MT data ready), to the next place (P2, MT sending data).

To translate various environmental conditions, network congestion, software and or hardware issues, and so on, in a first approximation, we simulated different message loss rate values ranging from zero (0) to 0.97 by triggering the transition T4, under varying conditions. In future works, this message loss rate could be related to realistic values in specific scenarios, considering the 5G NR V2X link. In addition to the different message loss rate values, the model operates under specific assumptions, including a transition delay up to 5 ms and a CAM period of 200 ms as referenced in previous studies [12,18,27]. The CAM period is the time interval during which the master train transmits its updated CAM to the slave train. These parameters are critical for accurately reflecting the dynamics of communication in real-world scenarios. They can be modified. The transition delay is the time it takes for each transition to complete after it becomes enabled in the CPN model. The Max Delay is equal to 500 ms, which represents the maximum allowable delay to receive a CAM with no error before emergency braking. The Max Gap is the maximum time allowed between received messages before emergency braking (1000 ms). Table 1 summarizes the simulation parameters. These parameters can be varied in order to reflect dif-

Table 1. The input parameters

Parameters	Values
Message loss rate, MLR	0.0 to 0.97
CAM period	200 ms
Transition delay	0 to 5 ms
Maximum delay	500 ms
Maximum gap	1000 ms

Table 2. 5G NR V2V Platooning benchmark requirement values of 3GPP and 5G AA

Description	Values
Inter-packet arrival time	50 to 200 ms
CAM period with radio reliability 95%, 1 retransmission	100 to 200 ms
Latency (varied scenarios)	10 to 500 ms
Cooperative awareness time for 90–95% radio reliability	100 ms to 1 s
Data rate per vehicle for Cooperative awareness	5–96 kbps
Cooperative sensing time for > 95% radio reliability	3 ms to 1 s
Cooperative maneuver time for > 99% radio reliability	<3 ms to 100 ms

ferent scenarios. Furthermore, due to the absence of performance requirements for wireless communication with VCTS at present, our study references requirements found for automotive applications, specifically for the Third Generation Partnership Project Vehicle-to-Everything (3GPP V2X) [27,28] and Fifth Generation Automotive Association (5G AA) [12] standards. Their relevance values are summarized in Table 2.

5.2 Simulation Metrics and Parameter Definitions

This section outlines the definitions of the metrics used to evaluate the CPN model. It includes their corresponding mathematical formulations and highlights their relevance to safety in virtual coupling and train-to-train communication systems.

End-to-End Delay – refers to the total time taken for a message to travel from the MT (T1) to the ST (T7). In the context of wireless communication, it represents system latency, the time required for data to reach its destination. This metric is especially vital in real-time applications, where on-time data delivery is necessary to ensure the information remains actionable. Minimizing delay is crucial for time-sensitive operations. Its mathematical expression for single and multiple messages is summarized in Eqs. 1 and 2, respectively.

$$\text{End-to-End Delay} = t_{\text{receive}} - t_{\text{sent}} = T7_{\text{timestamp}} - T1_{\text{timestamp}} \tag{1}$$

where: $t_{\text{receive}} = T7_{\text{timestamp}}$ is the received time of the message by the slave train and $t_{\text{sent}} = T1_{\text{timestamp}}$ is the time of the message sent by the master train.

$$\text{Average End-to-End Delay} = \frac{(\sum (T7_{\text{timestamp}} - T1_{\text{timestamp}}))}{(\text{Number of T7 messages})} \tag{2}$$

Thus, the average end-to-end delay becomes the mean of these delays across all messages.

Average Inter-message Gap - states the mean interval between successive messages received by the slave train. Unlike metrics that measure the transmission time of individual messages, this metric focuses on the frequency of message reception. It indicates how trains regularly exchange information such as position, speed, and braking curves, which is essential to maintain real-time situational awareness. A shorter gap implies more frequent updates, which is especially important in high-risk contexts such as high-speed operations or dense traffic. In contrast, a longer gap may be acceptable in low-risk scenarios but can lead to outdated data during emergencies, potentially increasing the risk of accidents or delays. This metric is mathematically defined based on the timestamps of messages received by the slave train, known as T7 events. The gap is calculated as the time difference between two consecutive T7 timestamps.

For the $i_{(th)}$ gap:

$$\text{gap}_i = T7_{(i+1)} - T7_i \qquad\qquad for\ i = 1, 2, 3, \cdots, n-1 \qquad (3)$$

where: T7 is a sorted list of timestamps when messages are received (T71, T72, T73...) and n is the total number($\#$) of T7 events.

Therefore, the Average Inter-Message Gap stands for the average of all these gaps:

$$\text{Average Inter Message Gaps} = \sum_{(i=1)}^{(n-1)} \frac{T7_{(i+1)} - T7_i}{(n-1)} \qquad (4)$$

Percentage of Safe Gaps – quantifies the portion of message intervals that fall within an acceptable time threshold, known as the Maximum Gap (e.g., 1000 ms). So, it effectively quantifies how often the system can maintain the communication intervals required for safe operation under varying loss conditions. A gap is considered safe if the time between two consecutive messages does not exceed this threshold, ensuring that communication remains timely and does not jeopardize safety or operational performance. This metric is crucial because even if the average inter-message gap is low, occasional excessive delays could still obstruct the delivery of critical updates. A higher percentage of safe gaps indicates more consistent and reliable communication, which is essential for preventing safety-related issues. To evaluate this, each gap is classified as safe (1) if it is less than or equal to the maximum gap, or unsafe (0) if it exceeds it.

$$\text{safe gap}_i = \begin{cases} 1, & \text{if gap}_i \leq \text{Max Gap} \\ 0, & \text{otherwise} \end{cases} \qquad (5)$$

where: Max Gap is the maximum time allowed between messages to be safe (1000 ms). The percentage of safe gaps is the proportion of safe gaps multiplied by 100:

$$\text{Percentage of safe Gaps} = \sum_{(i=1)}^{(n-1)} \frac{\text{safe gap}_i}{n-1} \times 100 = \frac{(\# \text{ of gaps} \leq \text{Max Gap})}{n-1} \times 100$$

$$(6)$$

where n is the total count of messages received. Collectively, these metrics evaluate both the regularity and reliability of communication, ensuring that trains consistently receive the timely updates necessary for safe and efficient operation.

Throughput – denotes the number of error-free messages successfully delivered during the entire simulation period, measured in messages per second. This metric reflects how efficiently messages are transmitted from the master train to the slave train over time. High throughput indicates the system's ability to handle a large volume of message exchanges quickly, which is essential for real-time functions such as train coordination. Throughput can be represented as messages per second using Eq. 7 or, when considering message size, as bits per second using Eq. 8.

$$\text{Throughput} = \frac{\text{number of T7 events}}{\text{Total simulation time}} \tag{7}$$

where: Total simulation time = max (T7)-min(T1)

$$\text{Throughput} = \frac{\text{number of T7 events} \times \text{message size}}{\text{Total simulation time}} \tag{8}$$

Message Delivery Ratio (MDR) – represents the ratio of messages that the slave train successfully receives out of the total messages sent. This metric reflects the reliability of the communication system in ensuring message delivery, which is vital for safe train operation. A high MDR signifies that nearly all messages are reaching their destination, supporting effective and safe coordination. In contrast, a low MDR suggests frequent message loss, which can compromise safety and lead to potential delays or accidents.

$$MDR = \frac{\text{number of successfully delivered messages}}{\text{Total number of messages sent}} = \frac{\text{\# of T7 events}}{\text{\# of T1 events}} \tag{9}$$

MDR can also be written in terms of Message Loss Rate (MLR) as: MLR is the proportion of messages that are lost (nor delivered at the slave train) out of all messages sent.

$$MLR = \frac{\text{Number of lost messages}}{\text{Total number of messages sent}} \tag{10}$$

where:

$$MLR = \frac{\text{Total number of sent messages - Number of delivered messages}}{\text{Total number of messages sent}}$$

$$MDR = 1 - \frac{\text{number of delivered messages}}{\text{Total number of messages sent}} = 1 - MLR \tag{11}$$

Percentage of Safe Delivery – indicates the proportion of messages that reach the slave train within the maximum permissible delay (Max Delay: 500 ms), making them timely and usable for real-time decision-making. A message is considered safely delivered if it arrives quickly enough to allow timely action, such as braking to prevent a collision or adjusting speed. Timeliness is crucial; even successfully delivered messages are ineffective if they arrive too late. For instance, an emergency braking alert must be received almost immediately. A high percentage of safe deliveries demonstrates that the communication system is not only dependable but also responsive enough to support critical safety functions in real time.

$$\%\text{age of Safe Delivery} = \frac{\#\text{ of messages delivered within time limit}}{\#\text{ of successfully delivered messages}} \times 100$$
$$= \frac{\#\text{ of T7 events where}\,(T7 - T1) \leq \text{Max Delay}}{\#\text{ of T7 events}} \times 100$$

$$(12)$$

Combined, the Message Delivery Ratio and Percentage of Safe Delivery provide a comprehensive measure of both the reliability and timeliness of train communication, key factors in preventing accidents and ensuring smooth, efficient operations.

6   Simulation Results and Discussion

The simulation graph in Fig. 4 illustrates the relationship between end-to-end delay, average Inter-message gap versus message loss rate in the context of T2T communication for CAM exchange. The graphs show that the end-to-end delay and average inter-message gap remain relatively low, stable, and consistent below 100 ms for MLR values below approximately 0.3 and 0.2, respectively. They slightly increase with increasing message loss rate up to 0.6 MLR value, indicating minimal retransmission overhead. However, as the MLR increases beyond 0.6, the delay and gap increase rapidly due to the retransmission required to ensure successful message delivery. This exponential growth indicates that the communication reliability and continuity significantly degrade or deteriorate. In T2T communication scenarios, where CAMs must be delivered in real-time to support situational awareness and safety applications, such delays and high message gaps can severely affect system performance. Therefore, maintaining a low MLR is essential. Below the MLR value of 0.2, the end-to-end delay is below 100 ms, and the inter-message gap becomes lower than the periodicity of 200 ms, even if there is one retransmission of the message in case of loss.

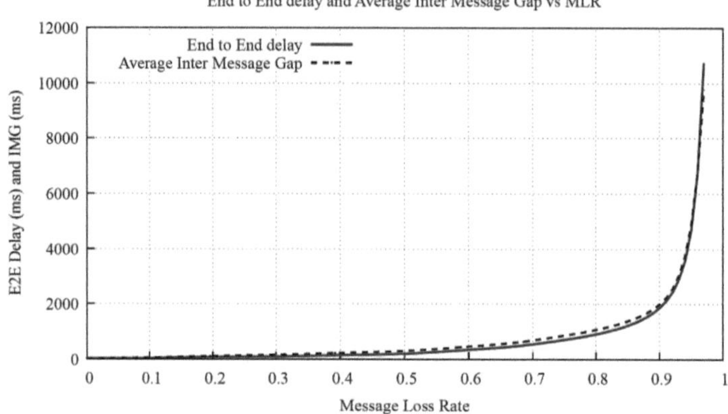

Fig. 4. End-to-End Delay, Average Inter-message gap versus Message Loss Rate

Moreover, Fig. 4 also shows the evolution of the end-to-end delay and average inter-message gap versus MLR. Our scenario considers messages sent sequentially, ensuring each is received before sending the next message to maintain strict timing and avoid overlaps or missed messages. This concept would naturally lead to the end-to-end delay and average inter-message gap being almost similar. The results are compliant with 5G NR V2X requirements in the vehicular context (Table 2).

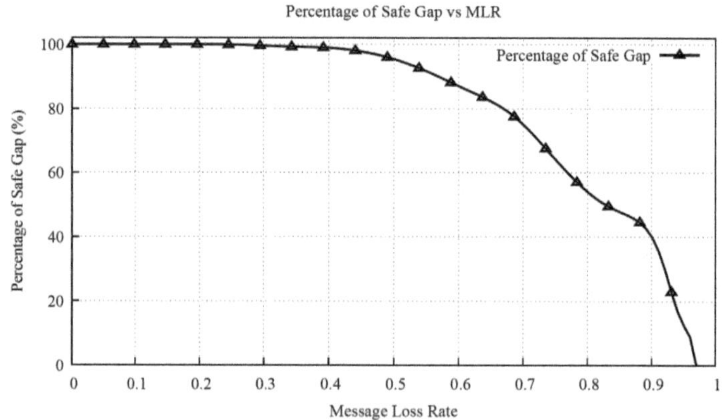

Fig. 5. Percentage of Safe Gap versus Message Loss Rate

Figure 5 illustrates how the percentage of safe gaps varies with the MLR. As shown in the graph, the percentage of safe gaps is nearly 100% at low message loss rates (MLR < 0.4), indicating highly reliable and timely message delivery. However, as the MLR increases beyond 0.4, the percentage of safe gaps begins to decline suddenly and approaches 0% as the MLR near to 1. This behaviour reflects the diminishing capacity of the system to maintain communication intervals that fall within the acceptable safety margins as reliability degrades. The results emphasise that the proposed communication model performs more than (>) 95% reliably at low to moderate MLR levels. This also achieves the requirements we proposed in Table 2 in the case of vehicular applications. However, at higher MLRs, the decline in safe gaps signifies openings in safety thresholds, emphasising the critical need to limit message loss in real deployments through robust error correction, redundancy, or prioritisation mechanisms.

Figure 6 shows the impact of message loss rate on the system throughput. The graph shows a step decline in throughput as the MLR increases. At very low MLRs (close to 0), the system achieves its maximum throughput, approximately 55 msg/s, indicating highly efficient and reliable data transmission. However, as the MLR increases beyond nearly 0.1, throughput rapidly degrades, falling below 10 msg/s by the time MLR reaches 0.2. Beyond this point the throughput goes near zero, suggesting that the network becomes practically unusable for real-time communication. This behaviour emphasises the critical dependence of throughput on network reliability because throughput serves as a direct indicator of how effectively the communication channel supports the intended message flow. When throughput drops significantly, even if some messages are delivered with low delay, the volume and consistency of message delivery are inadequate, which is unacceptable for safety-critical applications. This result aligns with the benchmarks stated in Table 2, which targets very high reliability (>95%).

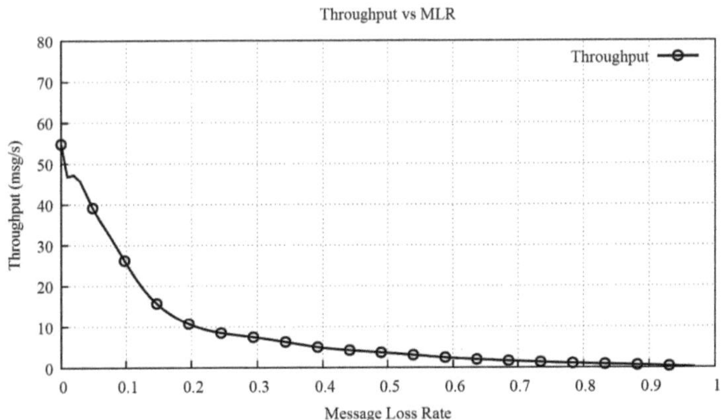

Fig. 6. Throughput versus Message Loss Rate

Figure 7 presents the relationship between message delivery ratio (MDR) and message loss rate. As expected, the graph shows a linear and inverse proportional relationship. When the message loss rate is 0, the MDR is 1 (in other words, 100% of messages are delivered successfully). As MLR increases, MDR declines, reaching nearly 0 when MLR approaches 1. This behaviour shows that as more messages are lost, fewer are delivered successfully, which is a direct and spontaneous relationship. From the graph, it is clear that the system performs well only when MLR is minimal (under ≈0.1) or with reliability >95%. Beyond this point, MDR degradation becomes critical, indicating a loss of reliability. This analysis aligns with the trends observed in the above Fig. 4, 5, and 6, where delay, message gaps, safe operation, and throughput deteriorated as MLR increased. We can observe that, below the MLR value 0.1, the results meet the requirements stated in Table 2 demanded by 3GPP V2X and 5G AA standards for real-time vehicular control systems and cooperative awareness.

Figure 8 shows the relationship between MLR and the Percentage of Safe Gaps, which indicates how effectively messages are delivered without compromising system safety. As illustrated in Fig. 8, the percentage of safe delivery remains consistently high (nearly 100%) for lower MLR values (approximately MLR <0.3). This suggests that at lower message loss rates, almost all messages are delivered within acceptable safety margins if we refer to the requirements stated in Table 2. In the reverse case, as the MLR increases beyond approximately 0.3, the percentage of safe delivery begins to decline more noticeably. The degradation becomes abrupt when MLR exceeds 0.5, and by the time MLR approaches 1.0, the percentage of safe delivery rapidly declines to 0%. This decline illustrates the system's inability to maintain reliable communication with high message loss rates, undermining operational safety.

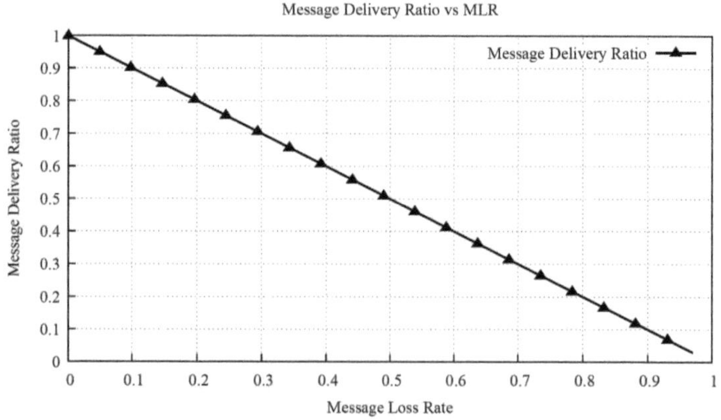

Fig. 7. Message Delivery Ratio versus Message Loss Rate

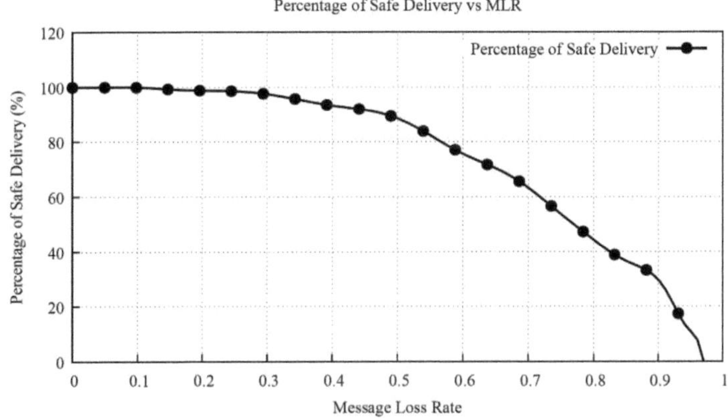

Fig. 8. Percentage of Safe Delivery versus Message Loss Rate

7 Conclusion

This study presented a simulation model of CAM exchanges for T2T communications in the VCTS process. This model is based on the coloured CPN IDE tool and considers only one retransmission. It is a tool to evaluate the dependability of Train-to-Train (T2T) wireless communication based on 5G NR-V2X. We focus in particular on the impact of message loss rate (MLR) on key safety-related performance metrics such as end-to-end delay, inter-message gaps (intervals), throughput, message delivery, and safe communication reliability. These first simulation results were analysed to quantify how increasing MLR affects the chosen metrics. As expected, the increase of MLR affects the metrics and shows deterioration of the CAM exchanges. These results show that it will be important to increase the number of retransmissions or to add other mechanisms, such as error corrections and prioritisation mechanisms. We observed that the results are consistent with the existing ones for 5G NR V2X automotive evaluation scenario for urban intersection environment, that we considered as a benchmark shown in Table 2. In future work, we will introduce in the CPN model some 5G NR V2X characteristics (blind or non blind packet retransmissions, specific bearer with guaranteed PER...) and the obtained performances in realistic railway environments. It will be important to take into account the KPI values at Physical layer including retransmissions processes inherent to 5G standard. Taking into account the characteristics of the technology, the model can be extended to account for multiple retransmissions at application layer within a bounded time interval called an acceptable time interval of messages, ensuring that safety-critical messages are delivered reliably before triggering the emergency braking. Additionally, varying the transmission periodicity between trains will allow a more realistic evaluation of communication performance under different operational scenarios. This will be vital to define potential requirements adapted to VCTS operation in railway environments, such as the maximum allowable number of retransmissions per periodicity interval, thereby supporting both safety and efficiency in VCTS implementations.

Acknowledgments. The work of F. Flammini was partly supported by the Swiss State Secretariat for Education, Research and Innovation (SERI) under contract no. 23.00321 (Academics4Rail) and 24.00528 (PhDs EU-Rail); those projects have been selected within the European Union's Horizon Europe research and innovation program under GA no. 101121842 and 101175856. The work of the other co-authors was carried out under the EU-funded Academics4Rail project GA 101121842. However, views and opinions expressed are those of the authors only and do not necessarily reflect those of the European Union or Europe's Rail Joint Undertaking. Neither the European Union nor the granting authority can be held responsible for them.

References

1. Aoun, J., Goverde, R.M., Nardone, R., Quaglietta, E., Vittorini, V.: Analysis of safe and effective next-generation rail signalling systems. Transp. Res. Part C Emerg. Technol. **162**, 104573 (2024). https://doi.org/10.1016/j.trc.2024.104573
2. Stickel, S., et al.: Technical feasibility analysis and introduction strategy of the virtually coupled train set concept. Sci. Rep. **12**(1), 4248 (2022). https://doi.org/10.1038/s41598-022-08215-y
3. Versluis, N.D., Quaglietta, E., Goverde, R.M., Pellegrini, P., Rodriguez, J.: Real-time railway traffic management under moving-block signalling: a literature review and research agenda. Transp. Res. Part C Emerg. Technol. **158**, 104438 (2024). https://doi.org/10.1016/j.trc.2023.104438
4. García-Loygorri, J.M., et al.: The wireless train communication network: Roll2Rail vision. IEEE Veh. Technol. Mag. **13**(3), 135–143 (2018). https://doi.org/10.1109/MVT.2018.2844408
5. Lopez, I., Goikoetxea, J., Arriola, A., Zabala, I., Priego, R.: Field tests of an LTE-based wireless train backbone in metro environments. In: 2018 16th International Conference on Intelligent Transportation Systems Telecommunications (ITST), pp. 1–6. IEEE (2018). https://doi.org/10.1109/ITST.2018.8566951. Accessed 03 May 2025
6. Chai, M., Su, H., Liu, H.: Long short-term memory-based model predictive control for virtual coupling in railways. Wirel. Commun. Mob. Comput. **2022**, 1–17 (2022). https://doi.org/10.1155/2022/1859709
7. Jia, D., Ngoduy, D., Vu, H.L.: A multiclass microscopic model for heterogeneous platoon with vehicle-to-vehicle communication. Transp. B Transp. Dyn. **7**(1), 311–335 (2019). https://doi.org/10.1080/21680566.2018.1434021
8. Li, L., Song, H., Ma, J., Dong, H.: Description and analysis of train-centric communication based autonomous train control system. In: 2022 IEEE 25th International Conference on Intelligent Transportation Systems (ITSC), pp. 3315–3320. IEEE (2022). https://doi.org/10.1109/ITSC55140.2022.9922576
9. Lehner, A., Strang, T., Unterhuber, P.: Train-to-train propagation at 450 MHz. In: 2017 11th European Conference on Antennas and Propagation (EUCAP), pp. 2875–2879. IEEE (2017). https://doi.org/10.23919/EuCAP.2017.7928155

10. Gómez, A.A., et al.: Performance analysis of ITS-G5 for smart train composition coupling. In: 2018 16th International Conference on Intelligent Transportation Systems Telecommunications (ITST), pp. 1–7. IEEE (2018). https://doi.org/10.1109/ITST.2018.8566840

11. Molla, D.M., et al.: Evaluation of V2X technologies for the connectivity of small autonomous vehicles on secondary railway lines. IEEE Access **13**, 116170–116187 (2025). https://doi.org/10.1109/ACCESS.2025.3585300

12. 5G-V2X Direct Communication Evaluation Approach: An Automotive Analysis 5GAA Automotive Association White Paper (2024). https://5gaa.org/content/uploads/2024/07/5gaa-wi-nr-v2x-eval.pdf. Accessed 04 May 2025

13. E. Std. Railway applications-Communications, signalling and processing systems-Safety related electronic systems for signalling. Eur. Comm. Electrotech. Stand. CENELEC (2019). http://www.tc278.csrzic.com/qbw/upload/file/20240708/17204276749660594569.pdf. Accessed 04 May 2025

14. Su, H., Wang, D., Su, L.: Fuzzy FMECA risk evaluation and its applications in Chinese train control systems based on cloud model. J. Intell. Fuzzy Syst. **37**(1), 1299–1309 (2019). https://doi.org/10.3233/JIFS-182745

15. Ahmad, W., Hasan, O., Pervez, U., Qadir, J.: Reliability modeling and analysis of communication networks. J. Netw. Comput. Appl. **78**, 191–215 (2017). https://doi.org/10.1016/j.jnca.2016.11.008

16. Pathak, G., Li, H., Math, C.B., De Groot, S.H.: Modelling of communication reliability for platooning applications for intelligent transport system. In: 2016 IEEE 84th Vehicular Technology Conference (VTC-Fall), pp. 1–6. IEEE (2016). https://doi.org/10.1109/VTCFall.2016.7881092

17. Song, H., Liu, J., Schnieder, E.: Validation, verification and evaluation of a train to train distance measurement system by means of colored petri nets. Reliab. Eng. Syst. Saf. **164**, 10–23 (2017). https://doi.org/10.1016/j.ress.2017.03.001

18. Verma, S., Ghazel, M., Berbineau, M.: Model-based dependability evaluation of a wireless communication system in a virtually coupled train set. IFAC-Pap. **54**(2), 179–186 (2021). https://doi.org/10.1016/j.ifacol.2021.06.045

19. Fu, L.: Analysis of virtual coupling control parameters based on colored Petri net. In: 2024 3rd International Conference on Electronics and Information Technology (EIT), pp. 260–267. IEEE (2024). https://doi.org/10.1109/EIT63098.2024.10762064

20. Lin, J., Yue, Q., Liu, X.: Optimization and modeling of high-speed flying train communication system based on colored petri nets. In: 2021 IEEE International Conference on Power, Intelligent Computing and Systems (ICPICS), pp. 158–163 (2021). https://doi.org/10.1109/ICPICS52425.2021.9524226

21. Li, R., Wu, D.: A CPN-based reliability analysis of a wireless communication system in a virtually coupled train set. In: 2023 China Automation Congress (CAC), pp. 1954–1959. IEEE (2023). https://doi.org/10.1109/CAC59555.2023.10451448

22. Yong, Z., Sirui, Z.: Typical train virtual coupling scenario modeling and analysis of train control system based on vehicle-vehicle communication. In: 2020 IEEE 6th International Conference on Control Science and Systems Engineering (ICCSSE), pp. 143–148. IEEE (2020). https://doi.org/10.1109/ICCSSE50399.2020.9171984

23. Liu, X., Jin, D., Zhang, T.: Simulation-based evaluation of handover mechanisms in high-speed railway control and communication systems. In: 2020 Winter Simulation Conference (WSC), pp. 3176–3187. IEEE (2020). https://doi.org/10.1109/WSC48552.2020.9383954

24. Abdollahi Pour, M.: Methods of risk estimation in production systems- literature review (2024). https://www.politesi.polimi.it/handle/10589/226751. Accessed 04 May 2025
25. Jensen, K.: A brief introduction to coloured Petri Nets. In: Brinksma, E. (ed.) TACAS 1997. LNCS, vol. 1217, pp. 203–208. Springer, Heidelberg (1997). https://doi.org/10.1007/BFb0035389
26. Qiao, W., et al.: Reliability analysis of CTCS-3 security services based on 5G-R using timed colored Petri nets. In: International conference on Electrical and Information Technologies for rail Transportation (2024). https://doi.org/10.1007/978-981-99-9315-4_22
27. Kosmanos, D., Chaikalis, C., Savvas, I.K.: 3GPP V2X 5G V2X scenarios: performance of QoS parameters using turbo codes. In: Telecom, pp. 174–194. MDPI (2022). https://doi.org/10.3390/telecom3010012
28. Ali, Z., Lagén, S., Giupponi, L., Rouil, R.: 3GPP V2X NR V2X mode 2: overview, models and system-level evaluation. IEEE Access **9**, 89554–89579 (2021). https://doi.org/10.1109/ACCESS.2021.3090855

Safe Maintenance of Railways Using COTS Mobile Devices: The Remote Worker Dashboard

Tommaso Zoppi[1]([⊠]) [iD], Innocenzo Mungiello[2], Andrea Ceccarelli[1], Alberto Cirillo[2], Lorenzo Sarti[2], Lorenzo Esposito[2], Giuseppe Scaglione[2], Sergio Repetto[2], and Andrea Bondavalli[1]

[1] Department of Mathematics and Informatics, University of Florence, Viale Morgagni 67/A, 50134 Florence, Italy
tommaso.zoppi@unifi.it
[2] R&D Department of Rete Ferroviaria Italiana, RFI, Naples Afragola ,, Italy

Abstract. The railway domain is regulated by rigorous safety standards to ensure that specific safety goals are met. Often, safety-critical systems rely on custom hardware-software components that are built from scratch to achieve specific functional and non-functional requirements. Instead, the (partial) usage of Commercial Off-The-Shelf (COTS) components is very attractive as it potentially allows reducing cost and time to market. Unfortunately, COTS components do not individually offer enough guarantees in terms of safety and security to be used in critical systems as they are. In such a context, RFI (Rete Ferroviaria Italiana), a major player in Europe for railway infrastructure management, aims at equipping track-side workers with COTS devices to remotely and safely interact with the existing interlocking system, drastically improving the performance of maintenance operations. The paper [10] describes the first effort to update existing (embedded) railway systems to a more recent cyber-physical system paradigm. Our Remote Worker Dashboard (RWD) pairs the existing safe interlocking machinery alongside COTS mobile components, making cyber and physical components cooperate to provide the user with responsive, safe, and secure service. Specifically, the RWD is a SIL4 cyber-physical system to support maintenance of actuators and railways in which COTS mobile devices are safely used by track-side workers. The concept, development, implementation, verification and validation activities to build the RWD were carried out in compliance with the applicable CENELEC standards required by certification bodies to declare compliance with specific guidelines. This is an extended abstract of the journal paper [10].

Keywords: Safety · Security · SIL4 · Railway · CPS · track-side maintenance · mobile devices · CENELEC · COTS

1 Railway Maintenance

The railway domain is based on embedded hardware-software systems that were built decades ago, and that are being maintained and updated along the evolution of the applicable standards as the *European Rail Traffic Management System/European Train Control System* (ERTMS/ECTS, [4, 8]). Indeed, recent technologies offer many additional

© The Author(s), under exclusive license to Springer Nature Switzerland AG 2026
M. H. ter Beek et al. (Eds.): RSSRail 2025, LNCS 16236, pp. 177–181, 2026.
https://doi.org/10.1007/978-3-032-10762-6_14

opportunities to improve control systems by remotely providing critical functionalities in a completely safe manner. Unfortunately, railway control systems are not generally willingly updated due to (*i*) the reluctance of authorities and (*ii*) the cost and effort to design, develop, implement, verify and validate a system that must comply with CEN-ELEC [1, 2, 3] (now [11]) standards and has to be approved by a certification body before installation and operation. Moreover, Commercial Off-The-Shelf (COTS) components that may meet specific needs at a cheaper price are usually designed without safety in mind, and therefore cannot be employed as they are. As a result, control systems in the railway domain work properly and are maintained efficiently, but do not fully exploit novel technologies.

RFI (Rete Ferroviaria Italiana), the company which manages railway infrastructure in Italy, has undergone a process to renew the current procedure to maintain rails, connected devices, and actuators. Maintenance activities are currently planned and coordinated via a *Worker Dashboard* (WD), which is located in the central offices of train stations and requires track-side workers to physically move there whenever they initiate and conclude each maintenance action. The WD shows the state of actuators (e.g., railway switches) and other devices in the station as a *synoptic* diagram, often referred to as *mimic panel*. After physical access to the WD, track-side workers phone the control room operators through a dedicated and protected phone line for any information which is not available on such synoptic. Moreover, to block transit of trains in the track segment or actuator to be maintained, the workers may need to move to a separate—albeit close to the WD— room which contains the key cabinet. This cabinet contains switch-lock keys for each area or actuator in the station, which have to be removed by track-side workers before starting operations and re-inserted only when concluding maintenance.

2 Motivation

Italian railways cover approximately 2,200 stations and a total of 16,723 km (10,391 mi) of active lines, 45% of which have double railway tracks [9]. The left of Fig. 1 shows the topology of the railway network, and allows identifying (i) stations, (ii) main lines, which have high traffic and good infrastructure quality, and (iii) secondary lines, which have less traffic and are responsible for connecting medium or small regional centers. Maintaining such safety-critical and cyber-physical infrastructure poses mechanical and electrical challenges, but also has to guarantee the personal safety of track-side workers, customers, and personnel on trains, trying to minimize delays due to maintenance operations. For instance, the schedule of planned maintenance operations for a secondary line of approximately 200 km in length (e.g., see right of Fig. 1, length of 198 km), or rather the 1.18% of the overall extension of Italian railways [9], usually allocates between 450 and 500 operations per month. These 477 maintenance operations (i.e., 15.4 operations as daily average) require disconnecting one or more actuators or physical components from the railway network, temporarily preventing the transit of trains to guarantee personal safety of track-side workers. Consequently, reducing maintenance time does not only improve the throughput of those operations, but also reduces delays due to train re-routing.

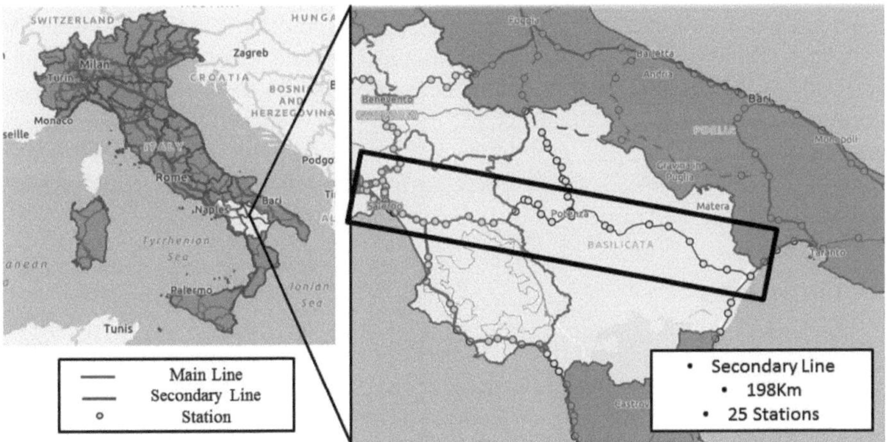

Fig. 1: Diagram of Tracks, Railways and Stations in Italy, highlighting a secondary line [9, 10].

3   A Remote Worker Dashboard

To improve and optimize such frequent operations, *RFI* is promoting the usage of COTS tablets and smartphones to (*i*) eliminate the need to physically access the WD and the key cabinet to acquire the physical token, (*ii*) provide remote access to the synoptic of the station to the track-side worker, and (*iii*) reduce the need of phone calls with the control room operator. It is worth mentioning that such an update will dramatically improve the efficiency of maintenance operations, minimize train delays and reduce workers' movements—which indeed have to be tracked [7]—between the train station and railways, with positive impact on the personal safety of the workers themselves.

As such, [10] introduces a SIL4 Remote Worker Dashboard (RWD) to support maintenance of railways, which connects and orchestrates physical components to provide the track-side worker with responsive, safe, and secure services, with clear economic benefits in the medium-long term period. The RWD is structured as depicted in the figure (Fig. 5 in the journal paper [10]). The left part of the picture depicts components (Computer-Based Interlocking CBI, Local Server LS) that: (*i*) are located in a premise of the station whose access is severely controlled; (*ii*) are intrinsically safe as they are designed, developed, verified and validated as SIL4 and (*iii*) can rely on secured (wired) connections that shield them from network threats.

Instead, the right part of the picture represents devices and interconnections lying in a "non-safe area", where components are individually built without safety in mind. Therefore, they may independently fail, or may be subject of attacks, which may also impact communication channels. The non-safe region of Fig. 2 embraces the global (web)server GS, the Local Web Server of the station (LWS), and two personal COTS devices available to the worker: A Worker TaBlet (WTB) and a Worker Smartphone (WS). GS and LWS are physically located in the station's premises and protected by a firewall to ensure security against network intrusions and therefore do not belong to the non-secure area. Moreover, each worker is responsible of mobile devices WTB and WS and they have to immediately notify the IT department of the railway manager if either of the two devices is lost or unavailable.

Aside from the system architecture, the paper [10] describes Concept, System Definition, Hazard and Risk Analysis, System Architecture, and some details on implementation and V&V activities, focusing on mechanisms to guarantee safety and/or security according to the CENELEC EN50126 [2] lifecycle. A dedicate discussion is directed towards explaining how COTS mobile devices can be safely used in the RWD without customization, as it is instead common practice in other railway systems [5, 6], providing additional relevance and novelty of the concept and design of the RWD.

4 Conclusions

The Remote Worker Dashboard (RWD) enhances current maintenance of railway infrastructures. RWD allows reducing maintenance time, minimizing delays on train schedule, and increasing safety of track-side workers. The RWD will support workers in managing maintenance operations through safe and secure interaction with the existing Computer-Based Interlocking. Workers can take advantage of personal COTS mobile devices to interact with the system, with clear advantages in terms of safety and time needed to fulfil operations.

To the best of our knowledge, RWD is the first cyber-physical railway system that embeds COTS mobile devices as tablets and smartphones without requiring rugged hardware or special configurations thanks to a consistent and coordinated system engineering effort of both the system owner and the consultants.

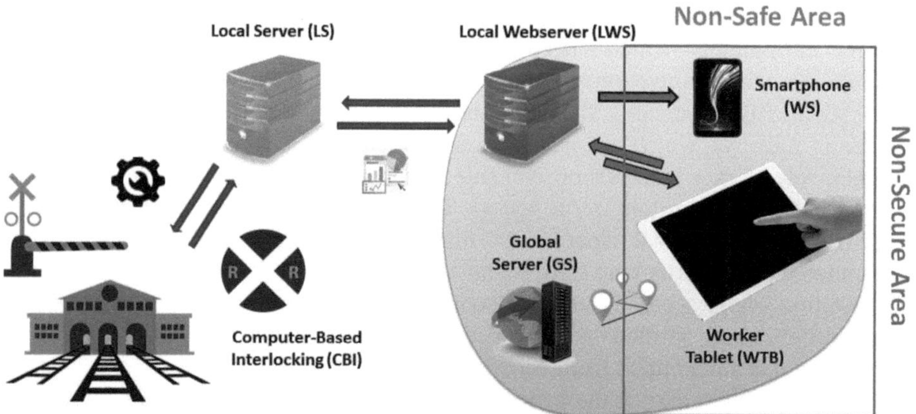

Fig. 2: Final Architecture of the RWD [10]. Components that lie in Non-safe or Non-Secure areas do not have to comply with safety or security requirements.

Acknowledgements. This work has been funded by RFI - Rete Ferroviaria Italiana S. p. A.

References

1. CENELEC, EN 50159.: Railway applications - Communication, signalling and processing systems - Safety-related communication in transmission Part 2 (2011)

2. CENELEC EN 50126.: Railway applications - The specification and demonstration of Reliability, Availability, Maintainability and Safety (RAMS) part 1 (2017)
3. CENELEC EN 50128.: Railway applications - Communication, signalling and processing systems - Software for railway control and protection systems (2012)
4. Bloomfield, R.: Fundamentals of european rail traffic management system-ertms. 165–184 (2006)
5. Ceccarelli, A., et al.: Design and implementation of real-time wearable devices for a safety-critical track warning system. High-Assurance Systems Engineering (HASE), 14th Symp. on. IEEE (2012)
6. Alam, M.M., Elyes, B.H.: Surveying wearable human assistive technology for life and safety critical applications: standards, challenges and opportunities. Sensors **14**(5), 9153–9209 (2014)
7. Wang, T., Wang, W., Liu, A., Cai, S., Cao, J.: Improve the localization dependability for cyber-physical applications. ACM Transactions on Cyber-Physical Systems. **3**(1), 1–21 (2018)
8. Lim, H.W., Temple, W.G., Tran, B.A.N., Chen, B., Kalbarczyk, Z., Zhou, J.: Data integrity threats and countermeasures in railway spot transmission systems. ACM Transactions on Cyber-Physical Systems. **4**(1), 1–26 (2019)
9. RFI – La Rete oggi (online). https://www.rfi.it/it/rete/la-rete-oggi.html
10. Zoppi, T., et al.: Safe maintenance of railways using COTS mobile devices: the remote worker dashboard. ACM Transactions on Cyber-Physical Systems. **7**(4), 1–20 (2023). https://doi.org/10.1145/3607193
11. CENELEC, EN 50716: Railway Applications - Requirements for Software Development, CENELEC (2023). (replaces the EN 50128 and EN 50657 standards, along with all their amendments and corrections)

Run-Time Monitoring of ERTMS/ETCS Control Flow by Process Mining

Francesco Vitale[1(✉)] , Tommaso Zoppi[2] , Francesco Flammini[2,3] ,
and Nicola Mazzocca[1]

[1] University of Naples Federico II, Naples, Italy
`{francesco.vitale,nicola.mazzocca}@unina.it`
[2] University of Florence, Florence, Italy
`{tommaso.zoppi,francesco.flammini}@unifi.it`
[3] University of Applied Sciences and Arts of Southern Switzerland, Lugano,
Switzerland
`francesco.flammini@supsi.ch`

Abstract. Ensuring the resilience of computer-based railways is increasingly crucial to account for uncertainties and changes due to the growing complexity and criticality of these systems. Although their software relies on strict verification and validation processes following well-established best-practices and certification standards, anomalies can still occur at run-time due to residual faults, system and environmental modifications that were unknown at design-time, or other emergent cyber-threat scenarios. This paper explores run-time control-flow anomaly detection using process mining to enhance the resilience of ERTMS/ETCS L2 (European Rail Traffic Management System/European Train Control System Level 2). Process mining allows learning the actual control flow of the system from its execution traces, thus enabling run-time monitoring through online conformance checking. In addition, anomaly localization is performed through unsupervised machine learning to link relevant deviations to critical system components. We test our approach on a reference ERTMS/ETCS L2 scenario, namely the RBC/RBC Handover, to show its capability to detect and localize anomalies with high accuracy, efficiency, and explainability.

Keywords: train control systems · dependability · fault-tolerance · software reliability and radio block center

1 Introduction

The European Rail Traffic Management System (ERTMS)[1] is a European standard setting the specification of both architecture and functions for interoperable, efficient, and dependable railways. The European Train Control System

---

[1] https://www.era.europa.eu/domains/infrastructure/european-rail-traffic-management-system-ertms_en.

(ETCS) standardizes the Automatic Train Protection (ATP) subsystem [16]. ERTMS/ETCS has different levels of operation, which determine how the on-board equipment of trains exchanges key information with the trackside subsystems. In this paper, we address ERTMS/ETCS L2, which uses wireless communication between on-board equipment and the Radio Block Center (RBC), based on the Euroradio protocol, to ensure continuous signalling. Train position is determined through Eurobalises and sent to the RBC via the Position Reports (PRs); RBC computes and transmits to the trains the so-called Movement Authority (MA), when full supervision is active (i.e., after start of mission and in case of no failures).

ERTMS/ETCS L2 must undergo strict verification and validation processes according to well-established best-practices, internal standards, and certification requirements. These include extensive requirements engineering, modeling and formal verification also using model-checking [3,7,9,14,16,20], as well as simulation and testing [2,15,24,29,30,32]. However, the coverage of these activities can never be complete due to several factors, such as: (1) the usage of natural language specification that might have ambiguities; (2) the high level of complexity undermining full formal verification and testing coverage, (3) heterogeneity in components developed by different manufacturers using diverse software versions and implementations. In such a scenario, residual or interaction faults, unexpected or uncontrolled modifications, system or environmental uncertainties, different specification interpretation or implementation across multiple manufacturers, emergent cyber-threats, as well as any other "unknown unknowns", pose threats that might affect the correct execution of ERTMS/ETCS L2 procedures and generate failures. Generally speaking, functional, environmental and technological changes during system operation require appropriate means to ensure resilience, i.e., the persistence of dependability when facing changes [21].

To address the problem of ensuring dependability in the presence of unexpected events possibly corrupting ERTMS/ETCS L2 control flow, we propose an approach for run-time monitoring and anomaly detection through process mining, which encompasses a set of explainable algorithms to model the so-called normative behavior (i.e., process discovery), and to check any deviations during system operation (i.e., conformance checking) [1]. In fact, process mining allows:

- Modeling the execution of ERTMS/ETCS L2 procedures under normal conditions through process discovery;
- Collecting run-time ERTMS/ETCS L2 control-flow and checking execution correctness against the normative execution model through conformance checking.

The characterization of ERTMS/ETCS L2 procedures under normal conditions from actual execution traces helps bridge the gap between specifications/models and actual system implementations. Although model-driven engineering is a widely adopted practice when developing safety-critical systems, ensuring strict consistency between system models and their software implementations is challenging due to the system's complexity and the concurrent operation of multiple developers [31,36]. As a result, some degree of divergence between specifications/models and the actual software is often unavoidable. This makes the characterization of the system's control flow from execution traces particularly valuable. In addition, while traditional rule-based methods (e.g., decision trees) provide a static representation of if–else rules [37] and more complex machine learning methods (e.g., recurrent neural networks) either lack an explicit representation of control-flow patterns or the ability to provide a process-based, trustworthy explanation of the deviations from prescriptive behavior [1,26], process mining explicitly allows capturing behavioral patterns—such as concurrent and exclusive control flow—through process discovery algorithms. Thereby, process discovery allows building prescriptive process models using well-known and interpretable formalisms, such as the Petri net. Finally, the approach enables resilience to changes, uncertainties, and any "unknown unknowns" as it combines data-driven insights with model-based analyses, taking concrete steps toward the development of an explainable run-time monitor. More specifically, conformance checking algorithms can pinpoint local diagnoses when comparing run-time control-flow with the prescriptive process model built with process discovery, supporting the root cause analysis of abnormal behavior.

Process mining has been applied for anomaly detection in several domains, including business processes of organizations [22,35], software applications [11,25], computer networks [18,28], and cyber-physical systems [23,34]. Notably, process mining has been also applied using an ERTMS/ETCS dataset generated from a high-level description of one use-case scenario in [12,35]. However, previous work did not thoroughly analyze ERTMS/ETCS L2 use cases or investigate process mining support for their development, monitoring, and the explanation of control-flow deviations from prescriptive specifications. In contrast, we propose a dedicated methodology that systematically combines behavior characterization, run-time monitoring, and anomaly detection and explanation. Our approach leverages offline ERTMS/ETCS L2 simulation or execution to extract a high-fidelity execution model of the target use case, integrates run-time execution with online conformance checking, applies machine learning-based post-processing of conformance diagnoses using clustering algorithms, and ultimately labels and localizes anomalies to pinpoint the faulty ERTMS/ETCS L2 components.

This paper is structured as follows. Section 2 establishes the background on key dependability concepts, ERTMS/ETCS L2, machine learning and process mining; Sect. 3 describes the proposed methodology for run-time monitoring of ERTMS/ETCS control flow; Sect. 4 shows the application of the methodology to RBC/RBC Handover, the chosen ERTMS/ETCS L2 scenario; Sect. 5 evaluates the anomaly detection and localization capabilities of the proposal; and Sect. 6 draws the conclusions and presents future work.

2   Background and Motivation

This section establishes the preliminary definitions used throughout the paper, and background information on ERTMS/ETCS L2, process mining, and machine learning.

2.1 Preliminary Definitions

Traditional definitions of **dependability** typically emphasize either "the ability to deliver service that can justifiably be trusted" or "the ability to avoid service failures that are more frequent and more severe than is acceptable" [4]. These definitions encompass a broad range of strategies for achieving dependability, including fault prevention, fault tolerance, fault removal, and fault forecasting. However, they do not explicitly address a key concept that is central to this paper: resilience. **Resilience** refers to a system's ability to continue delivering correct service in the face of changes in its run-time environment, including functional, environmental, and technological changes [21].

To achieve resilience in modern computer-based railways, including those based on ERTMS/ETCS L2, we propose to add specific software monitors performing **run-time control-flow anomaly detection**. Anomaly detection is a broad research area that aims to find "patterns in data that do not conform to a well defined notion of normal behavior" [8]. Different types of anomaly detection address different types of anomalies. In this paper, we address control-flow anomalies, namely those anomalies that manifest as unknown, skipped, and wrongly-ordered activities of event logs from computer-based systems [35]. In addition, we aim to perform control-flow anomaly detection at run-time, including when the system is operating in non perfectly known/predictable conditions, hence subject to functional, environmental, and technological uncertainties. Finally, it is worth mentioning that we propose an **unsupervised** approach to anomaly detection and localization, as we aim to characterize normal behavior from reference execution traces of the target system, and localize anomalies based on the model-based diagnoses we perform against a reference process model of the software.

2.2 ERTMS/ETCS L2

ERTMS/ETCS is characterized by a certain level of operation, from 1 to 3, which defines the degree of automation performance, and the required trackside and on-board equipment [16]. In this paper, we focus on the most successful level of operation to date, which is level 2. At this level, the on-board system collects the train's position through Eurobalises, which are electronic beacons installed across the tracks. The PR is forwarded to the RBC, which is responsible for train separation; the RBC elaborates the MA based on track occupation. Figure 1 shows a common use-case in ERTMS/ETCS, namely the MA request and provision to supervise train traffic. This use-case can be implemented within the Start-of-Mission procedure, which is one of the procedures documented in specification SUBSET-026; such a subset prescribes the behavior of ERTMS/ETCS constituents in all reference operational scenarios. Each step, labeled 1 to 7, requires either exchanging information between the on-board equipment of the requesting and preceding trains with the RBC, or using the on-board modules to perform some kind of data processing. The most important task performed

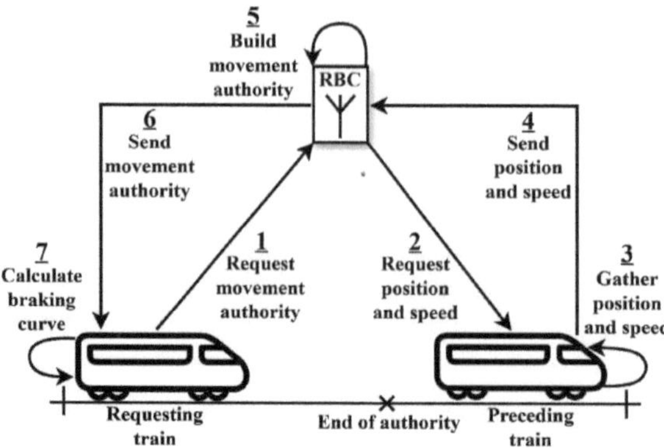

Fig. 1. Movement authority provision in ERTMS/ETCS L2.

on-board is the calculation of the so-called braking curve (also known as dynamic speed profile).

We assume that several types of run-time anomalies may occur across the many modules that compose ERTMS/ETCS L2, such as unexpected train data exchanged between the Driver Machine Interface (DMI) and the RBC through the Radio Transmission Module (RTM), mispositioning of balises, and issues in establishing connections with the RBC [6,30,32]. These anomalies may propagate across different components, and may influence other key modules, such as the European Vital Computer (EVC), which is the on-board component responsible for performing critical operations, such as calculating the braking curve.

Among the ERTMS/ETCS L2 operational scenarios of interest, we consider the RBC/RBC Handover, which is critical because it transfers train supervision to the "accepting" RBC from the "handing-over" RBC, when the train leaves the area covered by the handing-over RBC. The procedure includes: preannouncement of the transition by the handing-over RBC; registration to the new communication network; generation of movement authorities; announcement of the RBC transition; transfer of train supervision to the accepting RBC; and termination of the session with the handing-over RBC. There are several criticalities linked to the RBC/RBC handover use case:

- Different implementations of software modules developed by independent vendors;
- Software defects and unverified faulty edge-cases;
- Unpredictable environmental changes.

These aspects introduce uncertainties that cannot be completely avoided despite of strict model-checking and extensive testing activities.

2.3 Process Mining and Machine Learning

Process mining "aims to improve operational processes through the systematic use of event data" by mainly two types of algorithms: process discovery

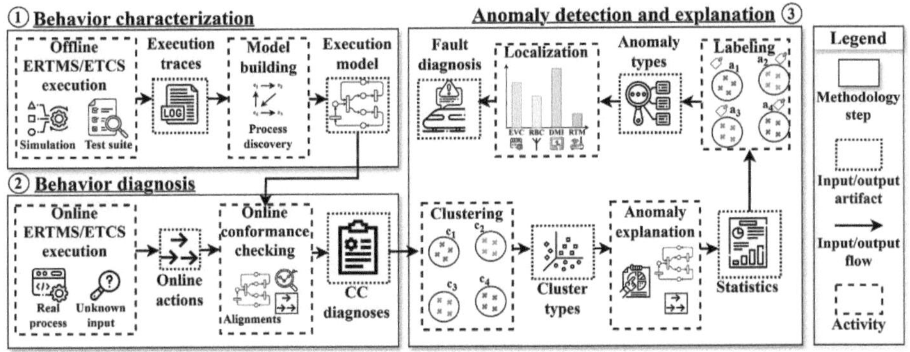

Fig. 2. The proposed methodology for run-time monitoring of ERTMS/ETCS control flow by process mining.

and conformance checking [1]. Process discovery attempts to build a normative behavioral model from historical event data collected by monitoring a reference application or process. Conformance checking aligns new event data to the normative model to diagnose any deviations from the control flow captured by the model. In addition, conformance checking can be performed online, i.e., it can be applied to streaming event data through, e.g., window-based approaches and prefix alignments [5,38].

Machine learning allows encoding data patterns into models. Traditional machine learning approaches capture patterns in data through rule-based learning, probabilistic modeling, linear and non-linear modeling, and clustering [37]. Advanced techniques include deep learning, which implements (deep) artificial neural networks mimicking the functioning of the human brain [13]. Machine learning algorithms also differ based on their learning paradigm (supervised, unsupervised, and semi-supervised) and degree of explainability [26].

Previous works have shown that conformance checking can be combined with unsupervised machine learning for explainable control-flow anomaly detection. The approach proposed in this paper is inspired by the work reported in reference [35], and proposes performing unsupervised run-time monitoring of ERTMS/ETCS L2 control flow through the combination of conformance checking and clustering.

3   Methodology

The methodology proposed in this paper aims to ultimately provide fault diagnosis at run-time through an explainable approach based on process mining and clustering. The methodology is organized into three steps, namely behavior characterization, behavior diagnosis, and anomaly detection and explanation.

3.1   Behavior Characterization

Offline ERTMS/ETCS Execution. The first step begins with offline ERTMS/ETCS execution, where a test suite is applied to a simulation environment or an actual system implementation. The simulation of ERTMS/ETCS systems can provide different types of high-level events that can be used to characterize the execution model of the target scenario. For example, di Tommaso et al. [30] simulated the Track Ahead Free (TAF) procedure with a trackside simulation environment. In this procedure, the RBC sends a TAF request to the train driver through the DMI to possibly grant a full supervision MA. Gaspari et al. [15] exemplified another remarkable simulation approach, involving the execution of abstract state machines representing several ERTMS/ETCS L3 scenarios to test the correctness of their models. The execution traces are collected to model the software behavior. We define a set of k traces as $\Sigma = \{\sigma_1, \sigma_2, \ldots, \sigma_k\}$, where each trace σ is an ordered sequence of events: $\sigma = \langle e_1, e_2, \ldots, e_{|\sigma|} \rangle \in \Sigma$, with e_j representing the j-th event. The definition of an event depends on the level of abstraction used in simulating ERTMS/ETCS L2. Since these systems involve distributed software components communicating over a railway network, events may correspond to specific software procedures executed by these components. This is a realistic representation, as safety-critical ETCS software is usually implemented in C/C++ [3,9,20].

Model Building. After the collection of execution traces, the model building activity applies a process discovery algorithm γ to find an execution model M from the set of traces representing the actual behavior of the system, i.e., $\gamma(\Sigma) = M$. There are many process discovery algorithms classified by their different learning approaches, including footprint-based and directly-follows-graph-based approaches that uncover local relationships between events (e.g., the α-miner and split miner), divide-and-conquer approaches that iteratively find relationships starting from the most general one (e.g., the inductive miner and partially ordered workflow language miner), and region-based approaches that obtain so-called regions from either state-based or language-based representations of the input log (e.g., the integer linear programming-based miner) [1]. Each process discovery algorithm has its own representational bias, which influences the quality of the resulting execution model. The execution model can be, e.g., a Petri net, a Business Process Modeling Notation (BPMN) model, or a process tree. The target formalism depends on the requirements of the applications. For example, a Petri net may be better suited for safety-critical environments due to its formal semantics. Hence, we consider the Petri net as the target formalism in the following.

3.2   Behavior Diagnosis

Online ERTMS/ETCS Execution. The second step is initiated by the online execution of an ERTMS/ETCS procedure with an unknown input. The real process is monitored throughout its execution. Such run-time monitoring can

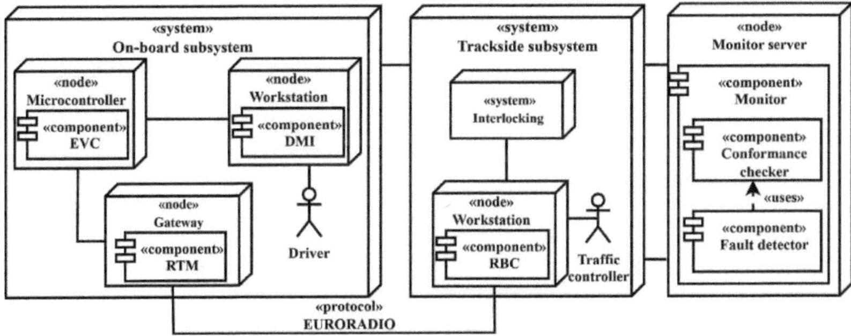

Fig. 3. An example deployment diagram showing the on-board and trackside subsystems communicating with each other and sending run-time events to a monitor server.

be performed in different ways. A plausible mechanism would be source-code instrumentation by well-defined logging rules, as proposed in [10]. This technique places logging rules to record specific events occurring in a program, such as interactions between objects, procedure calls, and the invocation of microservices. Its feasibility is due to the availability of source code in ERTMS/ETCS L2 implementations, as these systems require thorough white-box analyses to certify their safety levels. Figure 3 shows an example deployment diagram where the on-board and trackside subsystems communicate with each other and send run-time events to a monitor server. These run-time events configure a partial trace, and are checked against the execution model by a fault detector using a conformance checker that implements process mining techniques.

Online Conformance Checking. Similarly to process discovery, conformance checking can also be performed through a variety of algorithms, such as footprint-based, token-based, and alignment-based algorithms [1]. In this paper, we focus on alignment-based algorithms. These algorithms aim to build an alignment between a trace and the normative model by finding the path across it—the model trace—that either matches or is the best approximation of the trace. Using the approach in [35], the mismatches between the k actual traces and their corresponding model traces can be translated into "conformance checking diagnoses", i.e., tabular data $\mathcal{D} \in \mathbb{N}^{k \times m}$, where m is the cardinality of the set of activities $\mathcal{A}$. Each row of $\mathcal{D}$ represents the conformance checking diagnosis of a trace σ: $d_\sigma = \{d_1, \ldots, d_m\}$, where d_i is the number of misalignments associated with activity $a_i \in \mathcal{A}$. We aim to perform online conformance checking by employing a window-based approach [5], i.e., once a certain number of run-time events are collected from the system, these compose the partial trace and a partial alignment is computed. The partial trace is enlarged incrementally as more windows of activities are collected.

3.3   Anomaly Detection and Explanation

In the third phase, the conformance-checking diagnoses of non-conformant traces are analyzed to spot the occurrence of specific anomalies. As the data is unlabeled, the detection, explanation, labeling, and localization of anomalies are conducted in an unsupervised manner.

Clustering. The literature offers a wide variety of algorithms for unsupervised anomaly detection, including, but not limited to [17,39]: angle-based, neighbour(density)-based, statistical, neural networks, or clustering. Particularly, clustering is a type of unsupervised machine learning that aims at discovering clusters (i.e., subsets of data points, or diagnoses that are similar between each other) in training data, allowing to map a novel data point, or diagnosis d_σ, to a specific cluster, or no cluster at all (i.e., an outlier). Clustering techniques are particularly fitting for this study, as they partition the input space into "groups" that are easy to visualize and easier to understand than with other methods, which are not always transparent to the user. In our methodology, each tuple of diagnoses $d_\sigma \in \mathcal{D}$ is assigned to a cluster using one of the techniques above.

Anomaly Explanation. This step aims to explain the different clusters formed with $\mathcal{D}$, analyzing the misalignments of each tuple belonging to the different clusters. Specifically, given $C = \{c_1, c_2, \ldots, c_o\}$ the set of o clusters and $\mathcal{D}_c \subseteq \mathcal{D}$ the set of diagnoses belonging to $c \in C$, the anomaly explanation associated with cluster c is vector $s_c \in \mathbb{R}^m$ such that $s_c(i) = \sum_{j=1}^{l} d_j(i)$, where i is the i-th activity $a_i \in \mathcal{A}$. Next, given $COMP = \{comp_1, comp_2, \ldots, comp_p\}$ the set of p ERTMS/ETCS L2 components of the target scenario and $comp \in COMP$ a specific component, we compute $s_{c,comp} = \sum_{j \in \mathcal{A}_{comp}} s_c(j)$, which provides the amount of misalignments of the activities $\mathcal{A}_{comp} \subseteq \mathcal{A}$ linked to $comp$. $s_{c,COMP} = \{s_{c,comp_1}, s_{c,comp_2}, \ldots, s_{c,comp_p}\}$ is the anomaly explanation of cluster c. Finally, we calculate the probabilities of each component $comp$ for a given cluster c by computing $P(c, comp) = \frac{s_{c,comp}}{\sum_{comp_i \in COMP} s_{c,comp_i}}$. These values denote the probabilities that an anomaly occurred in the specific components, and are used in the subsequent labeling step.

Labeling. Once the probabilities of each cluster are computed, we are able to label the clusters based on the maximum probability. Specifically, if a cluster contains diagnoses that are more likely to have misalignments in a specific component, the cluster will be labeled as corresponding to an anomaly in such component. Note that this process of deriving explanations and compute the a-posteriori labeling of a clustering result does not require any knowledge of labels (thus it is entirely unsupervised) and solely relies on knowing which steps of the process are related to a specific component, which is something that can be easily derived by any functional specification of a problem, system, or protocol.

Anomaly Localization. When a new trace σ_{test} is collected from run-time monitoring, its diagnosis $d_{\sigma_{test}}$ is computed through online alignment-based conformance checking. Based on $d_{\sigma_{test}}$, the trace is assigned to the closest cluster and consequently labeled as a *comp*$_i$ anomaly if the closest cluster was previously labeled as containing diagnosis tuples affected by a fault in the i-th component. This completes the detection and explanation step, which uses diagnoses (non-conformances) of a trace with respect to its expected process flow to detect anomalies, diagnose their root cause, and localize their origin.

4 RBC/RBC Handover

In this section, we show the application of the three steps of the methodology shown in Fig. 2 to our ERTMS/ETCS L2 case study: the RBC/RBC Handover scenario.

4.1 Behavior Characterization

In this step, we simulate the RBC/RBC Handover scenario through a high-level description of its process according to the SUBSET-026 document of the ERTMS standard. First, we compiled the various sequences identified in the document under the chosen scenario into a BPMN model. Since the model describes a workflow from start to end, the model can be simulated, and various traces can be collected.

After the BPMN traces are collected, they are further pre-processed to mimic a realistic monitoring process of the computer-based system. Specifically, we aim to mimic the procedural programming paradigm, which is commonly found in the real implementation of ERTMS/ETCS systems. Using the activities of the traces generated through the BPMN model, our approach records the invocation of a procedure each time a new activity is executed as follows.

Let X be an ERTMS/ETCS component and $\mathcal{P}_X$ be the procedures implemented by X. One of the procedures is executed with a given probability for each distinct activity carried out by the component. It is expected that normal behavior follows a given control-flow with a high probability, whereas anomalous behavior involves the alteration of such normal control flow with the improper execution of other procedures. This is enforced using the following probability scheme. Let $\mathcal{A}_{HO}$ be the set of activities of the RBC/RBC Handover scenario, $\mathcal{X} = \{ARBC, HRBC, EVC, RTM\}$ the set of ERTMS/ETCS components involved in the use case, $\mathcal{P}_{a,X} = \{p_0, \ldots, p_{qx}\}$ the $q_X \in \mathbb{N}$ procedures implemented by $X \in \mathcal{X}$, and $\rho \in [0, 1)$ a real number. We define a procedure execution probability scheme PEP for each $\mathcal{P}_{a,X}$ associated with $a \in \mathcal{A}_{HO}$ that assigns probability values to the procedures so that one procedure is much more likely to be chosen than others, allowing the simulation of traces that are very similar to each other. In particular, let us consider a real number $\rho \in \mathbb{R}$ and the following function definition:

$$PEP : \mathbb{R} \times (\mathcal{P}_{a,X})^{q_x} \to \mathbb{R}^{q_x},$$

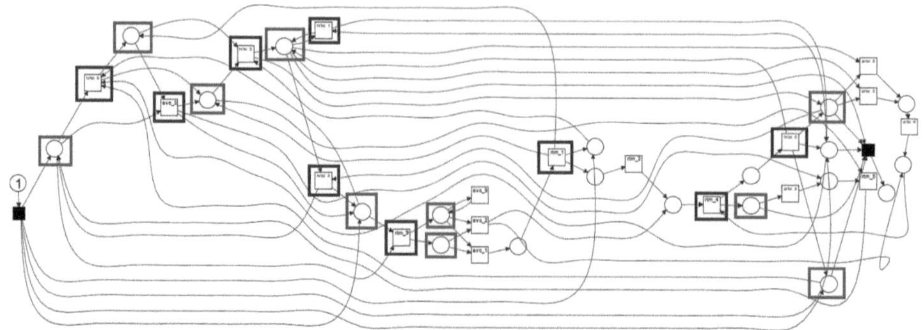

Fig. 4. The RBC/RBC Handover Petri net obtained through the integer linear programming-based miner during behavior characterization.

$PEP(\rho, p_0, \ldots, p_{qx}) = (pr_{p_0}, pr_{p_1}, \ldots, pr_{p_{qx}})$, where $pr_{p_0} = \rho$ and the other probabilities are equal to $\frac{1-\rho}{qx-1}$. For example, given $\mathcal{P}_{a,X} = \{p_0, \ldots, p_{qx}\}$, if $\rho = 0.99$, the application of PEP to $\mathcal{P}_{a,X}$ is such that p_0 is selected with 99% probability, whereas there is a 0.1% probability that other procedures are executed.

Following the procedure above, we generate the execution traces of RBC/RBC Handover as follows.

1. Set q_X for each component X involved in the RBC/RBC Handover use case;
2. For each activity $a \in \mathcal{A}_{HO}$, enforce a random order to the procedures that may be executed for that activity, i.e., generate $\mathcal{P}_{a,X}$;
3. Set $\rho = 0.99$;
4. Simulate $N_{norm} \in \mathbb{N}$ traces[2];
5. For each activity of the N_{norm} traces, sample a procedure through PEP using ρ.

In this preliminary setup, we have decided to set $q_X = 10$ for each component and generate $N_{norm} = 100$ traces. The dataset generation procedure has been published on the GitHub repository[3].

We used the integer linear programming-based miner with 75% tolerance to noise to build a workflow Petri net from the N_{norm} traces. Figure 4 shows the Petri net that the algorithm extracted. The Petri net contains two specific places: the source and the sink. The source place, marked with '1', allows triggering the first transition, whereas the sink place marks the end of the workflow. The red boxes outline those places with more than one outgoing arc, which means that in the presence of a single token in the place, only one of the outgoing paths can be followed—an exclusive control-flow pattern. The blue boxes outline those transitions with more than one outgoing arc, which means that multiple

---

[2] Popular simulation tools are **pm4py** (https://processintelligence.solutions/pm4py) and **ProM** (https://promtools.org/.

[3] https://github.com/francescovitale/pm_ertms.

concurrent paths are activated when the transition is triggered—a concurrent control-flow pattern. The Petri net has 21 places, 20 transitions and 78 arcs. The Woflan diagnosis [33] reports that there always exists a path leading to the sink and that there are no dead transitions.

4.2   Behavior Diagnosis

In this part, we aim to extract online actions from run-time traces and check them against the execution model obtained in the previous step. We can simulate run-time traces with the same procedure above. In particular, we simulated $N_{anom} = 400$ anomalous traces and injected control-flow anomalies. As there are 4 components, we split the N_{anom} traces into four sets of 100 traces, which we refer to as $N_{anom,ARBC}$ traces, $N_{anom,HRBC}$ traces, $N_{anom,EVC}$ traces, and $N_{anom,RTM}$ traces. Each set of traces is injected with a different type of anomaly. The injection procedure is as follows. Let X be one of the four components and let us consider its corresponding set of $N_{anom,X}$ traces. We scan the traces procedure-by-procedure and, if the procedure is executed by X, we randomly inject either a wrongly-ordered, skipped or wrong procedure control-flow anomaly. To account for the randomness of the simulation, we replicated the simulation ten times with different random seeds.

After we obtained the four sets of traces, we proceeded with the extraction of online actions by splitting each trace into multiple traces according to a window size. The number of online actions during this phase depends on the window size. We set three different window sizes, 5, 10 and 15, to evaluate the change in the results of the subsequent steps. For example, if a given trace has 20 traces and the window size is 10, it is split into 2 subtraces, where the first subtrace contains the first 10 online actions, whereas the second subtrace is the entire trace. Regardless of the window size, each subtrace is checked against the execution model to collect the conformance checking diagnoses to use in the subsequent steps.

4.3   Anomaly Detection and Explanation

The conformance checking diagnoses of the four sets of traces are clustered to identify the different anomalies. In particular, to evaluate the quality of different clustering techniques in correctly classifying the anomalies, we split the diagnoses into a training and a test set. We held out 25% of the diagnoses and used the training set to extract the clusters. Hence, there are 300 training diagnoses and 100 test diagnoses. Each cluster obtained from the training set was labeled with the type of anomaly injected. For example, all the clusters formed with the diagnoses of $N_{anom,ARBC}$ traces are labeled ARBC. The test diagnoses are subsequently assigned to each cluster and labeled accordingly. For completeness of our analysis, we selected multiple clustering algorithms, ensuring to select candidate clustering algorithms that are as diverse as possible between each other. We selected clustering algorithms that rely (e.g., K-Means) or do not rely on centroids (e.g., DBSCAN), algorithms that automatically derive the optimal number of clusters, and some that require the user to input the desired number of clusters as a parameter. Overall, we selected 10 algorithms: BIRCH, K-Means, Mini-Batch KMeans, Ward Hierarchical Clustering, Spectral Clustering, HDB-SCAN, DBSCAN, OPTICS, MeanShift, AffinityPropagation, whose implementation is available in the open-source Python library `scikit-learn`. Algorithms that required the number of clusters as input were exercised 5 times, each with the input parameter of 10, 30, and 50 clusters.

The conformance checking diagnoses collect the misalignments of the 40 possible procedures. These procedures are categorized according to the component that executes them: procedures 0 to 9: ARBC component; procedures 10 to 19: EVC component; procedures 20 to 29: HRBC component; procedures 30 to 39: RTM component, thus $comp = \{ARBC, EVC, HRBC, RTM\}$. For each cluster, the anomaly explanation s_c will be used to compute the quantities $s_{c,ARBC}$, $s_{c,EVC}$, $s_{c,HRBC}$, $s_{c,RTM}$, each quantifying the per-activity misalignment. Consequently, and regardless of the specific clustering algorithm, each cluster is labeled according to the process in Sect. 3.3 either as ARBC, EVC, HRBC or RTM.

5   Experimentation

Our experiments aim at evaluating the ability of the methodology to localize the different faults in the presence of control-flow anomalies.

5.1   Evaluation Metrics

There is a wide variety of metrics to measure the classification performance of multi-class classifiers [19], the most common being *accuracy*, typically used in its *balanced* formulation. Other commonly used metrics are those that are primarily meant for binary classification (e.g., precision, recall, F-measure, matthews correlation coefficient) but may be adapted to multi-class scenarios by performing an average per class. For this study, we choose the *balanced accuracy* to quantify the performance of clustering algorithms.

In addition to the classification metrics, there is a subset of metrics that aim at assessing the performance of clustering processes. These metrics stem from the idea that a cluster should contain all and only instances of a specific class. To evaluate such capability, two metrics are usually employed: homogeneity, which determines whether a cluster contains coherent data points, and completeness, which evaluates whether data points of a given class are elements of the same cluster. The V-measure [27] computes the harmonic mean of homogeneity and completeness. In this study, we use the V-measure to evaluate the quality of the clustering process.

Finally, we evaluate the effectiveness of the anomaly explanation mechanism discussed in Sect. 3.3. However, in this case, instead of computing the per-cluster explanation, we consider the explanation of each trace in the test set individually. Then, given a specific component, we sum all the test trace explanations, obtaining the four global anomaly explanations S_{ARBC}, S_{EVC}, S_{HRBC} and S_{RTM}.

Table 1. Anomaly detection results (best values are bolded in the table).

Window size	Metric	K-Means			WARD			Spectral			Birch			HDBScan
		10	30	50	10	30	50	10	30	50	10	30	50	–
5	Accuracy	0.61	0.78	0.82	0.68	0.80	0.83	0.61	0.80	0.83	0.62	0.74	0.76	0.69
	V-measure	0.32	0.52	0.56	0.42	0.56	0.59	0.32	0.53	0.57	0.33	0.48	0.50	0.37
10	Accuracy	0.75	0.86	0.88	0.70	0.87	0.89	0.77	0.87	0.89	0.72	0.85	0.86	0.61
	V-measure	0.52	0.64	0.68	0.47	0.69	0.72	0.54	0.66	0.70	0.50	0.67	0.66	0.35
15	Accuracy	0.81	0.89	0.91	0.75	0.88	0.89	0.82	0.92	**0.94**	0.77	0.88	0.87	0.34
	V-measure	0.63	0.73	0.75	0.57	0.71	0.72	0.61	0.77	**0.81**	0.58	0.73	0.70	0.09

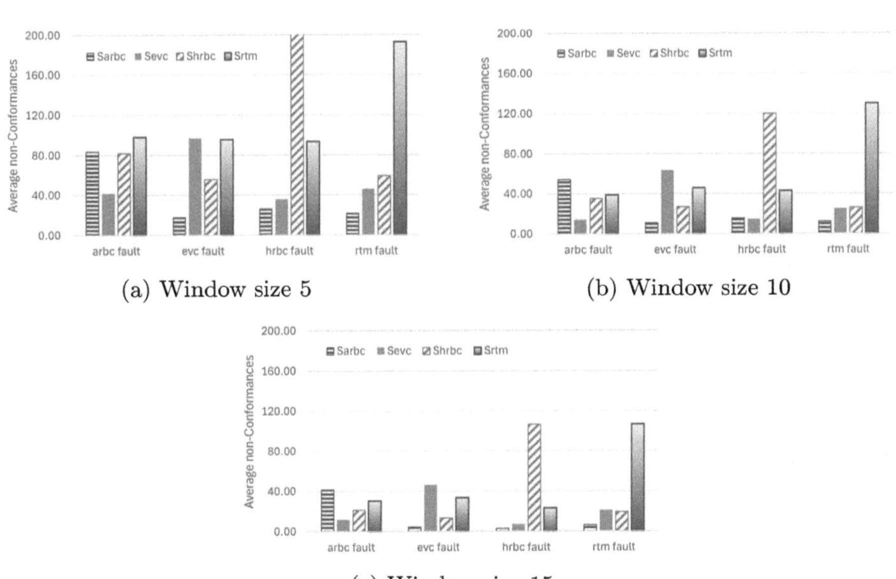

(a) Window size 5

(b) Window size 10

(c) Window size 15

Fig. 5. Spectral clustering with 50 clusters, averaged over experiments with different injected faults.

5.2 Anomaly Detection Results

Table 1 reports the anomaly detection results in terms of accuracy and V-measure for different window sizes and clustering algorithms. We limit our analysis to the best-performing clustering algorithms requiring the manual tuning of the number of clusters (K-Means, WARD, Spectral Clustering, and BIRCH) and the best-performing density-based clustering algorithm (HDBScan).

First, let us consider the impact of increasing the number of clusters in K-Means, WARD, Spectral Clustering and BIRCH on the evaluation metrics. Except for BIRCH, increasing the number of clusters leads to better performance, with Spectral Clustering peaking at 0.94 accuracy and 0.81 V-measure with 50 clusters. Such high performance is due to the ability of the algorithm to build specific, homogeneous, and complete clusters. However, it is worth noting that a higher cluster number increases the computational complexity and may lead to overfitting due to the specificity of the clusters being built. Therefore, selecting a lower number of clusters could be safer in terms of generalization capability and speed while maintaining a reasonably high accuracy, as Spectral Clustering achieves 0.82 accuracy and 0.61 V-measure with only 10 clusters.

Second, let us discuss the impact of the window size on the evaluation metrics. On the one hand, a window size equal to 5 leads to worse performance, with the lowest accuracy and V-measure being 0.61 and 0.32 for K-Means. On the other hand, increasing the window size leads to higher accuracy and V-measure across all the clustering algorithms—except for HDBScan, whose accuracy and V-measure, respectively, drop from 0.69 to 0.34 for window size equal to 5 and 0.37 to 0.09 for window size equal to 15. Hence, while K-Means, WARD, Spectral Clustering, and BIRCH are able to build better clusters through the additional conformance checking diagnoses yielded by a larger window size, HDBScan is unable to effectively use such information. In conclusion, it is worth noting that, despite the majority of algorithms achieving better accuracy and V-measure, increasing the window size generally leads to higher conformance checking times.

In conclusion, online conformance checking of the online traces with the Petri net in Fig. 4 allowed us to extract diagnoses that can be accurately handled by our clustering process to predict the fault that occurred in the system, achieving up to 0.94 accuracy and 0.81 V-measure.

5.3   Anomaly Explanation Results

The bar plots of Figs. 5a, 5b, and 5c show the anomaly explanations S_{ARBC}, S_{EVC}, S_{HRBC} and S_{RTM} for window sizes 5, 10, and 15, respectively. These results are based on the clusters built with Spectral Clustering using 50 clusters (the best clustering strategy from the previous discussion). S_{ARBC}, S_{EVC}, S_{HRBC}, and S_{RTM} are divided into four batches. Each batch collects the anomaly explanations related to the test traces of a specific fault type. For example, the first batch on the left-hand side of each bar plot collects the anomaly explanations of the $N_{anom,ARBC}$ traces.

Although it is expected that the activation of a fault within a specific component *comp* leads to high S_{comp} with a clear separation from the other explanations, some fault type-window size configurations fail to achieve this result. For example, the results of a window size equal to 5 shown in Fig. 5a show that S_{ARBC} is lower than S_{RTM} despite the activation of an ARBC fault. However, this does not occur for window sizes equal to 10 (Fig. 5b) and 15 (Fig. 5c), which is consistent with the accuracy and V-measure reported in Table 1. Still, while window sizes equal to 10 and 15 allow better localization of the ARBC and EVC faults, the separation of the different anomaly explanations is not so clear. On the other hand, the HRBC and RTM faults always lead to, respectively, high S_{HRBC} and S_{RTM}, and, in both cases, a very clear separation of anomaly explanations regardless of the window size. This suggests that faults in specific components are more likely to propagate to other components, making the labeling and localization of the fault more challenging in any window size scenario.

In summary, our explanation process allowed us to identify the misbehaving components of different online traces. The larger the window size, the more accurate the localization is with respect to the specific faulty component.

6   Conclusions

In this paper, we presented a novel approach for run-time control-flow anomaly detection in ERTMS/ETCS L2 using process mining. By leveraging execution traces and conformance checking, the behavior of the system can be monitored to identify deviations from expected execution models. Our method also integrates unsupervised machine learning to support anomaly detection and localization, offering insights into the root causes of observed deviations with a high degree of accuracy and explainability. The RBC/RBC Handover scenario has been chosen as a good-fitting use case of complex coordination tasks in train control; as such, it served as a reference case-study to validate our approach through a proof-of-concept, demonstrating its feasibility and effectiveness in realistic settings.

This work contributes to enhancing the dependability and fault-tolerance of safety-critical railway systems by bridging the gap between offline verification and online assurance. In line with the growing need for more resilient and intelligent railway software, our future research will focus on incorporating self-adaptive capabilities, wherein detected anomalies may trigger autonomous mitigation actions or adaptation strategies. Furthermore, the integration of our monitoring framework within digital twin architectures of ERTMS/ETCS subsystems is foreseen, enabling predictive diagnostics and closed-loop assurance [12, 34].

Ultimately, our goal is to contribute to a new generation of intelligent, trustworthy railway systems capable of continuous assurance in the face of evolving operational contexts and threats.

Acknowledgments. The work of Francesco Vitale and Nicola Mazzocca was partly supported by the Spoke 9 "Digital Society & Smart Cities" of ICSC - Centro Nazionale di Ricerca in High Performance-Computing, Big Data and Quantum Computing, funded by the European Union - NextGenerationEU (PNRR-HPC, CUP: E63C22000980007). The work of Francesco Flammini was partly supported by the Swiss State Secretariat for Education, Research and Innovation (SERI) under contracts no. 23.00321 (Academics4Rail) and 24.00528 (PhDs EU-Rail); those projects have been selected within the European Union's Horizon Europe research and innovation programme under grant agreements no. 101121842 and 101175856, respectively. The work of Tommaso Zoppi was partly supported by the Cognitive Safety with Point Clouds (CogniSafe3D - E!6085) Eurostars 3, Call 6 by the European Union. Views and opinions expressed are however those of the authors only and do not necessarily reflect those of the funding agencies, which cannot be held responsible for them.

Disclosure of Interests. The authors have no competing interests to declare that are relevant to the content of this article.

References

1. van der Aalst, W.M.P., Carmona, J.: Process Mining Handbook. Springer, Cham (2022)
2. Ameur-Boulifa, R., Cavalli, A., Maag, S.: From formal test objectives to TTCN-3 for verifying ETCS complex software control systems. In: Software Technologies, pp. 156–178 (2020)
3. Angeletti, D., Giunchiglia, E., Narizzano, M., Puddu, A., Sabina, S.: Using bounded model checking for coverage analysis of safety-critical software in an industrial setting. J. Autom. Reason. **45**, 397–414 (2010)
4. Avizienis, A., Laprie, J.C., Randell, B., Landwehr, C.: Basic concepts and taxonomy of dependable and secure computing. IEEE Trans. Dependable Secure Comput. **1**(1), 11–33 (2004)
5. Burattin, A.: Streaming process discovery and conformance checking, pp. 1–9. Springer (2020)
6. Cai, B., Liu, Y., Liu, Z., Chang, Y., Jiang, L.: Operation-oriented reliability and availability evaluation for onboard high-speed train control system with dynamic bayesian network. In: Cai, B., Liu, Y., Liu, Z., Chang, Y., Jiang, L. (eds.) Bayesian Networks for Reliability Engineering, pp. 109–133. Springer, Singapore (2020). https://doi.org/10.1007/978-981-13-6516-4_6
7. Campanile, L., Biase, M.S.d., Marrone, S., Raimondo, M., Verde, L.: On the evaluation of BDD requirements with text-based metrics: the ETCS-L3 case study. In: Intelligent Decision Technologies, pp. 561–571 (2022)
8. Chandola, V., Banerjee, A., Kumar, V.: Anomaly detection: a survey. ACM Comput. Surv. **41**(3) (2009)
9. Cimatti, A., et al.: Formal verification and validation of ERTMS industrial railway train spacing system. In: Computer Aided Verification, pp. 378–393 (2012)
10. Cinque, M., Cotroneo, D., Pecchia, A.: Event logs for the analysis of software failures: a rule-based approach. IEEE Trans. Software Eng. **39**, 806–821 (2013)
11. Cinque, M., Della Corte, R., Pecchia, A.: Discovering hidden errors from application log traces with process mining. In: 2019 15th European Dependable Computing Conference (EDCC), pp. 137–140 (2019)
12. De Benedictis, A., Flammini, F., Mazzocca, N., Somma, A., Vitale, F.: Digital twins for anomaly detection in the industrial internet of things: conceptual architecture and proof-of-concept. IEEE Trans. Industr. Inf. **19**(12), 11553–11563 (2023)
13. Dong, S., Wang, P., Abbas, K.: A survey on deep learning and its applications. Comput. Sci. Rev. **40**, 100379 (2021)
14. Flammini, F., Marrone, S., Iacono, M., Mazzocca, N., Vittorini, V.: A multiformalism modular approach to ERTMS/ETCS failure modelling. Int. J. Reliab. Qual. Saf. Eng. **21**(01), 1450001 (2014)
15. Gaspari, P., Riccobene, E., Gargantini, A.: A formal design of the hybrid European rail traffic management system. In: Proceedings of the 13th European Conference on Software Architecture, vol. 2, p. 156–162 (2019)
16. Ghazel, M.: Formalizing a subset of ERTMS/ETCS specifications for verification purposes. Transp. Res. Part C: Emerg. Technol. **42**, 60–75 (2014)

17. Goldstein, M., Uchida, S.: A comparative evaluation of unsupervised anomaly detection algorithms for multivariate data. PLoS ONE **11**(4), e0152173 (2016)
18. Hemmer, A., Abderrahim, M., Badonnel, R., François, J., Chrisment, I.: Comparative assessment of process mining for supporting IoT predictive security. IEEE Trans. Netw. Serv. Manage. **18**(1), 1092–1103 (2021)
19. Hossin, M., Sulaiman, M.N.: A review on evaluation metrics for data classification evaluations. Int. J. Data Min. Knowl. Manage. Process **5**(2), 1 (2015)
20. Karg, S., Raschke, A., Tichy, M., Liebel, G.: Model-driven software engineering in the openETCS project: project experiences and lessons learned. In: Proceedings of the ACM/IEEE 19th International Conference on Model Driven Engineering Languages and Systems, pp. 238–248 (2016)
21. Laprie, J.: Resilience for the scalability of dependability. In: Fourth IEEE International Symposium on Network Computing and Applications, pp. 5–6 (2005)
22. de Lima Bezerra, F., Wainer, J.: Algorithms for anomaly detection of traces in logs of process aware information systems. Inf. Syst. **38**, 33–44 (2013)
23. Myers, D., Suriadi, S., Radke, K., Foo, E.: Anomaly detection for industrial control systems using process mining. Comput. Secur. **78**, 103–125 (2018)
24. Nardone, R., et al.: An OSLC-based environment for system-level functional testing of ERTMS/ETCS controllers. J. Syst. Softw. **161**, 110478 (2020)
25. Pecchia, A., Weber, I., Cinque, M., Ma, Y.: Discovering process models for the analysis of application failures under uncertainty of event logs. Knowl.-Based Syst. **189**, 105054 (2020)
26. Rawal, A., McCoy, J., Rawat, D.B., Sadler, B.M., Amant, R.S.: Recent advances in trustworthy explainable artificial intelligence: status, challenges, and perspectives. IEEE Trans. Artif. Intell. **3**(6), 852–866 (2022)
27. Rosenberg, A., Hirschberg, J.: V-measure: A conditional entropy-based external cluster evaluation measure. In: Proceedings of the 2007 Joint Conference on Empirical Methods in Natural Language Processing and Computational Natural Language Learning (EMNLP-CoNLL), pp. 410–420 (2007)
28. Saint-Pierre, C., Cifuentes, F., Bustos-Jiménez, J.: Detecting anomalies in DNS protocol traces via Passive Testing and Process Mining. In: 2014 IEEE Conference on Communications and Network Security, pp. 520–521 (2014)
29. Su, H., Chai, M., Liu, H., Chai, J., Yue, C.: A model-based testing system for safety of railway interlocking. In: 2022 IEEE 25th International Conference on Intelligent Transportation Systems (ITSC), pp. 335–340 (2022)
30. di Tommaso, P., Flammini, F., Lazzaro, A., Pellecchia, R., Sanseviero, A.: The simulation of anomalies in the functional testing of the ERTMS/ETCS track-side system. In: Ninth IEEE International Symposium on High-Assurance Systems Engineering (HASE 2005), pp. 131–139 (2005)
31. Tröls, M.A., Mashkoor, A., Egyed, A.: Multifaceted consistency checking of collaborative engineering artifacts. In: 2019 ACM/IEEE 22nd International Conference on Model Driven Engineering Languages and Systems Companion (MODELS-C), pp. 278–287. IEEE (2019)
32. Valdivia, L.J., Solas, G., Añorga, J., Arrizabalaga, S., Adin, I., Mendizabal, J.: ETCS On-board unit safety testing: saboteurs, testing strategy and results. Promet - Traffic&Transp. **29**(2), 213–223 (2017)
33. Verbeek, H.M.W., Basten, T., van der Aalst, W.M.P.: Diagnosing workflow processes using Woflan. Comput. J. **44**(4), 246–279 (2001)
34. Vitale, F., Guarino, S., Flammini, F., Faramondi, L., Mazzocca, N., Setola, R.: Process mining for digital twin development of industrial cyber-physical systems. IEEE Trans. Industr. Inf. **21**, 866–875 (2025)

35. Vitale, F., Pegoraro, M., van der Aalst, W.M., Mazzocca, N.: Control-flow anomaly detection by process mining-based feature extraction and dimensionality reduction. Knowl.-Based Syst. **310**, 112970 (2025)
36. Weidmann, N.: Tolerant consistency management in model-driven engineering. In: Proceedings of the 21st ACM/IEEE International Conference on Model Driven Engineering Languages and Systems: Companion Proceedings, pp. 192–197 (2018)
37. Witten, I.H., Frank, E., Hall, M.: Data Mining: Practical Machine Learning Tools and Techniques, 4 edn. Morgan Kaufmann (2017)
38. van Zelst, S.J., Bolt, A., Hassani, M., van Dongen, B.F., van der Aalst, W.M.: Online conformance checking: relating event streams to process models using prefix-alignments. Int. J. Data Sci. Anal. **8**, 269–284 (2019)
39. Zoppi, T., Ceccarelli, A., Bondavalli, A.: Unsupervised algorithms to detect zero-day attacks: strategy and application. IEEE Access **9**, 90603–90615 (2021)

Industrial Experiences and Trams

Configurable Interlocking Verification

Alexei Iliasov[1], Dominic Taylor[2], Linas Laibinis[3],
and Alexander Romanovsky[1,4(✉)]

[1] The Formal Route Ltd., London, UK
`alexander.romanovsky@formal-route.com`
[2] Consilium Aquis Sulis Ltd., Bath, UK
[3] Institute of Computer Science, Vilnius University, Vilnius, Lithuania
`linas.laibinis@mif.vu.lt`
[4] Newcastle University, Newcastle upon Tyne, UK

Abstract. This short industrial paper discusses the challenge of precisely defining the scope of formal verification in industrial applications, to avoid both unintentional omission of verification of requirements and duplication of verification. It draws on the experience of using our formal verification technology, called SafeCap, in a substantial number of live railway signalling projects in the UK , and the solutions we are now developing. SafeCap uses safety invariants (safety properties) to formally and fully automatically verify the safety of site-specific configurations of railway interlockings using a dedicated symbolic theorem prover. The scope of this formal verification is a subset of the totality of site-specific interlocking configuration verification, which itself is a subset of the totality of signalling system verification. In the course of our work, it has also become apparent that there is a need to develop and use in practice different (often overlapping) sets of properties. There are various reasons for this: different railways use different safety standards from which the properties are developed; the standards themselves evolve; their is a need for versioning and change management of the properties during the continuous improvement of our tool. To this end, the paper puts forward the idea of defining the verification scopes (called *dialects*) together with a mechanism of introducing a scope as a set of verification properties which are tagged with the unique scope name. The paper uses various industrial scenarios we are facing in deploying SafeCap to demonstrate how this mechanism works in our commercial deployment.

1 Introduction

Railway signalling systems enable multiple trains to operate safely on a railway network at high speeds and serve many different destinations. At the heart of a railway signalling system is a device called an interlocking. Interlockings ensure that trains are only authorized to travel over infrastructure when it is safe for them to do so and that items of infrastructure that can change state, such as points, are only commanded to do so when safe.

© The Author(s), under exclusive license to Springer Nature Switzerland AG 2026
M. H. ter Beek et al. (Eds.): RSSRail 2025, LNCS 16236, pp. 203–212, 2026.
https://doi.org/10.1007/978-3-032-10762-6_16

Modern interlockings are computer based and consist of standard products configured for specific railway layouts. Safety thus depends on multiple elements working together:

- the hardware and software in the standard products;
- the interfaces from those standard products to devices, such as signals, by which train movements are authorized;
- the interfaces to devices, such as points, via which infrastructure can be moved or otherwise made to change state;
- the locations and specific types of signals, points and other signalling devices;
- the procedures by which signallers, drivers and other operators interact with the signalling system;
- the competence of those operators;
- the site specific functionality configured into the interlocking.

This paper concerns the application of formal verification to the last of these items: site-specific configuration of computer based interlockings.

One of the earliest forms of computer-based interlocking was the Solid State Interlocking (SSI) [1], developed in the UK in the 1980s through an agreement between British Rail and two signalling supply companies: Westinghouse and GEC General Signal. SSI and its successors are the predominant technologies used for computer-based interlockings on UK mainline railways. They also has applications overseas, including in India, Australia, New Zealand, France, Egypt, Serbia and Belgium.

In the last five years we have been applying a modern formal verification technology called SafeCap [2] to verify site-specific SSI configuration files, known as *geographic data*. SafeCap has been used in industrial signalling projects in the UK to verify geographic data in over 90 mainline interlockings that use SSI and successor technologies. This geographic data originates from multiple different suppliers and design offices and different time periods over the past thirty years.

Our approach to proving the safety of geographic data is based on expressing signalling principles as a collection of predicates constituting *safety invariants*, representing the railway layout (the schema) and source interlocking data as a *state transition system* that is required to comply with those predicates. We then generate and discharge proof obligations (i.e. verification conjectures) to establish that every system transition maintains the predefined safety invariants.

Safety invariants are derived from railway standards, of which there are three groups applicable to mainline railways in Great Britain: Network Rail company standards [3], Railway Group standards and Railway Industry standards [4]. These standards embody the lessons learnt from two centuries of railway experience, especially that learnt from serious accidents [5]. Not all railway standards pertain to railway signalling. Of those that do, only some of the clauses pertain to the functionality embodied in geographic data.

Our earlier paper describes how we systematically derive safety properties from standards and trace them to those standards [6]. Currently there are over 150 such invariants configured in SafeCap, some of which are generic to all mainline signalling systems in Great Britain, others of which pertain to specific types of signalling system.

This paper explores the idea of verification scopes to address broader topics of how to support structuring, selecting, changing and interpreting of safety properties.

2   Problem Statement

Our main efforts to maintain and improve SafeCap, since we ran the first commercial projects in the UK in 2020, have focused on improving and extending the properties and on developing supporting mechanisms and processes to help us in this work. In particular, there has been a clear demand to deal with several sets of properties. There are various reasons for this.

First of all, the standards from which properties are developed and to which they are traced change all the time. For example, the updates of the UK railway safety standards are issued quarterly.

In addition, there is a clear commercial need for SafeCap to conduct safety verification of interlockings developed to meet the standards as they were at the time of development. This happens, for example, when the newly designed or re-designed interlockings are on the fringes with interlockings developed earlier.

Another challenge we have encountered is the need to extend SafeCap with the verification of SSI interlockings in other countries. Due to the fact that the safety standards are different, we need to create a new set of properties to be used in SafeCap for every country.

Continuous improvement and extension of the property set used commercially is now critical for our business. The main reasons for conducting this work are

- to improve the quality of diagnostics we need to reduce the number of false positives using the experience gleaned from commercial projects;
- to fix the remaining bugs in the properties;
- to add new properties to extend the verification scope as the (current) scope of SafeCap formal verification is a subset of the complete scope of requirements for site-specific interlocking configuration specified in standards;
- to adjust the properties to the specific (sometimes very unusual or unpredictable) ways different engineers design data;
- to add new properties to deal with both ETCS (European Train Control System[1]) or non-ETCS data;
- to allow us to deal differently with properties of different maturity levels;
- to support phased development and extension of the property sets used in the tool to be certified and re-certified later.

Our earlier papers [7] and [6] describe the SafeCap improvements made during the first three years of its industrial use, including improvements of the properties, and propose a general approach to engineering properties, but they do not discuss systematic solutions for configuring and reconfiguring our tool by enabling the structuring of property sets or verification scoping.

---

[1] https://transport.ec.europa.eu/transport-modes/rail/ertms.

3   Scopes, Dialects, Features

The purpose of the scoping mechanism is to select appropriate verification properties among the set of all defined properties. It aims to address the following goals:

- picking properties that are necessary to fulfil stated verification objectives;
- excluding properties that are incompatible with a verified interlocking schema or data;
- differentiating between experimental and production-ready properties;
- selecting the correct variant of a multi-versioned property depending upon the nature of project under verification and the historic time frame of applicable safety standards.

Recall that inputs to a verification project are a digital schema and machine-readable signalling data (control program code). In addition to these, we shall require that a verification engineer explicitly states verification intent by defining a verification scope that we regard as a property *dialect*. In essence, a dialect is a rule identifying a subset of properties; thus, if P is an overall property set, a dialect corresponds to some set D, such that $D \subseteq P$.

Although dialects vary, they often share many common properties. Thus, it is convenient to identify smaller dialect build blocks that we call *features*. A feature, similar to a dialect, is a named rule identifying a property subset.

The mechanism for defining a dialect is based on annotating each property with a collection of *tags* and defining D via a tag matching predicate, denoted D_p. Property tags is a list of values $[t_1, t_2, \ldots]$, each one taking one the following forms:

- a simple tag in the form of a string literal, **tag-literal*;
- a regional dialect tag, **region(region-name)*;
- a historical time frame tag, **timeframe(date)*;
- a maturity level tag **maturity(level)*. There are three maturity levels forming a linear order: *initial < experimental < production*.

The tag matching predicate D_p is one of following expressions:

- a clause stating a positive match on a tag, *tag-literal*, or a negative match on a tag, *!tag-literal*. In the context of a given property, the positive match clause evaluates to truth if there is a matching simple tag in the property tag list. Symmetrically, negative match corresponds to the absence of such a tag;
- a regional dialect selector, *region(region-name-1, region-name-1, ...)*, evaluating to truth in case of the absence of **region(..)* tag or when the property-defined region matches one of the regions of the clause;
- a historical time frame selector, *timeframe(from, to)*. The match succeeds when the property tag list has no **timeframe* tag or specified date interval (*from, to*) contains the date defined in the **timeframe* tag;
- a maturity level selector *maturity(level-from, level-to)*, succeeding when the property specifies a maturity level L such that *level-from <= L <= level-to*;

- a reference to another matching predicate (a feature) $@p$;
- a conjunctive clause $f \wedge g$, where f and g references to other predicates;
- a disjunctive clause $f \vee g$;
- priority control brackets (f).

As an example, a predicate D_p could take the following form:

$$region(SSI\text{-}GB) \wedge$$
$$timeframe(1981, 2003) \wedge$$
$$colour\text{-}lamps \wedge autoworking \wedge \ldots$$
$$!flank\text{-}protection \wedge !ETCS \wedge \ldots$$

In the above example, the first line selects the British subset of SSI. The second line specifies the applicable historic period so that only properties within the defined historic range are included. The third line states that the selected property set must include properties with the tags *colour-lamps*, *autoworking* and so on. This prevents verification that is completely or partially vacuous (that is, not selecting any properties at all or none for some signalling principles). The final line states which properties must not be included in the resulting property set. If there are any properties matching the defined negative tags, they are removed, while the specified positive tag matching conditions (given on line three) are re-checked.

A definition of the form described above is given a label and saved in a collection of predefined *features* and *dialects*. A dialect is a predicate that is offered for selection to a verification engineer to define an overall verification scope, while a feature is a predicate referenced by other features and dialects. Therefore, features help to structure dialect predicate definitions into manageable and readable expressions.

As defined so far, the predicate D_p is computed without regard for the actual project under verification. In practice, a specific kinds of equipment and concepts defined in the digital railway schema as well as concrete code structures found in the signalling data can make properties:

- *extraneous*, where any conjectures generated (unnecessarily) from these properties are guaranteed to be discharged by the prover (such properties make verification run longer but do not, generally[2], result in false positives);
- *erroneous*, where conjectures may be undischarged and resultant violations reflected in verification are invariably false positives.

Hence, as an additional safeguard, on top of the property set D selected by a verification engineer, and during the production of a commercial verification report, we automatically compute two further constraints from the schema and data:

- $R^+ = t_1 \wedge t_2 \wedge \ldots$, the set of tags that *must* be included to achieve minimal valid verification coverage;

---

[2] In practice, verification is run with time and resource quotas so extraneous properties may in fact fail.

- $R^- =\, !n_1 \wedge !n_2 \wedge \ldots$, the set of tags that *must not* be included as they are incompatible with the schema or data design.

Taken together, R^+ and R^- make up the overall constraint $R = R^+ \wedge R^-$ that defines the minimal admissible property set consistent with the schema and data.

We then refine the engineer's dialect predicate as

$$D'_p = D_p \wedge R \wedge maturity(production)$$

The role of R^+ is to prevent *extraneous* properties by forcing the inclusion of properties that are relevant to the actual technology in the schema. Without this, a dialect might omit essential tags and yield vacuous verification results (e.g. covering no colour-light signalling rules even though the schema contains such equipment). The role of R^- is to prevent *erroneous* properties by excluding tags that contradict the schema and would otherwise give rise to false positives (e.g. attempting to verify ETCS properties in a non-ETCS interlocking). Together, R^+ and R^- act as an automatic safeguard, ensuring that the resulting property set is both non-vacuous and consistent with the verified project.

The resulting D'_p might yield an empty property set, indicating that the verification intent is incompatible with the schema and data of the project under verification. A typical case is selecting the timeframe range incompatible with the technology present on the schema.

4   Industrial Application of the Dialects

SafeCap is now used commercially for the verification of the UK SSI and SSI family interlockings with regular modifications and improvements of the verification scope to deal with changing standards, reduce false positives, add new properties and fix bugs.

Changing Standards and SafeCap. Railway standards evolve over time to reflect changing operational environments and evolving understanding of trade-off's between different safety risks. Sometimes standards become more restrictive: for example, modern interlockings generally provide overlaps for shunt routes whereas historically in some areas shunt routes has no overlaps. Other times standards become less restrictive: for example, historically points in overlaps beyond red signals (distances that are protected in case a train passes that signal) were detected in position before a train was allowed to approach that signal. However, this increases the impact of a point failure and hence the frequency with which trains need verbal authorization to move with very limited signalling protection. Therefore, in modern interlockings, points in overlaps are seldom detected in position.

New interlocking data is generally written in accordance with the latest standards. However, when modifying old interlocking data, it may not be cost-effective to update it to the latest standards. Whilst safety properties can be written to always cover the most restrictive case, this tends to result in excessive false positives. By contrast, dialects enable selection of the safety properties appropriate to the standards at the time the interlocking data was written.

Each successive update to standards is reviewed by two SafeCap engineers to identify any changes that affect safety properties. Where significant changes occur, the timeframe of affected properties and of the dialect that includes them can be updated to end immediately before the updated standard came into force and a new variant of a dialect created with a timeframe beginning at that date.

Different Railways and SafeCap. Whilst the high-level safety goals of railway signalling are the same everywhere, different railways adopt different standards. These reflect different ways of authorizing train movements, particularly through signal aspects, different operational procedures and different expectations of operators. Differences occur between railways in different countries, for example between British, French and German approaches to signalling. They also occur between different railways in the same country. For example between Network Rail and London Underground infrastructure in the UK or between practices in the different states and territories of Australia.

In some cases the differences are relatively minor, such as between mainline railways in Great Britain and Australia. In such cases, dialects enable a common set of properties to be developed with railway specific properties selected according to the specific application. For example, mainline railways in the UK and those in the state of Victoria have very similar underlying principles, but authorize trains to move through very different signal aspects. Properties pertaining to signal aspects thus apply to specific dialects whereas common properties apply universally.

Regression Testing and Property Variants. Continuous development and improvement of the properties is key to the commercial success of SafeCap. This development is naturally structured into baselines in which we use the dialect with the stable, already checked, properties in commercial projects. The new dialect, consisting of the properties modified and added since the the baseline, goes through a thorough process of design and evaluation, including regression testing. We use the previously completed commercial projects to ensure that the new dialect does not affect the correct outcomes of verification. All violations detected by the new and updated properties are manually analysed to make sure that these properties detect the existing violations correctly and provide sufficient and helpful diagnostics. In addition, we test the new dialect by seeding errors.

In addition, to aid diagnostics, we have started experimenting with subordinate dialects for which the verification scopes are subsets of the basic dialects.

During our work on the UK commercial projects we have developed two variants of the SSI dialect we widely use: one for the ETCS projects and another one for the non-ETCS projects. As an example of this, we have recently used the former to verify the full supervised mode in the Moorgate interlocking [8]. When we run the tool we select the required dialect manually.

Tool Certification. A clear definition of the verification scope is vitally important for tool certification. The claim about which safety violations the tool is qualified to verify should be justifiably made. In our work on a new tool, called Formal Rail, we use a phased approach. First, we are certifying the tool with the core set of properties (the core dialect) which have been used in our commercial projects in the last 5 years.

During the following re-certifications we will be providing the assurance arguments for the two dialects: the updated core which includes only the updated properties from the core and the new properties to be added. When the tool is used between these two certifications we verify data using two dialects: the core one for which the tool results are assured, and the non-certified dialect, with a warning that the outcomes of the verification are advisory.

5   Discussion

The concept of dialects allows us to configure and reconfigure the SafeCap tool to deploy different sets of verification properties. We are already using this approach in both commercial projects and in our experimental prototyping. This experience is helping us to refine the ideas and to develop more efficient and usable versions of the dialect support.

Dialects enable us to select different properties pertaining to overlaps according to the date of the standards to which interlocking functionality was designed. They also enable us to select different functionality according to whether trains are authorized to move via ETCS cab-signalling, lineside signals on UK mainlines or in the state of Victoria (Australia).

Development of new dialects to address changes to standards is fairly rare as, although the standards themselves change frequently, major changes to required interlocking functionality typically only occur of the order of every ten years. By contrast, dialects play a major role in enabling property sets to be customized to the needs of different railways. Creation of new properties and an associated dialect needs to be undertaken each time SafeCap is deployed on a different railway, but once done the new dialect can be applied repeatedly to interlockings on that railway.

There is now an experimental implementation supporting dialects in Safe-Cap, which is successfully used in extending the technology with verification of Victoria (Australia) SSI interlockings and in supporting two dialects for verification of ETCS and non-ETCS SSI data in the UK. The full support of dialects is being integrated into the new verification tool, called Formal Rail, which is now under development for certification. This dialect management system will incorporate a support for property and dialect change managements to deal with the various practical scenarios presented in Sect. 4.

Generation of comprehensive verification reports is critical to the commercial success of tools such as SafeCap. Given a dialect, schema and signalling data, our system builds a proof report by constructing necessary symbolic transition systems of the data, translating schema into a set-theoretic model, generating conjectures derived from safety properties, running the prover on those conjectures, extracting a proof log and, finally, building the proof report. The final report always includes a detailed description of the dialect used.

A dialect represents a property set formalising signalling principles that originate from standards and various regulatory documents. There are complementary yet importantly distinct aspects of a dialect - that of its *fidelity* and *fittingness*, and its signalling data verification *coverage*. The nature of the first aspect is such that we can only hope to study it in an indirect manner by noting any defects in verification reports and, through this experience, aiming to derive a development process that provides a high-quality set of formalised principles. The second aspect is more concrete and affords a directly measurable metric at the production stage. Notice that SafeCap detects signalling data that are not in agreement with the railway topology and signalling principles. So the verification coverage could be measured by how mutations of signalling data clauses are detected by formalised principles (our earlier paper discusses how this idea could be applied for analysing the coverage of control table verification [9]).

In conclusion we would like to clarify that to the best of our knowledge the concept of dialects as a mechanism for structuring verification property sets has been never discussed before, we are not aware of any work that treats these sets as the first class entities to be used for (re-)configuring verification tools.

References

1. Stratton, D.H: Solid State Interlocking. First edition, IRSE Booklet, 28. Institution of Railway Signal Engineers (IRSE). p. 20 (1988)
2. Iliasov, A., Taylor, D., Laibinis, L., Romanovsky, A.: Practical verification of railway signalling programs. IEEE Trans. Dependable Secure Comput. **20**(1), 695–707 (2023). https://doi.org/10.1109/TDSC.2022.3141555
3. Network Rail: Catalogue of Network Rail Standards, NR/CAT/STP/001 Issue 134, 7th December (2024). https://www.networkrail.co.uk/industry-and-commercial/third-party-investors/network-rail-is-open-for-business/reviewing-our-standards/
4. UK Railway Safety and Standards Board, RSSB: Standards Catalogue. https://www.rssb.co.uk/standards-catalogue#standards
5. Anderson, T., Rivett, R.: Lessons from railway accidents for autonomous road vehicles. In: 19th European Dependable Computing Conference (EDCC), pp. 85–88. IEEE (2024). https://doi.org/10.1109/EDCC61798.2024.00027
6. Iliasov, A., Taylor, D., Laibinis, L., Romanovsky, A.B.: Safety invariant engineering for interlocking verification. In: Ceccarelli, A., Trapp, M., Bondavalli, A., Bitsch, F. (eds.) Computer Safety, Reliability, and Security - 43rd International Conference, SAFECOMP 2024, Florence, Italy, September 18–20, 2024, Proceedings. Lecture Notes in Computer Science, vol. 14988, pp. 68–83. Springer (2024). https://doi.org/10.1007/978-3-031-68606-1_5

7. Iliasov, A., Taylor, D., Laibinis, L., Romanovsky, A.B.: The safecap trajectory: industry-driven improvement of an interlocking verification tool. In: Milius, B., Dutilleul, S.C., Lecomte, T. (eds.) Reliability, Safety, and Security of Railway Systems. Modelling, Analysis, Verification, and Certification - 5th International Conference, RSSRail 2023, Berlin, Germany, October 10–12, 2023, Proceedings. Lecture Notes in Computer Science, vol. 14198, pp. 117–127. Springer (2023).https://doi.org/10.1007/978-3-031-43366-5_7
8. Network Rail: The Northern City Line between Finsbury Park and Moorgate has become the first commuter railway in Britain to run without signals beside the track. (2025). https://www.networkrail.co.uk/stories/launching-britains-first-signals-free-commuter-railway/
9. Laibinis, L., Iliasov, A., Romanovsky, A.B.: Mutation testing for rule-based verification of railway signaling data. IEEE Trans. Reliab. **70**(2), 676–691 (2021). https://doi.org/10.1109/TR.2020.3047462

Automated Semantic Validation of Railway Signaling Data on the Basis of Schematron

Susanne Wunsch[1(✉)] , Birgit Jaekel[2] , Martin Lehnert[3] ,
Christoph Klaus[4], Jan Gruteser[5] , and Michael Leuschel[5]

[1] Chair of Traffic Process Automation, TUD Dresden University of Technology,
01062 Dresden, Germany
Susanne.Wunsch@tu-dresden.de

[2] German Centre for Rail Traffic Research, August-Bebel-Straße 10,
01219 Dresden, Germany
jaekelb@dzsf.bund.de

[3] Technical University of Applied Sciences Wildau, Hochschulring 1,
15745 Wildau, Germany
mlehnert@th-wildau.de

[4] Department for Principles of Control-Command and Signaling Technology,
DB InfraGO AG, Caroline-Michaelis-Straße 5-11, 10115 Berlin, Germany
Christoph.Klaus@deutschebahn.com

[5] Faculty of Mathematics and Natural Science, Institute of Computer Science,
Heinrich Heine University Düsseldorf, Universitätsstraße 1,
40225 Düsseldorf, Germany
{jan.gruteser,leuschel}@hhu.de

Abstract. This paper introduces a framework to ensure the semantic integrity of Control-Command and Signaling (CCS) design data, essential for reliable and efficient planning processes. Traditional XML Schema checks address syntax but fail to capture the complex logic required for CCS systems. To overcome this, we apply the Schematron standard to formally validate complex railway signaling rules.

Our approach is to translate natural language constraints into semi-formal semantic rules that are implemented and tested. We extend Schematron with technology- and domain-specific features, such as data indexing and advanced error reporting. These innovations enable scalability for large datasets while producing clear, actionable reports for signaling engineers, safety assessors, and infrastructure managers.

Applied to DB InfraGO's PlanPro data format, our framework automates processes that improve data quality, reduce human error, and accelerate CCS planning. By supporting formal workflows, it strengthens safety assurance and regulatory compliance, addressing key challenges in the railway domain. Its integration into the "Werkzeugkoffer" toolkit demonstrates its practical value in tackling the complexities of modern railway control systems.

1   Introduction

European railway infrastructure managers face the complex challenge of designing, building, and maintaining Control-Command and Signaling (CCS) systems. These systems integrate physical infrastructure with logical functions, including interlockings, train protection systems, or track alignment data. Operating within a stringent framework of laws, regulations, and specifications, their effective management is essential to ensuring safety and reliability.

The deteriorating state of railway infrastructure in many European countries, coupled with increasing project volumes and a shortage of domain experts, has exposed inefficiencies in CCS planning processes. In Germany, these processes often rely on manual workflows and computer-aided design software (CAD) that produce static PDF documents, hindering automation and enabling masked errors. To address these challenges, DB InfraGO developed PlanPro, a structured data format for CCS design that facilitates digital data management and automation [10].

The XML Schema Definition (XSD) serves as baseline for syntactic validation of XML-formatted PlanPro files. Additionally, semantic validation – based on expert knowledge and organizational specifications – is essential for maintaining data consistency, ensuring formal correctness, and guaranteeing content accuracy across varying levels of detail.

Semantic validation in transportation systems has been approached from different research directions. Tutcher et al. [14] demonstrated semantic data modeling using ontolology-based techniques with synthetic rules. Gruteser and Leuschel [6] explored the application of the B-method for validating railML files against custom rules, while earlier approaches using B (not targeting XML data in particular) are described in [1,12,13] and surveyed in [3]. In an article in the present proceedings, Dillmann and Hähnle [4] tackle validation of PlanPro datasets using SMT solvers. In the aviation sector, Wang et al. [15] applied Semantics of Business Vocabulary and Business Rules (SBVR) to AIXM data. Häußler et al. [7] focused on code compliance checks of railway Building Information Modeling (BIM) data using Business Process Model and Notation (BPMN) and Decision Model and Notation (DMN). Banerjee et al. [2] investigated ETCS design validation based on an attributed graph and logical constraints.

Unlike the mentioned approaches that require converting the data model or using non-native tools, our method performs validation directly within the XML ecosystem. We leverage the pattern-oriented Schematron standard [8], whose declarative, rule-based framework and XPath [16] expressions enable sophisticated, context-aware validation. This directly enhances data quality without the costly and error-prone process of data transformation by preserving original data integrity.

Our core contributions are:

- Test-driven implementation of semantic CCS rules (trivial to complex);
- Quality assurance by synthetic test files for pass, fail, and not-proven scenarios;
- Schematron Framework extended with XSLT 2.0 transformations and XPath 2.0 queries for advanced logic and features working on the XML data;

- Performance optimized for large files via data indexing (using the xsl:key element of XSLT);
- Rule implementation enhanced with generic functions and domain-specific variables;
- Specific XSLT stylesheets to generate user-friendly reports (PDF, HTML);
- Dynamically inject domain-specific terminology and context into tailored messages for different target groups.

The solution has been integrated as "PlaZ component" ("Plausibility and Admissibility Checking") into the "Werkzeugkoffer" toolkit [9,11] that visualizes PlanPro data sets. Developed for DB InfraGO, the tool is freely available upon registration[1], though this paper focuses on the theoretical concepts rather than tool specifics. Over one hundred rules have been implemented in Schematron covering ETCS balise groups, routes, signals, switches, derailers, flank protection, key locking devices, tracks, external object controllers, track layout and base objects.

In this paper we introduce the PlanPro format and describe the developed validation workflow, followed by key principles of the Schematron language and its application in the workflow. It concludes with key findings and future research directions.

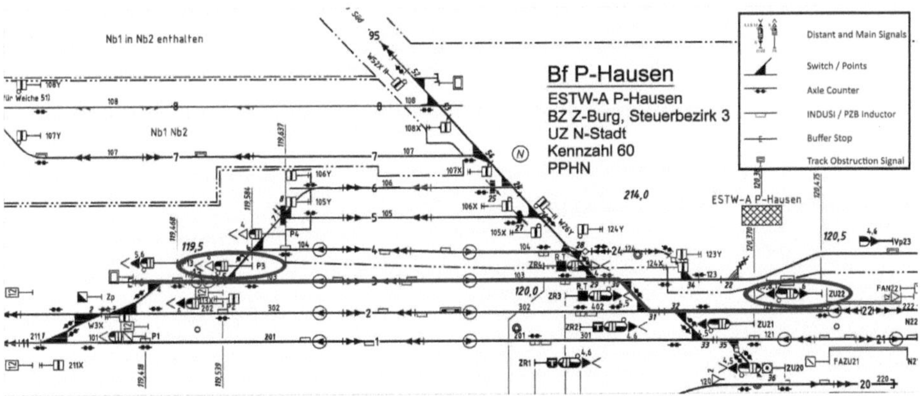

Fig. 1. Main part of the schematic track layout plan of P-Hausen; inner home signal ZU22, exit signal P3 and related route marked in red; related overlap marked in purple. (Color figure online)

2 PlanPro and Schematron

This chapter introduces the modeling concepts of the PlanPro data format as a foundation for applying formal validation concepts based on Schematron. The goal is to achieve semantic validation of PlanPro data sets.

---

[1] https://www.dbinfrago.com/web/schienennetz/dienstleistende/planpro/ digitale_lst_planung-11161508.

2.1 PlanPro - A Specialized Data Format for CCS Data Sets

PlanPro's data structure and types are modeled in Unified Modeling Language (UML) and automatically converted into an XML Schema Definition (XSD) enabling syntactic validation, identifying mismatched structures or incorrect data types. The sample file "P-Hausen" (schematic track layout in Fig. 1) demonstrates the use of the PlanPro format. It represents an advanced stage of planning for a complex railway station similar to a real-world German medium-sized station. Altogether, these are provided as open-source resources upon acceptance of the license agreements[2].

While the model was developed in German, the sample code in this paper is partially translated into English for clarity. However, XML elements are presented in their original German form to facilitate comparison with the XML Schema.

Listing 1 illustrates an adapted excerpt of the PlanPro file "P-Hausen" for traditional route logic. The route *(lines 19–29)* is a main regular route *(line 23)* on a route path *(lines 21, 13–18)* starting at a signal *(lines 16, 30–38)* and ending at a signal *(lines 17, 39–47)* with a route overlap *(lines 26, 2–12)*. The route overlap requires a nominal length (at minimum) of 69 meters *(line 5)* given a decisive gradient of -0.10 per mil *(line 6)* and maximum speed of 60 km/h *(line 9)*. The route path itself is designed for a maximum speed of 50 km/h *(line 15)*. The selected route overlap is determined as default for this route path *(line 25)*. The start signal of the route *(lines 16, 30–38)* is "60ZU22" *(line 33)* with the function of an inner home signal for the station *(line 36)*. The target signal of the route *(lines 17, 39–47)* is "60P3" *(line 42)* with the function of an exit signal *(line 45)*.

Note, that the number "60" is the code number of this station. Therefore, the signal names in the schematic plan leave this number out (cf. Fig. 1). "ZU22" is located on the right part and "P3" on the left part of the schematic plan.

The original sample file contains numerous additional attributes for the selected objects. For clarity, a simplified example is described in Listing 1 and illustrated in Fig. 2. The core design principle of the PlanPro model is already apparent.

Fig. 2. Simplified schematic track layout according to Fig. 1; inner home signal ZU22, exit signal P3 and related route marked in red; related overlap marked in purple. (Color figure online)

The modelling principle for PlanPro is modularization of traditional CCS objects regarding a certain set of properties, e.g. `Fstr_Zug_Rangier`, `Fstr_DWeg`,

---

Fstr_Fahrweg, resulting in distinct PlanPro objects. A traditional route is a combination of several PlanPro objects, avoiding duplications of the same properties. For instance, further routes may be defined reusing the same route path and signals but with different route overlaps. Therefore, identities and references play an important role for any data handling.

```
<PlanPro_Schnittstelle xmlns="http://www.plan-pro.org/modell/PlanPro/1.10.0.1">
  <Fstr_DWeg> <!-- route overlap -->
    <Identitaet><Wert>{GUID-1}</Wert></Identitaet> <!-- identity -->
    <Fstr_DWeg_Allg>
      <Laenge_Soll><Wert>69</Wert></Laenge_Soll> <!-- nominal length -->
      <Massgebende_Neigung><Wert>-0.10</Wert></Massgebende_Neigung> <!-- gradient -->
    </Fstr_DWeg_Allg>
    <Fstr_DWeg_Spezifisch>
      <DWeg_V><Wert>60</Wert></DWeg_V> <!-- maximum speed -->
    </Fstr_DWeg_Spezifisch>
    <ID_Fstr_Fahrweg><Wert>{GUID-2}</Wert></ID_Fstr_Fahrweg> <!-- refer to route path -->
  </Fstr_DWeg>
  <Fstr_Fahrweg> <!-- route path -->
    <Identitaet><Wert>{GUID-2}</Wert></Identitaet> <!-- identity -->
    <Fstr_V_Hg><Wert>50</Wert></Fstr_V_Hg> <!-- maximum speed -->
    <ID_Start><Wert>{GUID-3}</Wert></ID_Start> <!-- refer to start object -->
    <ID_Ziel><Wert>{GUID-4}</Wert></ID_Ziel> <!-- refer to target object -->
  </Fstr_Fahrweg>
  <Fstr_Zug_Rangier> <!-- route -->
    <Identitaet><Wert>{GUID-5}</Wert></Identitaet> <!-- identity -->
    <ID_Fstr_Fahrweg><Wert>{GUID-2}</Wert></ID_Fstr_Fahrweg> <!-- refer to route path -->
    <Fstr_Zug>
      <Fstr_Zug_Art><Wert>ZR</Wert></Fstr_Zug_Art> <!-- main regular route -->
      <Fstr_Zug_DWeg>
        <DWeg_Vorzug><Wert>true</Wert></DWeg_Vorzug> <!-- default overlap -->
        <ID_Fstr_DWeg><Wert>{GUID-1}</Wert></ID_Fstr_DWeg> <!-- refer to route overlap -->
      </Fstr_Zug_DWeg>
    </Fstr_Zug>
  </Fstr_Zug_Rangier>
  <Signal> <!-- signal -->
    <Identitaet><Wert>{GUID-3}</Wert></Identitaet> <!-- identity -->
    <Bezeichnung>
      <Bezeichnung_Tabelle><Wert>60ZU22</Wert></Bezeichnung_Tabelle> <!-- signal name -->
    </Bezeichnung>
    <Signal_Real>
      <Signal_Funktion><Wert>Zwischen_Signal</Wert></Signal_Funktion> <!-- inner home -->
    </Signal_Real>
  </Signal>
  <Signal> <!-- signal -->
    <Identitaet><Wert>{GUID-4}</Wert></Identitaet> <!-- identity -->
      <Bezeichnung>
        <Bezeichnung_Tabelle><Wert>60P3</Wert></Bezeichnung_Tabelle> <!-- signal name -->
      </Bezeichnung>
    <Signal_Real>
      <Signal_Funktion><Wert>Ausfahr_Signal</Wert></Signal_Funktion> <!-- exit signal -->
    </Signal_Real>
  </Signal>
</PlanPro_Schnittstelle>
```

Listing 1: An excerpt of a PlanPro data set showing a route (Fstr_Zug_ Rangier), a route path (Fstr_Fahrweg), a route overlap (Fstr_DWeg) and signals (Signal); the described route, route overlap, start and target signal marked in Fig. 1.

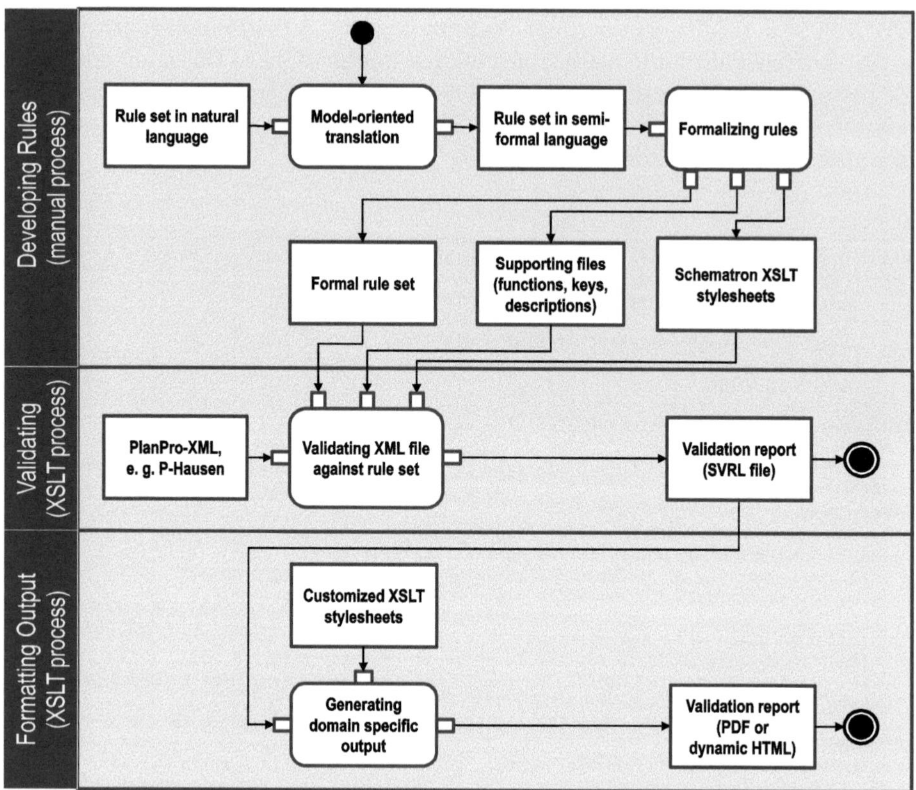

Fig. 3. Semantic validation process; The generated SVRL file in the middle lane can be used for debugging purposes. The second and third lanes are incorporated into the toolkit, accessible to the domain experts for validating PlanPro files.

The PlanPro model is designed for flexibility, allowing CCS design data to be provided at different maturity levels and across various disciplines. This leads to widespread use of optionality in XML elements and makes it necessary to check the presence of elements in different contexts using constraints. A common example are co-occurrence constraints, such as: "If attribute A exists, then attribute B must also exist; otherwise, B is optional." Based on these design principles, further validation is needed to ensure consistent and reliable data.

2.2   Validation Workflow

Validation of a PlanPro file involves the following sequential steps:

1. Grammatical correctness: Ensuring the XML is well-formed,
2. Syntactic validation: Verifying compliance with XSD,
3. Semantic validation: Checking adherence to predefined rules.

Whereas the first and second step are typically integrated into tools dealing with data, the third step – the semantic validation – comprises a series of activities, illustrated in Fig. 3 and explained in the following list:

1. **Model-oriented translation:** Rules are derived from engineering rulebooks, specifications, additional guidelines, or common practices by several domain experts in a domain-specific natural language. After prioritization and further detailing, the most relevant rules are prepared and manually translated by a trained domain expert for the platform specific PlanPro model, incorporating actual PlanPro objects, its relations and types. Accompanied by further metadata, this targets unambiguous formalization as a base for clear rule implementation.

2. **Formalizing rules:** The rules in semi-formal language enable the implementation in enhanced Schematron by another domain expert with strong background in XML technologies. In case of interpretation, there are discussions and adjustments between both experts. If required, supporting features are extended for a certain rule, e.g. establishing new `keys`, new additional `functions` or `descriptions`. Rule development involves creating synthetic PlanPro test files to verify correct functionality based on XML schema compliance. This testing approach follows a dual strategy: first, the rule's target is evaluated using PlanPro objects deliberately designed to both match and not match the constraint criteria. Second, for matching objects, verification ensures that the rule generates appropriate messages for non-compliant PlanPro objects while remaining silent for compliant ones (counterexample testing). Nevertheless, if the semi-formal rule with its metadata were interpreted in a wrong way, this quality check may also fail.

3. **Validating XML file:** The core semantic validation is an XSLT process, which transforms the input PlanPro XML file based on the semantic validation engine into a validation report in form of an XML file (Schematron Validation Report Language - SVRL) including detailed information about which rules passed or failed, along with specific error or warning messages. For rule development and debugging purposes, the internal SVRL output provides sufficient diagnostic information, skipping the user-friendly output transformations.

4. **Generating domain-specific output:** We developed specific XSL scripts for transforming the SVRL report into actionable documents for domain experts, namely via Extensible Stylesheet Language Formatting Objects (XSL-FO) and a Formatting Objects Processor (FOP) into *PDF format* as official document and including customized Cascading Style Sheets (CSS) and JavaScript (JS) libraries into *HTML format* as flexible platform enabling filtering and sorting features.

Most of these steps are designed for use with an XSLT processor, where the result forms the input for the next step. For developing and debugging of rules, activities 1 to 3 are conducted. Given a semantic validation engine as XSL script, activities 3 and 4 are incorporated into the "Werkzeugkoffer" toolkit for productive use by domain experts.

2.3 The Schematron Language

Schematron, as ISO/IEC 19757–3 standard [8], is a language for defining patterns for XML documents. Based on natural language assertions invoking an external query language (XPath2 [16] as recommended), it enables the generation of error messages[3]. Schematron may handle complex validation scenarios, including relational and conditional element sequences, conditional data types, mathematical operations, dependencies on content, number, order, or existence of elements or attributes.

Schematron's reliability is further supported by its open-source XSLT transformations. A custom XSLT framework has been developed for PlanPro framework that extends the capabilities of the standard Schematron. The source code is available on GitHub[4].

Listing 2 illustrates an example of a Schematron rule. The demonstrated structure, functionality, and application to the PlanPro data model will be explained in the following paragraphs, whereby our extensions to the standard Schematron will be mentioned.

Schematron Pattern. All PlanPro rules are implemented in separate Schematron `pattern` files in order to enable the `abstract pattern` mechanism for improving maintainability and reducing redundancy.

Abstract patterns define generic rules that are to be instantiated for specific properties. For PlanPro, this approach is used to apply similar rules to different project states, such as:

- **As-built state "LST_Zustand"** – the current state of CCS.
- **Target state "LST_Zustand_Ziel"** – the planned state of CCS.

Listing 3 presents the definition for this mechanism utilizing the parameter "state", that is activated in the second activity (cf. Sect. 2.2). The `iso:pattern/`@id attribute serves as identifier. After expansion, the original (abstract) pattern becomes inactive. In our case, two independent patterns provide almost equal validation rules for different context. Each occurrence of the defined parameter "state" (denoted as `$state`) is substituted, not limited to `iso:rule/@context` attribute.

Namespaces. The Schematron namespace *(line 2)* is required anyway, the XSL namespace *(line 3)* is declared for our extension (`xsl:if, xsl:value-of`) in the assertion, that generates custom messages with stronger expressiveness than the built-in `iso:value-of`. The PlanPro namespace *(line 4)* is declared for several additional XML attributes and XML elements, that facilitate metadata.

---

[3] Integrating other severity categories enables further types of messages, such as "warning" and "information".

[4] https://github.com/susi-wunsch/schematron.

Metadata. For rule development and maintenance, patterns use metadata nodes such as `planpro:arbeitspaket` *(line 6)* to assign a work package `planpro:version` *(line 6)* for a release, or `iso:title` *(line 7)* for a natural language heading. We extended the `iso:p` element *(lines 8–23)* with a flexible sub-structure to include more domain-specific properties, improving rule organization and comprehension.

```xml
<?xml version="1.0" encoding="UTF-8"?>
<iso:pattern xmlns:iso="http://purl.oclc.org/dsdl/schematron"
             xmlns:xsl="http://www.w3.org/1999/XSL/Transform"
             xmlns:planpro="http://www.plan-pro.org/regeln/struktur"
             abstract="true" id="ID278" fpi="{GUID-6}"
             planpro:arbeitspaket="Routes" planpro:version="1.10.0.1">
  <iso:title>One-time definition of a default route overlap per route path</iso:title>
    <iso:p>
      <planpro:description>
        If a route path is used as a traversed part of main routes including a route
            overlap, a default route overlap must be defined in exactly one of these main
            routes. This condition also applies if there is only one main route with a
            route overlap for this route path.

        For all Fstr_Zug_Rangier with Fstr_Zug_Rangier.Fstr_Zug.Fstr_Zug_DWeg with
            Fstr_Zug_Rangier.Fstr_Zug.Fstr_Zug_DWeg.ID_Fstr_DWeg -> Fstr_DWeg.
            Fstr_DWeg_Spezifisch and same Fstr_Zug_Rangier.ID_Fstr_Fahrweg there has to be
            exactly one Fstr_Zug_Rangier.Fstr_Zug.Fstr_Zug_DWeg.DWeg_Vorzug == 'true'.
      </planpro:description>
      <planpro:test>
        <planpro:success>
          For the route path, there is exactly one main route with a default route overlap.
        <planpro:success>
        <planpro:error>
          For the route path, there are either no or multiple main routes with a default
              route overlap.
        </planpro:error>
      </planpro:test>
      <planpro:output>Fstr_Fahrweg</planpro:output>
    </iso:p>
    <iso:rule role="error"
      context="Fstr_Fahrweg[ancestor::$state][fx:Fstr-278(current(), ancestor::$state)]">
      <iso:let name="route"
        value="key('route-for-routePath', Identitaet/Wert, ancestor::$state)"/>
      <iso:let name="routeOverlapDefault"
        value="$route[Fstr_Zug/Fstr_Zug_DWeg/DWeg_Vorzug/Wert='true']"/>
      <iso:let name="routeOverlapNoDefault"
        value="$route[not(Fstr_Zug/Fstr_Zug_DWeg/DWeg_Vorzug/Wert='true')]"/>
      <iso:assert diagnostics="guid type area structure s1 s2 s3"
        test="count($routeOverlapDefault)=1">For the route path, there are either no or
    multiple main routes with a default route overlap.
        <xsl:if test="$routeOverlapDefault">
          The following main routes serve a default route overlap:
          <xsl:value-of select="$routeOverlapDefault/Identitaet/Wert" separator=" / "/>.
        </xsl:if>
        <xsl:if test="$routeOverlapNoDefault">
          The following main routes serve no default route overlap:
          <xsl:value-of select="$routeOverlapNoDefault/Identitaet/Wert" separator=" / "/>.
        </xsl:if>
      </iso:assert>
    </iso:rule>
</iso:pattern>
```

Listing 2: A Schematron rule applying to a route path (`Fstr_Fahrweg`).

```
1  <pattern is-a="ID278" id="ID278-LST_Zustand">
2    <param name="state" value="LST_Zustand"/>
3  </pattern>
4  <pattern is-a="ID278" id="ID278-LST_Zustand_Ziel">
5    <param name="state" value="LST_Zustand_Ziel"/>
6  </pattern>
```

Listing 3: Schematron abstract patterns for rule ID278.

The first paragraph of planpro:description *(line 10)* contains the rule in a domain-specific natural language (cf. first activity in Sect. 2.2). The second paragraph *(line 12)* shows the translated rule in semi-formal language (cf. first activity). Both, the positive and negative result are formulated in natural language within planpro:success *(lines 15–17)* and planpro:error *(lines 18–20)*. The PlanPro object that will be checked for the message is stated in planpro:output *(line 22)*.

Schematron's role attribute *(line 24)* is facilitated in a customized way for designating a certain severity, like "error", "warning" or "information".

Schematron Rule with Context.

Each iso:rule *(lines 24–41)* is applied to a specific context *(line 25)* defined as an XPath [16] expression including possible predicates for filtering purposes which are by definition linked by logical AND. The context determines the XML elements (or attributes) to which the rule applies.

In Listing 2 the iso:rule targets the Fstr_Fahrweg node *(line 25)*, as described for the abstract pattern. The second predicate requires a custom XSL function (fx:Fstr-278, cf. Listing 4) with two parameters to return true().

```
1  <xsl:key name="routeOverlap" match="Fstr_DWeg" use="Identitaet/Wert"/>
2  <xsl:key name="route-for-routePath" match="Fstr_Zug_Rangier" use="ID_Fstr_Fahrweg/Wert"/>
3
4  <xsl:function name="fx:Fstr-278" as="xs:boolean">
5    <xsl:param name="current" as="node()"/>
6    <xsl:param name="context" as="node()"/>
7    <xsl:value-of
8      select="if (key('route-for-routePath', $current/Identitaet/Wert, $context)
9        [Fstr_Zug/Fstr_Zug_DWeg
10          [key('routeOverlap', ID_Fstr_DWeg/Wert, $context)/Fstr_DWeg_Spezifisch]])
11            then true() else false()"/>
12  </xsl:function>
```

Listing 4: An XSL function constraining the rule context predicate (fx:Fstr-278), completed with required XSL keys.

On the one hand, such custom functions enable re-usability for several rules with similar constrained context. On the other hand, applying functions allows for enhanced constraining concepts, e.g. with recursive functions.

Typed parameters (cf. Listing 4, *lines 5, 6*) support clean coding, so that mismatched values result in an exception requiring debugging. The return value of the function is evaluated in `xsl:value-of` (cf. Listing 4, *lines 7–11*) within an `if-then-else` XPath expression.

Validating relationships among multiple PlanPro objects requires careful consideration of the PlanPro data model and the node connections established through the GUID (Global Unique Identifier) values (a 35 character string). Aiming at improved processing time, we extended the Schematron standard with the application of `xsl:key`.

In Listing 4 (*lines 1, 2*) `xsl:keys` are created, that will be processed for any `matching` XML element of the PlanPro file storing the `use` value if available. This kind of pre-computation is done irrespective of the relevance for any rule. The usage of the keys may be observed in Listing 2 *(line 27)* or Listing 4 *(lines 8, 10)*. Precise path definitions, avoiding wildcards (NameTests), further optimize computational efficiency during XML document validation.

Schematron Assertions and Variables. Schematron `let` variables enhance rule clarity and re-usability by decomposing complex logic into smaller, manageable components incorporating strong XPath expressions (cf. Listing 2, *lines 26–31*). Based on well defined variables, the assertion `test` may be lean coded (cf. Listing 2, *line 33*).

The `test` attribute within an `assert` (cf. Listing 2, *lines 32–40*) or `report` node specifies the condition to be evaluated. If the condition fails (for `assert`) or succeeds (for `report`), the corresponding message (cf. Listing 2, *lines 33–39*) is included in the validation report.

For PlaZ, each `assert` or `report` is encapsulated in a separate `rule` to ensure all relevant messages are included in the validation report. The decision to use `assert` or `report` depends on ease of comprehension and rule maintenance.

Schematron Diagnostics. The `diagnostics` mechanism in Schematron (cf. Listing 2, *line 32*) is heavily utilized to enrich validation reports with context-sensitive information. *Diagnostics* variables are populated with dynamic content during the validation process. This information is used to generate user-friendly validation reports.

2.4   The Schematron Validation Workflow

The semantic validation process for PlanPro files involves a series of steps, each tailored to ensure the accuracy and usability of the validation results. As mentioned in Sect. 2.3 there are only minor changes to the Open Source Schematron XSL scripts, which build the basis of the whole validation process. Fig. 4 illustrates the workflow, which includes the following steps:

1. **Including Schematron Files** Modularized files are incorporated in the first step, which simplifies the management of complex rule sets and enables the reuse of common rules and supporting files across multiple schemas.

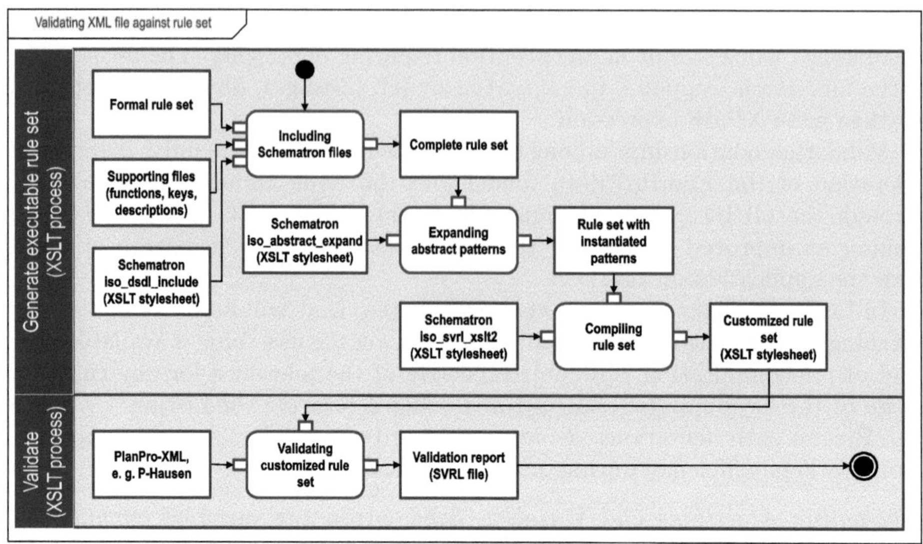

Fig. 4. Schematron Validation Process.

2. **Expanding Abstract Patterns** Schematron's parameterized templates create reusable validation logic that transcends specific element names. These abstract constructs function as macros, instantiated across multiple contexts with different parameters to reduce code duplication while maintaining validation consistency throughout complex document structures.
3. **Compiling the Rule Set** The expanded and included Schematron rules are compiled into an (executable) XSLT stylesheet. This step transforms the comprehensive rule set into a concrete validation engine that can process XML files.
4. **Validating XML file against rule set** During this step, the validation engine checks the XML file against the defined rules, generating a validation report in Schematron Validation Report Language (SVRL) format. The report includes detailed information about which rules passed or failed, along with specific error or warning messages.

These steps are designed for use with an XSLT processor, where the result forms the input for the next step. The first three steps have to be executed, if changes are made to the rule set; otherwise, the fourth step can be used independently for any semantic validation of PlanPro files.

2.5   The Schematron Validation Report

The report (cf. Fig. 3, Validation report as SVRL file) includes detailed information about which rules passed or failed, along with specific error or warning messages.

```
 1  <svrl:schematron-output xmlns:fx="http://tu-dresden.de/vlp/schematron/functions"
 2                           xmlns:planpro="http://www.plan-pro.org/regeln/struktur"
 3                           xmlns:svrl="http://purl.oclc.org/dsdl/svrl"
 4                           schemaVersion="ISO19757-3">
 5    <svrl:active-pattern document="PlanPro-samples/broken-sample.xml"
 6      id="ID278-LST_Zustand_Ziel" fpi="{GUID-6}"
 7      name="One-time definition of a default route overlap per route path"
 8      planpro:arbeitspaket="Routes" planpro:version="1.10.0.1">
 9      <svrl:text>
10        <planpro:description>
11          If a route path is used as a traversed part of main routes including a route
                overlap, a default route overlap must be defined in exactly one of these main
                routes. This condition also applies if there is only one main route with a
                route overlap for this route path.

12
13          For all Fstr_Zug_Rangier with Fstr_Zug_Rangier.Fstr_Zug.Fstr_Zug_DWeg with
                Fstr_Zug_Rangier.Fstr_Zug.Fstr_Zug_DWeg.ID_Fstr_DWeg -> Fstr_DWeg.
                Fstr_DWeg_Spezifisch and same Fstr_Zug_Rangier.ID_Fstr_Fahrweg there has to be
                exactly one Fstr_Zug_Rangier.Fstr_Zug.Fstr_Zug_DWeg.DWeg_Vorzug == "true".
14        </planpro:description>
15        <planpro:test>
16          <planpro:success>For the route path, there is exactly one main route with a default
                route overlap.<planpro:success>
17          <planpro:error>For the route path, there are either no or multiple main routes with
                a default route overlap.</planpro:error>
18        </planpro:test>
19        <planpro:output>Fstr_Fahrweg</planpro:output>
20      </svrl:text>
21    </svrl:active-pattern>
22    <svrl:fired-rule role="error"
23      context="Fstr_Fahrweg[ancestor::LST_Zustand_Ziel][fx:Fstr-278(current(),
              ancestor::LST_Zustand_Ziel)]"/>
24    <svrl:failed-assert test="count($routeOverlapDefault)=1"
25      location="/*:PlanPro_Schnittstelle[namespace-uri()='http://www.plan-pro.org/modell/
26      PlanPro/1.10.0.1'][1]/LST_Zustand_Ziel[1]/Fstr_Fahrweg[127]">
27        <svrl:text>For the route path, there are either no or multiple main routes with a
                default route overlap. The following main routes serve no default route overlap:
                {GUID-2}.</svrl:text>
28        <svrl:diagnostic-reference diagnostic="guid">{GUID-2}</svrl:diagnostic-reference>
29        <svrl:diagnostic-reference diagnostic="type">Fstr_Fahrweg</svrl:diagnostic-reference>
30        <svrl:diagnostic-reference diagnostic="area">Planung</svrl:diagnostic-reference>
31        <svrl:diagnostic-reference diagnostic="structure">02</svrl:diagnostic-reference>
32        <svrl:diagnostic-reference diagnostic="s1">Route path</svrl:diagnostic-reference>
33        <svrl:diagnostic-reference diagnostic="s2">60ZU22</svrl:diagnostic-reference>
34        <svrl:diagnostic-reference diagnostic="s3">60P3</svrl:diagnostic-reference>
35    </svrl:failed-assert>
```

Listing 5: A Schematron validation report.

The sample in Listing 1 validates successfully with no messages. In order
to require the given rule to fail, the conditions for the rule context have to be
met, whereas the assertion test shall fail. This may be achieved by deleting the
default toggle for the route overlap *(line 25)*. After doing this, the PlanPro file
still conforms to the XSD.

Listing 5 shows the output of such a Schematron process as a SVRL file
containing all `active-patterns` *(lines 5–21)* which were executed including their
metadata as well as all `fired-rules` *(lines 22–23)* which were applied to the
context nodes. Additionally, an error report for each `failed-assert` *(lines 24–
35)* or `successful-report` is given containing the `location` *(lines 25–26)* as

```
1   <iso:diagnostic id="s1">
2     <xsl:variable name="objectType" select="ancestor-or-self::*[parent::Container]"/>
3     <xsl:choose>
4       <xsl:when test="$objectType/self::Fstr_Fahrweg">
5         <xsl:value-of select="'Route path'"/>
6       </xsl:when>
7       <xsl:otherwise>
8         <xsl:value-of select="$objectType/local-name()"/>
9       </xsl:otherwise>
10    </xsl:choose>
11  </iso:diagnostic>
12  <iso:diagnostic id="s2">
13    <xsl:variable name="objectType" select="ancestor-or-self::*[parent::Container]"/>
14    <xsl:choose>
15      <xsl:when test="$objectType/self::Fstr_Fahrweg">
16        <xsl:value-of select="key('Signal', $objectType/ID_Start/Wert, parent::*)
17        /*/Bezeichnung_Tabelle/Wert"/>
18      </xsl:when>
19      <xsl:otherwise>
20        <xsl:value-of select="$objectType/(Bezeichnung/*/Wert)[1]"/>
21      </xsl:otherwise>
22    </xsl:choose>
23  </iso:diagnostic>
24  <iso:diagnostic id="s3">
25    <xsl:variable name="objectType" select="ancestor-or-self::*[parent::Container]"/>
26    <xsl:choose>
27      <xsl:when test="$objectType/self::Fstr_Fahrweg">
28        <xsl:variable name="currentTarget" select="$objectType/../*[Identitaet/Wert =
29        $objectType/ID_Ziel/Wert]"/>
30        <xsl:choose>
31          <xsl:when test="$currentTarget/self::Signal">
32            <xsl:value-of select="$currentTarget/*/Bezeichnung_Tabelle/Wert"/>
33          </xsl:when>
34          <xsl:when test="$currentTarget/self::Markanter_Punkt">
35            <xsl:value-of select="$currentTarget/*/Bezeichnung_Markanter_Punkt/Wert"/>
36          </xsl:when>
37          <xsl:otherwise><xsl:value-of select="''"/></xsl:otherwise>
38        </xsl:choose>
39      </xsl:when>
40      <xsl:otherwise><xsl:value-of select="''"/></xsl:otherwise>
41    </xsl:choose>
42  </iso:diagnostic>
```

Listing 6: Schematron Diagnostic definitions.

XPath expression according to the XML file and the report message `svrl:text` *(line 27)*. The `diagnostics` variables *(lines 28–34)* were filled with content.

Diagnostics Mechanism. As the `diagnostics` variable names were listed in the `assert` or `report` nodes inside the `rule` nodes (cf. Listing 2, *line 32*), they may provide static customized content as typically described for the Schematron language. Facilitating the fact that the whole Schematron rule set is compiled by an XSLT stylesheet (cf. Fig. 3, third activity), mutable content for these Schematron `diagnostics` can be provided as shown in Listing 6.

Incorporating Standard XSLT2 [17] language elements (`xsl:*`) inside the Schematron `diagnostic` element enables a powerful expressiveness for enriching the validation report with context-sensitive information. The diagnostic values "s2" and "s3" (cf. Listing 5, *lines 33–34*) are filled with the appropriate values

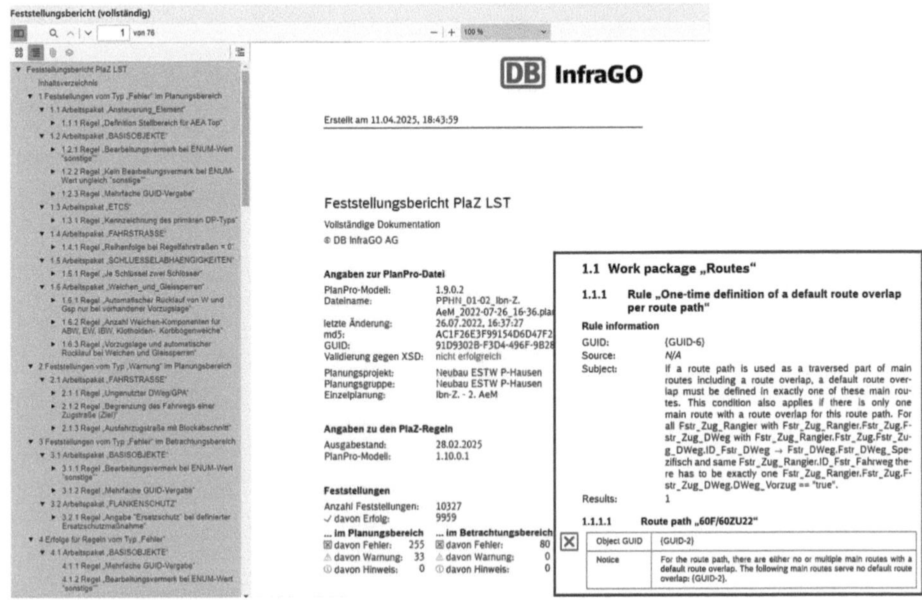

Fig. 5. A Validation Report as PDF document for P-Hausen in German, the cover page and excerpt of the rule with error message developed in the paper.

from our sample (cf. Listing 1, *lines 33, 42*) based on the definitions (cf. Listing 6, *lines 16, 30*).

User-Friendly Output Formats. The validation report as SVRL is meant for internal use. It is further processed into user-friendly output formats, such as a PDF document (Fig. 5) and an HTML document (Fig. 6), both provided in the Plan-Pro toolkit software for the domain experts [10]. The custom XSL stylesheets were developed from scratch for this use case and rely only on the validation report (SVRL) with not further visiting the original PlanPro file. This output generation is technically separated from the core validation process.

These output formats ensure that validation results are accessible and actionable for both technical and non-technical stakeholders. For example, the HTML report enables interactive exploration of validation messages, while the PDF report provides a formalized document for submission and archiving. Incorporating the logo and fonts of DB InfraGO, both output formats are streamlined with its corporate design.

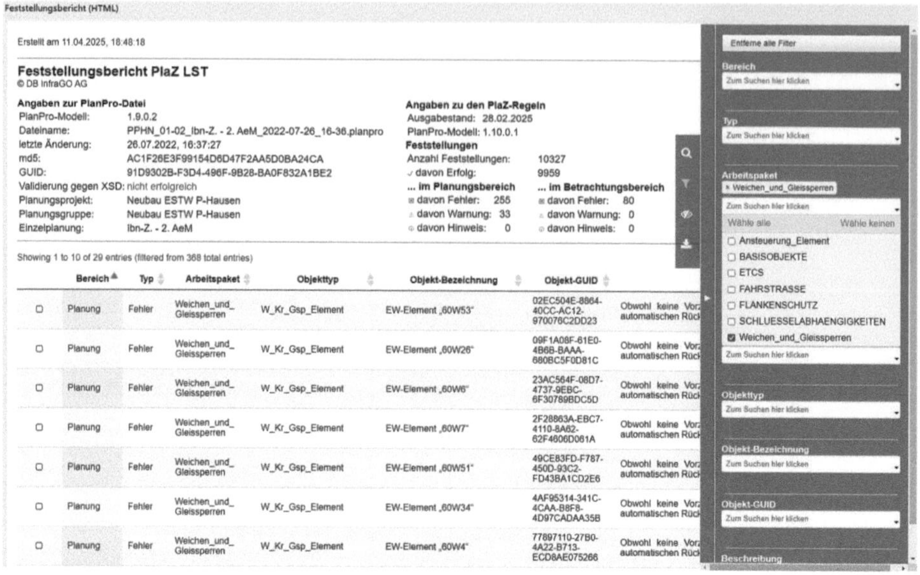

Fig. 6. An HTML Validation Report for P-Hausen in German, deploying filtering.

3   Conclusion

We presented a validation framework for CCS data, which is developed based on Schematron. In our work, we established a tailored workflow for the rule development incorporating quality checks with synthetic test files and adjusted the standard Schematron stylesheets for our concerns and provide the results as open source software. In order to achieve better performance and more reasonable results and dynamic domain-specific details for given validation messages, we integrated several XSL concepts into the workflow. Based on the validation results, we developed further XSL transformations for generating documents, that are easy to understand for domain experts in their daily work. The validation framework enables improving the quality of data sets and accelerating quality checks. By this, it is possible to save resources (processing time, error correction effort) and reduce costs. In the field of CCS this goal is of exceptional importance.

The ability to transfer the validation approach from the CCS domain to other fields of application in the railway domain is obvious. Furthermore the solution described in this paper can be applied to many use cases of data sets outside the railway domain, too. Similar approaches have been applied in other critical systems domains, such as aviation with the Aeronautical Information Exchange Model (AIXM) [5]. These parallels demonstrate the potential for cross-domain applications of rule-based data validation frameworks.

Although the PlaZ framework supports the implementation of any desired rule for validating PlanPro files, certain limitations have been identified that impact its performance and usability. As the complexity of the design grows, the file size expands, leading to longer processing times. One real-world PlanPro XML file in an early planning stage encompasses about 80 MB, containing about 39,000 objects within about 2,357,800 lines. It was recently checked against 110 rules performing about 50,000 tests in 3.5 minutes resulting in 850 errors or warnings. This issue is further exacerbated by the addition of rules for semantic validation, which aim to cover a broader range of PlanPro objects.

To mitigate the limitations, optimizations in the Schematron/XPath/XSLT implementation have been employed, resulting in reduced processing times. However, improving performance remains an ongoing objective, particularly as the scope of validation expands.

Another limitation is the scarcity of programmers with expertise in both Schematron and railway-specific requirements. This skills gap poses a challenge for the continued development and maintenance of the PlaZ component. Addressing this issue is critical to ensuring the long-term sustainability and adaptability of the framework.

As CCS design operates within a safety-critical domain, achieving certification for the tools used by design engineers and safety assessors is a key goal. Certification criteria may include validating results through independent tools that produce identical outcomes. Exploring alternative approaches such as [6] to achieve the same validation results would significantly support certification efforts and enhance trust in the method, respectively the applications.

References

1. Badeau, F., Chappelin, J., Lamare, J.: Generating and verifying configuration data with OVADO. In: Proceedings RSSRail 2022, pp. 143–148 (2022). https://doi.org/10.1007/978-3-031-05814-1_10
2. Banerjee, M., et al.: A Tool-chain for the verification of geographic scheme data. In: Milius, B., Collart-Dutilleul, S., Lecomte, T. (eds.) Reliability, Safety, and Security of Railway Systems. Modelling, Analysis, Verification, and Certification, pp. 211–224. Springer Nature Switzerland, Cham (2023). https://doi.org/10.1007/978-3-031-43366-5_13
3. Butler, M., Körner, P., Krings, S., Lecomte, T., Leuschel, M., Mejia, L.-F., Voisin, L.: The first twenty-five years of industrial use of the B-Method. In: ter Beek, M.H., Ničković, D. (eds.) FMICS 2020. LNCS, vol. 12327, pp. 189–209. Springer, Cham (2020). https://doi.org/10.1007/978-3-030-58298-2_8
4. Dillmann, S., Hähnle, R.: SMT-based verification of railway plannings. In: Proceedings RSSRail (2025)
5. Data verification – AIXM, Website (2025). https://aixm.aero/page/data-verification, Accessed 11 Apr 2025
6. Gruteser, J., Leuschel, M.: Validation of railML Using ProB. In: Engineering of Complex Computer Systems: 28th International Conference, ICECCS 2024, Limassol, Cyprus, June 19–21, 2024, Proceedings, pp. 245–256. Springer-Verlag, Berlin, Heidelberg (2024). https://doi.org/10.1007/978-3-031-66456-4_13
7. Häußler, M., Esser, S., Borrmann, A.: Code compliance checking of railway designs by integrating BIM, BPMN and DMN. Autom. Constr. (2021). https://doi.org/10.1016/j.autcon.2020.103427

8. ISO/IEC 19757-3:2020, Information technology - Document Schema Definition Languages (DSDL) - Part 3: Rule-based validation using Schematron
9. Klaus, C.: Specification of a test tool for the automated testing of CCS engineering data in XML format. Ph.D. thesis, Dresden University of Technology (2024). https://nbn-resolving.org/urn:nbn:de:bsz:14-qucosa2-906663
10. Klaus, C.: Digitale LST-Planung in aktuellen Projekten. Deine Bahn, pp. 12–17 (2025)
11. Klaus, C., Jaekel, B., Wunsch, S., Lehnert, M.: The automated semantic validation of planning data for signalling systems using Schematron. Signalling Datacommun. 03, 14–22 (2018). https://eurailpress-archiv.de/SingleView.aspx?show=143849
12. Lecomte, T., Burdy, L., Leuschel, M.: Formally checking large data sets in the railways. CoRR abs/1210.6815 (2012), proceedings of DS-Event-B 2012, Kyoto
13. Lecomte, T., Deharbe, D., Prun, E., Mottin, E.: Applying a formal method in industry: a 25-Year trajectory. In: Cavalheiro, S., Fiadeiro, J. (eds.) SBMF 2017. LNCS, vol. 10623, pp. 70–87. Springer, Cham (2017). https://doi.org/10.1007/978-3-319-70848-5_6
14. Tutcher, J., Easton, J.M., Roberts, C.: Enabling data integration in the rail industry using RDF and OWL: the racoon ontology. ASCE-ASME J. Risk Uncertainty Eng. Syst., Part A: Civ. Eng. (2017). https://doi.org/10.1061/AJRUA6.0000859
15. Wang, X., Tian, Y., Fu, S., Musila, C.M.: Research on semantic verification method of AIXM data based on SBVR. In: Liang, Q., Wang, W., Mu, J., Liu, X., Na, Z. (eds.) Artificial Intelligence in China, pp. 260–271. Springer Nature, Singapore (2023). https://doi.org/10.1007/978-981-99-1256-8_31
16. World Wide Web Consortium (W3C): XML Path Language (XPath) 2.0 (Second Edition) (2016). https://www.w3.org/TR/xpath20/
17. World Wide Web Consortium (W3C): XSL Transformations (XSLT) Version 2.0 Second Edition) (2021). https://www.w3.org/TR/xslt20/

Efficient Derivation of Optimal Signal Schedules for Multimodal Intersections

N. Bertocci, L. Carnevali[(✉)] , L. Scommegna , and E. Vicario

Department of Information Engineering, University of Florence, Florence, Italy
{nicola.bertocci,laura.carnevali,leonardo.scommegna,
enrico.vicario}@unifi.it

Abstract. This is an extended abstract of the journal paper [2]. Specifically, we illustrate an approach to efficiently derive optimal signal schedules for multimodal intersections among vehicle flows and right-of-way tram lines, minimizing the maximum expected percentage of queued vehicles of each flow. We model trams by Stochastic Time Petri Nets (STPNs), capturing periodic tram departures and bounded delays and travel times with general (i.e., non-Exponential) distribution, and we model vehicles by finite-capacity vacation queues, with general vacation times determined by the intersection availability. For each vehicle flow, we study the expected queue size, deriving both its transient behavior and its steady-state distribution at multiples of the hyperperiod (resulting from nominal tram arrival times and vehicle traffic signals). By doing so, we study the behavior of each vehicle flow over arbitrary-duration intervals by performing transient analysis for the hyperperiod duration, starting from the steady-state distribution of the expected queue size. Experimental results on case studies of real complexity with time-varying parameters show the approach effectiveness at identifying optimal traffic signal schedules, notably exploring in few minutes hundreds of schedules requiring tens of hours in Simulation of Urban MObility (SUMO).

Keywords: Multimodal intersections · optimal signal schedules · stochastic time Petri nets · finite-capacity vacation queues with general vacation time · Simulation of Urban MObility (SUMO) · software tools and libraries

1 Motivation

Tramways help to meet the needs of urban transport by increasing passenger volume and improving environmental sustainability [1]. At the same time, tramways significantly impact road traffic by reducing the available space and by typically having right of way at *multimodal* intersections. Thus, mitigation measures are needed, notably optimizing traffic signals to minimize the duration of the intervals of intersection unavailability for road transport. To this end, quantitative evaluation of stochastic models capturing behavior of road traffic and tram traffic at multimodal intersections can effectively support early assessment and runtime

© The Author(s), under exclusive license to Springer Nature Switzerland AG 2026
M. H. ter Beek et al. (Eds.): RSSRail 2025, LNCS 16236, pp. 231–236, 2026.
https://doi.org/10.1007/978-3-032-10762-6_18

adaptation of design choices, notably exploiting widespread smart technologies for online estimation of traffic parameters and tram delays [12], so as to maximize expected capacity or minimize expected queue lengths and delays [6].

2   Related Works

Quantitative evaluation methods supporting operation and management of urban transportation systems perform simulation and analysis of traffic signals [11] by exploiting stochastic models with different abstraction level, ranging from variants of Petri Nets (PNs) [21] to cellular automata [20] and car following representations [18]. In particular, *microscopic* models mainly capture behavior of individual vehicles and drivers as well as possible interactions among them, while *macroscopic* models represent global or aggregated features of traffic flows.

Methods that leverage microscopic models include the approach of [8], which exploits Time Petri Nets (TPNs) to model multiple signalized intersections, representing deterministic durations of traffic light phases, periodic arrival times of vehicles, and uncertain travel times comprised between a minimum value and a maximum value, though not associated with a probability distribution. In [4,5], a stochastic time Petri net models a road-tramway intersection with periodic tram departures, explicitly modeling each state of the queue of vehicles, and thus roughly estimating the average queue size over time by grouping car arrivals into platoons. Other approaches support rule-based simulation of signal policies at signalized intersections under different traffic demands [10], definition of model predictive control policies [23] for connected multimodal signalized intersections between vehicles and bicycles, development of traffic control policies [14] in the VISSIM simulation tool [28], and, simulation of urban mobility through cellular automata to optimize traffic schedules at signalized intersections [30] Optimization problems are also solved to coordinate tram timetables and signal timing at intersections with vehicle flows [16,25] and to minimize tram travel times and dwell times for a two-way line [32]. As a common trait, none of these approaches based on microscopic models captures both periodic tram departures and general (i.e., non-exponential) tram delays and travel times.

Methods that leverage macroscopic models exploit mixed integer linear programming to derive optimal traffic light control strategies [33], the input-output approach to predict delay and maximum queue length over time for each vehicle flow [24], the shockwave theory to analyze the dynamics of formation and dissipation of queues at isolated signalized intersections [27], and hybrid Petri nets to coordinate the traffic lights of multiple intersections [7,9]. As a common trait, these approaches typically model the vehicle flow dynamics and the temporization of traffic signal schedules, while not capturing periodic tram departures.

Methods requiring advanced technologies for accurate estimation of vehicle position and movements [13] as well as machine learning methods requiring availability of large amounts of mobility data [31] are out of scope with respect to our contribution, for which sensors detecting tram passage and statistics of inter-arrival and travel times of vehicles and trams are sufficient for model definition.

3   Contribution

We illustrate an efficient and accurate analytical approach to derive optimal traffic signal schedules for multimodal intersections among road transport flows and right-of-way tram lines, minimizing the maximum expected percentage of queued vehicles of each flow with respect to sequence and duration of traffic light phases. Specifically, we define a compositional approach combining the analyses of a *microscopic* model of tram traffic and a *macroscopic* model of road traffic:

- We model tram traffic by stochastic time Petri nets, representing periodic inter-arrival times as well as general bounded delays and crossing times, facilitating fitting of operational data. We perform numerical analysis based on the method of stochastic state classes [15] to compute the transient probability that the intersection is available for vehicle flows.
- We model road traffic by finite-capacity vacation queues [3,17,29], with general vacation time (i.e., duration of the intervals of intersection unavailability for vehicles) determined by the transient probability that the intersection is not available for vehicle flows, and with exponential inter-arrival times and service times (i.e., times needed to leave the intersection). We solve the set of ordinary differential equations characterizing the queue behavior to derive the expected queue size over time for each vehicle flow.

At multiples of the hyper-period (resulting from nominal tram arrival times and vehicle traffic signals), the distribution of the expected queue size of each vehicle flow reaches a steady state. We derive this distribution by performing steady-state analysis of the discrete time Markov chain embedded at multiples of the hyper-period in the continuous-time birth-death process characterizing the queue behavior. Since the steady state is reached within few hyper-periods, we derive the expected queue size over time by performing transient analysis starting from the steady-state distribution and lasting for the hyper-period duration.

We explore traffic signal schedules as they vary in sequence and duration of traffic light phases, and we exploit our approach to select the one that minimizes the maximum expected percentage of queued vehicles of each flow. We compare with SUMO [19] to assess accuracy and computational load of our approach, considering road-tramway intersections of real complexity. Results show that the approach achieves comparable accuracy, while requiring a computation time up to nearly four orders of magnitude lower than that of SUMO, notably evaluating in few minutes hundreds of schedules requiring tens of hours in SUMO.

We implemented our approach in the OMNIBUS library, exploiting the SIRIO library [26] of the ORIS tool [22]. OMNIBUS designed to facilitate code usability, maintainability, and extensibility, and available open source under the AGPLv3 licence at https://github.com/oris-tool/omnibus.

In particular, Fig. 1 shows a graphical representation of an intersection among a bidirectional tram line and three vehicle flows ϕ_1^{veh}, ϕ_2^{veh}, and ϕ_3^{veh}, with the same leaving rate and different arrival rates, and with queue capacity equal to 31. We consider 390 different traffic schedules for this intersection, obtained by varying the sequence of duration of phases, and we exploit our approach to rank the

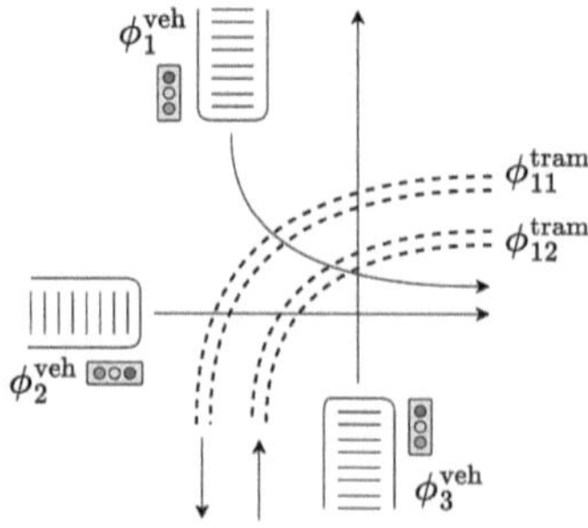

Fig. 1. A graphical representation of an intersection among three vehicle flows and a bidirectional tram line.

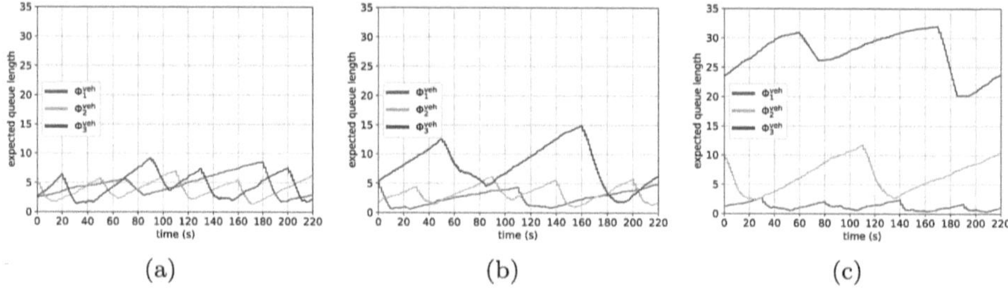

(a)   (b)   (c)

Fig. 2. Expected number of queued vehicles over time for each flow of the intersection of Fig. 1, computed through SUMO simulation (25 runs) for: a) the best schedule, b) the schedule in median position, and c) the worst schedule.

schedules according to the maximum expected percentage of queue occupation of any flow within an assigned time interval. Figure 2 shows the expected number of queued vehicles over time of each vehicle flow, computed through SUMO simulation (25 runs) over the considered time interval for the best schedule (which has maximum expected percentage of queue occupation equal to 0.297), for the schedule in median position (which has maximum expected percentage of queue occupation equal to 0.556), and for the worst schedule (which has maximum expected percentage of queue occupation equal to 1.0). As expected, the best schedule tends to balance the expected percentage of queue occupation of the three vehicle flows. Conversely, under the worst schedule, the queue of flow ϕ_3^{veh} (green curve in Fig. 2c) tends to saturation, and the expected queue size of flow ϕ_2^{veh} (orange curve) is always larger than that of flow ϕ_1^{veh} (blue curve).

Acknowledgement. This work was partially supported by the European Union under the Italian National Recovery and Resilience Plan (NRRP) of NextGenerationEU, partnership on "Telecommunications of the Future" (PE00000001 - program "RESTART"), and by the MUR PRIN 2022 PNRR P2022A492B project ADVENTURE (ADVancEd iNtegraTed evalUation of Railway systEms) funded by the European Union - NextGenerationEU.

References

1. ACEA: The 2030 urban mobility challenge. Technical Report (2016)
2. Bertocci, N., Carnevali, L., Scommegna, L., Vicario, E.: Efficient derivation of optimal signal schedules for multimodal intersections. Simulation Modelling Practice and Theory, p. 102912 (2024). https://doi.org/10.1016/j.simpat.2024.102912
3. Bolch, G., Greiner, S., De Meer, H., Trivedi, K.S.: Queueing networks and Markov chains: modeling and performance evaluation with computer science applications. John Wiley & Sons (2006)
4. Carnevali, L., Fantechi, A., Gori, G., Vicario, E.: Analysis of a road/tramway intersection by the ORIS tool. In: International Conference on Verification and Evaluation of Computer and Comm. Systems, pp. 185–199. Springer (2018)
5. Carnevali, L., Fantechi, A., Gori, G., Vicario, E.: Stochastic modeling and analysis of road-tramway intersections. Innovations Syst. Softw. Eng. $16(2)$, 215–230 (2020)
6. Cheng, C., Du, Y., Sun, L., Ji, Y.: Review on theoretical delay estimation model for signalized intersections. Transp. Rev. $36(4)$, 479–499 (2016)
7. Di Febbraro, A., Giglio, D., Sacco, N.: Urban traffic control structure based on hybrid Petri nets. IEEE Tr. Int. Tran. Sys. $5(4)$, 224–237 (2004)
8. Di Febbraro, A., Giglio, D.: On representing signalized urban areas by means of deterministic-timed Petri nets. In: International Conference on Intelligent Transportation Systems, pp. 372–377 (2004)
9. Di Febbraro, A., Sacco, N.: On modelling urban transportation networks via hybrid Petri nets. Control Eng. Practices $12(10)$, 1225–1239 (2004)
10. Dion, F., Hellinga, B.: A rule-based real-time traffic responsive signal control system with transit priority: application to an isolated intersection. Trans. Res. Part B: Methodol. $36(4)$, 325–343 (2002)
11. Eom, M., Kim, B.-I.: The traffic signal control problem for intersections: a review. Eur. Transp. Res. Rev. $12(1)$, 1–20 (2020). https://doi.org/10.1186/s12544-020-00440-8
12. Faria, R., Brito, L., Baras, K., Silva, J.: Smart mobility: a survey. In: International Conference on IoT for the Global Community, pp. 1–8. IEEE (2017)
13. Guo, Q., Li, L., Ban, X.J.: Urban traffic signal control with connected and automated vehicles: a survey. Trans. Res. Part C: Emerg. Technol. 101, 313–334 (2019)
14. He, Q., Head, K.L., Ding, J.: Multi-modal traffic signal control with priority, signal actuation and coordination. Trans. Res. Part C: Emerg. Technol. 46, 65–82 (2014)
15. Horváth, A., Paolieri, M., Ridi, L., Vicario, E.: Transient analysis of non-Markovian models using stochastic state classes. Perform. Eval. $69(7–8)$, 315–335 (2012)
16. Ji, Y., Tang, Y., Du, Y., Zhang, X.: Coordinated optimization of tram trajectories with arterial signal timing resynchronization. Trans. Res. Part C: Emerg. Technol. 99, 53–66 (2019)
17. Kleinrock, L., Gail, R.: Queueing Systems: Theory, vol. 1. Wiley, New York (1975)
18. Li, Y., Sun, D.: Microscopic car-following model for the traffic flow: the state of the art. J. Contr. Theory and Appl. $10(2)$, 133–143 (2012)
19. Lopez, P.A., et al.: Microscopic traffic simulation using SUMO. In: International Conference on Intelligent Transportation Systems, pp. 2575–2582. IEEE (2018)
20. Maerivoet, S., De Moor, B.: Cellular automata models of road traffic. Phys. Rep. $419(1)$, 1–64 (2005)
21. Ng, K.M., Reaz, M.B.I., Ali, M.A.M.: A review on the applications of Petri nets in modeling, analysis, and control of urban traffic. IEEE Trans. on Int. Transp. Sys. $14(2)$, 858–870 (2013). https://doi.org/10.1109/TITS.2013.2246153

22. Paolieri, M., Biagi, M., Carnevali, L., Vicario, E.: The ORIS tool: quantitative evaluation of non-Markovian systems. IEEE Trans. Softw. Eng. **47**(6), 1211–1225 (2021)
23. Portilla, C., Valencia, F., Espinosa, J., Nunez, A., De Schutter, B.: Model-based predictive control for bicycling in urban intersections. Trans. Res. Part C: Emerg. Technol. **70**, 27–41 (2016)
24. Sharma, A., Bullock, D.M., Bonneson, J.A.: Input-output and hybrid techniques for real-time prediction of delay and maximum queue length at signalized intersections. Transp. Res. Record **2035**(1), 69–80 (2007)
25. Shi, J., Sun, Y., Schonfeld, P., Qi, J.: Joint optimization of tram timetables and signal timing adjustments at intersections. Trans. Res. Part C: Emerg. Technol. **83**, 104–119 (2017)
26. SIRIO Library: (2024). https://github.com/oris-tool/sirio
27. Stephanopoulos, G., Michalopoulos, P.G., Stephanopoulos, G.: Modelling and analysis of traffic queue dynamics at signalized intersections. Trans. Res. Part A: General **13**(5), 295–307 (1979)
28. Stevanovic, J., Stevanovic, A., Martin, P.T., Bauer, T.: Stochastic optimization of traffic control and transit priority settings in VISSIM. Trans. Res. Part C: Emerg. Technol. **16**(3), 332–349 (2008)
29. Tian, N., Zhang, Z.G.: Vacation queueing models: theory and applications, vol. 93. Springer Science & Business Media (2006)
30. Tonguz, O.K., Viriyasitavat, W., Bai, F.: Modeling urban traffic: a cellular automata approach. IEEE Comm. Maga. **47**(5), 142–150 (2009)
31. Wei, H., Zheng, G., Gayah, V., Li, Z.: A survey on traffic signal control methods. arXiv preprint arXiv:1904.08117 (2019)
32. Zhang, T., Mao, B., Xu, Q., Feng, J.: Timetable optimization for a two-way tram line with an active signal priority strategy. IEEE Access **7**, 176896–176911 (2019)
33. Zhang, Y., Su, R.: An optimization model and traffic light control scheme for heterogeneous traffic systems. Trans. Res. Part C: Emerg. Technol. **124**, 102911 (2021)

A Zero Latency Handover Scheme for Autonomous Tram Signaling in a 5G Scenario

Dinesh Tamang[1]([⊠]) [ID], Giulio Bartoli[1] [ID], Andrea Abrardo[1] [ID], and Gianluca Mandò[2]

[1] University of Siena, Siena, Italy
{dinesh.tamang2,giulio.bartoli,abrardo}@unisi.it
[2] Hitachi Rail GTS, Florence, Italy
gianluca.mando@urbanandmainlines.com

Abstract. Autonomous Tram (AT) systems are an emerging application requiring mission critical services to ensure safe and continuous operation. Key functions such as positioning, track occupancy detection, and obstacle perception depend on uninterrupted communication and mobility support. Leveraging the capabilities of 5G networks is thus crucial to support these functions. In this paper, we investigate the applicability of 5G Ultra-Reliable Low Latency Communications (URLLC) services for AT use case, with a particular focus on mobility challenges. We begin by conducting a comprehensive 5G coverage analysis in a real urban deployment to identify limitations in handover (HO) performance, which may compromise service reliability and, consequently, the accuracy and timeliness of positioning and perception functions. To address this, we propose a 5G Dual Connectivity Handover (DC HO), offering seamless transitions compared to classical 4G-based HO solutions. The proposed HO mechanism is validated through extensive simulations, comparing key performance metrics such as latency and reliability against classical 4G HO approach. Results demonstrate that the 5G DC HO strategy meets the stringent requirements of URLLC, thus enabling reliable support for AT operations in dynamic environments and safeguarding the critical services of positioning, track management, and environment perception.

Keywords: Soft Handover · Autonomous Tram · Dual Connectivity · URRLC

1 Introduction

Fifth-generation (5G) wireless networks represent a transformative leap in wireless communications, designed to support a broad range of scenarios with diverse performance requirements. Unlike previous generations, 5G aims to deliver not only higher rate communications, represented by enhanced Mobile

© The Author(s), under exclusive license to Springer Nature Switzerland AG 2026
M. H. ter Beek et al. (Eds.): RSSRail 2025, LNCS 16236, pp. 237–254, 2026.
https://doi.org/10.1007/978-3-032-10762-6_19

Broad Band (eMBB) but also defines two other critical use cases; Ultra-Reliable Low Latency Communications (URLLC) and massive Machine-Type Communications (mMTC) [1]. These capabilities enable new applications such as autonomous vehicles, real-time remote surgery, smart cities, and large-scale Internet of Things (IoT) deployments. In this regard, 5G emerges as a game changer in railway communication, with high reliability, low latency, and high throughput supporting mission-critical scenarios with predefined requirements. In terms of service requirements, the advanced New Radio Vehicle to Everything (NR-V2X) use cases demand stringent end-to-end latency and reliability requirements. For remote driving, a reliability level of 99.999% and a latency of 1 ms are essential. Coordinated driving necessitates a reliability of 99.9% and a latency of 10 ms. Short-distance platooning requires an even higher reliability of 99.99% and a latency of 10 ms. In comparison, Long Term Evolution (LTE) V2X use cases fall short, offering a reliability not exceeding 99% and latency ranging from 5 to 100 ms [2–4].

A critical challenge in realizing the full potential of 5G lies in maintaining seamless connectivity as users move across the network. The process of Handover (HO), which enables a User Equipment (UE) to switch its connection from one cell to another without service disruption, becomes more complex in 5G due to factors like ultra-dense deployments, heterogeneous network architecture, and operation in high-frequency bands with limited coverage [5]. Improperly managed HOs can lead to service interruptions, degraded Quality of Service (QoS), and even dropped calls, which are especially detrimental for latency-sensitive and mission-critical applications. Moreover, the dense deployment of cells and reuse of Physical Cell Identifiers (PCIs) can cause interference and confusion during HO, resulting in increased failure rates. To address these issues, 5G incorporates advanced mechanisms such as Multi Connectivity (MC), allowing a UE to maintain simultaneous connections to multiple cells, thereby enabling smoother transitions and reduced interruption times [6]. Additionally, Self-Organizing Networks (SON) provide automated optimization of network parameters, including PCI allocation and HO settings, to enhance mobility robustness and reduce manual configuration overhead [7]. Therefore, mobility management in 5G networks is a critical challenge, particularly in scenarios involving frequent HOs in dense urban areas. In tramway systems, where frequent transitions across cell boundaries are inevitable, MC significantly reduces HO latency and packet loss by enabling seamless data flow during the transition. This is particularly crucial for latency-sensitive and reliability-critical applications such as real-time obstacle detection, localization, and autonomous control, which require uninterrupted connectivity.

The remainder of the paper is organized as follows. Section 2 reviews the state-of-the-art on 5G HO solutions for reliable communication and discusses related work. Section 3 discusses the stringent communication requirements for Autonomous Tram (AT), and states the main contributions of this work. Section 4 details the measurement campaign conducted for 5G coverage analysis, detailing the measurement setup, recorded signal data, power analysis, and the HO problem in a multi-PCI scenario. Section 5 describes the proposed DC HO approach. Finally, Sect. 6 presents the main simulation results and provides a detailed discussion. Finally, Sect. 7 concludes the paper by summarizing the key findings.

2   State of the Art

One of the key benefits of using MC in a tramway system lies in how it significantly improves HO performance. As trams move through different coverage zones—especially in dense urban areas with frequent cell boundaries—they face frequent HOs, which can lead to communication interruptions or large delays, MC mitigates this by allowing the onboard unit to maintain simultaneous connections to multiple cells. Instead of dropping one connection before establishing another (as in traditional hard HO), the tram can perform smooth transition between cells while data flows continuously across both links. This results in reduced HO latency and minimal packet loss, which is especially important for applications like real-time obstacle detection, positioning, or autonomous control that depend on uninterrupted connectivity.

Many works in the literature focus on HO decision algorithms and execution mechanisms to improve mobility in 5G. Challenges arise due to fast fading, high user speeds, and new technologies like Ultra Dense Network (UDN), massive Multiple Input Multiple Output (MIMO), SONs, and millimeter-wave communications, leading to imprecise measurements, frequent HOs, and control/user plane splits [7]. Various solutions have been proposed, including optimal eNodeB selection using spatiotemporal estimation [8], fuzzy Q-learning for mobility robustness optimization [9], and schemes like mobility anchors to reduce signaling load [10]. Reinforcement learning-based HO approaches also show promising performances in determining the best policy [11]. However, due to 5G's complexity, the best algorithm is still undetermined. Moreover, the work in the paper [19] presents a user-centric dynamic Radio Access Network (RAN) selection method and traffic load adaptation, thereby achieving energy-efficient high-quality health monitoring in a heterogeneous network.

Nowadays, MC is usually associated with the concept of Cloud-RAN (C-RAN) which enables centralized baseband processing of signals collected from multiple remote radio heads. However, Device-to-Device (D2D) and drone-assisted access are also considered to be other forms of MC. Generally speaking, MC adopts space diversity to ensure ultra-reliability without increasing the latency at the price of the complex cooperation in networking. Paper [12] proposes a MC method in the C-RAN to reduce mobility-related link failures and improve the cell-edge throughput. Huq et al. [13] propose a C-RAN and D2D combined architecture to handle the associated fronthaul delay of C-RAN. They believe that the architecture can be deployed in licensed and unlicensed bands with almost "zero delay". The availability of alternative connectivity options, such as D2D links, cellular connectivity and drone-assisted access is discussed in [14]. Improvements were up to 40 percent in link availability and reliability with the use of proximate connections on top of the cellular-only baseline are verified.

A significant gap exists in the evaluation of URLLC solutions using realistic, tram-specific channel models and mobility patterns. Many studies rely on statistical or simplified propagation models that fail to capture the actual radio frequency conditions a tram would experience on its route. Achieving these targets in a practical tramway deployment remains a significant challenge, heavily dependent on network architecture, radio propagation conditions, and mobility management, which is the main focus of this work.

3   Communication Requirements and Tram-Specific Challenges for ATs

The deployment of ATs imposes stringent URLLC requirements, where latency is the critical bottleneck for safe operation. While these requirements align with those for autonomous road vehicles, the unique operational profile of trams introduces distinct challenges that are often overlooked in broader vehicular communication studies. Safety-critical functions for ATs—including obstacle detection, emergency braking, remote intervention, and coordination with traffic management systems—demand exceptionally low latency to guarantee timely actuation. In accordance with 3GPP URLLC and ITU-T IMT-2020 specifications, the communication system must target an end-to-end latency below 1 ms with a reliability of 99.999% [18].

Unlike autonomous cars operating in dynamic road networks, ATs follow predefined tracks within controlled corridors. While this fixed-route operation adds predictability, it also creates unique communication challenges that form the core focus of our research. The high-speed, linear movement along a fixed route guarantees frequent cell transitions. The network topology along the track dictates a predictable yet rapid sequence of HOs. This makes minimizing HO interruption time and eliminating associated latency spikes, absolutely critical for service continuity. Current research often evaluates HOs in generic mobile scenarios, not this specific high-stress, predictable pattern. Tram lines are often embedded in dense urban environments, creating urban canyon effects characterized by complex multipath propagation, non-line-of-sight conditions, and rapid signal degradation. These challenging radio conditions can severely impact signal quality and HO reliability, a problem exacerbated by the tram's fixed path which may consistently traverse these poor coverage zones.

AT communication comprises both periodic and event-driven traffic. Periodic transmissions (e.g., position updates, system health monitoring) require consistency but have moderate latency sensitivity. In contrast, event-driven traffic (e.g., emergency alerts for obstacle detection) demands near-instantaneous delivery. For the simulations in Sect. 6, a nominal load of 250 Kbps is assumed, sufficient for transmitting processed data (e.g., object detections, position estimates) but not raw sensor streams, thus reflecting a latency-sensitive safety-critical communication profile.

In summary, meeting the URLLC demands for ATs requires solutions tailored to their specific challenges: fixed routes causing frequent HOs and urban canyon propagation. This paper addresses these gaps by evaluating a robust HO mechanism within a simulation environment calibrated by real-world data from a tram-relevant scenario.

3.1 Main Contribution

To address the above discussed challenges, this work moves beyond generic models with a data-driven approach. The key contributions of this work are summarized follows:

- We conducted a comprehensive measurement campaign along the T1 tram-line in Florence, collecting 5G Synchronization Signal Block (SSB) signals to analyze real-world 5G coverage characteristics in an urban tramway environment. This study revealed the presence of a multi-PCI scenario, highlighting the challenges of frequent HOs in urban mobility systems.
- We implemented and evaluated a 5G MC based Dual Connectivity HO (DC HO) mechanism using a system-level 5G-air-simulator. Leveraging the measurement data, we simulated urban tram communication in a multi-cell environment and compared the performance of the proposed 5G DC HO approach against conventional LTE HO. The results demonstrate notable gains in terms of latency reduction and reliability improvement.

4 Coverage Analysis of 5G Signals in Florence T1 Tramline

We investigate commercial 5G coverage along Tramline T1 in Florence, Italy, using SSB signals from Vodafone operating in band n78 (GSCN-7950, 3.6 GHz). The study analyzes 5G signal behavior along the T1 trajectory, focusing on SSBs defined by 3GPP Release 15. These signals are crucial for initial access, synchronization, and system information broadcast. The captured SSBs follow pattern C with 30 kHz subcarrier spacing, 20 ms periodicity, and occupy 7.2 MHz bandwidth (20 RBs $\times$ 12 subcarriers).

4.1 Installation of SDR USRP E312 on the Tram 1013

We used NI USRP E312 Software-Defined Radio (SDR) [15], deployed onboard the moving tram 1013, as shown in Fig. 1. The E312 supports a frequency range of 70 MHz to 6 GHz and up to 56 MHz instantaneous bandwidth, making it suitable for 5G NR. Its embedded Zynq-7000 SoC with ARM processors and FPGA enables real-time baseband processing, essential for synchronization and decoding [15].

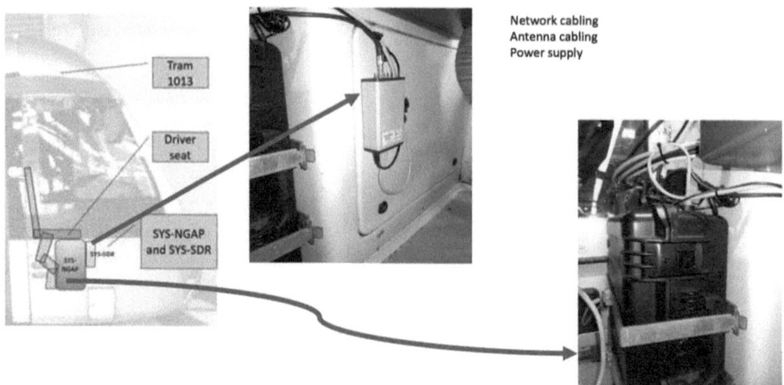

Fig. 1. SDR system installed on the Tram

The SDR was configured to operate at the desired 5G NR carrier frequency, and the received waveform was sampled and processed using the MATLAB 5G Toolbox [16]. SSBs were detected by correlating the signal with known Primary Synchronization Signal (PSS) and Secondary Synchronization Signal (SSS) sequences, enabling initial cell search and beam detection under realistic conditions. IQ samples were recorded with a length of four times that of the SSB block duration. Upon detection, we measured Synchronization Signal-Reference Signal Received Power (SS-RSRP) for each SSB. The device operated in standalone mode and was powered independently on the tram. A dedicated Python script automated the acquisition and logging of IQ samples to the onboard SD card.

4.2   Measurement Analysis and Multi-PCI Scenario

To understand the radio environment challenges faced by a moving tram, we conducted an extensive 11-hour measurement campaign on March 10, from 06:00 to 17:00, continuously collecting SSB data along the entire T1 tram line in Florence. A key finding was the detection of 148 unique PCIs. In 5G NR, the PCI is a critical parameter that allows UE to distinguish between different gNBs and is fundamental for cell selection, reselection, and the HO process. It is derived from the PSS/SSS broadcast by each cell.

The complex cellular landscape is visualized in the heatmap in Fig. 2, which plots the measured SS-RSRP in dBm. The x-axis represents the acquisition time (corresponding to the tram's position along its route), and the y-axis lists all detected PCI values. The color of each cell indicates the signal strength, with yellow representing high power (strong signal) and blue representing low power (weak signal).

This heatmap is crucial for diagnosing HO challenges, as it reveals:

- **Temporal Variations in Cell Dominance:** The shifting yellow patterns show how different cells become the strongest source of signal as the tram moves.

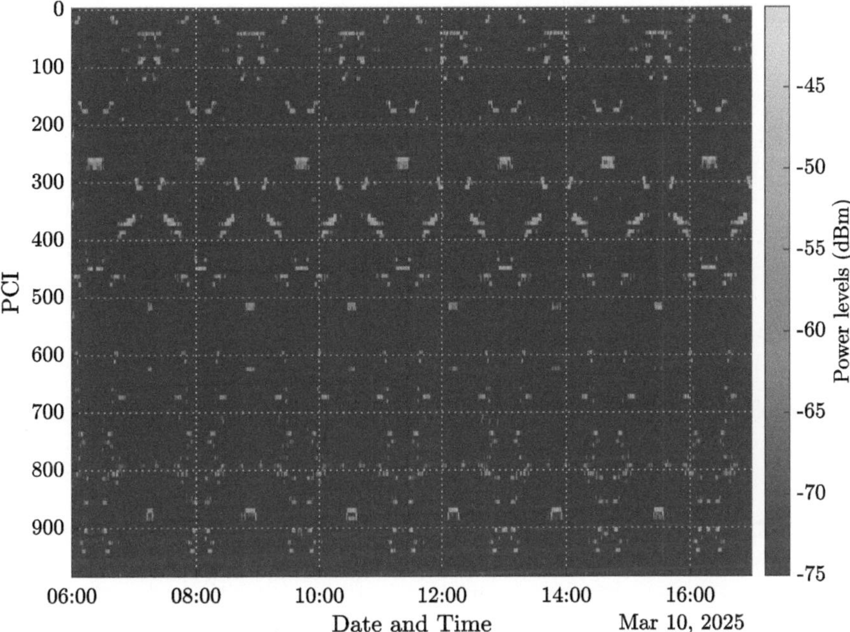

Fig. 2. Heatmap of SS-RSRP measurements for all detected PCIs over the 11-hour measurement campaign. The temporal and spatial dynamics of cell coverage along the tram line are clearly visualized.

- **Extensive Overlapping Coverage:** Multiple PCIs are frequently detected simultaneously at comparable power levels. This dense and overlapping network deployment, while beneficial for coverage, creates a complex environment where the UE must constantly evaluate the best connection, significantly increasing the likelihood of frequent and potentially unnecessary HO triggers.

To delve deeper into the HO behavior, we focus on a specific 12-minute interval and analyze the two strongest PCIs, as their interaction is most likely to trigger a HO. Figure 3 shows the SS-RSRP measurements for these two cells, sampled every 100 ms. The plot clearly illustrates a classic HO scenario: the signal from the current Serving gNB (S-gNB), i.e., PCI-343, experiences a gradual degradation, while the signal from a neighboring Target gNB (T-gNB), i.e., PCI-344, strengthens. This crossing point is the critical moment where a HO decision must be made to maintain a quality connection (Fig. 5).

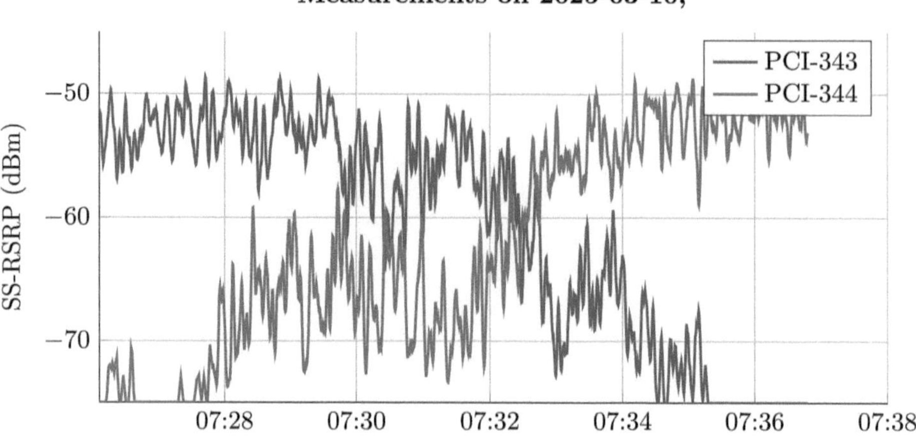

Fig. 3. SS-RSRP evolution for the two dominant PCIs over a 12-minute trajectory segment. The converging power levels demonstrate a clear HO opportunity zone where the UE must transition from the weakening PCI-343 (S-gNB) to the strengthening PCI-344 (T-gNB).

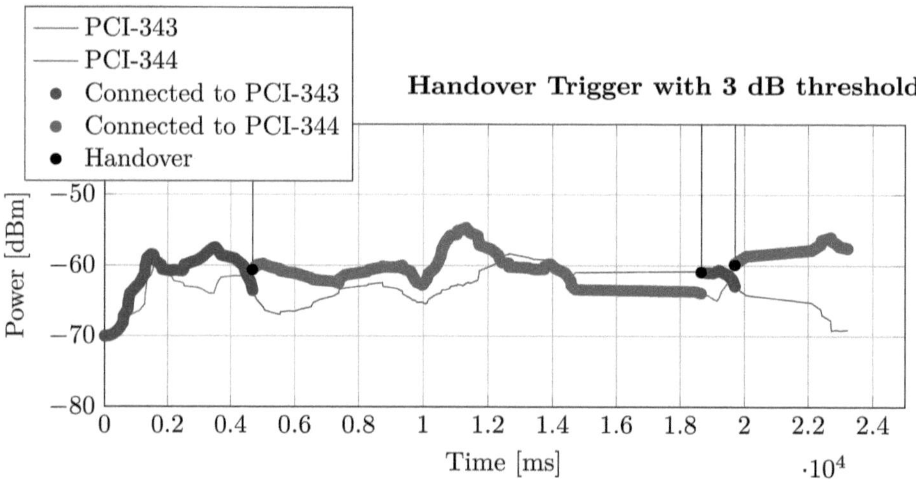

Fig. 4. High-resolution (20-second) view of power levels and HO instances. The black circles mark three separate HO events triggered based on a 3 dB margin threshold, highlighting the ping-pong effect that can occur in dense networks with similar signal strengths.

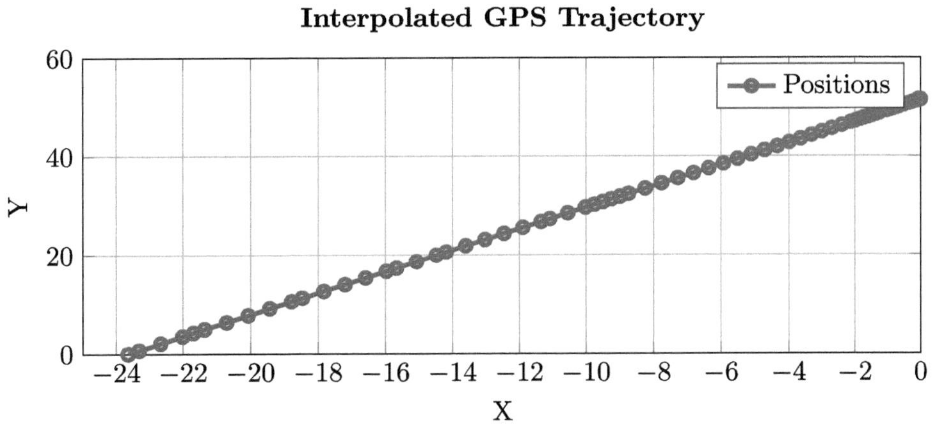

Interpolated GPS Trajectory

Fig. 5. Cartesian coordinate plot of the tram's GPS trajectory during the analyzed measurement period related to Fig. 4

Figure 4 zooms in on a critical 20-second window from the previous data, overlaying the precise HO triggering instances. Using a common HO margin threshold of 3 dB, we observe three distinct HOs between the same two PCIs (343 and 344). This "ping-pong" effect, where the UE rapidly switches back and forth between two cells, is a direct consequence of their highly similar and fluctuating signal strengths in an overlapping coverage area, as identified in the initial heatmap.

In conventional LTE systems, each of these HOs is a "hard" HO, requiring the UE to fully break its connection with the S-gNB before establishing a new one with the T-gNB. This process inevitably causes a brief but significant communication interruption (on the order of tens of milliseconds). For URLLC applications fundamental to modern tram signaling systems (e.g., train-to-ground communication for positive train control), such interruptions are unacceptable, as they can jeopardize safety and operational efficiency, as detailed in Sect. 3.

5 DC HO For Improved Reliability and Latency

MC stands as a fundamental technique for enabling URLLC, forming the core contribution of this work. As previously established, MC provides a pathway to ultra-reliable transmissions by facilitating robust HOs that eliminate interruptions for user plane data. The procedure is executed incrementally: one carrier is transitioned at a time from the source to the target node, ensuring the UE perpetually maintains at least one active connection. Throughout this process, packet duplication can be employed, guaranteeing that identical data packets are available at both the source and target nodes, thereby enabling interruption-free transmission to the UE. This mechanism is formally termed a soft HO or DC HO, characterized by the UE's sustained MC.

5.1 Development of a Discrete Event Simulator: The DC HO Module

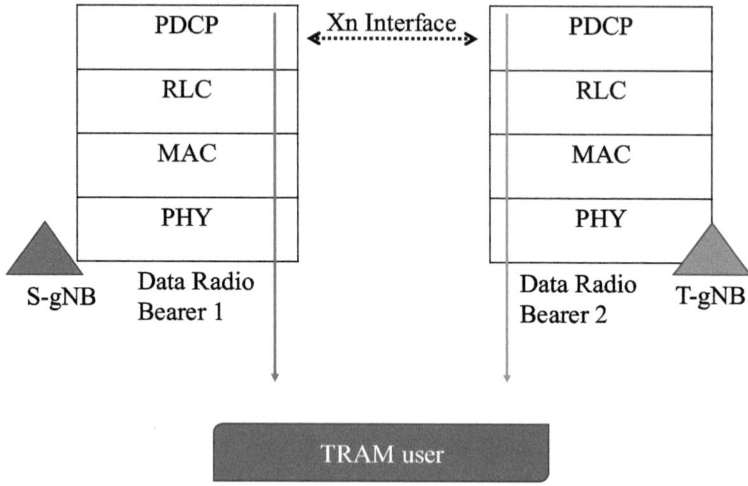

Fig. 6. Schematic diagram of the developed DC soft HO procedure, illustrating the involved protocol stack.

To rigorously address the challenge of HO interruptions, we employed a customized version of the 5G-air-simulator [17], a discrete-event simulation platform tailored for modeling Urban Macro (UMa) Scenarios. The 5G-air-simulator is an open-source, end-to-end packet-level simulator for simulating 5G air interface. It features comprehensive implementations of both control and data planes, incorporating sophisticated and standard-compliant Radio Resource Management (RRM) methodologies. Furthermore, it integrates advanced technical components essential for accurate 5G modeling, including a calibrated link-to-system interface, Block Error Rate (BLER) models for physical error evaluation, and support for MIMO and massive MIMO (mMIMO) features.

A primary contribution of this paper is the implementation and integration of a DC HO module into the simulator's existing hard HO framework. Our developed DC HO mechanism is designed to provide reliable, interruption-free HOs by introducing a form of Radio Resource Control (RRC) diversity. In this architecture, the RRC entity within the UE is responsible for maintaining simultaneous connections with two distinct gNBs.

The implemented HO process operates as follows: The UE continuously measures the received power from neighboring cells and reports these measurements to its Serving gNB (S-gNB) every Transmission Time Interval (TTI). As the UE approaches a cell border, the received signal level from the S-gNB degrades. A HO event is triggered once the signal received from a Target gNB (T-gNB) exceeds that from the S-gNB by a predefined $Hysteresis_{margin}$. Under the coordination of the S-gNB, the UE then synchronizes with the T-gNB. A new Data Radio Bearer (DRB) is activated for the data flow, and the UE's application layer begins generating packets for this new path starting from the next packet creation instant.

To accurately model the signaling and processing overhead inherent in establishing a new DRB, we introduce a fixed delay of 10 ms in our simulations. This value reflects a typical setup latency observed in practical 5G systems operating under DC configurations. Consequently, the simulator models a scenario where, after a delay of $(10 + x)$ ms (where x is the offset for the next application layer packet arrival time), the node begins dual transmission.

A critical aspect of this design is the role of the Packet Data Convergence Protocol (PDCP) layer, which is responsible for data duplication via bearer splitting. As illustrated in Fig. 6, a packet is only dropped if both of its duplicated versions are lost, effectively achieving a link-layer diversity order of two. During the dual transmission phase, the UE continues to measure the received power from both the S-gNB and T-gNB every TTI. The criteria for terminating the DC and completing the HO are based on the following conditions:

- **Case 1: Finalize HO to T-gNB.** If the power received from the T-gNB exceeds that from the S-gNB by $Hysteresis_{margin}$, dual transmission is terminated. The connection to the S-gNB is dropped in the subsequent TTI. Since the UE is already connected to the T-gNB, this final step incurs zero additional delay.
- **Case 2: Revert to S-gNB (Ping-Pong Mitigation).** If the power received from the S-gNB exceeds that from the T-gNB by the threshold $Hysteresis_{margin}$, the DC link is deactivated. The UE reverts to transmitting solely with its original S-gNB, thus avoiding an unnecessary HO—a common issue known as the ping-pong effect.
- **Case 3: Maintain Dual Transmission.** If neither condition is met, the UE continues to receive duplicated packets from both gNBs, preserving the high-reliability link until a clear decision can be made.

5.2 Calibration of the 5G-Air-Simulator Using Measured SS-RSRP from the Two Distinct PCIs

To ensure accurate modeling of mobility and HO dynamics between two neighboring 5G cells, we meticulously calibrated our discrete event simulator using measured SS-RSRP values. This calibration process involves converting RSRP measurements to Signal-to-Interference-plus-Noise Ratio (SINR) values and mapping them to the simulator's internal physical layer abstraction model. The core of this mapping utilizes the Mutual Information Effective SINR Mapping (MIESM) method, which condenses the per-resource-block SINRs into a single effective SINR value that reflects the overall radio channel quality. This effective SINR is then used to estimate the BLER for each transmitted data block via pre-defined SINR-BLER curves, ultimately determining the probability of successful reception or discard. This channel quality information is fed back to the gNB via Channel Quality Indicator (CQI) reports, enabling dynamic link adaptation. The simulator's full-stack implementation includes stochastic MAC layer behavior, Hybrid Automatic Repeat Request (HARQ) protocols, and dynamic Modulation and Coding Scheme (MCS) selection—all responding to the varying SINR inputs.

SINR Estimation from RSRP Measurements. Given the unavailability of direct SINR measurements in our dataset, we derived the SINR by treating the SS-RSRP from the serving cell's Physical Cell Identity (PCI) as the desired signal power. Under the assumption of no interference and full bandwidth utilization—a valid simplification for initial calibration and isolation of noise effects—the instantaneous SINR represented by γ in dB is calculated as:

$$\gamma_{\text{measured}} = \text{RSRP}_{\text{serving}} - N_0 \tag{1}$$

where $\text{RSRP}_{\text{serving}}$ is the reference signal received power from the serving PCI, and N_0 is the thermal noise power in dBm, computed as:

$$N_0 = -174 + 10 \log 10(B) + \text{NF}. \tag{2}$$

Here, B is the system bandwidth in Hz, and NF is the receiver noise figure in dB. The measurements were conducted with a subcarrier spacing (SCS) of 30 kHz. Consequently, the total bandwidth B is given by:

$$B = N_{\text{RB}} \times 12 \times 30 \times 10^3, \tag{3}$$

where N_{RB} is the number of resource blocks, and each resource block comprises 12 subcarriers.

Furthermore, to emulate the inherent randomness of a fading channel not captured by a single RSRP trace, we introduce seed-dependent stochastic perturbations. For each simulation seed, the derived γ at every spatial point is perturbed by adding an independent Gaussian random variable:

$$\gamma_{\text{final}} = \gamma_{\text{measured}} + \mathcal{N}(0, \sigma^2). \tag{4}$$

The standard deviation σ (e.g., set to 1 dB) controls the degree of variability, effectively modeling small-scale fading, subtle interference fluctuations, scheduling effects, and diverse channel realizations encountered in actual deployments. This approach ensures that each simulation run represents a unique channel instantiation, enabling robust and statistically significant performance evaluation despite being grounded in a single underlying RSRP measurement trace.

Finally, the calibration process derived from downlink SS-RSRP measurements is a spatially accurate map of channel quality, quantified as γ_{final}. For the purpose of simulating and analyzing HO performance, we leverage this downlink-derived γ_{final} value as the direct trigger for HO instances. This approach is justified by the principle of *spatial reciprocity*. Therefore, the HO triggering mechanism is implemented as an A3-like event, a standard in 3GPP mobility management:

$$\gamma_{\text{final,T}-\text{gNB}} > \gamma_{\text{final,S}-\text{gNB}} + \text{Hysteresis}_{\text{margin}}, \tag{5}$$

This provides a robust foundation for analyzing end-to-end performance during HO in a realistic propagation environment, enabling a meaningful evaluation of the HO algorithm's behavior.

6   Simulation Results and Discussions

In this section, we detail the simulation scenario, present the main experimental results, and provide a comprehensive discussion of the findings.

6.1   Simulation Scenario

In this study, we consider a simplified yet representative use case consisting of two adjacent cells, with a tram traversing from the coverage area of one cell into that of the other. As the tram approaches the cell boundary, a HO is triggered due to the degradation of the received signal power from the serving base station. This scenario has been simulated under multiple independent instances to analyze HO behavior in both 4G LTE and 5G systems.

Traffic was modeled using a Constant Bit Rate (CBR) source with a transmission rate of 250 Kbps to ensure consistent and controlled packet generation across all simulation runs. The primary objective of this simulation is to evaluate the impact of HO execution at the cell edge in terms of packet latency, allowing for a direct comparison between the performance of the traditional LTE HO and the 5G DC HO mechanisms. Each simulation run lasted for 20-seconds and repeated using different random seeds to generate statistically diverse instances, thereby verifying the system performance across several seeds. The key simulation parameters adopted for this scenario are summarized in Table 1.

6.2   Results and Discussions

In Figs. 7 and 8, we report packet delays as a function of user distance revealing the fundamental difference between the two technologies. The 4G HO where the connection to the serving gNB is broken before a new one is established, creates a clear point of failure. This is evidenced by a distinct peak in packet delays as the user crosses the cell border, indicating a period of service interruption and increased latency. In stark contrast, the 5G case shows no such increase in delay during the HO. This is a direct result of the DC scheme, where the UE simultaneously maintains connections with both the source and target nodes. The effective delay is calculated as the minimum of the delays from these two parallel transmissions, ensuring the user experiences the best possible performance without any interruption.

Table 1. Parameters for the considered scenario

Parameter	Value
Environment	UMa suburban
Number of cells	2
Inter-site distance	577,m
Number of sectors	3
Simulation time	20 s
Number of transmitting beams	32
Number of receiving beams	1
Bandwidth	20 MHz
Center Frequency	3.7 GHz
Traffic Type	CBR
UE transmitting power	23 dBm
Antenna height	25 m
Number of tram	1
Transport protocol	UDP
Data Rate	250 Kbps
User Speed	8 m/s
RLC Retransmission	10 ms
User Height	3.5 m
$\text{Hysteresis}_{margin}$	3 dB

This performance gap is further quantified through statistical analysis of 100 simulation runs. We report in Figs. 9 and 10 the histogram of delays for both cases. It is evident that 5G shows a tight, consistent distribution of values, all remaining within a few milliseconds. The 4G histogram, however, reveals a much wider spread with a long tail, including multiple instances of delays exceeding 10 ms. This visual data translates into the key figures presented in Table 2: 5G achieves a lower average delay (μ) of 0.0027 s compared to 4G's 0.0043 s. More importantly, 5G exhibits a dramatically lower standard deviation (σ) of 0.0004 versus 4G's 0.0058. This order-of-magnitude difference in variance proves that 5G not only provides lower latency on average but also delivers it with far greater consistency and predictability, a critical requirement for advanced applications.

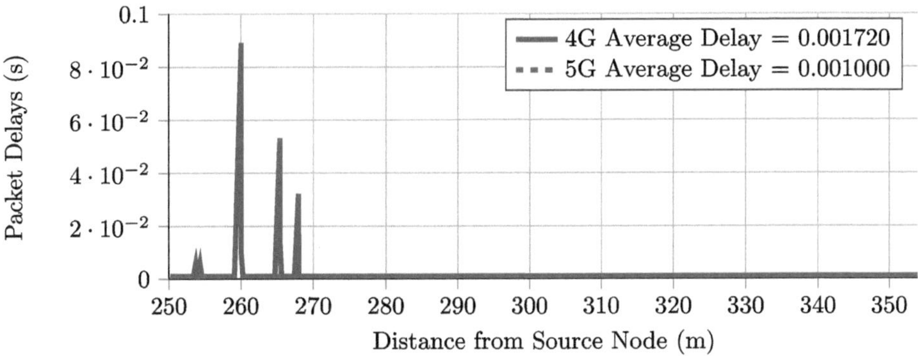

Fig. 7. 5G Vs 4G HO (instance 1)

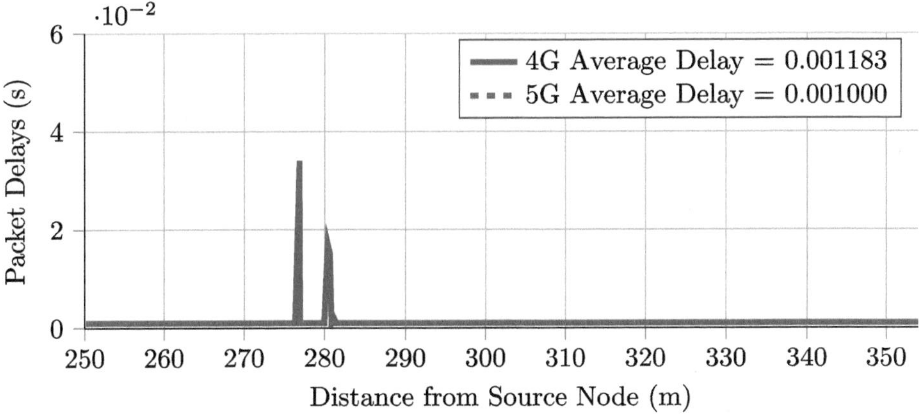

Fig. 8. 5G Vs 4G HO (instance 2)

Beyond latency, 5G also provides a substantial advantage in user throughput, offering a higher link capacity of 361.13 Kbps compared to 209.20 Kbps for 4G. Finally, the results confirm that the 5G system achieves perfect reliability (a value of 1) in this single tram scenario, outperforming the 99.9867% reliability of the 4G system. This enhancement is a direct consequence of the soft HO mechanism. The inherent redundancy of receiving the same packet from two different nodes means that even if one link fails during the HO, the packet can still be received successfully via the other, making the connection robust and minimizing service disruption.

At large, the results comprehensively show that the 5G HO mechanism, enabled by dual connectivity and soft HO, provides a superior user experience by simultaneously offering lower latency, higher consistency, greater throughput, and enhanced reliability compared to the traditional 4G HO process.

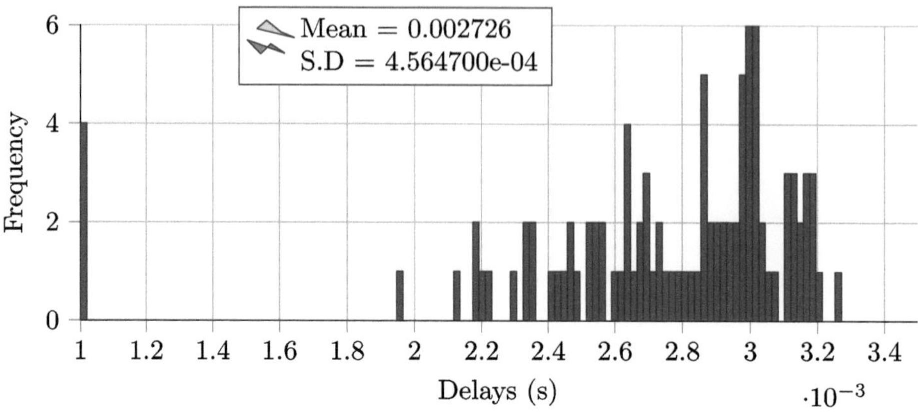

Fig. 9. Histogram of delays for 5G

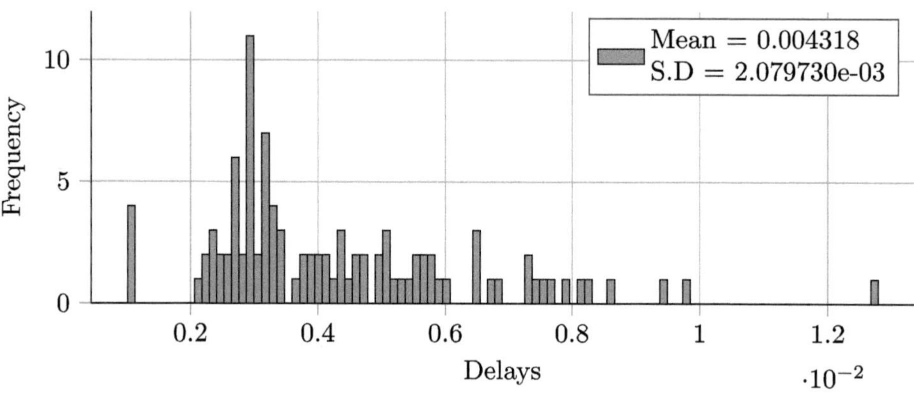

Fig. 10. Histogram of delays for 4G

Table 2. Performance analysis with simulation runs $= 100$

Configurations	μ(s)	σ	Link Capacity(Kbps)	Reliability
5G	0.0027	0.0004	361.13	1
4G	0.0043	0.0058	209.20	99.9867

7 Conclusions

In this paper, we have demonstrated the applicability and necessity of 5G HO mechanisms over traditional LTE approaches for providing URLLC services for tramway communication in an urban environment. By leveraging real-world 5G signal measurements to study signal behavior and common HO challenges, we employed a customized version of 5G air-simulator for our performance evaluation.

Our computer simulations conclusively proved the superiority of 5G DC HO compared to traditional 4G HO. The results show that mission-critical tram communications indeed require the advanced HO capabilities provided by 5G DC in multi-PCI scenarios, particularly for maintaining service continuity and meeting stringent reliability requirements. This case study with a single UE serves as valuable reference for future planning and dimensioning of full-scale autonomous tram services, providing insights into optimal cell planning strategies—including gNB placement, bandwidth requirements, and antenna configurations—as well as critical mobility management aspects.

A key area for future investigation involves optimization of HO decision algorithm parameters, particularly fine-tuning hysteresis margin for HO initiation and DC mode termination. This optimization will be essential for fully realizing the potential of AT network slices as integrated components of the broader 5G ecosystem.

References

1. 3rd Generation Partnership Project (3GPP), 3GPP TR 23.501 V17.1.1: Technical Specification Group Services and System Aspects; System Architecture for the 5G System (5GS) (Release 17), Technical Report V17.1.1, Technical Specification Group Services and System Aspects (2021)
2. 5GAA Automotive Association, C-V2X Use Cases Volume II: Examples and Service Level Requirements, Technical Report, 5GAA (2020)
3. Bagheri, H., et al.: 5G NR-V2X: toward connected and cooperative autonomous driving. IEEE Commun. Stand. Mag. **5**(1), 48–54 (2021)
4. Alliance, N.G.M.N.: V2X, White Paper v1.0. White Paper, NGMN Alliance (2018)
5. Tayyab, M., Gelabert, X., Jäntti, R.: A survey on handover management: from LTE to NR. IEEE Access **7**, 118907–118930 (2019). https://doi.org/10.1109/ACCESS. 2019.2937405
6. Haghrah, A., Abdollahi, M.P., Azarhava, H., Niya, J.M.: A survey on the handover management in 5G-NR cellular networks: aspects, approaches and challenges. EURASIP J. Wirel. Commun. Netw. **2023**(1), 1–57 (2023). https://doi.org/10. 1186/s13638-023-02261-4
7. 3rd Generation Partnership Project (3GPP), 3GPP TS 32.500 V18.0.0: Telecommunication Management; Self-Organizing Networks (SON); Concepts and Requirements (Release 18)," Technical Specification, 3GPP Technical Specification Group Services and System Aspects (2024)
8. Bilen, T., Duong, T. Q., Canberk, B.: Optimal eNodeB estimation for 5G intra-macrocell handover management. In: Proceedings of the 12th ACM Symposium on QoS and Security for Wireless and Mobile Networks, pp. 87–93. ACM (2016). https://doi.org/10.1145/2988272.2988284
9. Wu, J., Liu, J., Huang, Z., Zheng, S.: Dynamic fuzzy Q-learning for handover parameters optimization in 5G multi-tier networks. In: 2015 International Conference on Wireless Communications and Signal Processing (WCSP), pp. 1–5. IEEE (2015)
10. China Telecom, Huawei: Consideration on mobility anchor solution. 3GPP RAN3 87, R3-150016 (2015)

11. Yajnanarayana, V., Rydén, H., Hévizi, L., Jauhari, A., Cirkic, M.: 5G handover using reinforcement learning. arXiv preprint: arXiv:1904.02572 (2019)
12. Tesema, F.B., Awada, A., Viering, I., Simsek, M., Fettweis, G.P.: Mobility modeling and performance evaluation of multi-connectivity in 5G intra-frequency networks. In: Proc. IEEE Globecom Workshops (GC Wkshps), San Diego, CA, USA, pp. 1–6 (2015)
13. Huq, K.M.S., et al.: Enhanced C-RAN using D2D network. IEEE Commun. Mag. **55**(3), 100–107 (2017)
14. Orsino, A., et al.: Effects of heterogeneous mobility on D2D- and drone-assisted mission-critical MTC in 5G. IEEE Commun. Mag. **55**(2), 79–87 (2017)
15. USRP E312 Datasheet. https://kb.ettus.com/E310/E312. Accessed 26 May 2025
16. PCI Detection Using SDR. https://www.mathworks.com/help/5g/ug/5g-nr-synchronization-signal-capture-using-software-defined-radio.html. Accessed 26 May 2025
17. Martiradonna, S., Grassi, A., Piro, G., Boggia, G.: 5G-air-simulator: an open-source tool modeling the 5G air interface. Comput. Netw. **173**, 107151 (2020). https://doi.org/10.1016/j.comnet.2020.107151
18. International Telecommunication Union (ITU), ITU-R Guidelines for Evaluation of Radio Interface Technologies for IMT-2020. Technical Report M.2412, ITU (2017)
19. Awad, A., Mohamed, A., Chiasserini, C.-F.: User-centric network selection in multi-RAT systems. In: Proc. IEEE Wireless Communications and Networking Conference Workshops (WCNC Wkshps), pp. 1–6 (2016)

Fusion^2: Achieving SIL4 Onboard Positioning for Autonomous Trams

Gianluca Mandò[1], Luigi Rucher[1], Alessandro Fantechi[2],
and Gloria Gori[2(✉)]

[1] Hitachi Rail GTS, Florence, Italy
{gianluca.mando,luigi.rucher}@urbanandmainlines.com
[2] DINFO, University of Florence, Florence, Italy
{alessandro.fantechi,gloria.gori}@unifi.it

Abstract. Autonomous rail systems, including driverless trams, are gaining traction due to their potential to enhance efficiency, capacity, and operational cost-effectiveness. A central requirement for safe operation of autonomous tram vehicles is achieving ultra-reliable positioning accuracy, which traditionally relies on costly, infrastructure-heavy solutions like trackside beacons or GPS, alongside sensor fusion algorithms that often fail to meet the stringent requirements of Safety Integrity Level 4 (SIL4). These limitations create a significant barrier to the widespread adoption of autonomous light rail systems. This paper introduces the Consistency Check and Best performance Selection (CCBS) algorithm, a novel fully onboard solution that enhances data reliability for rail positioning and velocity estimation systems. Our method validates and combines outputs from multiple sensors, leveraging a sophisticated consistency check and a data performance selection mechanism to achieve a SIL4 level – even when individual data streams do not. This entirely onboard approach significantly improves positioning and velocity estimation accuracy and offers substantial cost and maintenance efficiencies by eliminating the need for trackside infrastructure.

1 Introduction

Autonomous transportation is rapidly becoming a reality, exemplified by significant achievements in the rail sector. For instance, in Australia's Pilbara region, the world's heaviest autonomous vehicle—a 2-kilometer-long freight train—navigates between mine and port without human intervention, leveraging advanced sensing and control systems to operate safely in challenging environments, and demonstrating the substantial potential of autonomous rail systems in controlled environments. However, achieving full autonomy in urban Light Rail Transport (LRT) systems presents diverse challenges. These systems operate within dynamic and crowded cityscapes, interacting with diverse traffic modalities and complex infrastructure including tunnels, bridges, and grade crossings. Furthermore, ensuring ultra-reliable and precise positioning is paramount for safe autonomous decision-making, requiring adherence to stringent Safety Integrity Level 4 (SIL4) requirements [4,5].

© The Author(s), under exclusive license to Springer Nature Switzerland AG 2026
M. H. ter Beek et al. (Eds.): RSSRail 2025, LNCS 16236, pp. 255–264, 2026.
https://doi.org/10.1007/978-3-032-10762-6_20

Traditional positioning solutions for LRT face significant limitations. These include reliance on expensive and maintenance-intensive trackside infrastructure or susceptibility of Global Positioning Systems (GPS) to signal degradation in urban canyons and tunnels. While sensor fusion algorithms are critical for autonomous systems, individual sensors often struggle to deliver the continuous, high-integrity data streams required for SIL4 certification, particularly in the challenging electromagnetic and physical environments characteristic of urban rail operations [3].

This paper proposes to exploit duplication of positioning equipment in order to improve the integrity of positioning data provided by the simplex equipment, namely its *Integrity Risk*, by a careful combination of the statistical properties of the data provided by the duplicated equipment. By leveraging a novel 'Fusion^2' approach, which carefully combines the statistical properties of data from two independent sensor fusion chains, we demonstrate how to enhance reliability, reduce the Integrity Risk (IR) from 10^{-5} for individual chains to 10^{-10} for the combined output, and provide robust fault detection even under non-nominal conditions. This methodology ensures adherence to stringent Safety Integrity Level 4 (SIL4) requirements for urban LRT.

The remainder of the paper is structured as follows. Section 2 briefly reviews the positioning solutions provided by current sensor fusion technologies. Section 3 explains the proposed approach, Sect. 4 describes the mitigation strategy when non-nominal condition are detected, Sect. 5 validates the approach through simulation results and Sect. 6 concludes the paper.

2   Positioning in a Challenging Environment

The positioning solution we refer to is the NGAP (Next Generation Autonomous Positioning) product, an innovative localization system for trams, but that can conceptually work as an independent library. NGAP uses a sensor fusion algorithm to integrate data from various onboard sensors, including RADARs, inertial navigation units and GNSS (Global Navigation Satellite System) receivers.

NGAP offers an alternative to traditional tram localization methods based on odometers and RFID/loop tags, by enhancing positioning accuracy and enabling autonomous tram operations. It computes the tram's speed using RADARs instead of odometers and captures dynamic parameters like acceleration and angular velocity via IMUs (Inertial Measurement Units). The system determines the tram's absolute position using GNSS data, further refined by sensor fusion. (see Fig. 1)

Indeed, NGAP uses a Sensor Fusion Algorithm (SFA) to determine the position and speed of a tram by integrating data from multiple onboard sensors: IMU, RADAR, and a GNSS receiver. The SFA relies on a method called strap-down inertial navigation, enhanced by an Unscented Kalman Filter, which combines these sensor inputs for precise positioning. [2,9–11].

For speed measurement, NGAP primarily uses the RADAR and IMU, while GNSS is used to establish the tram's absolute position. The IMU tracks the

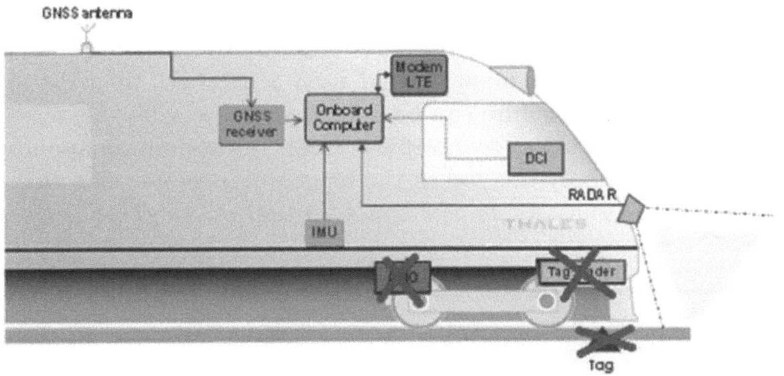

Fig. 1. Conceptual diagram of NGAP on-board sensor equipment for tram localization.

relative position through a process known as *dead reckoning* [8], which estimates the tram's movement based on a known starting location from the GNSS fix.

During operation, the sensor data is processed asynchronously: the SFA continuously evaluates new inputs from the sensors. The IMU provides relative position updates, the RADAR corrects speed measurements, and GNSS updates refine the tram's absolute position. In periods between GNSS updates, the SFA uses data from the IMU and RADAR to estimate the traveled distance and aligns this estimate with the track's centerline to maintain accuracy.

This dynamic and iterative approach allows the SFA to accurately navigate the tram along the guideway, offering improved precision and reliability checks.

The quality of position information is expressed by means of the *protection level*, also known as the boundary of uncertainty, a crucial concept in navigation and positioning systems. The protection level, computed by the estimation algorithm together with the position estimate, gives a quantifiable measure that defines the level of confidence or assurance in the accuracy of a position estimate. In essence, the protection level establishes a boundary around the calculated position, indicating the maximum potential error or uncertainty associated with that estimate.

This boundary serves as a safety margin, acknowledging that errors can arise from various sources, such as sensor inaccuracies, environmental conditions, or algorithm limitations. The larger the protection level, the greater the uncertainty in the position estimate, and vice versa. This parameter is particularly vital in safety-critical applications, such as autonomous navigation or transportation systems, where ensuring a reliable and secure position is paramount.

In NGAP, the SFA periodically provides an estimator of the actual position $\hat{s}$, which is described by a Gaussian random variable defined as $\hat{s} \sim N(s, \sigma)$, together with its Protection Level (PL). Alternatively this can also be expressed as the true position s perturbed by a Gaussian error $N(0, \sigma)$. PL is a statistical bound error that guarantees that the probability of the (unknown) real position error exceeding PL is smaller than or equal to a target value (called *integrity risk* (IR)). In other words, the interval $[s - \mathrm{PL}, s + \mathrm{PL}]$ contains the real position with probability greater or equal to $1 - IR$ (e.g. $1 - 10^{-5}$). The *alert limit (AL)* is the maximum value of PL allowed, that is, if $PL > AL$, then the measure is considered failed and the failure can be detected. These safety requirements are inspired by their aeronautical counterparts [6,8]. In the railway application, the protection level is actually defined as the length of a section of a line. For this reason, it is referred to as *Along The Track Protection Level (ATPL)*.

3   Safety Enhancement by Duplication

In sensor fusion theory, independent sensor fusion chains, estimating the same parameters, can be combined and compared in order to extract new added value information that help to improve estimation accuracy and its reliability. Starting with a number of sensor fusion chains, each supposed to be with a nominal error model (Gaussian distribution, unbiased and with a nominal standard deviation), the objective is to combine them in order to improve final estimation, bound the error and check and control if any non-nominal condition happens. Here, we discuss the case with two chains for simplicity reasons, but the approach can easily be extended to more chains, creating the so-called *binary fusion trees.*

Linear combination can be used to combine the two chains. In statistical signal processing, Linear Transformations are often used for their capability to preserve in the trasformation results, some important aspects of statistical characterization (e.g., Gaussian distributions) and for their capability of simplifying momentum computations of the resulting process. In our case, we refer to linear algebraic transformations, but the principle holds for any linear transformation (e.g., derivation, integration). It will help in the following three aspects:

1. improving final estimation accuracy, weighting the different estimators differently in order to compensate for losses in accuracy;
2. creating an error over bound by leveraging an estimation differences that eliminates the unknown parameter under estimation and provide only predictable error component;
3. together with other estimation techniques (e.g., Maximum Likelihood Estimation) and leveraging differences between estimates, in detecting and managing non-nominal condition cases.

The Consistency Check and Best Performance Selection is an algorithm and software library, initially developed for NGAP, that follows these principles on two chains. The algorithm applies to any pair of inputs, each composed by a location estimator and a protection level, agnostic to the actual algorithms employed in the previous stages of the chain.

In the specific application described in the paper, two instances of the Sensor Fusion Algorithm (SFA) are combined in an architecture resembling the classical 2oo2 (two-out-of-two) configuration (see Fig. 2)[1]. Each SFA instance processes

---

[1] In the current implementation, the two SFA chains are run on the same computer, but the software is then replicated on a 2oo2 hardware configuration to protect against hardware faults.

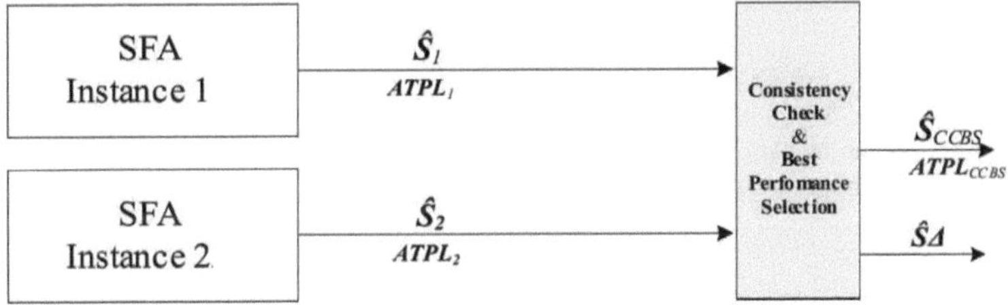

Fig. 2. SFA chains with difference estimator.

data from a separate set of sensors and provides an independent estimate of the tram's position. The linear combination of the data provided by the two SFA instances can be seen as a further fusion step, hence the name Fusion^2.

Each SFA provides an estimator of the actual position together with its protection level:

$$(\hat{s_1} \sim N\left(s_1, \sigma_1\right), ATPL_1) \ \text{ and } \ (\hat{s_2} \sim N\left(s_2, \sigma_2\right), ATPL_2) \tag{1}$$

With reference to Fig. 2, downstream of two instances of SFA, the *best performance selection* block is introduced to obtain, using a linear combination of the two estimators, a third estimator with its corresponding protection level to ensure an Integrity Risk (IR) not exceeding 10^{-10}. The third estimator is defined as $\hat{s}_{\text{ccbs}} = \mathbf{a}\hat{s}_1 + \mathbf{b}\hat{s}_2$, where the coefficients $\mathbf{a}$ and $\mathbf{b}$ are such that $\mathbf{a} + \mathbf{b} = 1$. It can be demonstrated that the variance of the estimator is minimized for the following values of $\mathbf{a}$ and $\mathbf{b}$:

$$a = \frac{\sigma_2^2}{\sigma_1^2 + \sigma_2^2} \ \text{ and } \ b = \frac{\sigma_1^2}{\sigma_1^2 + \sigma_2^2} \tag{2}$$

The consistency check and best performance selection block (CCBS) is designed so that the output is an estimator with the following characteristics:

$$\hat{s}_{CCBS} = \left(\frac{\sigma_2^2}{\sigma_1^2 + \sigma_2^2}\right)\hat{s_1} + \left(\frac{\sigma_1^2}{\sigma_1^2 + \sigma_2^2}\right)\hat{s_2} = a\hat{s_1} + b\hat{s_2} \tag{3}$$

Each SFA, by providing its own ATPL, ensures that the probability of the error $(\hat{e}_{s_1}, \hat{e}_{s_2})$ exceeding the ATPL without being detected is less than 10^{-5}:

$$P\left\{|\hat{e}_{s_1}| > ATPL_1 \mid \text{ not detected }\right\} < 10^{-5} \tag{4}$$

$$P\left\{|\hat{e}_{s_2}| > ATPL_2 \mid \text{ not detected }\right\} < 10^{-5} \tag{5}$$

Measurement errors from physically separated sensors are considered Gaussian and statistically independent (this assumption is usually accepted in observation and control theory, and underpins many models and methodologies in the literature). This is also constantly verified and checked by specific algorithms during the input phase. Therefore, two different sets of input sensors are processed by the same estimation process, producing estimates with estimation errors that are still independent of each other. However, in real-world scenarios, this independence may not be absolute, as the sensors are observing the same underlying physical event from spatially proximate locations. Consequently, a residual statistical dependence may exist, albeit typically negligible for practical purposes.

Diversity is adopted in the implementation of the two chains to minimize the probability of common cause errors. Hence, the two SFA chains are considered independent. Independence already suggests that the following intuitive result holds:

$$P\{|\hat{e}_{s_1}| > ATPL_1 \wedge |\hat{e}_{s_2}| > ATPL_2 \mid \text{not detected}\} < 10^{-10} \tag{6}$$

Indeed, it can be formally proved that:

$$P\{|\hat{e}_{CCBS}| > ATPL_{CCBS} \mid \text{not detected}\} < 10^{-10} \tag{7}$$

when the detection is made comparing $ATPL_{CCBS}$ with an Alert Limit which is 1.035 times the AL fixed as a requirement for a single chain.

The integrity risk of 10^{-10} is then used to estimate the probability of hazardous failure events of the positioning system, according to [8], which takes into account also timing parameters, that we have ignored here for brevity. Indeed, such estimation turns out to comply with Safety Integrity Level SIL4 [5].

4   Non-nominal Conditions Mitigation Strategy

Table 1. Table of Conditions and Error Distributions

Case	Condition	Error Distribution	Mean μ	Std. Dev. σ
0	Nominal	Gaussian	0	σ_{si}
1	Non-nominal	Gaussian	$\neq 0$	σ_{si}
2	Non-nominal	Gaussian	0	$> \sigma_{si}$
3	Non-nominal	Gaussian	$\neq 0$	$> \sigma_{si}$
4	Non-nominal	Non Gaussian	–	–

The output from the Consistency Check and Best Performance Selection (CCBS) block can be affected by faults in the SFA chains. In these *non-nominal conditions* the real statistical characterizations of the estimator's errors does not correspond to the assumptions: a fault in one of the two chains causes a non Gaussian estimator or it is still a Gaussian estimator but with bias and/or with a degradation of the accuracy. If we assume independence and a single fault among the two chains (as typically assumed in duplication, due to the extremely low probability of double faults), we can identify the non-nominal situations listed in Table 1, classified by the three failure modes of the faulty chain: non Gaussian error distribution, non-zero mean and larger standard deviation.

The CCBS block discriminates the non-nominal cases by means of specific tests. First, gaussianity test on the difference between the two estimates can detect whether the error distribution of one chain is non Gaussian.

To this aim, the difference random variable is constructed as follows:

$$\hat{s}_\Delta = |\hat{s_1} - \hat{s_2}| \tag{8}$$

Non-gaussianity of $\hat{s}_\Delta$ can be detected through specific gaussianity tests: MLE estimation of mean and standard deviation are continously monitored. To do this, being the single estimators correlated processes, a specific decorrelation time^2 needs to be taken in order to get uncorrelated samples for the MLE estimations. To this aim, a moving window collecting some hundreds of samples of $\hat{s}_\Delta$ is implemented by CCBS.

The non-nominal cases in which both estimates have a Gaussian error distribution can be detected either by checking whether they have a zero mean, and, again, exploiting the $\hat{s}_\Delta$ variable.

It is however necessary to impose an upper limit on the value that $\hat{s}_\Delta$ can take. This maximum limit is called the "overbound" and is computed as:

$$P_{\text{overbound}} = P\{\hat{s}_\Delta > \text{overbound}\} \tag{9}$$

where $P_{\text{overbound}}$ is the probability that the difference variable takes a value exceeding the pre-established over bound limit.

From the previous equation, we obtain the following formulation for the "overbound" variable:

$$\text{overbound} = \sqrt{\sigma_1^2 + \sigma_2^2} * Q^{-1}\left(\frac{P_{\text{overbound}}}{2}\right) \tag{10}$$

where Q is the Q-function (tail distribution function) of the standard normal distribution.

Note that in Nominal Condition both chains produce statistical characterizations of the estimation error that can be assumed Gaussian, unbiased and with known accuracy. In this case a best estimate is obtained by the linear transformation of Eq. 3. The difference between the two estimates will represent the natural error overbound for the estimation error.

In the Non-Nominal case 1 (to which we limit our discussion for brevity) both estimation chains produce an error distribution assumed to be Gaussian and with known accuracy, but biased. A best estimation can be still obtained

---

^{2} A decorrelation time is indeed considered in our internal implementation, ensuring that the samples used for MLE are sufficiently spaced in time to reduce statistical dependence. This approach is consistent with standard practices in signal processing and estimation theory, where temporal separation is used to approximate independence between samples [1].

by the linear transformation of the estimations given by Eq. 3, with minimal standard deviation, but biased. Calculating (estimating) the bias, the difference between estimates will still represent a natural error over bound for the best estimation error. Similar reasoning can be used for the other cases.

The overbound value represents an additional margin to contain the uncertainty estimated as output from the CCBS block, particularly for non-nominal conditions where one of the two estimation chains might be affected by bias.

This means that the optimal estimator resulting from the CCBS will be characterized by an uncertainty that is bounded within the protection level (calculated based on the desired Integrity Risk) adjusted according to the error bound value; this holds true as long as the output diagnostics, designed to monitor the deviation between the two estimators, do not detect the exceeding of the over bound threshold. In such an event, the output position estimator of the CCBS would indeed be declared no longer usable in the application context.

The above-mentioned diagnostics is nothing more than a hypothesis test conducted on a sample of the difference variable.

Summarizing, the CCBS block not only provides a new minimum variance estimator based on a linear combination of the two input estimators (outputs of the two SFAs) but also implements a consistency check, verifying that the two estimators do not deviate beyond a certain threshold.

Additionally, the CCBS block provides an ATPL that ensures an IR of 10^{-10}, starting from the IR of 10^{-5} for each SFA.

5   Validation Strategy

Within the patent application process [7], a validation of the approach has been carried on through extensive simulation. Simulations have been performed to evaluate the effectiveness of the proposed Consistency Check and Best Performance Selection (CCBS) approach in enhancing the accuracy of positioning data. The simulation cases reported in the following were conducted considering a 10 km line, assuming an average tram speed of 40 km/h. The experimental setup considers both nominal and non-nominal conditions, including scenarios with error correlation between the individual SFA chains.

Figures 3 and 4 show the cases of detected nominal and non-nominal conditions (case 1) respectively. Specifically in nominal condition case we can see that the optimum estimator preserves the zero mean in error and has reduced σ value. When the non-nominal condition has been detected, one of the two SFA chains exhibits a bias (indicated as a $\Delta = 1, 2$m shift). The figures present the error distributions of the two independent SFA chains and that of the optimal estimator derived from their combination via the CCBS approach. The results demonstrate that the CCBS successfully mitigates the bias for the optimal estimate. The probability density functions also confirm the reduction in uncertainty for the optimal combined estimator.

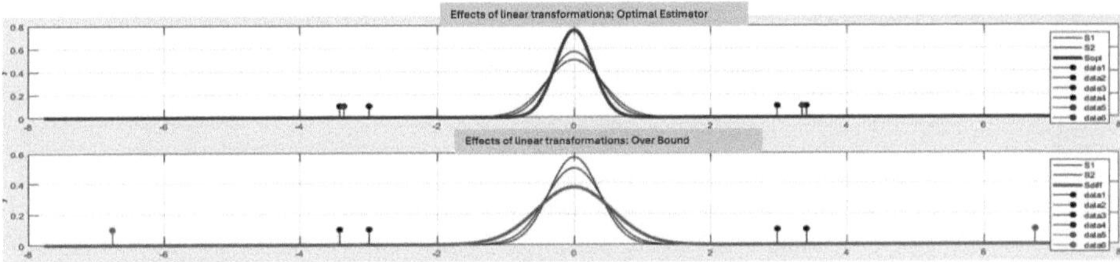

Fig. 3. Nominal conditions.

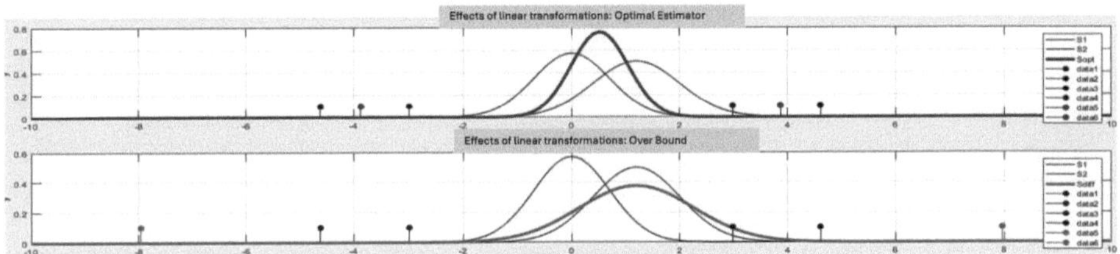

Fig. 4. Non-nominal conditions.

6   Conclusions

This paper has presented a novel approach to enhance the integrity and reliability of positioning data for autonomous urban Light Rail Transport (LRT) systems, addressing the SIL4 requirements. By exploiting the function of Next Generation Autonomous Positioning (NGAP) sensor fusion chains, our proposed Consistency Check and Best Performance Selection (CCBS) methodology statistically combines independent position estimators to significantly reduce the Integrity Risk (IR) from 10^{-5} per individual chain to 10^{-10} for the Fusion^2 output.

Building on these promising results, industrial developments are currently underway to implement the proposed solution in real-world operational environments. These activities aim to validate the system's performance on trains in active service, assessing its robustness and reliability under practical conditions. Due to the nature of these developments, further details are subject to industrial confidentiality.

Future work will focus on refining the fusion algorithms, expanding the scope of operational scenarios, and integrating the system into broader autonomous driving architectures. These steps are essential to support the transition from research to deployment in safety-critical railway applications.

References

1. Bar-Shalom, Y., Li, X.R., Kirubarajan, T.: Estimation With Applications to Tracking and Navigation: Theory Algorithms and Software. John Wiley & Sons (2001)

2. Basile, D., Fantechi, A., Rucher, L., Mandò, G.: Statistical model checking of hazards in an autonomous tramway positioning system. In: Collart-Dutilleul, S., Lecomte, T., Romanovsky, A. (eds.) Reliability, Safety, and Security of Railway Systems. Modelling, Analysis, Verification, and Certification, pp. 41–58. Springer International Publishing, Cham (2019)

3. Carnevali, L., Giandomenico, F.D., Fantechi, A., Gnesi, S., Gori, G.: Quantitative dependability evaluation of train control systems in presence of uncertainty: a systematic literature review. IEEE Trans. Intell. Transp. Syst. **26**(4), 4298–4314 (2025). https://doi.org/10.1109/TITS.2025.3530112

4. CENELEC: EN 50126-1: Railway Applications – The Specification and Demonstration of Reliability, Availability, Maintainability and Safety (RAMS) - Part 1: Generic RAMS Process (2017)

5. CENELEC: EN 50126-2: Railway Applications – The Specification and Demonstration of Reliability, Availability, Maintainability and Safety (RAMS) – Part 2: Systems Approach to Safety (2017)

6. ESA: Navipedia - Integrity. https://gssc.esa.int/navipedia/index.php/Integrity#Protection_Level. page last edited July (2018)

7. Hitachi Rail GTS Italia S.r.l.: Sistema e metodo per migliorare la precisione e ridurre l'incertezza nella determinazione dei parametri cinematici di un veicolo ferroviario mediante la combinazione di catene di sensor fusion (3 2025), PCT phase, n. PA107399IT01-HITACHI RAIL GTS ITALIA S.R.L

8. Legrand, C., Beugin, J., Conrard, B., Marais, J., Berbineau, M., El-Miloudi, E.: Approach for evaluating the safety of a satellite-based train localisation system through the extended integrity concept. In: Proceedings of ESREL 2015 - European Safety and Reliability Conference (2015)

9. Mandò, G., Giambene, G.: LTE system design for urban light rail transport. In: Fantechi, A., Lecomte, T., Romanovsky, A.B. (eds.) Reliability, Safety, and Security of Railway Systems. Modelling, Analysis, Verification, and Certification - Second International Conference, RSSRail 2017, Pistoia, Italy, 14–16 November 2017, Proceedings. Lecture Notes in Computer Science, vol. 10598, pp. 17–33. Springer (2017). https://doi.org/10.1007/978-3-319-68499-4_2

10. Selvi, D., Meli, E., Allotta, B., Rindi, A., Capuozzo, A., Rucher, L.: Feasibility analysis of positioning and navigation strategies for railway and tramway applications. IFAC-PapersOnLine **53**(2), 15680–15686 (2020). https://doi.org/10.1016/j.ifacol.2020.12.2557. 21st IFAC World Congress

11. Tamang, D., Martiradonna, S., Abrardo, A., Mandò, G., Roncella, G., Boggia, G.: Architecting 5G RAN slicing for location aware vehicle to infrastructure communications: The autonomous tram use case. Comput. Networks **200**, 108501 (2021). https://doi.org/10.1016/J.COMNET.2021.108501

Formal Modelling and Analysis

Compositional Model Checking of Railway Interlocking Systems Featuring Flank Protection

Anne E. Haxthausen[1]($\boxtimes$) , Alessandro Fantechi[2] , and Gloria Gori[2]

[1] DTU Compute, Technical University of Denmark, Lyngby, Denmark
`aeha@dtu.dk`
[2] University of Florence, Firenze, Italy
`{alessandro.fantechi,gloria.gori}@unifi.it`

Abstract. Model checking techniques applied to the verification of railway interlocking systems may fail to scale. Compositional methods have been proposed to reduce the size of networks to be model checked. In this paper we extend the scope of a previously defined compositional method to systems employing flank protection, not supported in the original method because flank protection requires a coordination of distant points. The extension comprises soundness results for this new context and a decomposition strategy able to divide a network into sub-networks of minimal size.

Keywords: Formal Methods · Model Checking · Compositional Verification · Interlocking Systems · Flank Protection

1 Introduction

Model checking techniques have often been applied to the verification of railway interlocking systems (see, e.g., [1,5,9,21]). However, the *state space explosion* phenomenon limits the scalability of this approach, making automatic verification of railway interlocking systems for large networks demanding in terms of computing resources and may even fail [4].

Abstraction techniques have typically been adopted to limit state space explosion in model checking. Abstraction should preserve the desired properties, while the adopted abstraction technique is often defined specifically for the kind of system and properties under examination. For interlocking systems, convenient abstractions are based on the *locality* principle [8,22]: properties concerning the safe allocation of a route to a train are typically not influenced by other train movements over network elements that are distant from, and not interfering with, the considered route. Locality of a safety property can be used to limit the state space by abstracting away such "distant movements".

The locality principle is at the base of *compositional* approaches to the verification of interlocking systems of large networks: the network is divided into two

M. H. ter Beek et al. (Eds.): RSSRail 2025, LNCS 16236, pp. 267–285, 2026.
https://doi.org/10.1007/978-3-032-10762-6_21

(or more) sub-networks, to which model checking is applied, with a substantial reduction of state space explosion [2,3,7,10–14].

The soundness of compositional safety verification guarantees that, when properly cutting a network, proving safety for the sub-networks suffices to prove safety for the full network. In this way, the task of proving safety for a large network can be reduced to the task of verifying safety for sub-networks of a size manageable by the model checker.

One question posed by the application of a compositional approach is about how and where to decompose the network. While the approach described in [10–12] is grounded on pragmatic domain-related criteria for the definition of how and where to perform a cut of a network, our previous work [6] has studied the conditions under which a network can be decomposed into a collection of sub-networks of the finest possible granularity, that belong to a library of pre-verified "elementary networks".

The conditions given by our previous paper include a ban of *flank protection*. Flank protection is an extra safety mechanism common in the design of interlocking systems, to enforce safety also in the case in which trains do not strictly respect signals, due to a driver's misbehaviour or accidental inability to brake. Since flank protection relates the position of points on a route to the position of possibly distant points, it violates the locality principle.

In this paper we release the ban on flank protection, first proving that the compositional verification method of [7] is still sound, provided that the points related by flank protection are in the same sub-network: this restricts the way in which a network can be safely decomposed. The decomposition strategy of [6] is changed accordingly to fulfil the new restricted requirements for cutting. The decomposition strategy still leads to sub-networks of minimal size, but not all of them are elementary.

Paper Overview. After a description of the RobustRailS verification method in Sect. 2 and a summary of the compositional verification method in Sect. 3, Sect. 4 recalls the decomposition strategy of [6]. Then, in Sect. 5, flank protection is introduced and in Sects. 6–7, the compositional verification method and the decomposition strategy are generalised to allow for flank protection. Section 8 draws conclusions and states ideas for future work.

2   The RobustRailS Verification Method and Tools

In the RobustRailS research project[1] that was accompanying the Danish resignalling programme on a scientific level in 2012–2017, a formal method with tools support for automated, formal verification of railway interlocking systems was developed [17–20].

---

[1] http://robustrails.man.dtu.dk.

About the Considered Interlocking Systems. An *interlocking system* is a signalling system component that is responsible for safe routing of trains through (a fraction of) a railway network under its control.

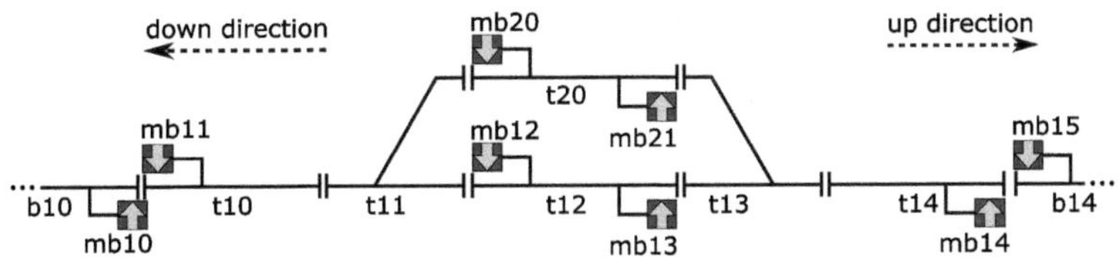

Fig. 1. A railway network layout example. From [18].

In Fig. 1 an example of a railway network layout for a small station is given. As it can be seen, it consists of (1) train detection sections that are either linear sections (like t10) or switchable points (like t11) having a STEM side and two branching sides called PLUS and MINUS (e.g. t11 has its STEM next to t10 and its PLUS branch next to t12 and its MINUS branch next to t20, respectively); (2) markerboards[2] (like mb10). There is zero or one markerboard in each end of a linear section and a markerboard can only be seen when leaving the section, (e.g. mb10 is visible in direction UP – see the direction arrows at the top of the figure). At the borders of a network, there are always two linear sections (like b10 and t10) with a signal configuration having an *entry signal* on the border section and an *exit signal* on the section next to the border section. Furthermore, networks are assumed to be *loop-free*[3]. A *route* in a network is a sequence of consecutive sections from one signal to the next signal, visible in the same direction. For instance, in the network of Fig. 1 the sections t10, t11, t12 constitute a route in the UP direction from mb10 to mb13.

About the Tool. The RobustRailS tool, *RR-T*, can be used to verify that an interlocking system instance controlling a certain railway network is safe by providing the following as input to the tool: (1) a generic, formal, behavioural model of the interlocking system and generic safety properties, as well as (2) a specification of the network under its control.[4] The tool then checks that the input is statically well-formed (represents a topologically legal railway network),

---

[2] We are considering modern ERTMS level 2 based interlocking systems for which there are no physical signals. They are replaced by markerboards, and in the control system there are virtual signals associated with the markerboards. Throughout the paper we use the term *signal* as a synonym for *markerboard*.

[3] A network is *loop-free*, if there are no physically possible path through the network containing the same section more than once.

[4] Throughout this paper, as generic model and safety properties, we are using those from [20]. The properties are the *no collision* and *no derailment* properties, shared by the vast literature on interlocking verification.

it instantiates the generic model and generic safety properties with the network description, and finally it verifies that the instantiated model satisfies the instantiated safety properties, by means of a bounded model checker performing a k-induction proof.

3   A Method for Compositional Verification

In this section we recall the compositional method proposed in [7]. It assumes that flank protection is not adopted. To introduce the method, we first define what is a *cut* of a network, and how sub-networks are generated by the cut.

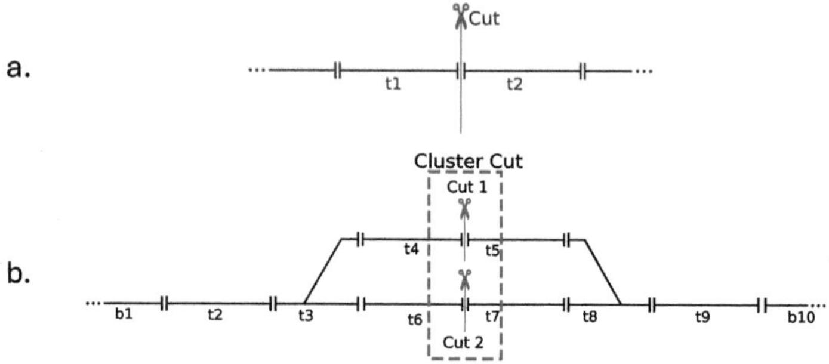

Fig. 2. Example of cuts from [7]: (a) a single cut and (b) a cluster cut.

Cut Specifications. A *single cut* is a cut that can be performed between any two neighbouring, non-border sections $t1$ and $t2$ in a network N. An example of a single cut is shown in Fig. 2.a. The *specification* of that single cut is the pair $(t1, t2)$. To divide a network into two parts, it is not always enough to perform a single cut, but a *cluster cut* consisting of several single cuts may be needed. An example of a cluster cut is shown in Fig. 2.b. The *specification* of a *cluster cut* is the set of specifications of each of its single cuts. A cut is *legal* if it divides the network into exactly two parts and no route is cut by more than one single cut.

Decomposing a Network According to a Cut Specification. Given a well-formed network N and a legal cut specification, the network can be decomposed into two networks as follows:

- if a single cut is between linear sections $t1$ and $t2$, first divide the network N between $t1$ and $t2$, obtaining two sub-networks N_{-1} and N_{-2}, and then add to N_{-1} and N_{-2} at the respective cut a border section, and also an entry and an exit markerboard at that border, if there were not already markerboards placed around the cut. By doing so, two well-formed networks are obtained:

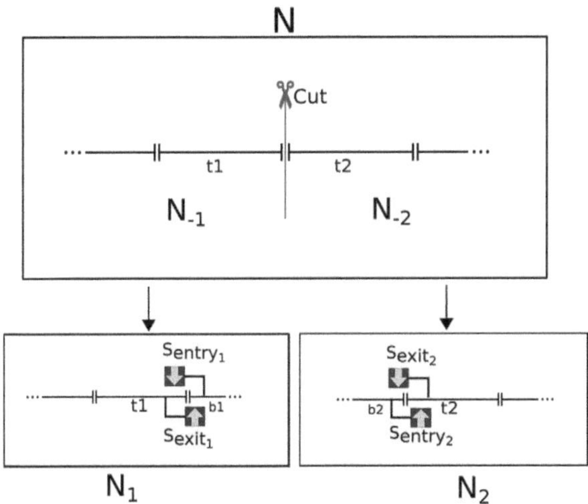

Fig. 3. An example of a decomposition of a network into two networks. From [7].

N_1 and N_2. Figure 3 shows how a network is decomposed into two networks by a single cut $(t1, t2)$. It can be seen how N_1 is obtained from the sub-network N_{-1} on the left-hand side of the cut by adding a border section $b1$ and border markerboards s_{entry_1} and s_{exit_1}. N_2 is obtained in a similar way. When it is clear from the context, sometimes we also call the resulting networks N_1 and N_2 *sub-networks*;

- if a single cut is between a linear section $t1$ and a point p, the decomposition is treated as if there were an additional linear section $t2$ between $t1$ and p, and the cut specification were $(t1, t2)$;
- if a single cut is between two points $p1$ and $p2$, the decomposition is treated as if there were two additional linear sections $t1$ and $t2$ between $p1$ and $p2$, and the cut specification were $(t1, t2)$.
- if the cut is a cluster cut, the above rules are simultaneously applied to each of its single cuts.

Method Steps. Using a legal cut allows to perform compositional verification in these steps:

1. Decompose a network N according to a legal cut specification, achieving two networks N_1 and N_2.
2. For $i = 1, 2$, apply the RobustRailS tool (RR-T) to N_i to instantiate the chosen generic model and generic safety properties and verify that the instantiated model satisfies the instantiated safety properties.

In [7] it is proved that this method is *sound*. Soundness means that in order to prove safety of the model instance for the whole network, it is sufficient to verify safety for the model instances for the two sub-networks formed by a legal cut.

4   A Decomposition Strategy

Using the presented compositional verification method leaves the question: which cuts should be made in order to decompose a network into small networks that are fast to verify? In this section we recall the idea, proposed in [6], of providing a library of pre-verified, elementary networks and a strategy for dividing a given network into sub-networks of which as many as possible are elementary.

4.1   Elementary Networks

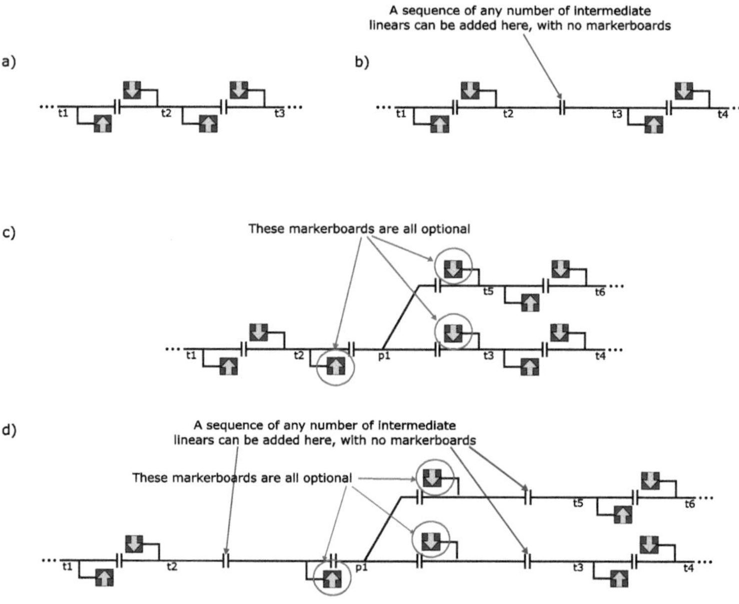

Fig. 4. Patterns for elementary networks. From [7].

As elementary networks, we allow the network patterns shown in Fig. 4: $(a)-(b)$, that is, a sequence of linear sections having only the required markerboards at the two borders; $(c)-(d)$, that is, one point surrounded by linear sections and the required markerboards, plus optional markerboards directly facing the point. All patterns admit an unbounded number of linear elements at the indicated positions. Model instances of the networks of Fig. 4 have been model checked to be safe, for all the admitted combinations of presence of markerboards, but without the presence of the admitted extra linear sections. Moreover, a result from [7] allows us to add an unbounded number of linear sections at the indicated specific positions without impacting safety. Hence, we can conclude that *model instances for all elementary networks are safe.*

4.2   Decomposing a Network

Given a network, now the idea is to search for places to make legal cuts, one by one, such that the network can be divided into parts that are either *elementary* networks or *non-decomposable* networks (that is, non-elementary networks that cannot be decomposed by any cut(s) without breaking the rules for legal cuts). In the ideal case that the decomposition leads to networks that are all elementary, no additional model checking is needed for verifying the safety of the whole network.

As an example, consider the network shown in Fig. 5. By making the three cuts (two single cuts $(083, PM02U)$ and $(PM02U, PM03U)$ and the cluster cut $\{(802, PM04U), (801, PM04U)\}$) shown by green lines, one by one, it yields four elementary networks N_1^1, N_1^2, N_1^3, and N_2^3 shown in Fig. 14 in Appendix A.

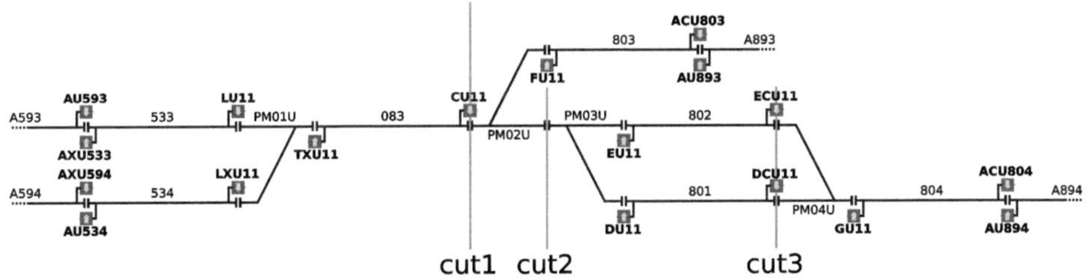

Fig. 5. Cuts shown on a network (LVR1). From [6].

The process defined in [6] for finding such cuts for a network N is as follows:

1. Start searching from the neighbour (linear section) l of some border section b of N. The search direction is from l towards the next adjacent element in the direction opposite to b.
2. Follow the sections from l one by one as long as they are linear and do not have any markerboard attached until one of the following happens:
   (a) If a linear section next to a border is reached, no cut should be made, as the considered network is an elementary linear network.
   (b) If two consecutive, linear sections $l1$ and $l2$ are found, and at least one of them has a markerboard facing the other, then a decomposition using the cut $(l1, l2)$ should be made. As a consequence, the sub-network containing $l1$ will by construction be an elementary linear network. The search for further cuts should then continue from $l2$ in the other sub-network.
   (c) If a point p is found, then we should continue to search for cuts on the two other sides of p. This search depends on from which side p was found: the stem or one of the branching sides. In both cases the search also depends on whether the two other sides are connected or not.[5] We refer to [6] for

____

[5] Two sides of point p are said to be *connected* if there is a path in the undirected graph of the not yet visited part of the network that goes between those two sides of p.

a detailed account on how the following cases produce the cuts shown in Fig. 14 in Appendix A.

i. If coming from the stem side of p, and the two other sides are not connected, then we should search for cuts in each of the two other sides. The search here is similar to the search starting from a border, except that if a second point is found, a single cut must be made just *before* that point. The two searches may hence lead to totally zero, one or two single cuts, dividing the network into (1) an elementary point network containing p and (2) zero, one or two additional sub-networks in which a search for cuts must be recursively performed.

ii. If coming from the stem, and the two branching sides are connected, then a similar search is made in each of the branches. In this case two single cuts (one in each branch) will be found and these must be combined in a cluster cut (in order to divide the network into two parts) leading to an elementary network containing p and a sub-network to which the search for cuts must be recursively applied.

iii. If coming from a branching side of p, and the stem and the other branching side are not connected, searches for cuts in the other branch and on the stem side must be performed in a similar way to case i above.

iv. If coming from a branching side of p, and the stem and the other branching side are connected, the search to be performed is similar to case ii, except that in some cases it is not possible to find a legal cluster cut: that happens if a potential cluster cut divides a route into three parts[6]. In such a case we say that N is *unbreakable* from the border b from where the search started, and we should then start a search from another border to see if a cut can be found from there. Should N be *unbreakable* from all borders, it is *non-decomposable*.

In [6] this strategy was formally specified in the RSL language and then implemented in C++ as a decomposer tool. Experiments showed that the execution time using the decomposer was a very small fraction of the time needed to verify the full network using the RobustRails Tools.

5   Flank Protection

In railway interlocking systems, specific extra mechanisms may be included in interlocking systems to enforce safety also in the case in which trains do not strictly respect signals, due to a driver's misbehaviour or accidental inability to brake. In the *Flank Protection* mechanism, during allocation of a route, points and signals not belonging to the route are properly set in order to avoid hostile train movements into the route at an incident point. In this paper, we consider only flank protection by points (see [16] for flank protection by signals).

---

[6] Note that when coming from the stem, we do not have such a problem, as a route cannot pass through a point via its two branches.

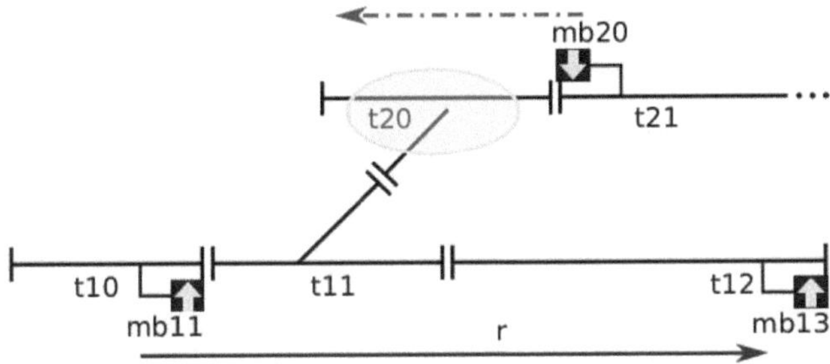

Fig. 6. Example of flank protection: $t20$ in PLUS flank protects $t11$ of route r. From [19].

In the example of Fig. 6, locking route r requires the point $t20$ to be in the PLUS (straight) position in order to protect the flank of route r by a train accidentally passing the closed $mb20$ signal. In this case point $t20$ is said to *flank protect* point $t11$ of route r. We also say that $t20$ in its PLUS position protects $t11$ in its PLUS position, and we use the notation $((t11, PLUS), (t20, PLUS))$ to specify that. It can be seen that likewise point $t11$ can *flank protect* point $t20$ of the dotted route, i.e. $((t20, PLUS), (t11, PLUS))$ holds.

Remote Flank Protection. According to Pachl [15], flank protection should be provided by elements that are directly adjacent to the route to be protected, but sometimes this is not possible and the protecting element must be further away, in which case it is said to be a *remote flank protection*. An example is shown in Fig. 7, where point $p3$ in the PLUS position cannot be protected by $p2$, but (partially) by $p1$ in the PLUS position. Note that also $p2$ in PLUS is protected by $p1$ in PLUS, and $p1$ in PLUS is protected by $p2$ in PLUS.

Conflicting Protections. In some cases the possible protection for two points in the same route are in conflict, i.e. the two points have the same point p as protecting point, but in different positions. Such a point is called a *self-selective protective point* [15]. In such a case at most one of the flank protections can be chosen for the route. For instance, for route $A1D1$ in Fig. 8, $p1$ in PLUS position can be protected by $p2$ in PLUS position, while $p4$ in MINUS position can be protected by $p2$ in MINUS position. These two protections of $p1$ and $p4$ are in conflict, as $p2$ cannot be in PLUS and MINUS position at the same time. Therefore, for route $A1D1$ it is not possible to protect both $p1$ and $p4$ by points and the railway engineer must choose at most one of the conflicting protections.

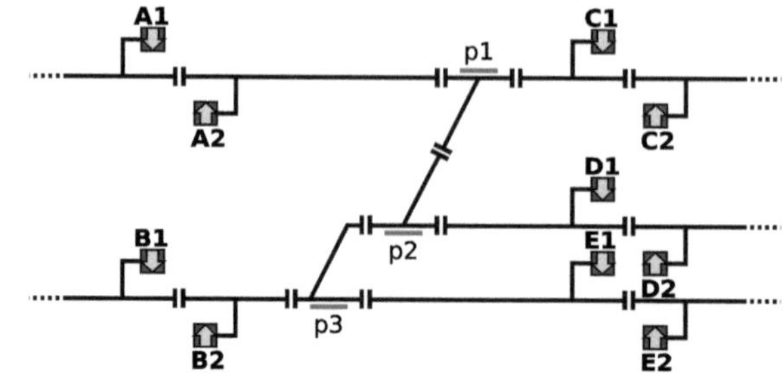

Fig. 7. Example of remote flank protection.

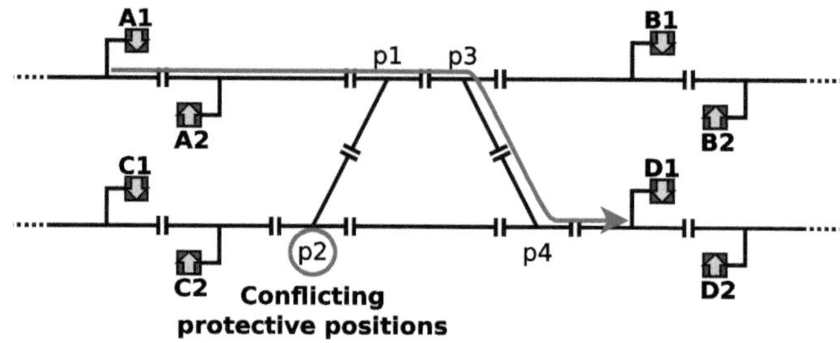

Fig. 8. Example of conflicting protections.

6   Compositional Verification Allowing Flank Protection

In this section we explore how the compositional method presented in Sect. 3 can be generalised to support systems using flank protection.

6.1   Cuts and Decomposition Revisited

In this section we re-define what it means for a cut to be legal, and we give examples of illegal and legal cuts. The decomposition of a network according to a cut specification and the steps of the compositional method are still as defined in Sect. 3.

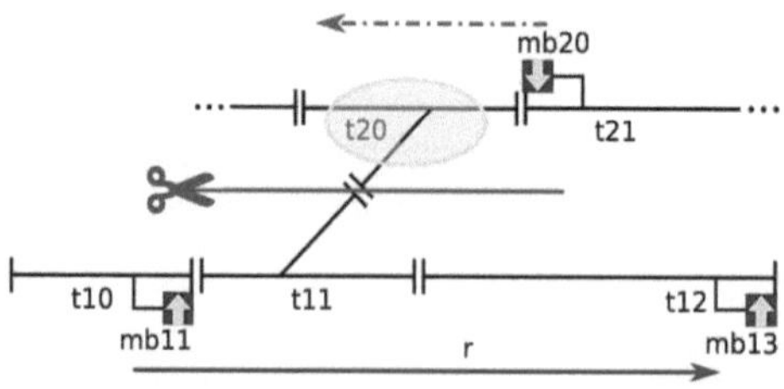

Fig. 9. Illegal cut through a flank protection. Based on [19].

Consider the example of Fig. 9 where locking of route r requires the point $t20$ to be in the PLUS position in order to protect the flank of route r. If both point $t20$ and route r lie in the same sub-network when a cut is operated, the extra condition on the point position has no impact on compositionality, but this is not the case for the drawn cut, which separates the protecting and the protected points. As discussed in [7], in this case compositional verification results do not fully hold, so we consider such a cut as not being legal: both elements should instead be in the same sub-network.

So the definition in Sect. 3 of what it means for a cut to be *legal* must be revised when flank protection is adopted. It is assumed that a railway engineer for each route has chosen which points in the route should be protected by which points and we let *fps* denote the flank protection relation containing all chosen flank protection pairs of all routes. A cut is *legal* for a chosen flank protection relation *fps* if it divides the network into exactly two parts, no route is cut by more than one single cut, and no *flank protecting* elements are separated by the cut from the sections they protect according to *fps*.

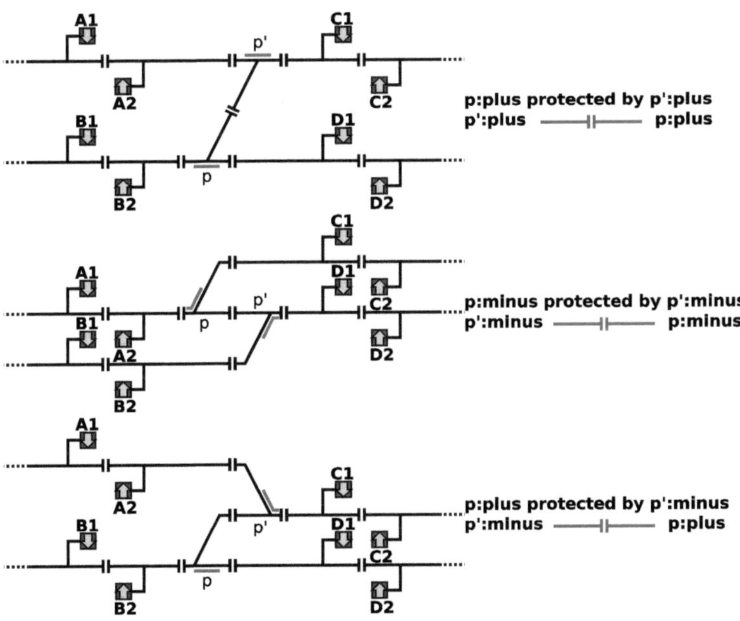

Fig. 10. Three minimal networks each containing two points p and p' flank protecting each other. Hence, (p, p') is an illegal cut for each of these networks.

Figure 10 contains three examples of networks, each containing exactly two points flank protecting each other and which therefore must not be separated. In the first network, the two points are connected on their MINUS sides, in the second by their PLUS sides, and in the third via a PLUS and a MINUS side.

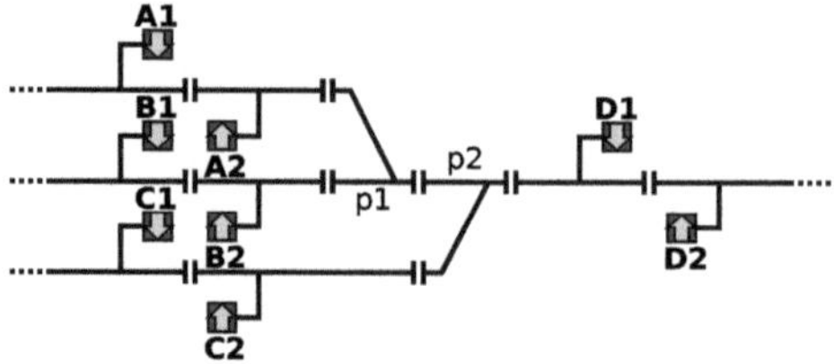

Fig. 11. A networks containing two points $p1$ and $p2$ not flank protecting each other. Hence, $(p1, p2)$ is a legal cut for this network.

Figure 11 shows a network containing two points connected by their STEM end and PLUS end, respectively, so they cannot be in flank protection relation. Therefore, a cut between the two points is legal. Decomposing the network according to this cut results in two elementary networks of pattern (c) in Fig. 4.

In general two points being in flank protection relation will always be connected via their branches and never via their stems, but in between the two points there can be linear sections (with or without signals) or even one or more points as can be exemplified by Fig. 7 where $p2$ is between $p1$ and $p3$, when all possible flank protections by points are chosen.[7] Having these flank protections, $p1$ and $p2$ as well as $p1$ and $p3$ must not be separated by a cut. Hence, $(p1, p2)$ and $(p2, p3)$ are not legal cuts.

6.2   Soundness Revisited

Theorem 1 (Soundness).   *The compositional method using the restricted notion of legal cuts as defined above for models supporting flank protection is sound.*

Proof. Most of the soundness proof in [7] for our original compositional method not supporting flank protection carries over to a proof of Theorem 1.

Due to the excessive length of such a proof, we briefly sketch here a rationale.

All parts, except the proof of Theorem 4.9 in [7] carry over. The proof of that theorem has been revisited[8], as part of it depends on the underlying model which is slightly changed to support flank protection: (1) the guard of the rule for allocating a route r checks that the route is not in conflict with other reserved routes, but the definition of route conflicts itself has changed. Now two routes are in conflict, not only if they are overlapping, but also if a protecting point of one route is either a point or a protecting point of the other route and the required setting of that point is different for the two routes. Furthermore, there

---

[7] That is, $fps = \{((p1, PLUS), (p2, PLUS)), ((p2, PLUS), (p1, PLUS)), ((p3, PLUS), (p1, PLUS))\}$. Note that $p3$ in PLUS cannot be protected by $p2$ as $p3$ is connected to $p2$'s stem side. Note also that the relation is not symmetric.

[8] On http://www.imm.dtu.dk/~aeha/RobustRailS/data/compositionalmethod/soundness-revisited-main.pdf, an internal technical note with proof details is provided.

is an extra guard condition requiring that each protecting point of the route is either already in the protecting position or it is not used by another train. (2) The actions of the same rule now not only request the points in r to be switched into correct position, but also the protecting points of r to be switched into their protecting positions. A key to the success of the proof is the fact that a point of a route and its protecting point will always be in the same sub-network, each with same required positions as in the full network.

7   Decomposition Strategy with Flank Protection

This section generalises our decomposition strategy presented in Sect. 4 to the case where flank protection is adopted.

7.1   Changes to the Decomposition Strategy

When flank protection is adopted, legal cuts do not allow to separate protecting points from the points they protect. Therefore, the strategy for decomposing a network in Sect. 4.2 must be updated to avoid such separations, taking a flank protection relation fps for a network into account.

For example, if a search is made from $t10$ in the network of Fig. 6, then the subsequent search for a cut on the MINUS side of $t11$ would have led to the cut $(t11, t20)$, if $t11$ and $t20$ had not been flank protecting each other in the PLUS position, but instead the search must continue from the MINUS side of $t20$, leading to normal searches on the STEM and PLUS sides of $t20$ (assuming that $t20$ is not in flank protection relation with other points than $t11$) as now the protecting point has been passed.

Note that while previously a search for cuts along a side of a point always led to the finding of none or one cut, now it can lead to more than one cut. For instance, in the example above, the new search for cuts on the MINUS side of $t11$ could lead to two cuts: one on the STEM side of $t20$ and one on the PLUS side of $t20$. On the PLUS side it could even lead to more than one cut, if $t20$ on the PLUS side had another protecting point.

Before providing a high-level description of our strategy for decomposing a network, we first establish the following definition.

Given a network N and a flank protection relation fps for N, we define a function $fpclass$ which generates an equivalence class partition of the points in N. This equivalence class partition is the least one fulfilling:

(1) if $((p, pos1), (p', pos2)) \in fps$, then p and p' are in the same class C and
(2) if $p \in C$ and $p' \in C$, then $\forall$ point p'' on a path between p and p', $p'' \in C$.

Note, if a point is not appearing in fps, then it is in a singleton class. We use the notation $class(p)(N, fps)$ for that class C in $fpclass(N, fps)$ for which $p \in C$. As an example, for the network in Fig. 12 and the shown fps, we have: $fpclass(N, fps) = \{\{p1, p2, p3\}, \{p4\}, \{p5\}\}$ and $class(p3)(N, fps) = \{p1, p2, p3\}$.

Step 1 and step 2 cases (a)-(b) of the strategy are all as before, but the search for cuts in step 2 case (c) (a point p is met from some of its three sides) should be modified: If point p is not in flank protection relation with any other point, the search is as usual. If point p is in flank protection relation with other point(s), then identify (1) the smallest sub-network N_{sub} that contains p and all other points in its equivalence class, $class(p)(N, fps)$, and (2) specify cuts that can cut this sub-network out. The execution of these cuts will divide the network into (1) N_{sub} and (2) n additional sub-networks in which a search for cuts must be performed, where n is the number of found cuts. The created network N_{sub} is a *minimal* network, with minimality defined as follows: A sub-network N_{sub} of N is *minimal*, if

1. (a) the set of points in N_{sub} is empty, or (b) the set of points in N_{sub} is a class in $fpclass(N, fps)$, and
2. (c) if N_{sub} contains two consecutive, non-border, linear sections, at least one of which has a signal facing the other section, then both sections are in the path between two points in the same class in N_{sub}.

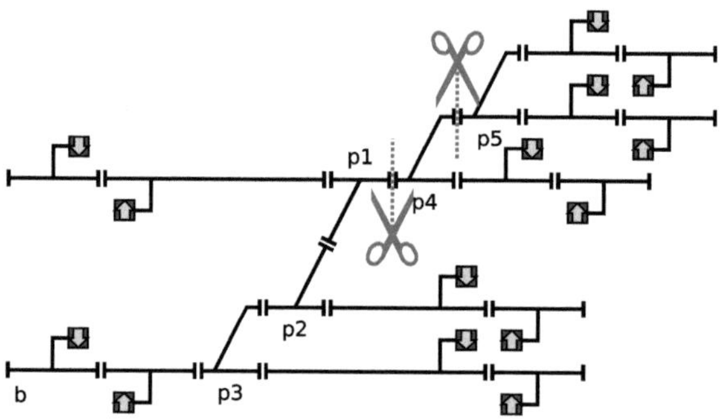

Fig. 12. A network with cuts found by decomposition with $fps = \{((p1, PLUS), (p2, PLUS)), ((p2, PLUS), (p1, PLUS)), ((p3, PLUS), (p1, PLUS))\}$.

Decomposition Example. Consider the network N in Fig. 12. We will now show how our strategy will decompose this network into three sub-networks when starting a search for cuts from border b. When the point $p3$ is met it is noticed that it is in flank protection relation with $p1$. Therefore, the smallest sub-network $N1$ containing the points in $class(p3)(N, fps) = \{p1, p2, p3\}$ is identified and it is found that only one cut, $(p1, p4)$ is needed to separate $N1$ from the remaining network. Then a search is made in the other resulting network. This search is normal as the points are not in any flank protection relation and it will find the cut $(p4, p5)$. After this cut is executed, no more cuts are found. Hence, the decomposition leads to three minimal networks of which two are elementary.

If flank protection had not been adopted, the original decomposition algorithm would, in addition to the cuts $(p1, p4)$ and $(p4, p5)$, have found two more cuts: $(p1, p2)$ and $(p2, p3)$, and hence have divided the network into 5 elementary networks rather than 2 elementary networks and 1 non-elementary network.

Table 1. Verification metrics for the RobustRails Tool (RR-T). Time is measured in seconds, memory in MB.

		Sub-networks	Verification Time	Memory usage
Without Flank	Full Network	1	41	357
Protection	Decomposed Network	5	15	93
With Flank	Full Network	1	36	346
Protection	Decomposed Network	3	11	188

Table 1 shows verification metrics for various model checking experiments for the network shown in Fig. 12. The first and third row of the table show the verification time and memory usage for checking the full network without and with flank protection, respectively. Row 2 shows the same metrics for the combined compositional verification of the five networks obtained by the decomposition algorithm for the case of no flank protection: the execution time is the sum of the execution times for the five sub-networks, and the memory usage is the maximum of the memory usages for the five sub-networks. Similarly, row 4 shows the metrics for the combined compositional verification of the three sub-networks obtained by the decomposition algorithm for the case of flank protection.

It can be seen that flank protection decreases both verification time and memory usage for the full network (which gives an indication that the state space is also smaller). Indeed, flank protection increases the conflicts between routes, shrinking the possible combinations of simultaenously allocated routes.

It can also be seen that in both cases the adoption of decomposition decreases verification time and memory usage already for this small example. Such gain is expected to be more significant for larger networks.

7.2   Elementary Networks Revisited

While the new strategy cannot decompose all well-formed networks into elementary sub-networks (as defined in Sect. 4)—since some sub-networks may contain pairs of protected-protecting points—it guarantees that any well-formed network will be decomposed into minimal sub-networks. Unfortunately, defining an extended set of elementary networks to address this limitation is not feasible.

Indeed, in Fig. 10 we saw examples of some minimal networks. They could have been candidates for an extended library of elementary networks, and so could the slightly larger network in Fig. 7. Now consider Fig. 13 in which a family of similarly structured networks is shown: they differ in the number n of parallel lines. They are all minimal and cannot be decomposed, as $p1$ will be in flank protection relation with all the other points. This family has an infinite number of networks, and each of these need to be model checked in order to be added to the library of elementary networks. Therefore, it is not possible to define a new (extended) complete set of elementary networks.

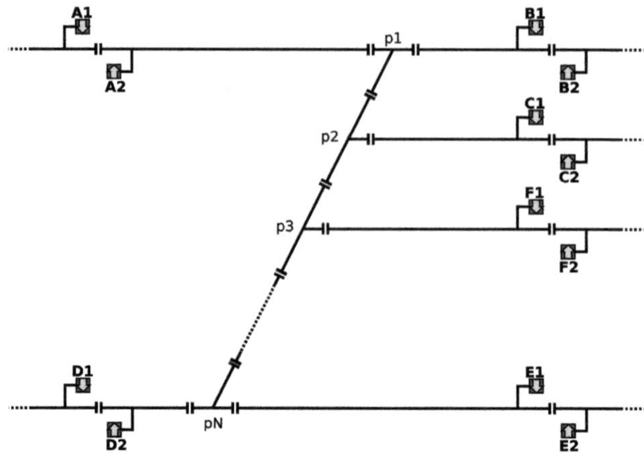

Fig. 13. Example illustrating an infinitely large family of minimal networks.

8   Conclusions

Contributions. In this paper we have exploited a previously defined compositional method for model checking the safety of interlocking systems and a strategy for automated decomposition, both assuming that there were no flank protection. We have extended the compositional method and the strategy to deal with flank protection as well. The generalised compositional method is proved to still be sound. The generalised division algorithm is able to divide a network into subnetworks of minimal size, but not all of these are elementary due to flank protection. This extension is particularly important, as flank protection is commonly used in practice.

This study also sheds light on the fact that flank protection breaks the locality principle, extending the conditions to be considered for allocating a route: this aspect is independent of the adopted modelling framework.

Future Work. Topics for future work on this research line include:

1. formalise and implement the new decomposition strategy in a new decomposer tool and make experiments with that,
2. extend the method to also allow markerboards to be used for flank protection (that would be straightforward), and
3. transfer the method to other verification methods, such as the Surrey/Swansea interlocking verification method described in [8,9].

While the goal of this paper has been to explore how the existing compositional method and decomposition algorithm could be extended to work for models including flank protection, a totally different line of research could be to investigate how to verify that a chosen flank protection is sufficient - so wrong deployment of flank protection could be caught.

Acknowledgements. The authors would like to thank (1) Jan Peleska and Linh H. Vu together with whom Anne Haxthausen developed the RobustRailS verification method and tools, (2) Hugo D. Macedo, who contributed to the initial work on the applied compositional method, (3) Sofie-Amalie Petersen and Óli Kárason Mikkelsen for having implemented the decomposer tool, and (4) Anna Nam Anh Nguyen and Ole Eilgaard for their network cutter tool which was integrated into the decomposer tool. The contribution by the second and third author was supported by the MUR PRIN 2022 PNRR P2022A492B project ADVENTURE (ADVancEd iNtegraTed evalUation of Railway systEms) and the MOST – Sustainable Mobility National Research Center and received funding from the European Union NextGenerationEU (PIANO NAZIONALE DI RIPRESA E RESILIENZA (PNRR) – MISSIONE 4, COMPONENTE 2, INVESTIMENTO 1.4 – D.D. 1033 17/06/2022, CN00000023). This manuscript reflects only the authors' views and opinions, neither the European Union nor the European Commission can be considered responsible for them.

A   Decomposition Example

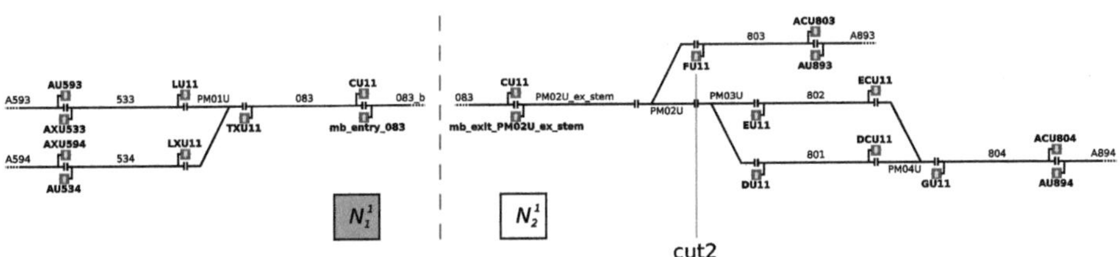

(a) Networks $N_1^1 + N_2^1$ resulting from decomposing the LVR1 network by *cut1*.

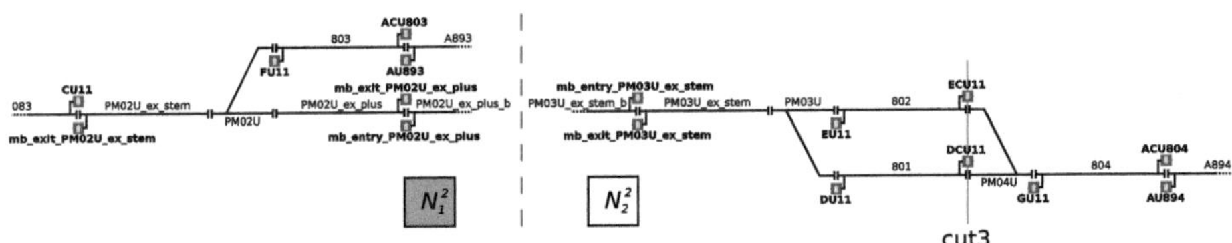

(b) Networks $N_1^2 + N_2^2$ resulting from decomposing N_2^1 by *cut2*.

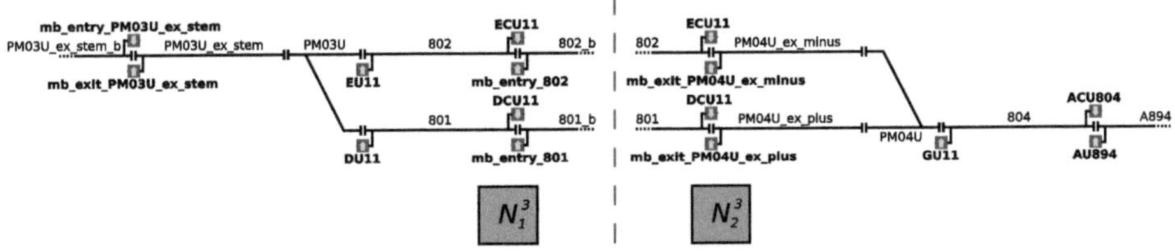

(c) Networks $N_1^3 + N_2^3$ resulting from decomposing N_2^2 by *cut3*.

Fig. 14. Decomposition of the LVR1 network in three steps according to the three cuts shown in Fig. 5. The four resulting green sub-networks N_1^1, N_1^2, N_1^3, and N_2^3 are elementary. From [6].

References

1. Cimatti, A., Giunchiglia, F., Mongardi, G., Romano, D., Torielli, F., Traverso, P.: Model checking safety critical software with SPIN: an application to a railway interlocking system. In: Ehrenberger, W.D. (ed.) Computer Safety, Reliability and Security, 17th International Conference, SAFECOMP'98, Heidelberg, Germany, 5–7 October 1998, Proceedings. LNCS, vol. 1516, pp. 284–295. Springer (1998). https://doi.org/10.1007/3-540-49646-7_22
2. Fantechi, A., Gori, G., Haxthausen, A.E., Limbrée, C.: Compositional verification of railway interlockings: comparison of two methods. In: Dutilleul, S.C., Haxthausen, A.E., Lecomte, T. (eds.) Reliability, Safety, and Security of Railway Systems. Modelling, Analysis, Verification, and Certification: Fifth International Conference, RSSRail 2022, Paris, France, 1–2 June 2022, Proceedings. LNCS, vol. 13294, pp. 3–19. Springer Nature Switzerland AG (2022)
3. Fantechi, A., Haxthausen, A.E., Macedo, H.D.: Compositional verification of interlocking systems for large stations. In: Cimatti, A., Sirjani, M. (eds.) Software Engineering and Formal Methods - 15th International Conference on Software Engineering and Formal Methods, Trento, Italy, 4–8 September 2017. LNCS, vol. 10469, pp. 236–252. Springer (2017)
4. Ferrari, A., Magnani, G., Grasso, D., Fantechi, A.: Model checking interlocking control tables. In: FORMS/FORMAT 2010 – Formal Methods for Automation and Safety in Railway and Automotive Systems, pp. 107–115. Springer (2010)
5. Haxthausen, A.E., Le Bliguet, M., Kjær, A.A.: Modelling and verification of relay interlocking systems. In: Choppy, C., Sokolsky, O. (eds.) Monterey Workshop 2008. LNCS, vol. 6028, pp. 141–153. Springer, Heidelberg (2010). https://doi.org/10.1007/978-3-642-12566-9_8
6. Haxthausen, A.E., Fantechi, A., Gori, G., Mikkelsen, Ó.K., Petersen, S.: Automated compositional verification of interlocking systems. In: Milius, B., Dutilleul, S.C., Lecomte, T. (eds.) Reliability, Safety, and Security of Railway Systems. Modelling, Analysis, Verification, and Certification - 5th International Conference, RSSRail 2023, Berlin, Germany, 10–12 October 2023, Proceedings. LNCS, vol. 14198, pp. 146–164. Springer (2023). https://doi.org/10.1007/978-3-031-43366-5_9
7. Haxthausen, A.E., Fantechi, A.: Compositional verification of railway interlocking systems. Form. Asp. Comput. **35**(1) (2023). https://doi.org/10.1145/3549736
8. James, P., Möller, F., Nguyen, H.N., Roggenbach, M., Schneider, S., Treharne, H.: Decomposing scheme plans to manage verification complexity. In: Schnieder, E., Tarnai, G. (eds.) FORMS/FORMAT 2014–10th Symposium on Formal Methods for Automation and Safety in Railway and Automotive Systems, pp. 210–220. Institute for Traffic Safety and Automation Engineering, Technische Univ. Braunschweig (2014)
9. James, P., et al.: Verification of scheme plans using CSP||B. In: Counsell, S., Núñez, M. (eds.) Software Engineering and Formal Methods, LNCS, vol. 8368, pp. 189–204. Springer (2014)
10. Limbrée, C., Cappart, Q., Pecheur, C., Tonetta, S.: Verification of railway interlocking - compositional approach with OCRA. In: Lecomte, T., Pinger, R., Romanovsky, A. (eds.) RSSRail 2016. LNCS, vol. 9707, pp. 134–149. Springer, Cham (2016). https://doi.org/10.1007/978-3-319-33951-1_10
11. Limbrée, C., Pecheur, C.: A framework for the formal verification of networks of railway interlockings - application to the Belgian railway. Electr. Commun. Eur. Assoc. Study Sci. Technol. **76** (2018)

12. Limbrée, C.: Formal verification of railway interlocking systems. Ph.D. thesis, UCL Louvain (2019)
13. Macedo, H.D., Fantechi, A., Haxthausen, A.E.: Compositional verification of multistation interlocking systems. In: Margaria, T., Steffen, B. (eds.) ISoLA 2016. LNCS, vol. 9953, pp. 279–293. Springer, Cham (2016). https://doi.org/10.1007/978-3-319-47169-3_20
14. Macedo, H.D., Fantechi, A., Haxthausen, A.E.: Compositional model checking of interlocking systems for lines with multiple stations. In: Barrett, C., Davies, M., Kahsai, T. (eds.) NFM 2017. LNCS, vol. 10227, pp. 146–162. Springer, Cham (2017). https://doi.org/10.1007/978-3-319-57288-8_11
15. Pachl, J.: Railway Operation and Control. VTD Rail Publishing (2002)
16. Peleska, J., Krafczyk, N., Haxthausen, A.E., Pinger, R.: Efficient data validation for geographical interlocking systems. Formal Aspects Comput. **33**(6), 925–955 (2021). https://doi.org/10.1007/s00165-021-00551-6
17. Vu, L.H., Haxthausen, A.E., Peleska, J.: A Domain-Specific Language for Railway Interlocking Systems. In: Schnieder, E., Tarnai, G. (eds.) FORMS/FORMAT 2014–10th Symposium on Formal Methods for Automation and Safety in Railway and Automotive Systems, pp. 200–209. Institute for Traffic Safety and Automation Engineering, Technische Universität Braunschweig (2014)
18. Vu, L.H., Haxthausen, A.E., Peleska, J.: A domain-specific language for generic interlocking models and their properties. In: Fantechi, A., Lecomte, T., Romanovsky, A. (eds.) Reliability, Safety, and Security of Railway Systems. Modelling, Analysis, Verification, and Certification: Second International Conference, RSSRail 2017, Pistoia, Italy, 14–16 November 2017, Proceedings. LNCS, vol. 10598, pp. 99–115. Springer, Cham (2017)
19. Vu, L.H.: Formal Development and Verification of Railway Control Systems - In the context of ERTMS/ETCS Level 2. Ph.D. thesis, Technical University of Denmark, DTU Compute (2015)
20. Vu, L.H., Haxthausen, A.E., Peleska, J.: Formal modelling and verification of interlocking systems featuring sequential release. Sci. Comput. Program. **133, Part 2**, 91–115 (2017)
21. Winter, K.: Symbolic model checking for interlocking systems. In: Flammini, F. (ed.) Railway safety, reliability, and security: technologies and systems engineering. IGI Global (2012)
22. Winter, K.: Optimising ordering strategies for symbolic model checking of railway interlockings. In: Margaria, T., Steffen, B. (eds.) ISoLA 2012. LNCS, vol. 7610, pp. 246–260. Springer, Heidelberg (2012). https://doi.org/10.1007/978-3-642-34032-1_24

Modelling Railway Networks with Bigraphs: Electrification, Failures, and Optimisation

Ricardo Almeida[✉][iD], Susmoy Das[✉][iD], Blair Archibald[iD], Muffy Calder[iD], and Michele Sevegnani[iD]

School of Computing Science, University of Glasgow, Glasgow, UK
`{ricardo.almeida,susmoy.das,blair.archibald,muffy.calder,`
`michele.sevegnani}@glasgow.ac.uk`

Abstract. Upgrading rail network infrastructure involves complex system design decisions that can be informed by suitably abstract models. Ideally, the modelling techniques support formal analysis e.g. of safety, security, resilience, and performance, the models are extensible, and they are accessible to both railway engineers and policy makers.

We propose using bigraphs—a diagrammatic formal model with user-defined entities and rewrite rules—as a visual and intuitive approach to extensible railway system modelling. An example is presented: electrification rollout and the adoption of battery-powered trains that includes the impact of (probabilistic) power blackouts and supports system-level optimisation e.g. selecting which track segments to electrify, without resorting to constraint programming languages. Formal analysis via model checking is used throughout.

This work represents a shift in the use of formal methods in railway engineering: from verifying isolated components such as signalling, to supporting formal, system-level design and decision-making.

Keywords: Model checking · Bigraphs · Markov Decision Processes · Discrete-Time Markov Chains · Rail Networks · Electrification

1 Introduction

Railway systems are inherently spatial, involving both static infrastructure and dynamic behaviour. We propose a diagrammatic approach to modelling based on Milner's bigraphs [13], a formalism capable of representing both spatial hierarchy and non-local connectivity as well as dynamic evolution through user-defined rewrite rules. The visual representations are also user-defined, so they can be intuitive and tailored to specific domains. Here, we employ a rich theory of bigraphs, employing conditional, probabilistic, and action-based extensions [3,4].

Bigraphs have previously been applied to verify properties such as safety, reliability, and predictability in location-aware, event-driven systems [12]—including applications in wireless sensor networks [16] and transportation [7]. Despite their visual nature, bigraphs retain formal rigour and support advanced reasoning

M. H. ter Beek et al. (Eds.): RSSRail 2025, LNCS 16236, pp. 286–302, 2026.
https://doi.org/10.1007/978-3-032-10762-6_22

techniques, such as (probabilistic) model checking. This makes them a strong complement to traditional formal methods in rail engineering, which have typically focused on low-level aspects like verifying segment locking [9,14]. In contrast, our work applies formal methods to higher-level system design.

An example bigraph of a simple rail network decomposed into track *segments* that can be considered collectively as *routes* is shown in Fig. 1. The train icon represents a train and a basic track segment is represented by a rectangle (it is common to mix meaningful diagrams with standard geometric shapes). The green links indicate contiguous track segments (within a route). The dashed rectangles (without shading) represent (possibly) disjoint parts of the system. Figure 1a is a bigraph representing two routes, the left route has two track segments, the first of which contains a train; the right route has only one segment, which does not contain a train. The gray filled rectangles in Fig. 1b abstract away an unspecified bigraph that might exist/connect there. The rule in Fig. 1b indicates that a train may move between the two connected segments. This simple model is developed further in Sect. 3, including a much richer definition of Segment.

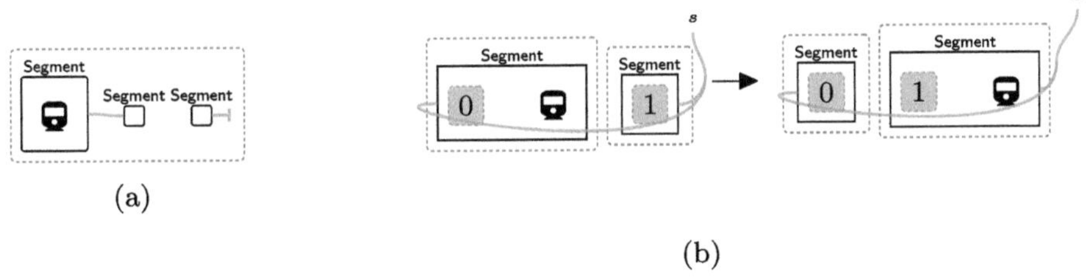

(a)

(b)

Fig. 1. (a) Bigraph model of a basic rail network composed of two routes, each of which is composed of track segments, which may or may not contain a train. Segments are connected by green links, which are ordered from left to right. (b) A rewrite rule that shows how trains can move between two connected segments. Everything else in the segments remains the same, and this is abstracted as simply 0 and 1. (Color figure online)

We make the following research contributions:

- **Bigraphs as an intuitive, diagrammatic modelling technique for rail networks.** We present a bigraph model of rail networks that includes partially electrified infrastructure and an energy mechanism. The bigraph model is highly parameterised and extensible and the underlying models are MDPs (Markov Decision Process). Formal analysis is via model checking and reward structures, using the BigraphER [15] tool.
- **Analysis of electricity failures.** We show how to quantify and analyse the impact of electricity failures on battery levels of the trains.
- **Optimal electrification strategies.** We develop an extension to the model that initially contains no electrified segments, and then explore all possible electrification combinations to find the ones that guarantee all trains reach their destination with a safe amount of charge left.

2   Bigraphs and Bigraphical Reactive Systems (BRSs)

Bigraphs specify models based on both spatial relationships—e.g. in Fig. 1 train entities (we denote either 🚊 or Train) are *nested* (i.e. placed inside) in rail Segments—, and non-local linking—e.g. a Segment has a single green link[1] determining the next segment to move to in a route. Nesting/Linking can be between arbitrary numbers of entities, e.g. an entity can have any number (including 0) children and a link can have any number of entities on it (these are hyperedges, not classic binary links). Links can either be open or closed, the former allowing the possibility for the link to be established/terminated dynamically as the system evolves. The entities in the model, and how they should nest/link, are fully user-specified and this makes them flexible to a wide variety of scenarios.

We allow parameterised entities [5], e.g. Charge(80), Charge(65), ..., that represent entities carrying some value[2].

Rather than needing to specify the entire bigraph of a complete system each time, special structures allow some information hiding. The dashed *unfilled* rectangles are *regions* that denote these two elements of the system might be[3] in two different spatial locations, the dashed *filled* rectangles denote there may be additional nested entities (including none), while the names above the bigraph denote that there may be other entities on this link.

Bigraphs represent the state of a system at a single point. To allow systems to evolve over time a *user can define* a set of rewrite rules (sometimes called reaction rules) that specify system behaviour. Rewrite rules have the form $L \longrightarrow R$, where L and R are bigraphs. This means that a match of L (within a larger) bigraph can be replaced by R to evolve to a new state. For example, Fig. 1b shows a rule that moves trains between segments. Here we have an L consisting of a 🚊 on a Segment linked to another Segment to its right, while R has the train on the right segment implying the train has moved to the next segment. We abstract away from entities using *sites*, which are like free variables, and we draw them as dashed gray filled rectangles. This allows the movement rule to be applied in general situations: regardless of what else is in the segments, the rule gets applied so long as there is at least a train while everything else in the segments (represented by sites 0 and 1) remains the same. We use parameterised rewrite rules to define families of rules for different parameter values.

We use Conditional Bigraphs [3] that allow constraints to be placed on elements inside sites (and in general wider context; but we only constrain sites here). For example, when defining a train-movement rewrite rule such as the one illustrated in Fig. 1b), we can guard it with if $\langle -, \boxed{\text{Charge}(0)}, \downarrow \rangle$ to ensure trains have charge in order to move. Here, $-$ means should not exist, Charge(0) is the bigraph we want to disallow, and $\downarrow$ means we disallow in the sites.

---

[1] In practice, we nest an additional entity rather than linking segments directly. See Sect. 3.

[2] In theory, this corresponds to defining distinct entities for each value.

[3] They may be either completely disjoint or siblings, but never nested below one another.

An initial bigraph, with a set of rewrite rules, is a bigraphical reactive system (BRS). To analyse a BRS, we start from the initial state and apply all possible rules at each step. When multiple rewrites are possible for a state, we apply all rules resulting in state-branching (looking at all futures). This generates a transition system representing how the system can evolve. We can later ask questions such as "Can my system reach this failure state?".

Sometimes, applying all rules is too strong. To gain more control, rewrite rules can be organised into *priority classes*. Rules with the highest priority are applied first, and only when there are no applicable rules do we try the next class (and so on). If several rules within a class are applicable we still get the branching behaviour.

The BigraphER tool we use supports instantaneous rules [5,15], that allow multiple rewrites to apply atomically without introducing intermediate states. These rules can enhance efficiency by removing redundant interleavings and intermediate states, yielding a smaller, more semantically meaningful transition system—beneficial for model analysis and verification.

We employ two extensions to conditional BRS. Reaction rules may include weights, resulting in *probabilistic bigraphical systems* (PBRS) and then further extended with non-deterministic actions, resulting in *action bigraphical reactive systems* (ABRS) [4], in which case the underlying model is an MDP (Markov Decision Process).

3   Diagrammatic Model of A Railway

We consider a simplified semi-electrified railway scenario as a proof of concept for our modelling approach. The rail network is divided into track segments of equal length (10 mi each), and each segment may be electrified or not. We assume identical battery-powered trains, but support 3 different routes. Routes may include stops at stations.

Time in the system advances in discrete units, or clock ticks, corresponding to 10 min each. At any given moment, each active train is either moving at a constant speed of 60 mi per hour or stopped at a station for exactly 10 min. This ensures a headway of 10 min between successive trains (i.e. the minimum time interval maintained between consecutive trains on the same route to ensure safety). These parameters could be adjusted by, e.g. increasing the granularity of how time increases to support trains moving at different speeds and other variants.

The model incorporates a simple energy mechanism: a train gains 10% charge for every electrified track segment it traverses or every 10-minute stop at an electrified station. If the segment/station is not electrified, the train loses 5% charge to traverse it.

In the next section we describe the bigraphical states of the model. The dynamic behaviour of the system, i.e. the transitions that define how to move between these states, is defined via rewrite rules in Sect. 3.2.

3.1   A Diagrammatic Model of Rail Network, Routes and Trains

Railways are spatial in nature and this is reflected in our bigraph model. Key entities are Segment and Train representing where trains are in the network and where they can move to. We first describe the basic entities and then how we model specific routes. An example model state is in Fig. 2 and we describe the key elements below. Links through waypoints WP are the routes the trains take, including their designated stops. For visual clarity, some of these links have been omitted as have links for activities such as timekeeping.

Each Segment has a name SName($name$), e.g. SName($T1$), a flag E determining if it is electrified: E.Yes or E.No. The segment might also contain a *single* Train[4]. As our Trains are battery-powered, they nest a Charge(n) that describes the percentage charge left.

The previous entities were largely physical in nature, e.g. the train on a track. We can also utilise additional entities within the same model to represent non-physical constructs such as routes.

We overlay routes onto segments by nesting waypoint entities (WP). Each waypoint contains a Next pointer that determines where a trains should go next on a route (or empty if the train is at a terminus). A series of linked waypoints then describes a single route. Each train contains a RouteN entity that points to the waypoint it should head to next on the route. The entity RStops denotes segments where a train might wait, e.g. a station. A segment may be a stop for some routes but not for others.

To allow discussions about specific routes, we store all route information in a R entity (within a separate Routes entity). Each R($name$) contains a Start linked to the first waypoint in this route; Trains, linking to all active trains on this route; and Stops, linking to any tracks where this route stops.

Trains also maintain some non-physical information such as an internal state machine that determine the next Action to perform: Wait to stay in the same segment, or Move to move to the next segment on the route (if one exists).

3.2   Rail Model Dynamics

So far we have considered only the static aspects of the system: describing trains, rail segments, routes, etc. We now define system dynamics as rewrite rules (Figs. 3 and 4).

All trains move synchronously over these steps, i.e. there is no interleaving of steps, and we enforce this using a global clock entity (updates only happen while a train's local clock is not at the most recent time) and instantaneous rules. This is similar in style to discrete event simulation. The mechanism of using a local clock ($LC(t)$) per agent alongside a global clock ($Clock(t)$) is inspired by Albalwe et al.'s work on modelling real-time systems using bigraphs [1].

---

[4] We are not modelling segment locking/signalling directly, but this could be added.

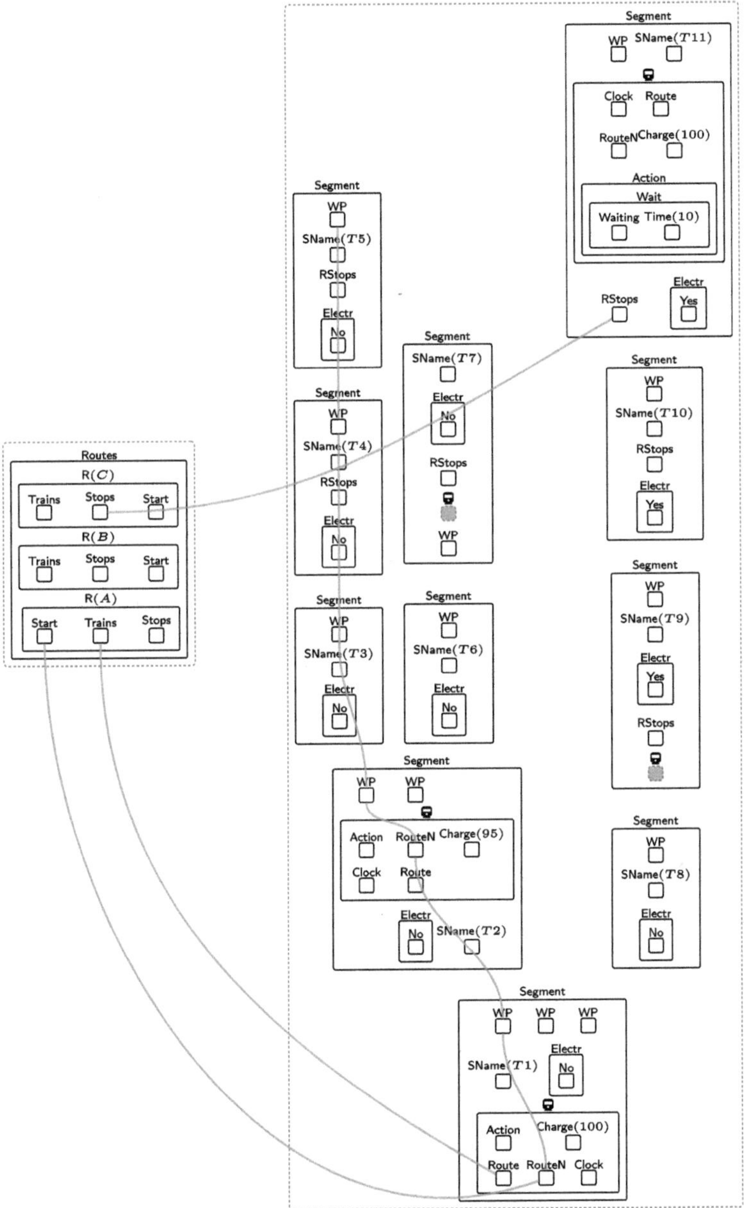

Fig. 2. (Partial) Example state of the Railway Bigraphical Reactive System, depicting five trains travelling along their respective routes (for simplicity, only a subset of links is shown). All trains depart with a full (100%) charge from $T1$ (e.g. note the link from Start in R(A) to RouteN). Trains lose charge when passing through non-electrified tracks (e.g. the train on $T2$), and regain it on electrified tracks such as $T11$. On $T11$, a train completing route C has recharged and, because this track corresponds to a designated stop (see the link from Stops in R(C) to RStops), it is currently waiting for 10 min before completing its route. Waypoints (WP) indicate the paths each route takes through the network, and the links collectively visualize the full structure of each route.

In detail, the steps are:

1. **Train Departures.** Timetabled departures are modelled by a parameterised rule, $\texttt{trains\_starts}(t, route)$(Fig. 3) that is only applicable when the global clock matches the departure time t for a route. It creates a new Train in the initial segment for that route (always $T1$ in our examples) given by Start. The Train is given 100% Charge, a clock set to the current global clock time, an empty Action, and the RouteN/Route pointers are updated to track the next waypoint and to denote this train is working on the given route.

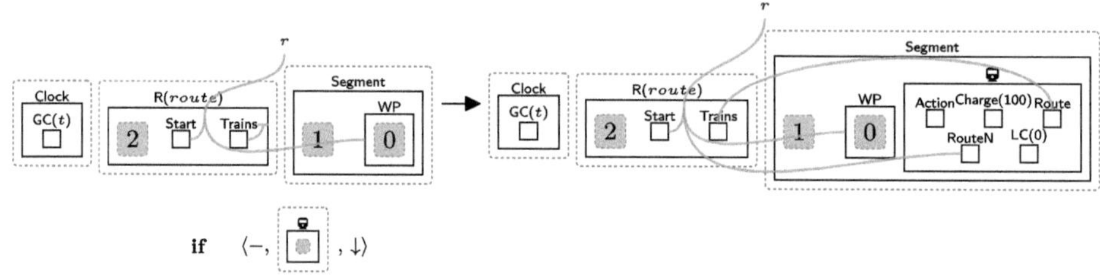

Fig. 3. The $\texttt{train\_starts}(t, route)$ rewrite rule.

2. **Battery Update.** While detailed battery modelling is an active research field in its own right [17,18], we intentionally abstract away from such complexity here. Our aim is to capture only the high-level charging and discharging behaviour through a simplified rule-based model. Modelled by three rules $\texttt{gain\_charge}(t, c)$ (Fig. 4), $\texttt{lose\_charge}(t, c)$, and $\texttt{keep\_charge}(t, c)$, each train gains 10% charge when on an electrified segment (e.g. tracks 9–11), loses 5% *moving* on a non-electrified segment, or maintains current charge if stopped. The rules all have the same form (and so we only show $\texttt{gain\_charge}$ here): match on the existing charge levels (Charge(c)) and segment setup, e.g. is it electrified, and perform the required update. Battery-update actions tag the Train with the token Update to signal readiness for the next step.

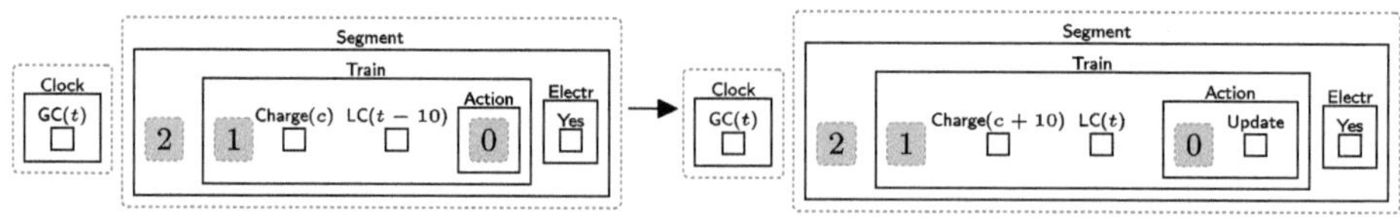

Fig. 4. The $\texttt{gain\_charge}(t, c)$ rewrite rule.

3. **Station-Wait Handling.** If the train's Action is currently set to Waiting, then we do no movement and instead consume the Update token and set Waiting to Over. If Over is already present, or the train was already moving, Action is updated to Action.Move.

4. **Train Movement.** Trains with a Move action are moved using the rule `move_train` (Fig. 5). This rule looks at the Next waypoint in a route and moves the train to the segment containing that waypoint. If there is no next waypoint, we are at a terminus and this rule does not apply.

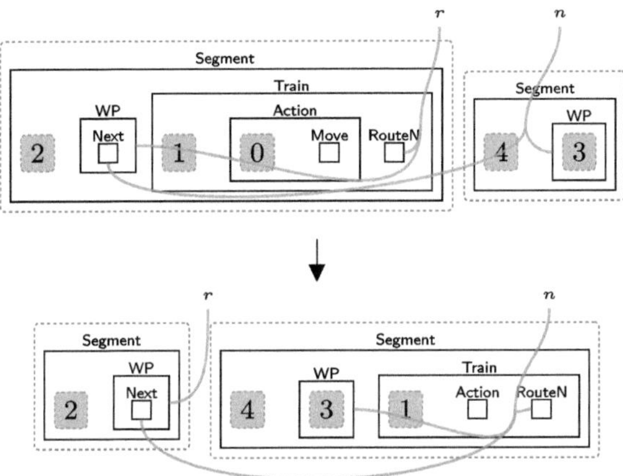

Fig. 5. The `move_train` rewrite rule.

5. **Station-Entry Handling.** The rule `stop_on_track` determines when the next action, e.g. the action in the next round, of a train should be to wait in a segment (to model station stops). The rule checks if a segment is a designated stop on the train's route using the Stops links in the Routes region and, if so, sets the train's Action to Wait.
6. **Train Exit.** Finally, the rule `train_ends` handles trains reaching their terminus. In this case, we find a waypoint with no Next and remove the train.

Once all rules have been applied, the global clock is incremented with the `tick(t)` rewrite rule (not shown) to restart the process.

3.3   Extension: (Probabilistic) Electric Track Failures

The previous sections describe a model of an electrified rail network that is assumed stable: i.e. there is always electricity if we require it. This is not always the case in practice, e.g. fully renewable supply in remote locations causing blackouts. A core benefit of the model is that we can easily extend it, by adding additional entities/rules, to consider failure cases.

Here, we use a probabilistic BRS, to capture (probabilistic) power failure on an electrified track segment. The extension requires only a single rule `electrical_failure` (that moves a segment from electrified to non-electrified). We do not include the inverse rule to re-enable the power, but this could be easily added if required.

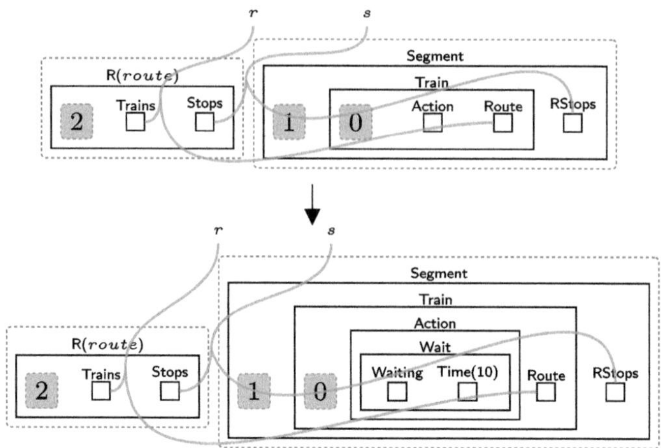

Fig. 6. The `stop_on_track`(*route*) rewrite rule.

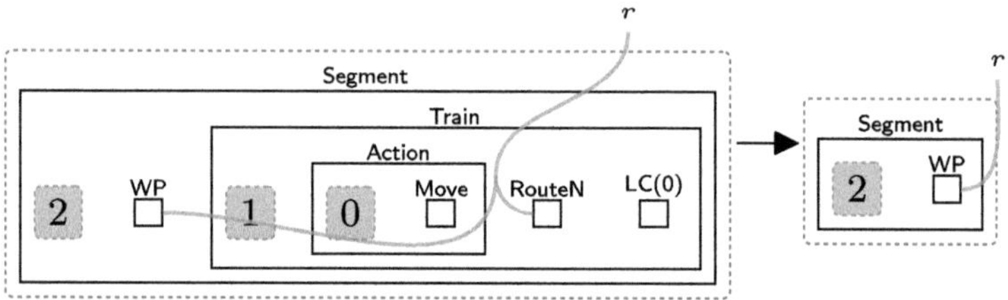

Fig. 7. The `train_ends` rewrite rule.

The `electrical_failure` becomes the second non-instantaneous rewrite rule in the PBRS (apart from `start_clock`), and we assign weights to both to tune the probabilities of either being applied. We give `electrical_failure` weight 0.01 and `tick` 1.0, making `tick`(t) 100 times more likely than `electrical_failure` when both can be applied. Note that these are not probabilities but probability weights, which are scaled relative to the number of matches possible. This means that in between train movements (when the only rewrite rules that can be applied are `tick` and `electrical_failure`), if there is only one electrified segment then the probability of it failing is 1%, and if there are four segments still electrified then the probability of any of them failing is 4%. We use these rules for probabilistic analysis in Sect. 4.1.

4   Model Analysis

We have implemented our model in BigraphER [15]: an open-source framework for constructing, manipulating, and executing bigraph models. For analysis, BigraphER supports model checking by generating a transition system—where states are bigraphs and transitions are rewrites (up to bigraph isomorphism).

The resulting transition system can be analysed using external (probabilistic) model checkers such as PRISM [10]. Our BigraphER model, and analysis scripts, are available online[5].

For analysis it is helpful to identify states that include bigraphs of interest, for example those where a train has run out of charge. In BigraphER, this is achieved using bigraph predicates which are essentially the left-hand sides of rewrite rules. States matching a predicate are labelled in the resulting transition system and these labels can be used in logical formulae when model checking. We use (Probabilistic) Computational Tree Logic ((P)CTL) [6,8] and its reward-based variant [11] to specify the properties of interest.

We can use a PCTL formula such as $\mathbf{P}_{=?}[\,\mathbf{F}\,\mathsf{oob}\,]$ to compute the probability of reaching a state where a train is out of battery (true when $\mathsf{Charge}(0)$) is satisfied ($\mathbf{F}$ corresponds to the *eventually* operator). The result for the above query on our model was 0, confirming that there are no possible executions in which a train ends up in an unsafe state stranded with no charge. Other predicates include checking if two trains are on the same segment which could have catastrophic consequences. The same set of predicates could also be used in this regard to validate/debug the model. We used predicates such as battery levels below (above) 0 (100), inspecting wrongful links, checking if we update the same information twice, etc.

4.1   Impact of Electricity Failures on Final Battery Charge

The additional `electrical_failure` rule of Sect. 3.3 models failure of an electrified segment, e.g. a blackout. As the probability of failure is configurable (via setting different relative weights) we can use this to ask how robust the battery rail system is. In this case, we use final battery charge as a proxy for robustness, i.e. we want to avoid trains running out of charge and blocking routes.

BigraphER can generate a discrete time Markov chain corresponding to the extended model. It has $2,140$ states, $5,776$ transitions and can be generated in a few minutes on a commodity laptop. We then ask "What is the probability of reaching scenarios when k segments have failed and a train has a particular battery level?", expressed as $\mathbf{P}_{=?}[\,\mathbf{F}\,\mathsf{charge\_fail}(n,c)\,]$, where n is the number of failures and c the charge level. Note that although four tracks may have failed, there can still be trains that do not use the failed tracks; hence, we can observe states where the battery levels of some trains remain at 100%. The same state may also reflect a lower battery level for the trains affected by the failures. The lowest battery level observed in our model is 80%. Additionally, since track segment failure is an extremely rare event (we have varied the weights assigned to the rule that disables electricity on tracks), we analyse the resulting proportions. For calculating these proportions, the probability of trains with a 100% battery level is used as the reference. For example, with one failure (under a failure weight of 0.01), we observe a $(0.87/0.94) \times 100 = 92.5\%$ probability of trains reaching battery levels of 80%. Let us consider the results when the failure

---

[5] https://zenodo.org/records/16895542.

Table 1. Impact of Track Failures on Battery Levels. Top values indicate the weights of the electricity failure rule; table entries show the probability of a train reaching each battery level given the number of track failures.

	Failure Rate														
	0.01					0.05					0.1				
	Number of Failures					Number of Failures					Number of Failures				
Battery	0	1	2	3	4	0	1	2	3	4	0	1	2	3	4
80%	0.79	0.87	0.67	0.33	0.07	0.33	0.64	0.79	0.89	0.89	0.13	0.39	0.62	0.80	0.99
85%	0.85	0.87	0.67	0.32	0.07	0.48	0.74	0.86	0.94	0.89	0.26	0.57	0.76	0.90	0.99
90%	0.92	0.91	0.68	0.32	0.07	0.69	0.88	0.92	0.95	0.88	0.51	0.78	0.88	0.93	0.99
95%	0.96	0.91	0.69	0.33	0.07	0.83	0.91	0.93	0.95	0.88	0.71	0.86	0.89	0.93	0.99
100%	1.00	0.94	0.72	0.34	0.07	1.00	0.97	0.97	0.97	0.87	1.00	0.95	0.95	0.96	0.99

weight is 0.01. With no segment failures, the proportion of trains reaching the lowest battery level is significantly lower. As the number of failures increases, the likelihood of trains reaching the minimum threshold also rises. For instance, with four track failures, all trains that began with a 100% charge ended with 80%, compared to 97%, 93%, and 92.5% for three, two, and one failures, respectively. For zero failures, this value drops to 79%. As the failure weight increases, the probability of trains reaching 80% grows sharply; e.g. at a failure weight of 0.1, this probability approaches one (0.99) (Table 1).

4.2 Optimal Electrification Strategy

The model introduced in Sect. 3.2 considers a network configuration in which some segments are electrified while others are not. In real-world settings, the decision to electrify parts of the railway network is a complex policy matter, influenced by a range of economic, environmental, and operational considerations. In this section, we explore a variant of the model aimed at identifying the optimal electrification strategy that ensures all scheduled trains reach their destinations with sufficient remaining battery charge. To support this analysis, we extend the initial bigraph with an energy-log region. For each route, this mechanism records a safe initial charge level that will ensure a train completes its journey while maintaining battery levels above a predefined threshold (*threshold_c*) at all times, represented by the MinBatt(*safe_c*) entity. We augment the Routes region with a Consumption entity, linked to the corresponding Log within the EnergyLog region. Additionally, each train starts its journey with the Lowest(100) entity, which will track the lowest battery level observed during the route.

To accommodate this functionality, we adapt the behaviour defined in Sect. 3.2 by introducing non-deterministic actions, transforming the BRS into an ABRS. This augmented system introduces an electrification phase prior to the original movement phase. In the electrification phase, we assume a predefined set of segment sequences, each of which may independently be electrified or not. The ABRS begins by branching over all possible combinations of electrification configurations (e.g. for three segment sequences, there are $2^3 = 8$ branches in total). Each branch proceeds to the movement phase, which need only consider one train journey per route. It advances as previously defined but with the following modifications:

- **Energy Log Creation** (after **Train Departures** and before **Battery Update**): When a train for a given route departs, a new Log is created under the corresponding EnergyLog region, initialized with MinBatt(100). This log remains open until this train completes its journey.
- **Battery Update**: This step is modified to account for battery depletion. If a train runs out of charge, its Charge(c) and Lowest(l) entities are replaced with OutOfBattery, preventing it from continuing.
- **Energy Log Completion** (between **Station Wait Handling** and **Train Movement**): If a train successfully completes its route (i.e. it did not deplete its battery), the log is closed with MinBatt($safe\_c$), where $safe\_c = initial\_c - lowest\_c + threshold\_c$. Thus, $safe\_c$ is a starting level of charge that accounts for the route discharges and guarantees the battery will remain within safe levels at all times.

The ABRS model described above has 623 states and 622 transitions and takes about a minute to generate. Note that, since instantaneous rules and failures not being modelled, many states are omitted, resulting in a smaller model compared to the PBRS. This reduction in the state space makes model checking more efficient.

4.3 Analysis of Optimal Electrification Strategy

In this section we consider how we can utilise the bigraph model to perform optimisation. The idea here is to show how the approach can be applied, and the results are likely not directly transferable to a real scenario given we only show a small rail topology.

For the next set of analysis, we assign reward structures to our models. A reward (dually cost) structure can be used to capture additional aspects of the system modelled by the MDP, such as track usage, battery levels, etc. We identify states to which we assign a reward using predicates. This would imply that leaving a state (which satisfies the predicate along) a path in the model will accumulate the associated reward. In the context of reward based model checking, *total reward* properties capture the accumulation of state and transition rewards over an entire (potentially infinite) path, similarly to *reachability* and *cumulative reward* properties. This is denoted in literature using **C** formulae [11]. For total rewards accumulated up until a time instant t, this is denoted as $\mathbf{C} \leq t$. In contrast, *instantaneous reward* properties evaluate the reward at a specific point in time. The reward property $\mathbf{I} = t$ assigns to each path the reward associated with the state it occupies precisely at time t. Due to non-determinism in MDPs, querying exact reward values is impossible. Instead, we analyse reward bounds by resolving non-determinism to either maximize or minimize accumulated rewards. While train routes and schedules are fixed and unaffected by non-determinism, metrics like battery charge are. These concepts will guide the analyses discussed below.

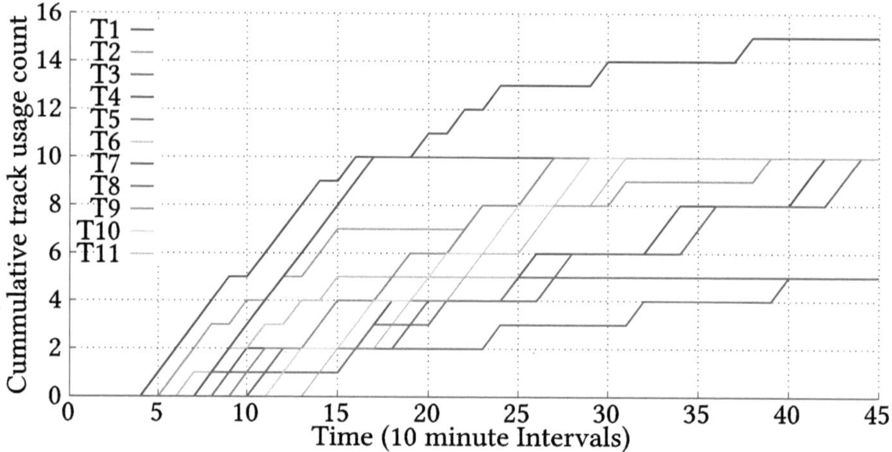

Fig. 8. Total number of times a track has been used as time progresses.

To analyse track usage, we employ total reward properties. A predicate identifies whether a track segment is live, i.e. currently occupied by a train—and a reward of 1 is accumulated each time this condition holds. Plotting the total rewards over time reveals increasing usage as more trains traverse the network. Segments with the highest accumulated rewards correspond to the most frequently used tracks. The results are shown in Fig. 8. Note, all trains considered in the time-table of our model reach the destination by $t = 45$.

Track 1 exhibits the highest cumulative reward, which also serves as a validation point, as all trains begin their journey from this segment. Tracks 7, 9, 10, and 11 follow as the next most frequently used, with Tracks 2, 4, and 5 showing similar reward values but at later timestamps. These delays indicate that trains using these tracks have already passed through earlier segments—potentially electrified—where they could recharge. This highlights the utility of the graph in guiding infrastructure planning: early-use, high-frequency segments should be prioritised for electrification, as they contribute more directly to sustained battery levels.

In contrast, tracks 3, 6, and 8 are used significantly less. Thus, electrifying tracks 7, 9, 10, and 11 emerges as a key insight. However, practical constraints such as installation costs must be considered (e.g. electrifying continuous segments is generally more efficient than isolated ones), which could make tracks

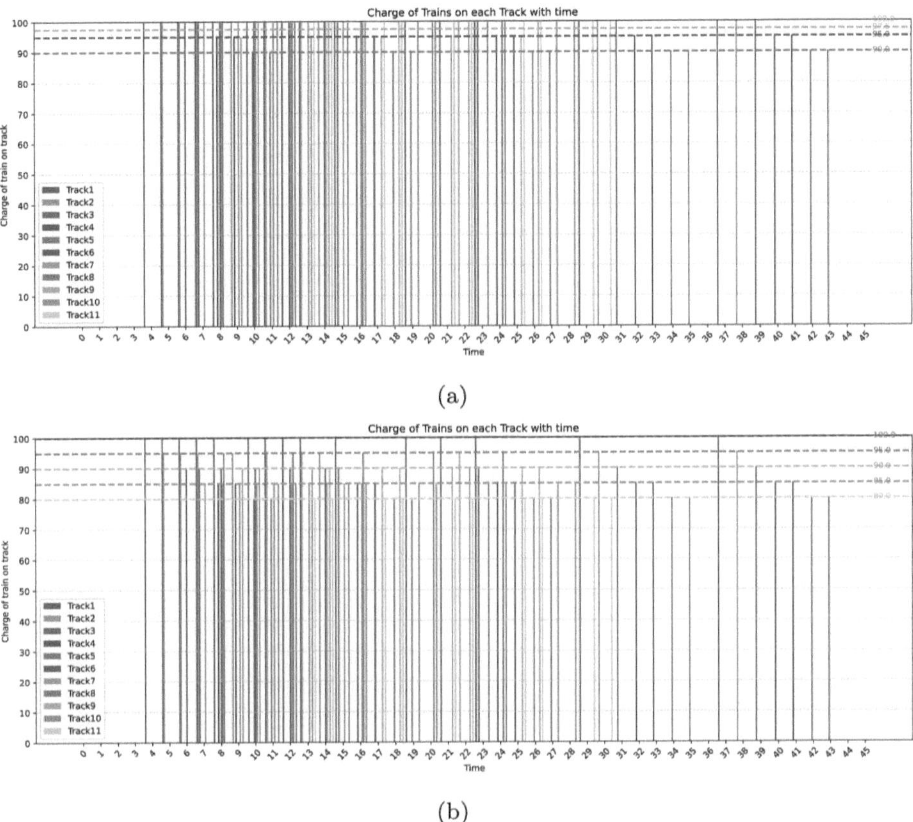

Fig. 9. Tower graph showing battery levels on trains when they are on a track at the t-th time. The dotted lines show the mean charge of trains on each track. (a) shows maximum rewards (electrified tracks), while (b) shows minimum rewards (non-electrified tracks).

9–11 good candidates for electrification. An additional insight concerns the safety of leaving a track segment non-electrified. To evaluate this, we examine the average battery level of trains upon entering each segment. A predicate accumulates a reward of x when a train with charge x occupies a segment, and this instantaneous reward is calculated over time. A value of zero at any time indicates no usage, not the presence of a train with no charge, which is impossible as previously established.

In Fig. 9, bars represent the battery levels of trains occupying each segment at time t, while the dotted line shows the average battery level, computed from non-zero values. Based on prior analysis, Tracks 2–8 show lower usage and are candidates for non-electrification. Specifically, Track 6 was modelled with optional electrification; this analysis supports the decision to leave it unelectrified, as trains traversing it maintain an average charge of 95% (Fig. 9b). This analysis reinforces confidence in the system's reliability, offering valuable guidance for future policy decisions. In the scenario where Tracks 9, 10, and 11 are electrified and Track 6 is not, the results demonstrate a resilience analysis. Specifically, we simulate a worst-case scenario in which no tracks are electrified—representing disruptions such as power outages or natural disasters. Even in such conditions, trains successfully complete their routes with an average battery level of 80%, assuming an initial charge of 100%.

The maximum reward values (Fig. 9a) anticipate future extensions beyond Track 11, informing infrastructure planning if those segments are electrified. This is further supported by a filtering mechanism that identifies underutilised tracks and evaluates the average battery levels on the remaining ones. Collectively, these findings provide a robust framework to guide policymakers in identifying which track segments can be safely excluded from electrification.

5   Conclusion and Future Work

This work explores the use of Bigraphical Reactive Systems (BRS) for modelling and analysing railway electrification strategies. We have demonstrated that bigraphs provide an intuitive and extensible formalism for representing both the structural and dynamic aspects of railway systems. Our model captures partially electrified infrastructure, introduces an energy-tracking mechanism to simulate battery usage, and is extended to handle probabilistic events such as power failures.

Using model checking, we validate key safety predicates, including that no train runs out of battery and no two trains occupy the same segment concurrently. We further introduced track failures as a modelling variable, enabling analysis of battery levels under adverse conditions and supporting resilience assessment. The modified ABRS allows us to model system dynamics and extract track usage patterns using reward structures, identifying segments with high cumulative usage and earlier utilisation—crucial indicators for prioritising electrification.

The ABRS is an extension in which electrification is not predefined but synthesised: the model systematically explores all possible configurations and identifies those that ensure all scheduled trains reach their destinations with sufficient remaining charge. This forms a basis for future design automation and optimisation.

Additionally, track-wise battery level analysis was conducted by monitoring each train's charge as it traverses the network under two extremes: when all tracks are electrified and when none are.

- In the non-electrified case, this serves as a resilience baseline, confirming that trains retain adequate charge (e.g. 80%) even under worst-case scenarios.
- In the fully electrified case, the results support future planning, indicating how battery levels evolve across the network and where additional electrification would have the most impact.

These insights guide selective electrification, helping balance safety, operational efficiency, and infrastructure cost. Several directions remain for further development:

- Improved Temporal aspects and Movement Modelling: Enhancing temporal granularity to represent variable train speeds and segment-specific speed limits would enable modelling of diverse services (e.g. high-speed, intercity, regional trains). This would support exploring trade-offs between travel segments offering higher speeds/shorter charges vs. lower speeds/longer charges.
- Electrification Case Study with Real-World Data: We plan to apply our approach to a real-world rail network segment currently under electrification consideration. Future work will focus on automatically generating the initial state of the bigraph (i.e. its topology) from network maps as shown in [2]. By assigning realistic costs to each segment, we can perform multi-objective strategy synthesis to identify the lowest-cost configuration that guarantees safe operations—validating the model's practical applicability.
- Operational Disruptions and Delay Propagation: Extending the model to handle complex disruptions such as train delays and their propagation across routes would further test its flexibility and support robust, fault-tolerant rail system design.
- Faults and Probabilistic Repairs: Incorporating initial/dynamic faults and probabilistic repair mechanisms would enable analysis of recoverability and survivability, enhancing the model's ability to support realistic and resilient system design.

These extensions progressively align the model with the characteristics of a Digital Twin (DT) by integrating real-world data, operational variability, and fault dynamics—enabling high-fidelity simulation and decision support for real rail systems.

Acknowledgments. This work is supported by the Engineering and Physical Sciences Research Council, under grant EP/Z533221/1 (TransiT: Digital Twinning Research Hub for Decarbonising Transport) and an Amazon Research Award on Automated Reasoning.

References

1. Albalwe, M., Archibald, B., Sevegnani, M.: Modelling real-time systems with bigraphs. Electr. Proc. Theor. Comput. Sci. **417**, 96–116 (2025). https://doi.org/10.4204/eptcs.417.6
2. Ang, K.R.R.: Building bigraphs of the real world (2025). https://arxiv.org/abs/2508.00003
3. Archibald, B., Calder, M., Sevegnani, M.: Conditional bigraphs. In: Gadducci, F., Kehrer, T. (eds.) ICGT 2020. LNCS, vol. 12150, pp. 3–19. Springer, Cham (2020). https://doi.org/10.1007/978-3-030-51372-6_1
4. Archibald, B., Calder, M., Sevegnani, M.: Probabilistic bigraphs. Formal Aspects Comput. **34**(2), 1–27 (2022). https://doi.org/10.1145/3545180

5. Archibald, B., Calder, M., Sevegnani, M.: Practical modelling with bigraphs. Form. Asp. Comput. (2025). https://doi.org/10.1145/3721142

6. Clarke, E.M., Emerson, E.A.: Design and synthesis of synchronization skeletons using branching-time temporal logic. In: Kozen, D. (ed.) Logics of Programs, Workshop, Yorktown Heights, New York, USA, May 1981. Lecture Notes in Computer Science, vol. 131, pp. 52–71. Springer (1981). https://doi.org/10.1007/BFB0025774

7. Das, S., Almeida, R., Archibald, B., Sevegnani, M.: Formal analysis of resilience in transport systems with bigraphs. In: Safety/Reliability/Trustworthiness of Intelligent Transportation Systems. SAFECOMP 2025 Workshops - CoC3CPS, DECSoS, SASSUR, SENSEI, SafetyNXT, SCSSS, SRToITS and WAISE, Stockholm, Sweden, 9 September 2025, Proceedings. Lecture Notes in Computer Science, Springer (2025 - To Appear)

8. Hansson, H., Jonsson, B.: A logic for reasoning about time and reliability. Formal Asp. Comput. **6**(5), 512–535 (1994)

9. Ingleby, M., Mitchell, I.: Proving safety of a railway signalling system incorporating geographic data. IFAC Proceedings Volumes **25**(30), 129–134 (1992). https://doi.org/10.1016/S1474-6670(17)49419-5, iFAC Symposium on Safety of Computer Control Systems (SAFECOMP'92), Zürich, Switzerland, 28-30 October 1992

10. Kwiatkowska, M., Norman, G., Parker, D.: PRISM 4.0: verification of probabilistic real-time systems. In: Gopalakrishnan, G., Qadeer, S. (eds.) CAV 2011. LNCS, vol. 6806, pp. 585–591. Springer, Heidelberg (2011). https://doi.org/10.1007/978-3-642-22110-1_47

11. Kwiatkowska, M., Norman, G., Parker, D.: Stochastic model checking. In: Bernardo, M., Hillston, J. (eds.) SFM 2007. LNCS, vol. 4486, pp. 220–270. Springer, Heidelberg (2007). https://doi.org/10.1007/978-3-540-72522-0_6

12. Lu, C., Zou, Q., Zhou, J.: Toward a modeling and analysis method of cyber-physical systems architecture evolution based on bigraph. Sci. Rep. **15**(8766) (2025). https://doi.org/10.1017/S089006041900012X

13. Milner, R.: The Space and Motion of Communicating Agents. Cambridge University Press (2009)

14. Morley, M.J.: Safety-level communication in railway interlockings. Sci. Comput. Program. **29**(1), 147–170 (1997). https://doi.org/10.1016/S0167-6423(96)00033-0, https://www.sciencedirect.com/science/article/pii/S0167642396000330, cOST 247, Verification and validation methods for formal descriptions

15. Sevegnani, M., Calder, M.: BigraphER: rewriting and analysis engine for bigraphs. In: Chaudhuri, S., Farzan, A. (eds.) CAV 2016. LNCS, vol. 9780, pp. 494–501. Springer, Cham (2016). https://doi.org/10.1007/978-3-319-41540-6_27

16. Sevegnani, M., Kabac, M., Calder, M., McCann, J.: Modelling and verification of large-scale sensor network infrastructures. In: 2018 23rd International Conference on Engineering of Complex Computer Systems (ICECCS), pp. 71–81 (2018). https://doi.org/10.1109/ICECCS2018.2018.00016

17. Vykhodtsev, A.V., Jang, D., Wang, Q., Rosehart, W., Zareipour, H.: A review of modelling approaches to characterize lithium-ion battery energy storage systems in techno-economic analyses of power systems. Renew. Sustain. Energy Rev. **166**, 112584 (2022). https://doi.org/10.1016/j.rser.2022.112584

18. Wang, Y., et al.: A comprehensive review of battery modeling and state estimation approaches for advanced battery management systems. Renew. Sustain. Energy Rev. **131**, 110015 (2020). https://doi.org/10.1016/j.rser.2020.110015

Formal Analysis of a Railway Signaling Block Designed in **AIDA**

Roberto Cavada[1], Alessandro Cimatti[1], Alberto Griggio[1], Christian Lidström[1], Gianluca Redondi[1(✉)], Matteo Tessi[2], and Dylan Trenti[1]

[1] Fondazione Bruno Kessler, Trento, Italy
`{cavada,cimatti,griggio,clidstrom,gredondi,dtrenti}@fbk.eu`
[2] Reti Ferroviarie Italiane, Rome, Italy
`m.tessi@rfi.it`

Abstract. Ensuring the correctness of control logic in railway systems is essential for safety and reliability. In this paper, we present an industrial case study on the formal verification of a software component responsible for managing signal color aspects in a railway interlocking system. We work within AIDA, a model-based design environment where generic control logics are specified in a controlled natural language, and which then drives the automatic generation of SysML models and executable code. In the first phase, we followed an approach based on the use of the Dafny prover, analyzing the model automatically generated from AIDA. This model includes both the Dafny counterpart of the control logics and its annotations. When Dafny failed to prove the expected properties, manual inspection highlighted the existence of some corner cases that led to the discovery of actual bugs. After revising the logic, Dafny still failed to prove the overall correctness. Hence, we replaced manual inspection with the model checking of a carefully reduced model, obtained by localization reduction and focusing on the most relevant classes and havoc-ing the behavior of the others. The model was derived from the summarizations of the methods in Dafny, and could be fully analyzed with the nuXmv model checker. The subsequent automated analysis was able to detect additional violations, and to pinpoint them in the form of easy-to-understand counterexample traces (instead of returning a *failed to prove* answer).

1 Introduction

Ensuring the correct behavior of railway signaling systems is essential for safety and operational reliability. This paper presents an industrial case study on the formal verification of the signal control functions, which is part of the development of a parameterized interlocking logic designed using the AIDA framework [1,5]. AIDA supports the specification in controlled natural language (CNL) of generic interlocking and protection procedures, and the subsequent model-based generation of SysML documentation and executable code generation. The components under verification in this case study implement the functions related

M. H. ter Beek et al. (Eds.): RSSRail 2025, LNCS 16236, pp. 303–312, 2026.
https://doi.org/10.1007/978-3-032-10762-6_23

to displaying different color signals in response to commands resulting from more complex operations carried out at a railway station, such as the creation and deletion of shunting routes, and the isolation of tracks for maintenance. The functions are critical since incorrect outputs could result in dangerous misinterpretations.

This case study illustrates the application of two complementary formal verification approaches: deductive verification using Dafny, and model checking with nuXmv. The deductive verification approach implemented in AIDA is based on the automatic generation of Dafny code and contracts from the CNL description of the control procedures. The idea is to obtain a proof of global, system-level properties of large logics by partitioning the verification into the compositional verification of local properties of individual transitions. Despite its effectiveness, the proof process may fail to prove that the global property holds, and understanding the reasons for such failures is a hard and labor-intensive task. In fact, the diagnostic information provided by the Dafny prover is basically limited to local counterexamples-to-induction; these are typically unable to pinpoint the issue at system level, which may result from the interaction of multiple components according to a domain-specific scheduling policy. We adopt model checking [3] as a complementary approach, able to analyze models representing the execution and the interactions of multiple transitions. In case of a violation, model checking is able to produce more meaningful counterexamples, in form of simulation traces that can be easily traced back to the debugging environment adopted by the signaling engineers. A key challenge is converting a large, global control procedure to a reduced, finite-state model that safely over-approximates its behavior. To this end, we adopt an abstraction based on localization reduction, where only components directly related to assertion violations are explicitly modeled; the rest of the system is disregarded, essentially havoc-ing its signals into non-deterministic inputs. Another characterizing feature of the abstract model is that it captures some important details (e.g., the phases) of the scheduling policy of the system components.

With the combined approach, we were able to find several property violations and fix them thanks to easy-to-understand counterexample traces. The case study offers some encouraging insights on how to combine two formal verification techniques, and is the starting point of a more systematic and synergistic integration of model checking techniques in the verification of AIDA logics.

There have been many applications of formal methods to the railway domain (see [2,10]). The SafeCap approach [13,14] targets the verification of railway control systems with different deductive and automated techniques, whereas the AIDA framework targets parameterized verification over all configurations. The work in [12] proposes methods to partition the verification of interlocking of large, specific stations. This work was inspired by the verification of an entire AIDA logic within Dafny [4], and in particular in the difficulties found in interpreting failed-to-prove results from Dafny. This case study focuses on a fragment of another, larger logic, and adopts a customized abstraction retaining necessary properties of the scheduling policy, enabling the use of model checking counterexamples to explain property violations.

2   Background

Railway Logics in AIDA. AIDA is a model-based design framework used in the development of railway interlocking systems [1,5]. The design process in AIDA is structured into two distinct stages, aligned with the VV development model [15]. The first stage focuses on the creation of a generic, parameterized system that remains independent of any specific station layout. In the second stage, the generic system is instantiated with concrete configuration data, which includes details on the station topology, such as the number of entities of each class and the connections between them. The toolchain automatically generates SysML models and executable code from the generic design, and offers testing and simulation capabilities.

In this framework, railway signaling engineers describe a control logic by defining classes in a domain-specific, controlled natural language (CNL). Each class instance operates as an extended finite-state machine (EFSM), featuring state locations, typed variables, and potentially references to other class instances it can interact with. The behavior of classes is governed by transitions, each equipped with guard conditions and effects.

At runtime, the system operates under an application-independent scheduler, that induces a structured duty cycle and defines the order in which transitions are triggered[1]. A cycle begins by reading the external inputs, such as manual commands from railway operators and the status of the trackside devices; then, the output variables for all class instances are initialized to a default value. The execution progresses in order through three phases. In the *manual* phase, each instance may execute at most one manual transition, if triggered by an operator command. In the *state* phase, each instance executes exactly one state transition based on its current state and guard conditions. The cycle end with the *automatic* phase, during which each instances responds to the commands issued by the other instances. Notice that an instance can execute multiple automatic transitions per cycle. At the end of each cycle, the scheduler aggregates the output values from all class instances and transmits them to the operator interfaces and to the trackside devices.

Dafny. Dafny is an imperative, object-oriented programming language with native support for formal specification and deductive verification [16]. In Dafny, program specifications, including pre- and postconditions, and loop invariants, are integrated directly as annotations the code. Annotated programs are automatically translated into verification conditions, which are discharged by an underlying SMT solver.

In the case of verification failure, Dafny can generate counterexamples as partial assignments of variables for which an assertion could not be proven. Proof failures can occur either because an assertion is violated or because Dafny lacks the sufficient information to complete the proof, e.g., because of missing axioms, and it is up to the user to interpret the counterexamples accordingly.

---

[1] Each transition is also linked to a specific scheduling phase.

Within the AIDA toolchain, the EFSM description of each class is automatically translated into a corresponding Dafny implementation. This translation preserves the structure of the executable code while augmenting it with contracts that precisely encode the intended behavior of each transition. To facilitate verification, the toolchain also generates auxiliary annotations such as loop invariants, which are essential for ensuring the automatic provability of the generated contracts.

nuXmv. nuXmv [3] is a state-of-the-art symbolic model checker designed for the analysis of both finite- and infinite-state transition systems. It offers comprehensive support for safety and temporal properties, and integrates multiple verification engines, including SAT-based bounded model checking and SMT-based unbounded verification.

One of the key advantages of model checking is its ability to exhaustively explore all reachable system states and automatically generate global proofs, or counterexample traces when property violations are detected. These traces provide concrete execution paths leading to the violation, offering significantly more intuitive debugging feedback compared to proof failures produced by deductive verifiers such as Dafny. Despite its versatility, nuXmv can face scalability issues when applied to large systems requiring unbounded quantification, such as the ones described in AIDA.

3   The Signal Component

Our long term goal is the verification of a large interlocking logic composed of 147 classes, more than 4800 methods, resulting in more than 190KLOC of MISRA C. Within the logic, we focus on the verification of the properties of a signaling component playing the critical role of managing and displaying signal color aspects. We now describe the structure and the behavior of the signal component. The signal component is implemented in AIDA as a class with three parameters (i.e., variables whose value depends on the configuration and remains fixed thereafter), two (constant) references to instances of other classes, and thirteen local variables of various types (Booleans, enumeratives, and integers). The two referenced classes are responsible for sending diagnostic commands and placing the signal into exclusion mode. The class can receive five distinct manual commands, and two distinct automatic commands from other classes. Additionally, it has ten input variables and five output variables.

The five output variables (CH1–CH5) correspond to output channels, responsible for encoding specific color aspects of the signal. Each channel can assume four different values (off, on, phase0 and phase180), and valid output configurations correspond to twelve possible color encodings, as detailed in Table 1.

The transition system of the class has seven manual transitions, one state transition, and four automatic transitions. While the output channels can only be modified by the logic of the signaling component, other internal variables can be set externally by the other classes (W transitions).

Table 1. Valid output of the signal component.

Aspect	CH1	CH2	CH3	CH4	CH5
None	off	off	off	off	off
●	on	off	off	off	off
○	off	on	off	off	off
○	off	phase0	off	off	off
●	off	off	on	off	off
○ ●	off	on	off	off	on
○ ◐	off	phase0	off	off	phase0
○ ◑	off	phase0	off	off	phase180
● ○	on	off	off	on	off
● ○	on	phase0	off	off	off
● ●	on	off	off	off	on
○ ○	off	on	off	on	off

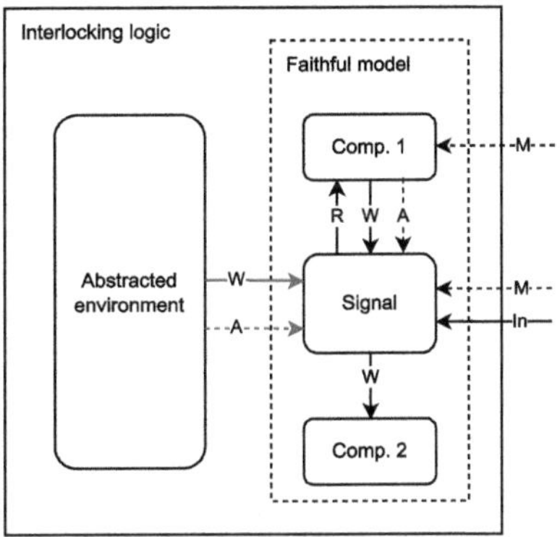

Fig. 1. Diagram of the abstract model. Arrows for **R**eads, **W**rites, **A**utomatic and **M**anual commands, and **In**puts, with red for nondeterministic values.

The verification objective, defined in collaboration with the signaling engineers, is to prove that, at the conclusion of every scheduler cycle, each signal instance activates its output channels to represent exactly one valid color aspect. See Table 1. We refer to this property as ϕ. The property is crucial for safety, as ambiguous or conflicting signals could lead to dangerous misinterpretations by an external display system.

The component behavior within the cycle is determined by the scheduler phases. During the initialization of each cycle, all output channels are reset to a safe "off" value. Then, during the manual phase, the component may process one of several operator-issued commands. These manual transitions primarily affect internal state variables and do not modify directly the output color. In the subsequent state phase, the component executes the only one state transition, activating a default color (red or yellow, depending on a parameter). During the automatic phase, the component deals with the commands received from other entities to update the displayed aspect. In nominal operation, these requests originate from route-setting components of the logic and undergo several validation checks, including checking fault conditions. Successful validation results in displaying the requested color, while failed checks trigger degradation to more restrictive aspects (e.g., green downgraded to yellow or red). The component also handles diagnostic commands that place it in exclusion mode, removing it from normal operational service while maintaining a specified display color.

4   Verification Process

Our goal is to prove that ϕ holds at the end of each cycle. To this end, we employed two different formal verification strategies: deductive verification, and model checking.

Deductive Verification in Dafny. The approach to verification with Dafny follows that of prior work [4], where the AIDA toolchain was used to generate the Dafny implementation of the class, along with method contracts summarizing the guard and effect of each transition. Then, the Dafny verifier was used to check that the implementations satisfy the contracts.

Once validated, the contracts were used to reason about the overall behavior of the class. As a base case, we verified that the initial output assignment, set at the beginning of each scheduler cycle, satisfied ϕ. The inductive proof was then structured around the three phases of the scheduler. Since the output channels are not modified externally, we could focus exclusively on transitions belonging to the signal class itself.

For the manual phase, it was simple to prove that the output channels remained unchanged, and thus it followed that ϕ held after this phase. For the state phase, we checked that executing the state transition from states resulting from the manual phase satisfied ϕ. This transition set the output channels to either red or yellow, both valid aspects, depending on the configuration. The automatic phase introduced some challenges. We initially attempted to verify that any single automatic transition, starting from a state outputting red or yellow, would result in a state satisfying ϕ. However, Dafny reported a violation, and generated a counterexample to induction, consisting of a pre- and post-state in which ϕ did not hold. A painful and time-consuming manual inspection revealed an actual bug: for certain class parameter values, if a color request was issued during the automatic phase but internal checks failed, the component tried to activate both yellow and red colors simultaneously resulting in an invalid output in which two conflicting aspects were active. The bug was confirmed using the logic simulator and subsequently fixed by the signaling experts, after which we could verify that each individual automatic transition, when executed from the end of the state phase, preserved ϕ.

However, this was insufficient to complete the inductive proof at the system level, since within a single scheduler cycle the component could perform multiple automatic transitions in response to commands. Dafny failed to verify that an arbitrary sequence of such transitions preserved ϕ. It was unclear if this failure was due to another flaw or reflected the need for stronger axioms, which motivated the complementary model checking approach described below.

Model Checking with nuXmv. Building a complete nuXmv model of the whole interlocking logic was considered not feasible, due to the fact that several other classes in the system may interact with the signal class, leading to state space explosion if modeled explicitly.

Instead, we decided to model faithfully only a single instance of the signal class, along with other two classes directly interacting with it. All other components were abstracted: their logic was not explicitly modeled, and, instead, all public variables they might affect were allowed to change nondeterministically. This abstraction, a form of localization abstraction [6,9], ensures that the environment can simulate arbitrary external interference while still enabling precise modeling of the core component and its immediate context.

The nuXmv model describes a single scheduler cycle. The initial state corresponded to the assignment of default output values at the start of the cycle. Then, all modeled entities executed transitions in scheduling order. Between each of these transitions, the model allowed a special transition in which the environment could nondeterministically update any public variables, effectively representing all possible external interactions. An image of the model is shown in Fig. 1. The abstraction is sound as it over-approximates the behavior: any run of the concrete logic can be simulated with a run of the nuXmv model.

The nuXmv statements symbolically describing the transitions were derived from the Dafny contracts, automatically generated by AIDA, that summarize the methods of the classes. This translation required two manual steps: first, adapting the syntax of variables and operators, and second, resolving cross-instance references, as the Dafny model is generic (i.e., not related to a specific configuration). As the signal class has only bounded references to other classes, no unbounded quantification was needed in the nuXmv model.

The model checker reported a counterexample to ϕ consisting of an 11-step execution trace. In this trace, the signal instance received two conflicting commands: one from a class modeled in the environment, and one from the diagnostic component. The signal class executed both transitions, resulting in two incompatible output channels being active simultaneously. The counterexample trace was shared with engineers, who confirmed the scenario on the railway yard simulator. The root cause was a missing check in one of the nominal transitions: it did not verify whether the signal had been excluded from service, and thus performed an update that should have been blocked.

Interestingly, after the logic was fixed, nuXmv was re-run, and another counterexample was found. In this case, the signal instance again executed two conflicting transitions, this time in response to two external commands from the environment. Upon inspection, it was determined that in a real deployment the other classes would have not been able to send those two commands in a same cycle. Yet, the counterexample showed that the class violated an implicit design principle, i.e., that its properties should not depend on the number of times its methods are called. Once we assumed that the environment would not send multiple commands in a single cycle, the property ϕ was successfully verified.

Discussion. The performance of the verification engines were not an issue. All experiments were conducted on a laptop with an `Intel Core i7-4600U` processor and `8 GB RAM`. The verification of the Dafny class contracts, automatically generated from AIDA, took 3 min and 33 s. Checking the property ϕ with Dafny required 12 s during the first attempt, and 7 s after the faulty transition was fixed, in the case of at most one automatic transition. The final nuXmv model consisted of 105 state variables, most of which were Boolean or enumerative, with a single integer variable. Model checking (with the ic3 algorithm) was completed in 6 s on the first run and 2 s after the design fix[2].

---

[2] Due to the proprietary nature of the logic, we cannot release the Dafny and nuXmv models.

Our case study highlighted the complementary strengths and limitations of deductive verification with Dafny and symbolic model checking with nuXmv, applied to the formal analysis of a real-world railway signal component.

Dafny allowed us to reason directly about the class implementation, which was generated automatically from the AIDA model along with contracts summarizing the behavior of each transition. This tight integration between model and code provides high confidence that the verified properties held in the logic. However, deductive verification still required considerable manual effort. The verification engineer had to devise inductive invariants and auxiliary lemmas to complete the proofs. Moreover, when verification failed, it was unclear whether the failure indicated a real bug or a missing lemma.

In contrast, model checking with nuXmv provided fully automated exploration of the abstracted model. Once the abstract model and property were defined, the tool either verified the property or returned a counterexample. This automation made nuXmv highly effective in discovering real issues, especially when proof-based methods failed due to missing invariants. Despite the second counterexample being spurious, it still highlighted another issue: the safety of the signal class was not enforced locally, but depended on assumptions about the environment's behavior. This lack of robustness suggests that the component was not designed defensively—an undesirable property in safety-critical systems, as components should enforce safety invariants independently of the environment.

Our experience underscores how deductive verification and model checking can synergistically address industrial-scale verification challenges. We are now formalizing this hybrid approach into a systematic workflow where: (i) Dafny's auto-generated contracts provide the foundation for deductive proofs; (ii) localization reduction focuses on critical components while abstracting environmental interference, enabling model checking techniques to be applied effectively; (iii) counterexamples or invariants from the model checker drive iterative refinement, whether as concrete bug reports or as indicators for deductive invariants.

5   Conclusion

We presented an industrial case study where we formally verified a signaling component developed in AIDA, a model-based framework for the development of railways applications. We adopted an approach combining automated deduction with model checking applied to an abstract model obtained by localization reduction. The two techniques offered complementary capabilities, and their integration proved highly effective in reducing the manual effort required with respect to the pure deductive approach adopted in [4]. Signaling engineers found the approach to be invaluable, as they uncovered issues missed by the traditional test-based approach.

In the future, we plan to work in three main directions. First, we want to integrate abstraction and invariant generation techniques, such as [7,11,12,17] to support proof production. Second, we will investigate the automated generation of sub-configurations for the generation and investigation of counterexamples.

Finally, we will work on temporally extended properties, including liveness, and the integration with test case and scenarios generation [8].

References

1. Amendola, A., et al.: A model-based approach to the design, verification and deployment of railway interlocking system. In: Margaria, T., Steffen, B. (eds.) ISoLA 2020. LNCS, vol. 12478, pp. 240–254. Springer, Cham (2020). https://doi.org/10.1007/978-3-030-61467-6_16
2. ter Beek, M.H.: Formal methods and tools applied in the railway domain. In: Bonfanti, S., Gargantini, A., Leuschel, M., Riccobene, E., Scandurra, P. (eds.) Rigorous State-Based Methods, LNCS, pp. 3–21. Springer, Cham (2024). https://doi.org/10.1007/978-3-031-63790-2_1
3. Cavada, R., et al.: The nuXmv symbolic model checker. In: Biere, A., Bloem, R. (eds.) Computer Aided Verification, LNCS, pp. 334–342. Springer, Cham (2014). https://doi.org/10.1007/978-3-319-08867-9_22
4. Cavada, R., et al.: Automated parameterized verification of a railway protection system with dafny. In: Piskac, R., Rakamarić, Z. (eds.) Computer Aided Verification. CAV 2025. LNCS, vol. 15934. Springer, Cham (2025). https://doi.org/10.1007/978-3-031-98685-7_17
5. Cavada, R., Cimatti, A., Griggio, A., Susi, A.: A formal IDE for railways: research challenges. In: Masci, P., Bernardeschi, C., Graziani, P., Koddenbrock, M., Palmieri, M. (eds.) Software Engineering and Formal Methods. SEFM 2022 Collocated Workshops, pp. 107–115. Springer, Cham (2023). https://doi.org/10.1007/978-3-031-26236-4_9
6. Cimatti, A., Griggio, A., Redondi, G.: Universal invariant checking of parametric systems with quantifier-free SMT reasoning. In: Platzer, A., Sutcliffe, G. (eds.) CADE 2021. LNCS (LNAI), vol. 12699, pp. 131–147. Springer, Cham (2021). https://doi.org/10.1007/978-3-030-79876-5_8
7. Cimatti, A., Griggio, A., Redondi, G.: Towards the verification of a generic interlocking logic: dafny meets parameterized model checking. CoRR **abs/2403.00087** (2024). https://doi.org/10.48550/arXiv.2403.00087
8. Cimatti, A., et al.: Model-based testing of railway interlocking systems. In: Margaria, T., Steffen, B. (eds.) Leveraging Applications of Formal Methods, Verification and Validation. Application Areas. ISoLA 2024. LNCS, vol. 15223, pp. 112–126. Springer, Cham (2025). https://doi.org/10.1007/978-3-031-75390-9_8
9. Clarke, E.M., Kurshan, R.P., Veith, H.: The localization reduction and counterexample-guided abstraction refinement. In: Manna, Z., Peled, D.A. (eds.) Time for Verification. LNCS, vol. 6200, pp. 61–71. Springer, Heidelberg (2010). https://doi.org/10.1007/978-3-642-13754-9_4
10. Ferrari, A., Beek, M.H.T.: Formal methods in railways: a systematic mapping study. ACM Comput. Surv. **55**(4) (2022). https://doi.org/10.1145/3520480
11. Frenkel, E., Chajed, T., Padon, O., Shoham, S.: Efficient implementation of an abstract domain of quantified first-order formulas. In: Gurfinkel, A., Ganesh, V. (eds.) Computer Aided Verification. CAV 2024. LNCS, vol. 14682, pp. 86–108. Springer, Cham (2024). https://doi.org/10.1007/978-3-031-65630-9_5
12. Haxthausen, A.E., Fantechi, A.: Compositional verification of railway interlocking systems. Form. Asp. Comput. **35**(1) (2023). https://doi.org/10.1145/3549736

13. Iliasov, A., Taylor, D., Laibinis, L., Romanovsky, A.: Formal verification of Signalling programs with SafeCap. In: Gallina, B., Skavhaug, A., Bitsch, F. (eds.) SAFECOMP 2018. LNCS, vol. 11093, pp. 91–106. Springer, Cham (2018). https://doi.org/10.1007/978-3-319-99130-6_7
14. Iliasov, A., Taylor, D., Laibinis, L., Romanovsky, A.: Practical verification of railway signalling programs. IEEE Trans. Dependable Secure Comput. **20**(1), 695–707 (2023). https://doi.org/10.1109/TDSC.2022.3141555
15. Jin-hua, L., Qiong, L., Jing, L.: The W-model for testing software product lines. In: 2008 International Symposium on Computer Science and Computational Technology, vol. 1, pp. 690–693 (2008). https://doi.org/10.1109/ISCSCT.2008.34
16. Leino, K.R.M.: Dafny: an automatic program verifier for functional correctness. In: Clarke, E.M., Voronkov, A. (eds.) LPAR 2010. LNCS (LNAI), vol. 6355, pp. 348–370. Springer, Heidelberg (2010). https://doi.org/10.1007/978-3-642-17511-4_20
17. Redondi, G., Cimatti, A., Griggio, A., Mcmillan, K.L.: Invariant checking for SMT-based systems with quantifiers. ACM Trans. Comput. Log. **25**(4), 1–37 (2024). https://doi.org/10.1145/3686153

Use of Certified Industrial Tools
for Formal Analysis and Monitoring
of Communications-Based Train Control
Systems

Dalay Almeida[(✉)] [iD]

CLEARSY, Aix-en-Provence, France
dalay.almeida@CLEARSY.com

Abstract. The B method has long been employed in the development of Communications-Based Train Control (CBTC) systems, providing strong traceability from requirements and system design to implementation, as well as mathematical guarantees that the system meets its safety requirements. However, integration and system testing are typically performed using a distinct environment, which weakens the traceability between requirements and test scripts compared to the traceability with the code. Additionally, once deployed, CBTC systems could benefit from continuous functional monitoring to further enhance safety, not only by verifying compliance with formal specifications, but also by identifying possible issues arising from human actions or material failures. In previous work, we proposed a methodology for analyzing and monitoring relay-based Railway Interlocking Systems using the certified tools of the CLEARSY Safety Platform (CSSP). In this paper, we extend that methodology to support computer-based railway systems, with a particular focus on CBTC. Our approach introduces a formally defined runtime monitor that can be integrated into the testing, and operational phases of the system lifecycle. This monitor acts as a safety layer that reinforces test campaigns and continues to check key system properties after deployment. Although our method was applied to a real industrial case that cannot be fully disclosed, we present a representative case study to demonstrate its feasibility and benefits in realistic scenarios.

Keywords: Formal Methods · B-method · Safety-Critical Systems · Software Verification · CBTC

1 Introduction

Since the METEOR project [6], the B method [1] has been applied in the development of several Communications-Based Train Control (CBTC) systems [8]. This method ensures strong traceability due to the close alignment between system requirements documentation and B abstract machines. Once implemented, it allows one to prove that the refinement is consistent with the abstract machine, ensuring compliance with the specified requirements. Consequently, while the

© The Author(s), under exclusive license to Springer Nature Switzerland AG 2026
M. H. ter Beek et al. (Eds.): RSSRail 2025, LNCS 16236, pp. 313–330, 2026.
https://doi.org/10.1007/978-3-032-10762-6_24

system's adherence to safety requirements can be rigorously verified, analysing the implementation in relation to the documentation is also facilitated.

Over the past decades, B has proven to be effective in the components in which it is applied [8]. However, many aspects of CBTC development could still benefit from formal methodologies, particularly integration and system testing. Although these tests are designed based on system documentation, differences in syntax and semantics between the languages used in these phases complicate the mandatory review process required in the development of safety-critical railway systems [11]. Moreover, once deployed, the system is no longer systematically tested by the development team. In this context, a continuous monitoring strategy based on safety requirements can enhance overall safety by enabling the ongoing analysis of both functional behaviour and potential dysfunctions.

In a previous paper, we presented a methodology for analysing and monitoring legacy relay-based Railway Interlocking Systems with respect to safety properties [2]. This methodology leverages the CLEARSY Safety Platform (CSSP) [14], a set of industrial safety-certified tools, to continuously verify compliance with system safety requirements. By formally specifying and implementing these requirements, the platform can be connected to the system's inputs and outputs to continuously verify compliance.

In this paper, we extend that work by detailing how CBTC safety requirements can be formally specified and implemented within the CSSP, as well as how the platform can be integrated into the CBTC environment. This integration not only enables system testing with strong traceability through a formal methodology but also provides a mechanism for continuous monitoring after deployment. In this context, the CSSP can be used to raise alerts whenever a safety requirement is violated, enhancing system safety and enabling timely corrective actions. Although our methodology was evaluated on an industrial system, confidentiality constraints prevent us from disclosing its details. Instead, we present a similar case study that accurately illustrates how the CSSP can be used to analyse and monitor a CBTC system based on its inputs and outputs.

It is important to emphasize that, although CBTC systems are classified at the highest safety integrity levels, there are human and material aspects (such as hardware components and physical interfaces) that are not directly controlled by the system. As most accidents stem from human or material causes [18], CBTC operation could benefit from continuous monitoring as a way to enforce safety requirements. Moreover, since the system is specified, implemented, and tested by humans, it is essential to adopt strategies that support the systematic creation, review, and execution of test scripts, reinforcing both functional correctness and robustness against dysfunctions. The strategy proposed in this paper does not aim to replace current development and verification methodologies for these already highly safe systems. Instead, it complements them by easing the testing process and introducing an additional safety layer focused on monitoring component interactions, verifying the correct functioning of hardware elements, and supporting proper system use during operation.

The literature offers a wide range of approaches for generating both tests and runtime monitors based on formal methods. In the domain of testing, prominent examples include automatic test generation from formal models [3,22], as well as approaches that incorporate formal analysis in fault detection and assurance [21]. For system monitoring, several runtime verification frameworks have been proposed [4,7,10,19,20], often focusing on compositionality, minimal intrusion, and monitor synthesis from formal specifications.

However, these works are typically domain-independent and focus on generic architectures, which may limit their direct applicability to industrial settings with strict certification requirements and well-established toolchains. Our work distinguishes itself by explicitly targeting the railway domain, where the adoption of formal methods has a long-standing tradition, but the integration of runtime monitors and automated testing strategies remains limited. Unlike general-purpose proposals, our methodology is grounded in actual industry practices: it reuses tools and technologies already certified and widely adopted in the railway sector, such as the B-method and the CLEARSY Safety Platform. This alignment with industry standards ensures that our solution is both deployable and certifiable, two key aspects often overlooked in academic proposals.

Furthermore, instead of generating tests or monitors from high-level models or newly introduced formalisms, we leverage the system's own formal requirement specifications, that can be written in B, as the basis for both test analysis and runtime verification. This traceability increases confidence in the monitor's correctness and reduces engineering effort by avoiding redundant artifacts. Additionally, our monitors operate in parallel with the CBTC system using certified minimal-intrusion techniques, following principles found in [7], but adapted to the constraints of the CBTC environment.

While most related work does not specifically address railway systems, there are notable exceptions worth mentioning. Colored Petri Nets have been used to model and verify CBTC procedures [17], and other studies have proposed safety monitors based on temporal logic and topological analysis [23]. Some efforts have focused on diagnostic tools [12] or wireless testbeds for CBTC experimentation [9]. These approaches, however, often rely on external modeling frameworks or custom hardware, whereas our methodology integrates directly into the existing CBTC development and testing pipeline, requiring no additional components or changes to system architecture. It introduces a lightweight, logic-based monitoring layer that builds on the system's own documentation and supports both design-time and runtime assurance.

In summary, our work fills a gap in the literature by offering a formal, certifiable, and industry-aligned methodology that enhances CBTC testing and monitoring using existing assets. It bridges academic principles with practical deployment concerns, enabling formal verification to extend beyond design and into the operational lifecycle of railway systems.

The remainder of this paper is structured as follows. Section 2 introduces the B-method and its application in CBTC system development. Section 3 presents the CLEARSY Safety Platform. Section 4 details our proposed strategy for analyzing and monitoring CBTC systems using the CSSP. Section 5 discusses additional considerations and practical aspects of the methodology. Finally, Sect. 6 concludes the paper and outlines future perspectives.

2   B-Method in the CBTC Development

To understand how the CBTC development process can be enhanced using the CLEARSY Safety Platform, it is first necessary to examine how the B-method is already integrated into this process. A CBTC system is composed of multiple subsystems, each of which can be further subdivided into smaller components. One of the main distinctions is between onboard and wayside components. The onboard system, in turn, consists of several modules, such as the odometry system (responsible for estimating position, speed, and acceleration) and the driver interface. Each of these subsystems is further divided into safety-related and non-safety-related parts during development, as defined in the system design documentation. The B-method is applied to every safety-related parts of the components to ensure compliance with safety requirements.

In this context, a typical CBTC development process follows a specialized V-cycle [11], as illustrated in Fig. 1. In this process, documentation is structured into two levels: system design, and component design. The safety aspects of each component are formally specified before development begins. The implementation phase includes both the refinement and coding of the formal specification for safety-related components, as well as the development of the non-safety-related parts. The ascending part of the V-cycle consists of the verification phases: formal proof of the specification, unit testing of individual components, and integration and system testing. Each of these verification steps corresponds to a specific document from the descending phase.

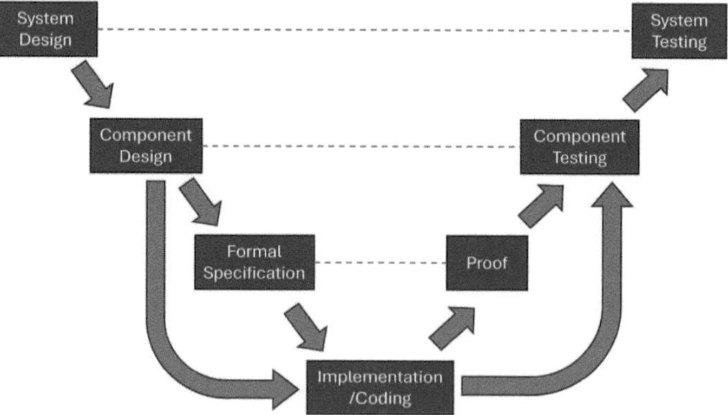

Fig. 1. The V-cycle used in the part of the CBTC development that uses the B-method

The B method includes tools to support system specification, formal proof, and implementation. Among them, Atelier B [13] has been the primary tool used over the past decades for developing CBTC systems. In this method, a system is first modeled using Abstract Machines, which may then be refined through optional Refinement Machines and eventually implemented in Implementation Machines. Each step is formally proven to ensure that the implementation preserves all properties specified at the abstract level. Machines are structured into clauses such as CONSTANTS, VARIABLES, INVARIANT, INITIALISATION, and OPERATIONS, each playing a specific role in the specification. The B proof rules rely on the contents of these clauses to establish model consistency and correctness. Once the model is concrete enough, Atelier B can automatically generate executable code.

In this context, the B-method plays a crucial role in the formal specification of the safety-related functions of the components. Among its many benefits, this formal approach enhances traceability by allowing requirements to be expressed in propositional logic and by ensuring, through formal proofs, that the implementation complies with these specifications.

For example, a system requirement stated in natural language as: *"If the train location is undetermined, an alarm indicating the loss of the train must be activated"* can be formally specified as:

```
(train_location = indet) => (train_lost_alarm = TRUE)
```

where `train_location` and `train_lost_alarm` are variables defined in the B abstract machine and propagated through to the system implementation. Since propositional logic is more structured and closer to natural language than a typical programming language, it simplifies the verification process, making it easier for reviewers to assess whether the system meets its documented requirements. Once the specification is validated, the formal proofs ensure that the implementation strictly adheres to the behaviour defined in the B abstract machines.

While formal development methods like B provide strong traceability from requirements to code, the same level of rigor is not typically applied to testing, particularly in unit, integration, and system-level tests. In practice, test scripts are often written in technical languages that are far from natural language, making them harder to review and validate, especially by non-developers. Tests are generally structured around actions and reactions, where actions are used to establish specific system states through inputs, and reactions check the outputs as well as selected internal variables deliberately made visible. While the formal specification provides a link between the code and the documentation, the test scripts' actions and reactions have a weak connection with the logic defined in the system and components design. In this context, a testing environment with strong traceability, supported by a monitoring mechanism that observes the system throughout its lifecycle, can greatly benefit both the development process and long-term system assurance.

3   The CLEARSY Safety Platform

The CLEARSY Safety Platform (CSSP) is the result of a project aimed at creating a comprehensive development environment for generating and proving bounded algorithmic software, as well as a secure and cost-effective platform for executing these applications while ensuring the highest level of safety. In this context, the CSSP encompasses not only a certified SIL4 single-board vital computer but also a software library incorporating all the safety principles required to achieve SIL4 execution and a fully integrated toolchain that supports system specification, proof, implementation, and deployment. By leveraging certified tools and a complete development framework, the CSSP facilitates the development of critical systems and streamlines their certification processes.

Nowadays, the CSSP is used to deploy numerous certified industrial systems operating worldwide. However, its use is not limited to industry, as many academic research projects utilize the academic version of the CSSP [15]. This version includes a development interface with a simulator of a simplified vital computer, enabling users to specify, implement, prove, and run safety-critical systems. Some research partners also have access to a physical version of this board. Both the simulated and physical boards are shown in Fig. 2.

Fig. 2. From left to right: the simulated and the real academic versions of the CLEARSY Safety Platform board

As an example of ongoing research, we recently demonstrated how the CSSP can be used to analyze and monitor legacy relay-based systems by connecting it to electrical Railway Interlocking Systems [2]. Given the power and compact size of the vital computer, we believe it is an ideal candidate for monitoring safety-critical CBTC systems. As B is used as the formal language for the development of these systems, the documentation is naturally structured to reflect its constructs and logic, further reinforcing this alignment. Moreover, since the abstract syntax and semantics of the B-method closely align with documented system requirements, the traceability between the CSSP monitoring system and the monitored system's documentation is strong, facilitating reviewer analysis.

4   CBTC Analysis and Monitoring

After decades of applying the B-method to CBTC system development, the process is well established, and resulting systems have been extensively tested, consistently demonstrating the expected safety behaviours [8]. However, as these systems are developed by humans, processes such as testing and review still require significant effort. In this section, we propose leveraging the B-method and CSSP certified tools to analyze CBTC systems based on their documentation, aiming to streamline testing and review. Additionally, the CSSP can act as a system monitor, enabling continuous analysis of system behaviour to mitigate human and component errors during both development and operation.

In this context, our methodology begins by formally specifying CBTC safety requirements in an abstract B machine. This specification is then used to develop a system capable of monitoring the execution of CBTC systems by analyzing their inputs and outputs. The process involves three main steps: (1) formalizing the safety requirements, (2) implementing the monitor, and (3) integrating the CSSP platform with the CBTC system. The examples discussed in this paper, along with the latest beta version of the CSSP extension for Atelier B, are available online[1]. While this beta version includes all the necessary tools to support the methodology described here, it is still under development and not yet publicly released. A stable version of Atelier B with the CSSP extension can be downloaded from the official website[2].

4.1   Formal Specification of the CBTC Safety Requirements

There are two main documents that describe CBTC requirements. Each company names these documents differently. In this paper, to maintain a generic approach, we refer to them as: *system design documentation* and *component design documentation*. The former describes the system functions in an abstract manner, while the latter focuses on detailing each function within each system component, specifying inputs, outputs, and even internal variables as support.

For example, a system design document may include a requirement stating: *"If the train speed exceeds the track section speed limit, the overspeed alarm must be activated."* This requirement represents a critical safety function but does not specify implementation details. In a more concrete document, the onboard component design documentation may refine this requirement as: *"If the train speed (`odo_train_speed`) received from the odometry component is higher than the speed limit set in the section component (`section_x_speed_limit`), the* `overspeed_alarm` *must be activated."* This document not only defines the variables (`odo_train_speed`, `section_x_speed_limit`, `overspeed_alarm`) but also specifies their origin and destination, clarifying inputs and outputs. In some cases, we have also seen a prototype of the code written in the documentation, such as:

```
IF odo_train_speed > section_x_speed_limit
THEN overspeed_alarm = true
```

This prototype has the potential to guide both the formal specification and the system implementation. This property regarding the train speed is used throughout the paper as an example for our methodology.

---

[1] https://github.com/CLEARSY/system-monitoring/tree/main.

[2] https://www.atelierb.eu/support-et-maintenance-atelier-b/telechargement/.

The B-method formal specification language allows the creation of variables and the use of these variables inside propositional logic expressions inside the B abstract machines. These expressions are used to enforce that the system or an operation meets the specified requirement. In this context, the speed limit safety requirement could be written in propositional logic as:

```
(odo_train_speed > section_x_speed_limit) => overspeed_alarm = true
```

This mathematical logical expression can be read exactly as the requirement expressed in the system design documentation, except that we are using variables described into the component design documentation to represent the train speed, speed limit and overspeed alarm.

This logical expression may be used inside the CSSP as a way to analyse the CBTC behaviour. In the CSSP environment, one may declare the inputs and outputs of the platform. In this case, instead of using variables in the logical expression, one may use the inputs and outputs of the board (which can be named during the creation of the B project). In this context, the abstraction offered by the B-method supports not only the specification of the safety properties in a logical format but also the detailing of the origin of this information as described in the documentation.

If the objective were to replace the onboard system with a CSSP board, the components would be connected as follows: the odometry and section would be linked to the board inputs, while the alarm would be connected to a board output. However, since the goal of the CSSP monitor is to analyze whether the CBTC meets the safety requirements, our methodology requires all these components to be connected to the CSSP board inputs. The same principle applies to the formal specification: every variable used in the logical safety requirements must be treated as an input. As the CSSP CBTC monitor will interface with the real CBTC system to verify whether its inputs and outputs comply with the specified requirements, the CSSP board must receive this data through the board inputs for analysis. In this context, the outputs of the CSSP board serve only to raise safety flags either after the analysis or during continuous monitoring.

The abstract machine of the overspeed alarm verification is presented in Fig. 3. While `odo_train_speed`, `section_x_speed_limit` and `overspeed_alarm` are inputs (specified in the visible inputs machine), `red_flag` is an output of the board that can be used to indicate whether the system meets the requirements. When this output has the value ON, it is activated. Otherwise, when it has the value OFF, it is deactivated. In this paper, we use the value ON to represent a red flag, i.e., the activation of a light and/or alarm to indicate that the system does not meet a safety requirement. Further details on the connection between the CSSP monitor and the CBTC system are discussed later in this section.

As presented in Fig. 3, in the CSSP B abstract machine, the requirement logic is specified within an operation called `user_logic`. This operation runs indefinitely on the platform, continuously receiving inputs and producing outputs in an infinite cycle (each cycle takes fractions of seconds). With this approach, the monitor can continuously analyze whether the CBTC system complies with

```
MACHINE
    logic
SEES inputs, g_types, g_operators, io_constants, lchip_interface, user_ctx
ABSTRACT_VARIABLES red_flag, board_0_02
INVARIANT red_flag : uint8_t & board_0_02 : uint8_t
INITIALISATION red_flag :: uint8_t || board_0_02 :: uint8_t
OPERATIONS
    user_logic =
    BEGIN
        red_flag :
        (red_flag : uint8_t &
        (not((odo_train_speed > section_x_speed_limit) => (overspeed_alarm = IO_ON))<=> red_flag = IO_ON) )
    END;

    po <-- get_red_flag =
    PRE po : uint8_t
    THEN po := red_flag
    END;

    po <-- get_board_0_02 =
    PRE po : uint8_t
    THEN po := board_0_02
    END
END
```

Fig. 3. CSSP specification of the overspeed alarm verification example with the user logic inside the red square (Color figure online)

the specified safety logic. However, in order to be able to use the CSSP CBTC monitor, one must implement the specified logic.

4.2   Implementation of the CSSP CBTC Monitor

The implementation of the specified monitor follows the natural B-method implementation strategy. In this paper, we focus on creating the implementation without an intermediary refinement machine. In order to implement the system, it is essential to ensure that the system states and state transitions are preserved. For instance, the overspeed alarm logic can be implemented in different ways, as long as the observable behaviour and the resulting system states remain consistent with the specification. A possible solution is:

```
user_logic =
BEGIN
    VAR train_speed, section_speed, alarm
    IN
        train_speed : (train_speed : uint8_t);
        section_speed : (section_speed : uint8_t);
        alarm : (alarm : uint8_t);

        train_speed <-- get_odo_train_speed;
        section_speed <-- get_section_x_speed_limit;
        alarm <-- get_overspeed_alarm;

        red_flag := IO_OFF;

        IF train_speed > section_speed
        THEN IF alarm = IO_OFF
            THEN red_flag := IO_ON
    END END END   END;
```

It is important to note that platform outputs are updated only at the end of each execution cycle. This allows variables to be freely manipulated within an operation, as only their final values, after completion, affect the outputs. When comparing abstract and implementation machines, one observes specific syntactic constraints imposed by the B method. In the Implementation machine, access to variables from other machines is restricted, requiring local variable declarations with explicit typing and values retrieved via corresponding getter operations. The implementation also enforces sequential instruction execution using the ";" operator and limits the use of unrestricted propositional and first-order logic. These restrictions help bridge the gap between formal specification and executable code, ultimately supporting automatic code generation.

Once the implementation machine is complete, Atelier B can automatically prove the required properties using its built-in rules, ensuring logical consistency. If some properties cannot be proven automatically, the tool offers an interactive prover that allows users to guide the process until all properties are verified. In some cases, errors in the specification or implementation must be corrected. These are highlighted by the prover, which pinpoints the expressions or conditions that could not be validated.

Atelier B can then be used to simulate the system on the CSSP platform or upload it directly to the physical hardware. In both cases, the implementation is translated into code following all certified procedures defined by the CSSP approach, then compiled and deployed to the simulator or target platform.

4.3   Integration Between the CSSP and the CBTC

Once compiled, the CSSP CBTC monitor can be used for either testing or monitoring CBTC systems. Each use case involves a different approach.

Testing with the CSSP. CBTC systems are tested at various levels. In our V-cycle, two of them are accessible to developers: component testing and system testing. Both rely on a simulator that replicates the CBTC system and its environment. This simulator emulates external components, manages message exchanges, and handles input/output signals. To execute a test, the user creates a script that sends commands to the system and reads its outputs. Additionally, certain internal variables are exposed, allowing verification of whether the system behaves as expected.

The overall testing strategy follows standard software testing practices: verifying each requirement during system tests and exercising all lines of code during component tests. In this context, developers design test scenarios to simulate specific environments and evaluate the system's response to particular requirements or variable states. For critical systems, it is also important to test all possible combinations of variables to ensure correct behaviour even under extreme or unlikely conditions. These scenarios are often long and repetitive—and this is where the CSSP approach can bring significant advantages.

In our CSSP CBTC testing approach, the CSSP board receives system inputs and outputs via its interfaces, allowing it to be connected directly to an existing CBTC simulator. This integration requires only a simple adapter capable of capturing the test scenario inputs and simulator outputs, then forwarding them to the CSSP board for analysis. Figure 4 illustrates the overall test setup and our CSSP-based strategy for testing CBTC systems. Rather than generating logs for human review, the CSSP actively compares the system's behavior—based on the provided inputs and observed outputs—against the formally specified requirements. Then, any alerts related to CBTC errors produced by the CSSP monitor can be forwarded to a handler. This "alert handler" may range from a complete system that collects, processes, and presents the test results, to a simple set of indicator lights.

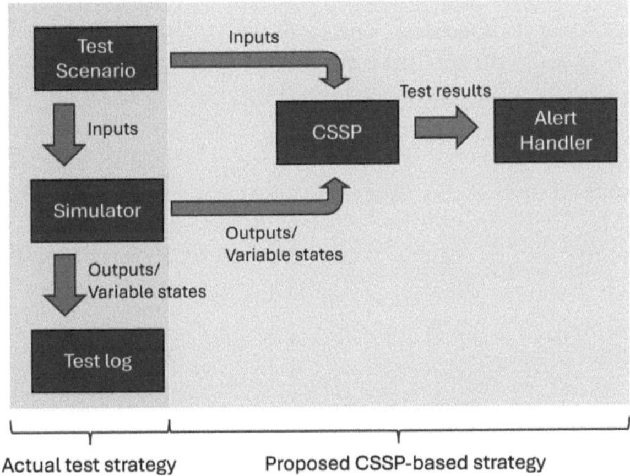

Fig. 4. A diagram presenting the actual and the proposed test strategies

There are two main benefits to using the CSSP during CBTC testing. First, the system can be continuously monitored against a set of safety properties, including those not explicitly targeted by the current test scenario. This introduces a layer of redundancy that enhances the overall robustness and reliability of the testing process. Second, the CSSP enables exhaustive testing by allowing developers to focus on systematically varying the inputs, while offloading the output analysis to the platform. For instance, instead of crafting a test where a human manually verifies the system's response as the train's speed increases, one can implement a simple loop that increases the speed at regular intervals, letting the CSSP automatically verify compliance with the safety requirements.

In our work, we were not able to connect the CSSP board directly to the CBTC simulators, as these systems rely on proprietary technology with limited access for external developers. However, based on other industrial experiences, several connection methods are feasible. For instance, the CSSP can interface with a server responsible for delivering inputs and collecting outputs. Since CBTC simulators are typically server-based (to allow access for all licensed developers), this presents a viable integration point. Moreover, as the simulator runs on a standard computer, a direct physical connection is also possible.

To conduct our case studies, we opted for an indirect approach by using the logs generated during testing. In this setup, the CSSP was fed with log data, allowing our monitor to analyse system behaviour throughout the test execution. This also illustrates a viable offline solution for asynchronous analysis, enabling a connection-free integration. Our experiments were carried out using the CSSP simulator within Atelier B, which also supports the use of a server to control system inputs and collect outputs. Although this setup illustrates the applicability of our methodology in an industrial context, we strongly recommend using the fully certified version of the CLEARSY Safety Platform for any concrete deployment. The certified version implements several safety principles and configurations that are essential for use in safety-critical environments.

In some cases, is important to consider that the CBTC system takes a few fractions of a second to produce outputs after receiving inputs. This delay is fixed, as the CBTC operates using a cycle-based execution strategy. Each component of the system has a defined cycle time that must be taken into account. In this context, the temporal gap between inputs and outputs may lead to the false detection of "dangerous states", since the system has not yet had time to react accordingly. As the CSSP also operates in cycles and supports the specification of time-based behaviour, it can be configured to wait for one CBTC cycle before raising an error:

```
user_logic =
BEGIN
VAR train_speed, section_speed, alarm, time, wait
IN
    train_speed : (train_speed : uint8_t);
    section_speed : (section_speed : uint8_t);
    alarm : (alarm : uint8_t);
  time : (time : uint32_t);
  wait : (wait : uint32_t);

    train_speed <-- get_odo_train_speed;
    section_speed <-- get_section_x_speed_limit;
    alarm <-- get_overspeed_alarm;

    red_flag := IO_OFF;
    time <-- get_ms_tick;

    IF train_speed > section_speed
    THEN
        IF timer = 0
        THEN timer <-- get_ms_tick
        END;
        IF alarm = IO_OFF
        THEN
            wait := time - timer;
            IF wait > 200
            THEN red_flag := IO_ON
END END END END END;
```

The operation `get_ms_tick` returns the elapsed time since the application started. In this example, the global variable `timer` stores the moment the train starts exceeding the speed limit. A global variable is needed to preserve its value across multiple CSSP cycles. The local variables `time` and `wait` are used to retrieve the current time and calculate how long the train has been overspeeding. The red flag is raised only if the alarm is not triggered within a time interval longer than the CBTC cycle (200 ms) after the overspeed condition begins.

The use of timed logic in this context is optional and depends on both the component under test and how the alert handler processes the information. If a component has a cycle time significantly longer than the CSSP's, timing must be considered as part of the system behavior, otherwise, the CSSP may observe and flag what it perceives as prolonged unsafe behavior across multiple cycles. Conversely, if the component's cycle is much shorter than the CSSP's, the system may raise an alert based on a transient state that lasts for only a single CSSP cycle. In such cases, timing constraints can be relaxed if brief delays are still within acceptable safety margins (as is often the case in CBTC systems). For instance, in the overspeed alarm scenario, if the CSSP output is connected to a light indicating the alarm status, the light may briefly flash when the alarm fails to activate immediately. This highlights the importance of aligning the monitoring logic with both system timing and the alert interpretation strategy.

Although not further explored in this paper, the abstract machine also supports the use of the variable `ms_tick` inside logical expressions. This variable underlies the operation `get_ms_tick` and can be used to specify timed behaviors directly within the B-method formalism, thereby combining its mathematical background with an explicit notion of time progression.

A final testing level, not covered in our V-cycle, is the in-loco testing. This stage involves deploying the CBTC system in a real-world environment, using actual trains. In this context, the CSSP is no longer connected to a simulator via software, but rather to the physical components of the train, effectively acting as a runtime monitor.

Monitoring the CBTC System. Once the CBTC system has successfully passed all test stages and reached a mature state, it is ready to be tested in real-world conditions and eventually deployed in operational environments. In both cases, the system can benefit from the integration of the CSSP monitor. The strategy at this stage is to connect the monitor to the same components interfaced by the CBTC, allowing it to receive the system's inputs and outputs directly via the board's input channels.

For example, to analyse the ongoing case study, the board must be connected to the Odometry, Section, and Alarm components (see Fig. 5), enabling the monitor to verify whether the exchanged information behaves as expected. In this setup, the CSSP board acts as an additional CBTC component, continuously monitoring system execution and raising alerts (represented here by the red light) whenever a hazardous state is detected.

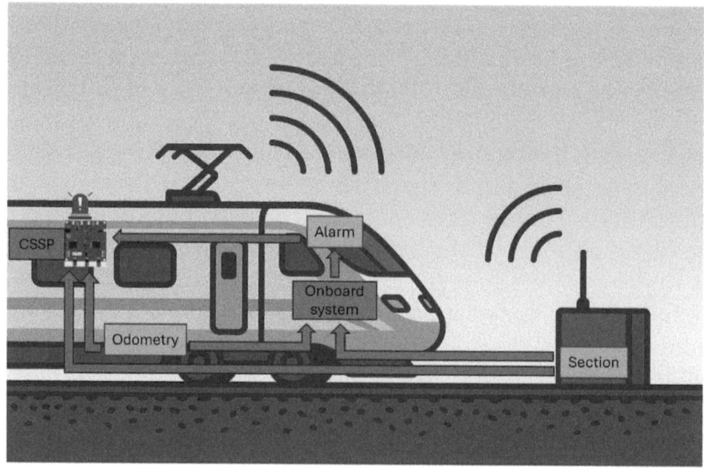

Fig. 5. A diagram presenting the proposed connections between the CBTC components and the CSSP

It is worth noting that CBTC systems already meet the highest safety integrity levels and are not expected to exhibit unsafe behaviour under normal conditions. We acknowledge this; however, human and material factors, which are external to the system's formal logic, may still lead to unexpected outcomes. Human operators, for instance, can access components and disable certain functions, while hardware may fail or degrade over time. In our case study, for example, the alarm can either be manually deactivated or become dysfunctional. In such situations, the corresponding safety property is no longer ensured. To address this, the monitor validates system inputs and outputs at runtime to ensure that the system behaves according to its formal B model. This runtime checking is crucial because external components or operator actions can influence overall safety in ways that static verification cannot capture. When inputs come from components outside the B specifications, they must be correctly mapped to the B representation to guarantee accurate monitoring, which is ensured by our methodology.

While other mechanisms within the CBTC system might preserve safety in such scenarios, our methodology aims to complement them by covering a broader set of safety requirements simultaneously. We see this as an additional safety layer that strengthens the system's ability to prevent accidents. It is also important to consider that most train incidents today are caused by human error or hardware failure [18]. In this context, our monitoring strategy contributes to addressing part of this risk and reinforcing the overall safety of CBTC systems.

5   Discussion

This section discusses key aspects of our methodology that were not covered in the previous sections. It focuses on the feasibility of the monitoring approach, its potential contributions to improving the V-cycle, and its positioning within the broader context of Software Engineering.

Regarding the limitations related to the B language, the variety of invariants that can be translated are limited by the subset of the B language supported by the CSSP. While complex data types such as functions, relations, or sets are not fully covered, the allowed notations are sufficient for CBTC purposes. A more in-depth analysis could be addressed in future work.

As for the use of the CSSP board as a monitor, it is important to consider its potential limitations and how they may impact our methodology. While using a server to provide the CSSP inputs significantly increases the number of accessible inputs (by creating 65536×2 virtual channels), the physical input capacity of a certified board remains limited to 32×2 connections. Since each CBTC component may involve hundreds of inputs, outputs, and internal variables, we recommend adopting server-like architectures to handle data exchange. However, CSSP boards also support interconnection, allowing multiple boards to be combined in order to expand their physical I/O capacity. If space constraints are not an issue, this remains a viable alternative.

In terms of cost, the CLEARSY Safety Platform was developed as part of the LCHIP project, which aimed to create a cost-effective solution for building certified safety-critical systems [16]. Consequently, our proposed approach tends to be more affordable, as the certified CSSP hardware is less expensive than other safety-grade computers available on the market. Moreover, since the B-method is already used during CBTC development, implementing a monitor based on this method does not require additional training. The monitor's logic can also be derived directly from the system's formal documentation, aligning with existing development activities and reducing the overall effort.

In this context, we suggest developing the monitor early in the lifecycle, specifically during the documentation phase. Based on a test-driven development approach, the system designer can define the key system constraints at the beginning of the V-cycle (see Fig. 6). These constraints can then be formally specified and continuously enforced throughout system testing and operation using our CSSP-based strategy. The cost of developing the monitor was not formally measured; however, the process closely resembles standard system development, as it involves translating requirements from natural-language documentation into formal logic. Since the system documentation already describes the system logic in an abstract way, we argue that the system designers are well-positioned to provide a formal specification of the requirements. Furthermore, given that these requirements are expressed using propositional logic, their implementation closely follows what is already outlined in the documentation.

The CSSP CBTC monitor, in this light, becomes a multi-purpose asset: it encapsulates the core logic of the system requirements, acts as a testing tool to enhance test coverage and quality, and serves as a runtime monitor throughout the system's operational lifecycle, adding a new layer of safety to CBTC systems. Additionally, although not explored in depth in this paper, our strategy aligns with the concept of Digital Twins [5]. Since the CSSP CBTC monitor operates as

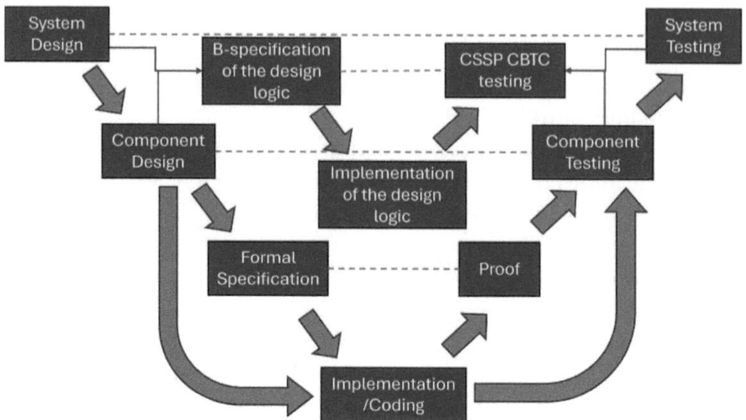

Fig. 6. Updated version of the V-cycle using the CSSP approach for CBTC testing and monitoring

a simplified, requirement-based replica of the actual CBTC system, validating its inputs and outputs, it can be understood as a digital twin: a virtual counterpart used to analyze and ensure correct system behaviour.

6   Conclusion and Perspectives

This paper presents a methodology for creating a CBTC monitor—a system that can be used either for testing or continuous monitoring of CBTC systems throughout their lifecycle. The methodology is grounded in established industrial CBTC development practices and leverages technologies already adopted in the railway domain, aiming to ensure both industrial applicability and certification readiness.

Our approach relies on the B-method, a formal specification language widely used in CBTC development, and on the CLEARSY Safety Platform (CSSP), a certified platform employed in various safety-critical railway applications. From the formal specification of safety requirements, we derive a monitor program that runs on the CSSP safety computer, connected to the CBTC system. This setup enables real-time verification of safety properties during operation. Additionally, we provide a solution integrated with CBTC simulators, making it suitable for both system and unit testing phases.

The key advantage of our approach is the creation of an independent safety layer that enhances both testing and runtime monitoring. In testing, it enables the analysis of system behaviour against a formally specified and traceable set of requirements. During operation, it improves safety by continuously checking for violations due to human error or system malfunctions, issuing alerts when safety properties are not satisfied.

Our initial case study was conducted using existing system test logs. As a next step, we plan to collaborate with industrial partners to connect the CSSP board to CBTC simulators for live execution testing. We also intend to expand our case study to include a broader set of safety requirements derived from real documentation. In the longer term, we aim to integrate the CSSP monitor into a live onboard CBTC installation, once the monitoring solution reaches a sufficient level of maturity.

While this work has focused exclusively on the railway domain, specifically CBTC system development, the underlying methodology is general and could be adapted to other safety-critical domains. One promising direction for future exploration is the renewable energy sector, particularly wind power systems, where continuous monitoring is crucial to maintain turbine health and operational safety. Such systems require the supervision of speed, direction, and component status, along with reliable fault detection and alert mechanisms. We believe our approach could bring added value to this field, and we plan to investigate its applicability further.

References

1. Abrial, J.R., Lee, M., Neilson, D., Scharbach, P., Sørensen, I.: The b-method. In: Prehn, S., Toetenel, H. (eds.) VDM '91 Formal Software Development Methods. VDM 1991. LNCS, vol. 552, pp. 398–405. Springer, Berlin, Heidelberg (1991). https://doi.org/10.1007/BFb0020001
2. Almeida, D., Jamain, F., Lecomte, T.: Formal analysis and monitoring of legacy safety-critical interlocking systems with the use of certified industrial Tools. In: Haxthausen, A.E., Serwe, W. (eds.) Formal Methods for Industrial Critical Systems. FMICS 2024. LNCS, vol. 14952, pp. 182–198. Springer, Cham (2024). https://doi.org/10.1007/978-3-031-68150-9_11
3. Balcer, M., Hasling, W., Ostrand, T.: Automatic generation of test scripts from formal test specifications. In: Proceedings of the ACM SIGSOFT'89 Third Symposium on Software Testing, Analysis, and Verification, pp. 210–218 (1989)
4. Barringer, H., Groce, A., Havelund, K., Smith, M.: An entry point for formal methods: specification and analysis of event logs. arXiv preprint arXiv:1003.1682 (2010)
5. Batty, M.: Digital twins. Environ. Plan. B Urban Anal. City Sci. **45**(5), 817–820 (2018)
6. Behm, P., Benoit, P., Faivre, A., Meynadier, J.M.: Meteor: a successful application of b in a large project. In: Wing, J.M., Woodcock, J., Davies, J. (eds.) FM'99 – Formal Methods. FM 1999. LNCS, vol. 1708, pp. 369–387. Springer, Berlin, Heidelberg (1999). https://doi.org/10.1007/3-540-48119-2_22
7. Berkovich, S., Bonakdarpour, B., Fischmeister, S.: Runtime verification with minimal intrusion through parallelism. Form. Methods Syst. Des. **46**(3), 317–348 (2015). https://doi.org/10.1007/s10703-015-0226-3
8. Butler, M., et al.: The first twenty-five years of industrial use of the b-method. In: ter Beek, M.H., Ničković, D. (eds.) Formal Methods for Industrial Critical Systems. FMICS 2020. LNCS, vol. 12327, pp. 189–209. Springer, Cham (2020). https://doi.org/10.1007/978-3-030-58298-2_8
9. Cao, Y., Niu, R., Xu, T., Tang, T., Mu, J.: Wireless test platform of communication based train control (cbtc) system in urban mass transit. In: 2007 IEEE International Conference on Vehicular Electronics and Safety, pp. 1–4. IEEE (2007)

10. Chen, F., d'Amorim, M., Roşu, G.: A formal monitoring-based framework for software development and analysis. In: Davies, J., Schulte, W., Barnett, M. (eds.) Formal Methods and Software Engineering. ICFEM 2004. LNCS, vol. 3308, pp. 357–372. Springer, Berlin, Heidelberg (2004). https://doi.org/10.1007/978-3-540-30482-1_31

11. EN 50128:2011 Railway applications – Communication, signalling and processing systems – Software for railway control and protection systems (2011)

12. Greco, J.A.: Predict, detect and react to signaling and train control failures with improved diagnostics achieved with a suite of data collection and analysis tools in a maintenance and diagnostic center. In: ASME/IEEE Joint Rail Conference, vol. 50978, p. V001T04A006. American Society of Mechanical Engineers (2018)

13. Lecomte, T.: Atelier b. Formal Methods Applied to Complex Systems: Implementation of the B Method, pp. 35–46 (2014)

14. Lecomte, T.: Programming the CLEARSY safety platform with B. In: Raschke, A., Méry, D., Houdek, F. (eds.) ABZ 2020. LNCS, vol. 12071, pp. 124–138. Springer, Cham (2020). https://doi.org/10.1007/978-3-030-48077-6_9

15. Lecomte, T., Deharbe, D., Fournier, P., Oliveira, M.: The clearsy safety platform: 5 years of research, development and deployment. Sci. Comput. Program. **199**, 102524 (2020)

16. Lecomte, T., et al.: Low cost high integrity platform. arXiv preprint arXiv:2005.07191 (2020)

17. Lin, Q., Xu, N.: Formal verification of train control procedures in train-centric cbtc system using colored petri nets. In: 2020 IEEE International Conference on Intelligent Rail Transportation (ICIRT), pp. 1–6. IEEE (2020)

18. Liu, X., Saat, M.R., Barkan, C.P.: Analysis of causes of major train derailment and their effect on accident rates. Transp. Res. Rec. **2289**(1), 154–163 (2012)

19. Pinisetty, S., Pradhan, A., Roop, P., Tripakis, S.: Compositional runtime enforcement revisited. Form. Methods Syst. Des. **59**(1), 205–252 (2021)

20. Reinbacher, T., Függer, M., Brauer, J.: Runtime verification of embedded real-time systems. Form. Methods Syst. Des. **44**, 203–239 (2014)

21. Rushby, J., De Moura, L.M., Hamon, G.: Formal methods for test case generation (Jan 4 2011), uS Patent 7,865,339

22. Wang, C., Pastore, F., Goknil, A., Briand, L.C.: Automatic generation of acceptance test cases from use case specifications: an nlp-based approach. IEEE Trans. Softw. Eng. **48**(2), 585–616 (2020)

23. Wang, H., Zhao, N., Ning, B., Tang, T., Chai, M.: Safety monitor for train-centric CBTC system. IET Intell. Transp. Syst. **12**(8), 931–938 (2018)